Guide
to
College
Reading

Why Do You Need This New Edition?

If you're wondering why you should buy the eighth edition of Guide to College Reading here are six good reasons!

1. A **New Contemporary Issues Minireader** contains six readings on current hot topics–such as smoker's rights, cell phones and driving safety, campus violence, and global warming—that you can use to build and improve your reading skills.

2. A **New Section on Word Mapping**—particularly helpful for visual learners—offers you a new way to improve your vocabulary using word maps and a dictionary.

3. A **New Section on Online Dictionaries** demonstrates the advantages of using online resources to quickly find the definitions of words while you are reading and to identify the right way to use and spell words as you write.

4. **New Vocabulary Exercises** offer you practice with using a dictionary to find the multiple meanings of words, the origins of words, and how to pronounce unfamiliar words correctly.

5. **Four New End-of-chapter Readings** about illegal immigration, the problems of families of soldiers in Iraq, animal cloning of human body parts, and prejudice in the classroom will stimulate you to think about these important issues while providing you with practice in understanding a writer's message.

6. **Updated Chapter Opening Images** featuring new photographs and cartoons illustrate what each chapter is about and help you connect with what you are going to learn.

Guide
to
College
Reading

Eighth Edition

Kathleen T. McWhorter

Niagara County Community College

PEARSON
Longman

New York   San Francisco   Boston
London   Toronto   Sydney   Tokyo   Singapore   Madrid
Mexico City   Munich   Paris   Cape Town   Hong Kong   Montreal

ACQUISITIONS EDITOR:	Kate Edwards
DEVELOPMENT EDITOR:	Gillian Cook
SENIOR SUPPLEMENTS EDITOR:	Donna Campion
MARKETING MANAGER:	Thomas DeMarco
PRODUCTION MANAGER:	Bob Ginsberg
PROJECT COORDINATION, TEXT DESIGN, AND ELECTRONIC PAGE MAKEUP:	Pre-Press PMG
COVER DESIGNER/MANAGER:	Wendy Ann Fredericks
COVER ART (LEFT TO RIGHT):	Photo by Wendy Ann Fredericks; Somos/Veer/Getty Images; Laurence Mouton/PhotoAlto/AgeFotostock; and Dictionary.com screenshot, © 2007, Lexico Publishing Group, LLC. All rights reserved.
PHOTO RESEARCHER:	Clare Maxwell
SENIOR MANUFACTURING BUYER:	Alfred C. Dorsey
PRINTER AND BINDER:	Worldcolor/Taunton
COVER PRINTER:	Phoenix Color Corporation

For permission to use copyrighted material, grateful acknowledgment is made to the copyright holders on pp. 575–585, which are hereby made part of this copyright page.

Visit us at www.ablongman.com

Student Edition ISBN-13: 978-0-205-60497-5
Student Edition ISBN-10:   0-205-60497-8
Annotated Instructor's Edition ISBN-13: 978-0-205-60504-0
Annotated Instructor's Edition ISBN-10:   0-205-60504-4

4 5 6 7 8 9 10—WCT—11 10 09

Brief Contents

Detailed Contents

Preface

The influx of nontraditional students into both two- and four-year colleges has enriched the educational scene; at the same time, it has made the preparation of these students for academic success an institutional priority. *Guide to College Reading*, Eighth Edition, is written to equip students of widely different backgrounds with the basic reading and critical-thinking skills needed to cope with the demands of academic work. It offers a completely new Contemporary Issues Minireader, including guidelines for how to read about controversial issues, a new section on word mapping, increased coverage of online dictionary use, additional vocabulary exercises for each end of chapter reading, and updated Internet activities for skill reinforcement. The eighth edition uses a visually appealing four-color design, including interactive chapter openers, that has been updated to make the text more easily accessible.

NEW TO THIS EDITION

Numerous changes and additions have been made in this eighth edition that update the book and address the changing needs of beginning college students.

- **New Contemporary Issues Minireader.** Comprising Part Six of the book, the minireader offers six new readings on topics of current interest: smoker's rights, cell phones and driving safety, campus violence, employee rights, media images of women, and global warming. Each reading begins with prereading questions and a vocabulary preview. Each reading is followed by comprehension and critical reading and thinking questions, words in context and vocabulary review exercises, a summarizing activity, and writing assignments.
- **New section on word mapping.** New to Chapter 4, this section teaches students a visual strategy for expanding their vocabularies. Word mapping, which requires students to use a dictionary to analyze a word's parts and discover multiple meanings and synonyms, and to write two sentences using the word, encourages intensive word study. It is particularly helpful for visual learners.

- **New section on online dictionary usage.** Because more students are using online dictionaries, a new section including sample Web pages has been added to Chapter 4. It explains the benefits of these online resources, which can be used to find the definitions of words while reading, to identify correct usage and spelling when writing, and to build and expand general vocabulary.

- **New vocabulary exercises.** Each end-of-chapter reading (Mastery Test 4) now features a new exercise, Studying Words, that provides students with practice using a dictionary to find the etymology, correct pronunciation, word parts, and multiple meanings of specific words.

- **New readings.** Four new end-of-chapter readings (Mastery Test 4) have been added on the topics of illegal immigration, problems faced by families of soldiers in Iraq, animal cloning of human body parts, and classroom stereotyping. A new contemporary short story by Becky Birtha, "Route 23: 10th and Bigler to Bethlehem Pike," has been added to the Fiction Minireader.

- **Updated Chapter Opening Images.** Each chapter starts with an image related to the content of the chapter to pique students' interest and engage them in the subject material. The majority of them have been replaced with new photographs and cartoons that illustrate chapter content using contemporary images.

- **Updated Four-Color Design.** An updated design has made the text more visually appealing and easier for students to navigate.

THE PURPOSE OF THIS TEXT

Guide to College Reading, Eighth Edition, addresses the learning characteristics, attitudes, and motivational levels of reading students. It is intended to equip students with the skills they need to handle the diverse reading demands of college courses. Specifically, the book guides students in becoming active learners and critical thinkers. This text adopts an encouraging, supportive, nonthreatening voice and an unassuming attitude toward learning. The text provides a variety of everyday examples and extensive exercises to encourage students to become involved and to apply the skills presented.

The chapters are divided into numerous sections; exercises are frequent but brief and explicit. The language and style are simple and direct; explanations are clear and often presented in step-by-step form. Reading topics and materials have been chosen carefully to relate to the students' interests and backgrounds, while exhibiting potential for broadening their range of experience. Many students have compensated for poor reading skills with alternate learning styles; they have become visual and auditory learners. To capitalize on this adaptation, a visual approach to learning, including four-color drawings, diagrams, and visual aids to illustrate concepts, is used throughout.

CONTENT OVERVIEW

The text is organized into six major sections, following the logical progression of skill development from vocabulary development to reading paragraphs, articles, essays, and chapters. It also proceeds logically from literal comprehension to critical interpretation and response. An opening chapter focuses on student success strategies, including such topics as attitudes toward college, concentration, learning styles, and comprehension monitoring.

- **Part One teaches students basic approaches to vocabulary development.** It includes contextual aids, analysis of word parts, pronunciation, word mapping, and the use of the dictionary and other reference sources.
- **Part Two helps students develop literal comprehension skills.** It emphasizes prereading techniques that prepare and enable the student to comprehend and to recall content. Previewing, activating background knowledge, and using guide questions are emphasized. The unit provides extensive instruction and practice with paragraph comprehension and recognition of thought patterns. An entire chapter is devoted to stated and implied main ideas; another entire chapter focuses on supporting details and transitions.
- **Part Three teaches students textbook reading skills.** Topics include textbook learning aids, chapter organization, ways to read graphics and technical material, reading and evaluating Internet sources, reading in various academic disciplines, and methods of organizing and retaining course content.
- **Part Four introduces critical reading and thinking skills.** It presents skills that enable students to interact with and evaluate written material, including material on the Internet. Topics include making inferences, identifying the author's purpose, recognizing assumptions, and distinguishing fact and opinion.
- **Part Five, "A Fiction Minireader," offers a brief introduction to reading fiction.** An introductory section discusses the essential elements of a short story, using Kate Chopin's "The Story of an Hour" as a demonstration. Three additional short stories with accompanying exercises and discussion questions are also included.
- **Part Six, "A Contemporary Issues Minireader," contains six articles on contemporary issues.** An introductory section offers strategies for reading about contemporary issues. Each reading is prefaced by an interest-catching introduction, previewing questions, and a vocabulary preview. Literal and critical

comprehension questions as well as a words-in-context exercise, a vocabulary review, a summarizing activity, and a writing exercise follow each selection.

SPECIAL FEATURES

The following features enhance the text's effectiveness and directly contribute to students' success:

- **Integration of Reading and Writing.** The text integrates reading and writing skills. Students respond to exercises by writing sentences and paragraphs. Answers to most questions for each reading selection also require composition. A writing exercise accompanies each reading selection in Part Six.

- **Reading as Thinking.** Reading is approached as a thinking process—a process in which the student interacts with textual material and sorts, evaluates, and reacts to its organization and content. For example, students are shown how to define their purpose for reading, ask questions, identify and use organization and structure as a guide to understanding, make inferences, and interpret and evaluate what they read.

- **Comprehension Monitoring.** Comprehension monitoring is also addressed within the text. Through a variety of techniques, students are encouraged to be aware of and to evaluate and control their levels of comprehension of the material they read.

- **Skill Application.** Chapters 2 through 13 conclude with four mastery tests that enable students to apply the skills taught in each chapter and to evaluate their learning.

BOOK-SPECIFIC ANCILLARY MATERIALS

- **Annotated Instructor's Edition.** The Annotated Instructor's Edition is identical to the student text but includes all answers printed directly on the pages where questions, exercises, or activities occur (ISBN: 0-205-60504-4).

- **Instructor's Manual.** An Instructor's Manual, including an Answer Key, accompanies the text. The manual describes in detail the basic features of the text and offers suggestions for structuring the course, for teaching nontraditional students, and for approaching each section of the text (ISBN: 0-205-60505-2).

- **Test Bank.** This new supplement features two sets of chapter quizzes and a mastery test for each chapter. It is printed in an 8-1/2 × 11 format that allows for easy photocopying and distribution (ISBN: 0-205-60506-0).

- **PowerPoint Presentations.** For the lab or electronic classroom, a Power-Point presentation is available for each chapter of *Guide to College Reading*. Each chapter's presentation consists of approximately 15 to 20 slides highlighting key concepts from the text, as well as additional activities. Download the presentations from our Website at **www.ablongman.com/mcwhorter.**

- **Companion Website.** We are proud to offer a complete Website to accompany *Guide to College Reading*. Visit this site for additional quizzes, readings, and Web resources for each chapter of the text at **www.ablongman.com/mcwhorter.**

THE LONGMAN DEVELOPMENTAL READING PACKAGE

Longman is pleased to offer a variety of support materials to help make teaching developmental reading easier for teachers and to help students excel in their course work. Visit **www.ablongman.com** or contact your local Longman sales representative for a detailed listing of our supplements package or for more information on pricing and how to create a package.

ACKNOWLEDGMENTS

I wish to express my gratitude to my reviewers for their excellent ideas, suggestions, and advice on this and previous editions of this text:

Alfradene Armstrong, Tougaloo College
Carla Bell, Henry Ford Community College
Dorothy Booher, Florida Community College at Jacksonville, Kent Campus
Diane Bosco, Suffolk County Community College
Beth Childress, Armstrong Atlantic University
Pam Drell, Oakton Community College, Des Plaines Campus
Shirley Hall, Middle Georgia College
Pam Hallene, Community College of Rhode Island

Kevin Hayes, Essex County College
Peggy Hopper, Walters State College
Danica Hubbard, College of DuPage
Suzanne E. Hughes, Florida Community College at Jacksonville
Jacqueline Jackson, Art Institute of Philadelphia
Arlene Jellineck, Palm Beach Community College
Jeanne Keefe, Belleville Area College
Patti Levine-Brown, Florida Community College at Jacksonville
Ann Mueller, Kishwaukee Community College
Sharyn Neuwirth, Montgomery College, Takoma Park Campus
Catherine Packard, Southeastern Illinois College
Kathy Purswell, Frank Phillips College
Dianne Schellack, Burlington County College
Jackie Stahlecker, St. Philips College
Mary Wolting, Indiana University–Purdue University at Indianapolis
Nora Yaeger, Cedar Valley College

I am particularly indebted to Gillian Cook, my development editor, for her energetic guidance and valuable advice and to Kate Edwards, acquisitions editor, for her enthusiastic support of this project.

KATHLEEN T. McWHORTER

How Do You READ?

R   Rate your attitudes

E   Evaluate your habits

A   Assess your skills

D   Decide how you learn

Directions: Rate how accurately each of the following statements describes you using a scale of 1 to 4, with 1 being Highly Accurate and 4 being Very Inaccurate.

R—Rate Your Attitudes	Highly Accurate	Somewhat Accurate	Somewhat Inaccurate	Very Inaccurate
1. I will become a successful student.	1	2	3	4
2. I have academic and career goals for the next several years.	1	2	3	4
3. I know it is up to me to learn what is needed in each of my courses.	1	2	3	4
4. I can visualize myself passing exams and earning good grades.	1	2	3	4
E—Evaluate Your Habits				
5. I enjoy spending my free time reading.	1	2	3	4
6. I expect reading assignments to be time-consuming and am committed to spending the time necessary to complete them.	1	2	3	4
7. I have little or no difficulty concentrating.	1	2	3	4
8. As I read textbooks, I try to decide what is important to learn.	1	2	3	4

1

A—Assess Your Skills	Highly Accurate	Somewhat Accurate	Somewhat Inaccurate	Very Inaccurate
9. When I read, I seldom meet words I don't know.	1	2	3	4
10. When I read, I look for main ideas and details that explain them.	1	2	3	4
11. I can usually remember what I read.	1	2	3	4
12. When I read, I question what I read and analyze the author's ideas.	1	2	3	4
D—Decide How You Learn				
13. I know my strengths and weaknesses as a learner.	1	2	3	4
14. I decide how to best learn something before I begin.	1	2	3	4
15. I use different study methods for different assignments.	1	2	3	4
16. I can describe my learning style.	1	2	3	4

If you checked one or more Somewhat Inaccurate or Very Inaccurate boxes in any section, then you will find Chapter 1 of this book especially useful in improving how you READ. The remaining chapters will focus on specific skills for strengthening your vocabulary, comprehension, and critical thinking skills.

Chapter 1

Successful Attitudes Toward Reading and Learning

THIS CHAPTER WILL SHOW YOU HOW TO

1 **Understand what is expected in college**

2 **Start with a positive attitude**

3 **Build your concentration**

4 **Analyze your learning style**

5 **Strengthen your comprehension**

Getting Started with . . .
Learning

Each photograph shows college students studying or learning. Which way would you prefer to study or learn? These photographs demonstrate that students learn in a variety of ways, ranging from study groups, to hands-on learning, to listening and note-taking. This chapter will help you discover how you learn most effectively and help you approach the reading and study demands of your courses successfully.

College is very different from any other type of educational experience. It is different from high school, job training programs, adult education, or technical training programs. New and different types of learning are demanded, and you need new skills and techniques to meet these demands. This chapter offers you ways to become a successful student. You will discover what is expected of you in college, learn how to improve your concentration, analyze how you learn, and strengthen your comprehension.

UNDERSTAND WHAT IS EXPECTED IN COLLEGE

Following is a list of statements about college. Treat them like a quiz, if you wish. Decide whether each statement is true or false, and write *T* for true or *F* for false in the space provided. Each statement will make you think about the reading and study demands of college. Check your answers by reading the paragraph following each item. As you work through this quiz, you will find out a little about what is expected of you in college. You will see whether or not you have an accurate picture of what college work involves. You will also see how this text will help you to become a better, more successful student.

_____ 1. For every hour I spend in class, I should spend one hour studying outside of class.

Many students feel that even one hour for each class (or 15 hours per week for students carrying a 15 credit-hour load) is a lot. Actually, the rule of thumb used by many instructors is two hours of study for each class hour. So you can see that you are expected to do a great deal of reading, studying, and learning on your own time. The purpose of this text is to help you read and learn in the easiest and best way for you.

_____ 2. I should expect to read about 80 textbook pages per week in each of my courses.

A survey of freshman courses at one college indicated that the average course assignment was roughly 80 pages per week. This may seem like a lot of reading—and it is. You will need to build your reading skills to handle this task. To help you do this, techniques for understanding and remembering what you read, improving your concentration, and handling difficult reading assignments will be suggested throughout this book.

_____ 3. There are a lot of words I do not know, but my vocabulary is about as good as it needs to be.

For each college course you take, there will be new words to learn. Some will be everyday words; others will be specialized or technical. Part One of this book will show you how to develop your vocabulary by learning new words, figuring out words you do not know, and using reference sources.

_____ 4. College instructors will tell me exactly what to learn for each exam.

College instructors seldom tell you exactly what to learn or review. They expect you to decide what is important and to learn that information. In Part Two of this text you will learn how to identify what is important in sentences and paragraphs and how to follow authors' thought patterns.

_____ 5. The more facts I memorize, the higher my exam grades will be.

Learning a large number of facts is no guarantee of a high grade in a course. Some instructors and the exams they give are concerned with your ability to see how facts and ideas fit together, or to evaluate ideas, make comparisons, and recognize trends. Parts Two and Three of this text will help you to do this by showing you how to read textbook chapters, use graphic aids, and organize and remember information.

_____ 6. The only assignments that instructors give are readings in the textbook.

Instructors often assign readings in a variety of sources including periodicals, newspapers, reference and library books, and Internet sources. These readings are intended to add to the information presented in your text and by your instructor. The six reading selections contained in Part Six will give you the opportunity to practice and apply your skills to readings taken from a variety of sources. These selections are similar to the outside readings your instructors will assign.

_____ 7. Rereading a textbook chapter is the best way to prepare for an exam on that chapter.

Rereading is actually one of the poorest ways to review. Besides, it is often dull and time-consuming. In Chapter 11, you will learn about four more-effective alternatives: highlighting and marking, outlining, mapping, and summarizing.

_____ 8. College instructors expect me to react to, evaluate, and criticize what I read.

Beyond understanding the content of textbooks, articles, and essays, students need to be able to criticize and evaluate ideas.

To help you read and think critically, Part Four of this text will show you how to interpret what you read, find the author's purpose, and ask critical questions.

_____ 9. The best way to read a textbook assignment is to turn to the correct page, start reading, and continue until you reach the end of the assignment.

There are numerous things you can do before you read, while you read, and after you read that can improve your comprehension and retention. These techniques for improving your comprehension and recall are presented throughout this text. For example, later in this chapter you will learn techniques for building your concentration. In Chapter 5 you will be shown how to preview, think about what you will read, and use questions to guide your reading. Chapter 11 will focus on techniques to use after you read to strengthen comprehension and recall.

_____ 10. You can never know whether you have understood a textbook reading assignment until you take an exam on the chapter.

As you read, it is possible and important to keep track of and evaluate your level of understanding. You will learn how to keep track of your comprehension, recognize comprehension signals, and strengthen your comprehension.

By analyzing the above statements and the correct responses, you can see that college is a lot of work, much of which you must do on your own. However, college is also a new, exciting experience that will acquaint you with new ideas and opportunities.

This text will help you to get the most out of college and to take advantage of the opportunities it offers. Its purpose is to equip you with the reading and learning skills necessary for academic success.

The opportunity of college lies ahead of you. The skills you are about to learn, along with plenty of hard work, will make your college experience a meaningful and valuable one. The remainder of this chapter will help you take four important steps to becoming a successful student. You will learn to develop a positive attitude, control your concentration, strengthen your comprehension, and analyze how you learn.

START WITH A POSITIVE ATTITUDE

Reading and studying are keys to college success and, later, to success on the job. In fact, many employers identify reading, thinking, and communicating as three essential skills for the workplace.

Becoming a Successful Student

Here are a few approaches that will help you become a successful college student:

1. **Be confident: send yourself positive messages.** Tell yourself that college is something you want and can do. Negative messages such as "I might not be able to do this" or "What if I fail?" will only get in the way. In fact, there is substantial evidence to suggest that negative thinking interferes with performance. In other words, you may be limiting your success by thinking negatively. Instead, send yourself positive messages such as "I can do this" or "I've studied hard, and I'm going to pass this test."

2. **Accept responsibility for your own learning.** Think of your instructors as guides. Fishing guides take you to where you are likely to catch fish, but they do not catch them for you. Similarly, your college instructors will lead you to the information you need to learn, but they will not learn for you. You must choose the strategies and techniques necessary to learn from your textbooks and college lectures.

3. **Visualize success.** Close your eyes and imagine yourself completing a long or difficult assignment or passing an upcoming exam. Just as athletes prepare for a competition by visualizing themselves finishing a marathon in record time or completing a difficult ski run, you should visualize yourself successfully working through challenging tasks.

4. **Set long-term goals for yourself.** You will feel more like working on assignments if you have things you are working toward. Goals such as "to get my own apartment," "to be able to quit my job at Kmart," or "to become a registered nurse" will help you focus and stick with daily tasks.

Becoming a Successful Reader

Reading can open up worlds of new ideas, show you different ways of looking at things, and provide a welcome escape from day-to-day problems. It is an opportunity to visit new places, meet new people and ideas, and broaden your experience. You will spend a great deal of time in college reading your textbooks and other assignments. Think of reading in a positive way. Here are a few approaches that will make reading work for you:

1. **Stick with a reading assignment.** If an assignment is troublesome, experiment with different methods of completing it. Consider highlighting, outlining, testing yourself, preparing vocabulary cards, or drawing diagrams, for example. You will learn these methods in later chapters.

2. **Plan on spending time.** Reading is not something you can rush through. The time you invest will pay off in increased comprehension.

3. **Actively search for key ideas as you read.** Try to connect these ideas with what your instructor is discussing in class. Think of reading as a way of sifting and sorting out what you need to learn from the less important information.

4. **Think of reading as a way of unlocking the writer's message to you, the reader.** Look for clues about the writer's personality, attitudes, opinions, and beliefs. This will put you in touch with the writer as a person and help you understand his or her message. Part Four of this book will offer suggestions to help you do this.

BUILD YOUR CONCENTRATION

Do you have difficulty concentrating? If so, you are like many other college students who say that lack of concentration is the main reason they cannot read or study effectively. Building concentration involves two steps: (1) controlling your surroundings, and (2) focusing your attention.

Controlling Your Surroundings

Poor concentration is often the result of distractions caused by the time and place you have chosen to study. Here are a few ideas to help you overcome poor concentration:

1. **Choose a place to read where you will not be interrupted.** If people interrupt you at home or in the dormitory, try the campus library.

2. **Find a place that is relatively free of distractions and temptations.** Avoid places with outside noise, friends, a television set, or an interesting project close at hand.

3. **Read in the same place each day.** Eventually you will get in the habit of reading there, and concentration will become easier, almost automatic.

4. **Do not read where you are too comfortable.** It is easy to lose concentration, become drowsy, or fall asleep when you are too relaxed.

5. **Choose a time of day when you are mentally alert.** Concentration is easier if you are not tired, hungry, or drowsy.

Focusing Your Attention

Even if you follow these suggestions, you may still find it difficult to become organized and stick with your reading. This takes self-discipline, but the following suggestions may help:

1. **Set goals and time limits for yourself.** Before you begin a reading assignment, decide how long it should take, and check to see that you stay on schedule. Before you start an evening of homework, write down what you plan to do

10/20

Eng. paper–revise $\frac{1}{2}$ hr.

Math probs. 1–10   1 hr.

Sociology
    read pp. 70–82 1 hr.

Figure 1-1   Goals and time limits

and how long each assignment should take. Sample goals for an evening are shown in Figure 1-1.

2. **Choose and reserve blocks of time each day for reading and study.** Write down what you will study in each time block each day or evening. Working at the same time each day establishes a routine and makes concentration a bit easier.

3. **Vary your reading.** For instance, instead of spending an entire evening on one subject, work for one hour on each of three subjects.

4. **Reward yourself for accomplishing things as planned.** Delay entertainment until after you have finished studying. Use such things as ordering a pizza, calling a friend, or watching TV as rewards after you have completed several assignments.

5. **Plan frequent breaks.** Do this at sensible points in your reading—between chapters or after major chapter divisions.

6. **Keep physically as well as mentally active.** Try highlighting, underlining, or making summary notes as you read (see Chapter 11). These activities will focus your attention on the assignment.

EXERCISE 1-1

Directions: Answer each of the following questions as honestly as you can. They will help you analyze problems with concentration. You may want to discuss your answers with others in your class.

1. Where do you read and study? _____

   What interruptions, if any, occur there? _____

2. Do you need to find a better place? _____

   If so, list a few alternatives. _____

3. What is the best time of day for you to read? (If you do not know, experiment with different times until you begin to see a pattern.)

_____

4. How long do you normally read without a break?

_____

5. What type of distraction bothers you the most?

_____

6. On average, how many different assignments do you work on in one evening?

_____

7. What types of rewards might work for you?

_____

EXERCISE 1-2   **Directions:** As you read your next textbook assignment, either for this course or another, be alert for distractions. Each time your mind wanders, try to identify the source of the distraction. List in the space provided the cause of each break in your concentration and a way to eliminate each, if possible.

_____

_____

_____

EXERCISE 1-3   **Directions:** Before you begin your next study session, make a list in the space provided of what you intend to accomplish and how long you should spend on each task.

Assignment   **Time**

1. _____   _____

2. _____   _____

3. _____   _____

ANALYZE YOUR LEARNING STYLE

Reading assignments are the primary focus of many college classes. Instructors make daily or weekly textbook assignments. You are expected to read the material, learn it, and pass tests on it. Class lectures and discussions are often based on textbook assignments. An important part of many college classes, then, is completing reading assignments.

Reading and understanding an assignment, however, does not mean you have learned it. In fact, if you have read an assignment once, you probably have *not* learned it. You need to do more than read to learn an assignment. Your question, then, is "What else should I do?" The answer is not a simple one.

Not everyone learns in the same way. In fact, everyone has his or her own individual way of learning, which is called *learning style*. The following section contains a brief Learning Style Questionnaire that will help you analyze how you learn and prepare an action plan for learning what you read.

LEARNING STYLE QUESTIONNAIRE

Directions: Each item presents two choices. Select the alternative that best describes you. In cases in which neither choice suits you, select the one that is closer to your preference. Write the letter of your choice in the space provided.

Part One

_____ 1. I would prefer to follow a set of
              a. oral directions.
              b. written directions.

_____ 2. I would prefer to
              a. attend a lecture given by a famous psychologist.
              b. read an article written by the psychologist.

_____ 3. When I am introduced to someone, it is easier for me to remember the person's
              a. name.
              b. face.

_____ 4. I find it easier to learn new information using
              a. language (words).
              b. images (pictures).

_____ 5. I prefer classes in which the instructor
              a. lectures and answers questions.
              b. uses films and videos.

_____ 6. To follow current events, I would prefer to
     a. listen to the news on the radio.
     b. read the newspaper.

_____ 7. To learn how to operate a fax machine, I would prefer to
     a. listen to a friend's explanation.
     b. watch a demonstration.

Part Two

_____ 8. I prefer to
     a. work with facts and details.
     b. construct theories and ideas.

_____ 9. I would prefer a job involving
     a. following specific instructions.
     b. reading, writing, and analyzing.

_____ 10. I prefer to
     a. solve math problems using a formula.
     b. discover why the formula works.

_____ 11. I would prefer to write a term paper explaining
     a. how a process works.
     b. a theory.

_____ 12. I prefer tasks that require me to
     a. follow careful, detailed instructions.
     b. use reasoning and critical analysis.

_____ 13. For a criminal justice course, I would prefer to
     a. discover how and when a law can be used.
     b. learn how and why it became law.

_____ 14. To learn more about the operation of a high-speed computer printer, I would prefer to
     a. work with several types of printers.
     b. understand the principles on which they operate.

Part Three

_____ 15. To solve a math problem, I would prefer to
     a. draw or visualize the problem.
     b. study a sample problem and use it as a model.

_____ 16. To best remember something, I
    a. create a mental picture.
    b. write it down.

_____ 17. Assembling a bicycle from a diagram would be
    a. easy.
    b. challenging.

_____ 18. I prefer classes in which I
    a. handle equipment or work with models.
    b. participate in a class discussion.

_____ 19. To understand and remember how a machine works, I would
    a. draw a diagram.
    b. write notes.

_____ 20. I enjoy
    a. drawing or working with my hands.
    b. speaking, writing, and listening.

_____ 21. If I were trying to locate an office on an unfamiliar campus, I would prefer
    a. a map.
    b. written directions.

Part Four

_____ 22. For a grade in biology lab, I would prefer to
    a. work with a lab partner.
    b. work alone.

_____ 23. When faced with a difficult personal problem, I prefer to
    a. discuss it with others.
    b. resolve it myself.

_____ 24. Many instructors could improve their classes by
    a. including more discussion and group activities.
    b. allowing students to work on their own more frequently.

_____ 25. When listening to a lecturer or speaker, I respond more to the
    a. person presenting the idea.
    b. ideas themselves.

_____ 26. When on a team project, I prefer to
    a. work with several team members.
    b. divide the tasks and complete those assigned to me.

_____ 27. I prefer to shop and do errands
          a. with friends.
          b. by myself.

_____ 28. A job in a busy office is
          a. more appealing than working alone.
          b. less appealing than working alone.

Part Five

_____ 29. To make decisions, I rely on
          a. my experiences and gut feelings.
          b. facts and objective data.

_____ 30. To complete a task, I
          a. can use whatever is available to get the job done.
          b. must have everything I need at hand.

_____ 31. I prefer to express my ideas and feelings through
          a. music, song, or poetry.
          b. direct, concise language.

_____ 32. I prefer instructors who
          a. allow students to be guided by their own interests.
          b. make their expectations clear and explicit.

_____ 33. I tend to
          a. challenge and question what I hear and read.
          b. accept what I hear and read.

_____ 34. I prefer
          a. essay exams.
          b. objective exams.

_____ 35. In completing an assignment, I prefer to
          a. figure out my own approach.
          b. be told exactly what to do.

To score your questionnaire, record the total number of *a*'s you selected and the total number of *b*'s for each part of the questionnaire. Record your totals in the scoring grid provided at the top of the next page.

Scoring Grid

Parts	Choice A Total	Choice B Total
Part One	_____	_____
	Auditory	Visual
Part Two	_____	_____
	Applied	Conceptual
Part Three	_____	_____
	Spatial	Verbal
Part Four	_____	_____
	Social	Independent
Part Five	_____	_____
	Creative	Pragmatic

Now, circle your higher score for each part of the questionnaire. The word below the score you circled indicates a strength of your learning style. The next section explains how to interpret your scores.

Interpreting Your Scores

The questionnaire was divided into five parts; each part identifies one aspect of your learning style. Each of these five aspects is explained below.

Part One: Auditory or Visual Learners   This score indicates whether you learn better by listening (auditory) or by seeing (visual). If you have a higher auditory than visual score, you tend to be an auditory learner. That is, you tend to learn more easily by hearing than by reading. A higher visual score suggests strengths with visual modes of learning—reading, studying pictures, reading diagrams, and so forth.

Part Two: Applied or Conceptual Learners   This score describes the types of learning tasks and learning situations you prefer and find easiest to handle. If you are an applied learner, you prefer tasks that involve real objects and situations. Practical, real-life examples are ideal for you. If you are a conceptual learner, you prefer to work with language and ideas; you do not need practical applications for understanding.

Part Three: Spatial or Verbal (Nonspatial) Learners   This score reveals your ability to work with spatial relationships. Spatial learners are able to visualize or mentally see how things work or how they are positioned in space. Their strengths may include drawing, assembling, or repairing things. Verbal learners lack skills in positioning things in space. Instead they rely on verbal or language skills.

Part Four: Social or Independent Learners   This score reveals whether you like to work alone or with others. If you are a social learner, you prefer to work with others—both classmates and instructors—closely and directly. You tend to be people-oriented and enjoy personal interaction. If you are an independent learner, you prefer to work alone and study alone. You tend to be self-directed or self-motivated and are often goal-oriented.

Part Five: Creative or Pragmatic Learners   This score describes the approach you prefer to take toward learning tasks. Creative learners are imaginative and innovative. They prefer to learn through discovery or experimentation. They are comfortable taking risks and following hunches. Pragmatic learners are practical, logical, and systematic. They seek order and are comfortable following rules.

Evaluating Your Scores

If you disagree with any part of the Learning-Style Questionnaire, go with your own instincts rather than the questionnaire results. The questionnaire is just a quick assessment; trust your knowledge of yourself in areas of dispute.

Developing a Learning Action Plan

Now that you know more about *how* you learn, you are ready to develop an action plan for learning what you read. Suppose you discovered that you are an auditory learner. You still have to read your assignments, which is a visual task. However, to learn the assignment you should translate the material into an auditory form. For example, you could repeat aloud, using your own words, information that you want to remember, or you could tape-record key information and play it back. If you also are a social learner, you could work with a classmate, testing each other out loud.

Table 1-1 on page 17 lists each aspect of learning style and offers suggestions for how to learn from a reading assignment. To use the table:

1. **Circle the five aspects of your learning style in which you received higher scores.** Disregard the others.
2. **Read through the suggestions that apply to you.**

TABLE 1-1   Learning Styles and Reading/Learning Strategies

If your learning style is . . .	Then the reading/learning strategies to use are . . .
Auditory	• discuss/study with friends • talk aloud when studying • tape-record self-testing questions and answers
Visual	• draw diagrams, charts, tables (Chapter 11) • try to visualize events • use films and videos, when available • use computer-assisted instruction, if available
Applied	• think of practical situations to which learning applies • associate ideas with their application • use case studies, examples, and applications to cue your learning
Conceptual	• organize materials that lack order • use outlining (Chapter 11) • focus on organizational patterns (Chapter 9)
Spatial	• use mapping (Chapter 11) • use outlining (Chapter 11) • draw diagrams, make charts and sketches • use visualization
Verbal (Nonspatial)	• translate diagrams and drawings into language • record steps, processes, procedures in words • write summaries (Chapter 11) • write your interpretation next to textbook drawings, maps, graphics
Social	• form study groups • find a study partner • interact with your instructor • work with a tutor
Independent	• use computer-assisted instruction, if available • purchase review workbooks or study guides, if available
Creative	• ask and answer questions • record your own ideas in margins of textbooks
Pragmatic	• study in an organized environment • write lists of steps, procedures, and processes

3. **Place a check mark in front of suggestions that you think will work for you.** Choose at least one from each category.

4. **List the suggestions that you chose in the box labeled Action Plan for Learning below.**

Action Plan for Learning

Learning Strategy 1 _____

_____

Learning Strategy 2 _____

_____

Learning Strategy 3 _____

_____

Learning Strategy 4 _____

_____

Learning Strategy 5 _____

_____

Learning Strategy 6 _____

_____

In the Action Plan for Learning box you listed five or more suggestions to help you learn what you read. The next step is to experiment with these techniques, one at a time. (You may need to refer to chapters listed in parentheses in Table 1-1 to learn or review how a certain technique works.) Use one technique for a while, and then move to the next. Continue using the techniques that seem to work; work on revising or modifying those that do not. Do not hesitate to experiment with other techniques listed in the table as well. You may find other techniques that work well for you.

Developing Strategies to Overcome Limitations

You should also work on developing styles in which you are weak. Your learning style is not fixed or unchanging. You can improve areas in which you scored lower. Although you may be weak in auditory learning, for example, many of your professors will lecture and expect you to take notes. If you work on improving your listening and note-taking skills, you can learn to handle lectures effectively. Make a conscious effort to work on improving areas of weakness as well as taking advantage of your strengths.

EXERCISE 1-4   **Directions:** For each learning strategy you listed in your Action Plan for Learning, write a brief evaluation of the strategy. Explain which worked; which, if any, did not; and what changes you have noticed in your ability to learn from reading.

PAY ATTENTION TO COMPREHENSION SIGNALS

Think for a moment about how you feel when you read material you can easily understand. Now compare that with what happens when you read something difficult and complicated. When you read easy material, does it seem that everything "clicks"? That is, do ideas seem to fit together and make sense? Is that "click" noticeably absent in difficult reading?

Read each of the following paragraphs. As you read, be aware of how well you understand each of them.

Paragraph 1

The **spinal cord** is actually an extension of the brain. It runs from the base of the brain down the center of the back, protected by a column of bones. The cord acts as a sort of bridge between the brain and the parts of the body below the neck. But the spinal cord is not merely a bridge. It also produces some behaviors on its own, without any help from the brain. These behaviors, called spinal **reflexes**, are automatic, requiring no conscious effort. For example, if you accidentally touch a hot iron, you will immediately pull your hand away, even before the brain has had a chance to register what has happened. Nerve impulses bring a message to the spinal cord (HOT!), and the spinal cord immediately sends out a command via other nerve impulses, telling muscles in your arm to contract and pull your hand away from the iron. (Reflexes above the neck, such as sneezing and blinking, involve the lower part of the brain rather than the spinal cord.)

—Wade and Tavris, *Psychology,* p. 82.

Paragraph 2

In an isolated antiworld, antipeople would go about their lives the same as we do. When an antiperson flipped an antiswitch, antiatoms in the antilightbulb would give off the same kind of light that you are using to read these words. There would be no annihilation going on, because there would be no ordinary matter involved. If, however, you happened to be transported to this antiworld, and tried to shake hands with your antiself, the two of you would disappear in a titanic explosion. In that explosion your bodies would be converted almost entirely into pure energy; all that would be left would be electromagnetic radiation and a thin cloud of particles.

—Trefil, "Greetings from the Antiworld," *Smithsonian,* p. 62.

Did you feel comfortable and confident as you read Paragraph 1? Did ideas seem to lead from one to another and make sense? How did you feel while reading Paragraph 2? Most likely you sensed its difficulty and felt confused. Some words were unfamiliar, and you could not follow the flow of ideas.

As you read Paragraph 2, did you know that you were not understanding it? Did you feel lost and confused? Table 1-2 lists and compares some common signals that are useful in monitoring your comprehension. Not all signals appear at the same time, and not all signals work for everyone. As you study the list, identify those positive signals you sensed as you read Paragraph 1 on the spinal cord. Then identify those negative signals that you sensed when reading about the antiworld.

Once you are able to recognize negative signals while reading, the next step is to take action to correct the problem. Specific techniques are given in the last section of this chapter.

TABLE 1-2   Comprehension Signals

Positive Signals	Negative Signals
Everything seems to fit and make sense; ideas flow logically from one to another.	Some pieces do not seem to belong; the ideas do not fit together or make sense.
You are able to understand what the author is saying.	You feel as if you are struggling to stay with the author.
You can see where the author is leading.	You cannot think ahead or predict what will come next.
You are able to make connections among ideas.	You are unable to see how ideas connect.
You read at a regular, comfortable pace.	You often slow down or lose your place.
You understand why the material was assigned.	You do not know why the material was assigned and cannot explain why it is important.
You can understand the material after reading it once.	You need to reread sentences or paragraphs frequently.
You recognize most words or can figure them out from context.	Many words are unfamiliar.
You can express the key ideas in your own words.	You must reread and use the author's language to explain an idea.
You feel comfortable with the topic; you have some background knowledge.	The topic is unfamiliar; you know nothing about it.

Directions: Read the following excerpt from a biology textbook on the theory of continental drift. It is intended to be difficult, so do not be discouraged. As you read, monitor your comprehension. After reading, answer the questions that follow.

In 1912, Alfred Wegener published a paper that was triggered by the common observation of the good fit between South America's east coast and Africa's west coast. Could these great continents ever have been joined? Wegener coordinated this jigsaw-puzzle analysis with other ecological and climatological data and proposed the theory of continental drift. He suggested that about 200 million years ago, all of the earth's continents were joined together into one enormous land mass, which he called Pangaea. In the ensuing millennia, according to Wegener's idea, Pangaea broke apart, and the fragments began to drift northward (by today's compass orientation) to their present location.

Wegener's idea received rough treatment in his lifetime. His geologist contemporaries attacked his naivete as well as his supporting data, and his theory was neglected until about 1960. At that time, a new generation of geologists revived the idea and subjected it to new scrutiny based on recent findings.

The most useful data have been based on magnetism in ancient lava flows. When a lava flow cools, metallic elements in the lava are oriented in a way that provides permanent evidence of the direction of the earth's magnetic field at the time, recording for future geologists both its north-south orientation and its latitude. From such maps, it is possible to determine the ancient positions of today's continents. We now believe that not only has continental drift occurred, as Wegener hypothesized, but that it continues to occur today. . . .

The disruption of Pangaea began some 230 million years ago in the Paleozoic era. By the Mesozoic era, the Eurasian land mass (called Laurasia) had moved away to form the northernmost continent. Gondwanaland, the mass that included India and the southern continents, had just begun to divide. Finally, during the late Mesozoic era, after South America and Africa were well divided, what was to be the last continental separation began, with Australia and Antarctica drifting apart. Both the North and South Atlantic oceans would continue to widen considerably up to the Cenozoic era, a trend that is continuing today. So we see that although the bumper sticker "Reunite Gondwanaland" has a third-world, trendy ring to it, it's an unlikely proposition.

—Wallace, *Biology,* p. 185.

1. How would you rate your overall comprehension? What positive signals did you sense? Did you feel any negative signals?

2. Test the accuracy of your rating in Question 1 by answering the following questions based on the material you read.

   a. Explain Wegener's theory of continental drift.

   b. Which two continents led Wegener to develop his theory?

   c. What recent finding has supported Wegener's theory?

   d. Describe the way in which Pangaea broke up and drifted to become the continents we know today.

3. In which sections was your comprehension strongest?

4. Did you feel at any time that you had lost, or were about to lose, comprehension? If so, go back to that paragraph now. What made that paragraph difficult to read?

5. Would it have been useful to refer to a world map?

6. Underline any difficult words that interfered with your comprehension.

WORK ON IMPROVING YOUR COMPREHENSION

At times, you will realize that your comprehension is poor or incomplete. When this occurs, take immediate action. Identify as specifically as possible the cause of the problem. Do this by answering the following question: "Why is this not making sense?" Determine if it is difficult words, complex ideas, organization, or your lack of concentration that is bothering you. Next, make changes in your reading to correct or compensate for the problem. Table 1-3 on page 24 lists common problems and offers strategies to correct them.

EXERCISE 1-6   **Directions:** Read each of the following difficult paragraphs, monitoring your comprehension as you do so. After reading each passage, identify and describe any problems you experienced. Then indicate what strategies you would use to correct these.

A. A word about food—in the simplest of terms, there are two kinds of organisms: those that make their own food, usually by photosynthesis (autotrophs, "self-feeders") and those that depend upon an outside-the-cell food source (heterotrophs, "other-feeders"). The autotrophs include a few kinds of bacteria, some one-celled eukaryotes (protistans), and all green plants. The heterotrophs encompass most bacteria, many protistans, all fungi, and all animals. Because this chapter is about animal nutrition, attention first will be given to examining the nature of food, then to how food is made available to cells.

—Norstog and Meyerricks, *Biology,* p. 193.

• Problem: _____

• Strategies: _____

B. The vestibular apparatus in the inner ear has two distinct components: the semicircular canals (three mutually perpendicular, fluid-filled tubes that contain hair cells connected to nerve fibers), which are sensitive to angular acceleration of the head; and the otolith organs (two sacs filled with calcium carbonate crystals embedded in a gel), which respond to linear acceleration. Because movement of the crystals in the otoliths generates the signal of acceleration to the brain and because the laws of physics relate that acceleration to a net force, gravity is always implicit in the signal. Thus, the otoliths have been referred to as gravity receptors. They are not the only ones. Mechanical receptors in the muscles, tendons and joints—as well as pressure receptors in the skin, particularly on the bottom of the feet—respond to the weight of limb segments and other body parts.

—White, "Weightlessness and the Human Body," *Scientific American Online,* p. 2.

• Problem: _____

• Strategies: _____

C. The objective of some tariffs is to protect an industry that produces goods vital to a nation's defense. In the case of a strategic industry, productive efficiency relative to that of other nations may not be an important consideration. The domestic industry—oil, natural gas, shipping, or steel, for example—may require protection because of its importance to national defense. Without protection, such industries might be weakened by foreign competition. Then, in an international crisis, the nation might find itself in short supply of products essential to national defense.

—Chisholm and McCarty, *Principles of Economics,* p. 443.

• Problem: _____

• Strategies: _____

TABLE 1-3   How to Improve Your Comprehension

Problems	Strategies
Poor concentration	1. Take limited breaks. 2. Tackle difficult material when your mind is fresh and alert. 3. Choose an appropriate place to study. 4. Focus your attention.
Words are difficult or unfamiliar.	1. Use context and analyze word parts. 2. Skim through material before reading. Mark and look up meanings of difficult words. Jot meanings in the margin. 3. Refer to the vocabulary preview list, footnotes, or glossary.
Sentences are long or confusing.	1. Read aloud. 2. Locate the key idea(s). 3. Check difficult words. 4. Express each sentence in your own words.
Ideas are hard to understand, complicated.	1. Rephrase or explain each in your own words. 2. Make notes. 3. Locate a more basic text that explains ideas in simpler form. 4. Study with a classmate; discuss difficult ideas.

Ideas are new and unfamiliar; you have little or no knowledge about the topic, and the writer assumes you do.	1. Make sure you didn't miss or skip introductory information.
	2. Get background information by referring to
	  a. an earlier section or chapter in the book.
	  b. an encyclopedia.
	  c. a more basic text.

The material seems disorganized or poorly organized.	1. Pay more attention to headings. 2. Read the summary, if available. 3. Try to discover organization by writing an outline or drawing a map as you read (see Chapter 11).
You do not know what is and is not important.	1. Preview. 2. Ask and answer guide questions. 3. Locate and underline topic sentences (see Chapter 6).

LEARNING STYLE TIPS

If you are a(n) . . .	Then improve your comprehension by . . .
Auditory learner	Reading aloud
Visual learner	Visualizing paragraph organization
Applied learner	Thinking of real-life situations that illustrate ideas in the passage
Conceptual learner	Asking questions

SELF-TEST SUMMARY

How can you develop a positive attitude toward reading?	You can begin to develop a positive attitude if you think of reading as an active process of looking for important ideas and unlocking a writer's message, and if you realize to do this successfully you cannot rush through it.
What can you do to control your concentration?	Building concentration involves two steps: 1. Control your surroundings by wisely choosing your time and place of study and avoiding distractions. 2. Focus your attention on the assignment by setting goals and rewarding yourself for achieving them by working in planned, small time blocks with frequent breaks, and by getting actively involved in the assignment.
What is learning style?	Learning style refers to your profile of relative strengths as a learner. Its five components are: 1. Auditory or visual learner 2. Applied or conceptual learner 3. Spatial or verbal learner 4. Social or independent learner 5. Creative or pragmatic learner
How can knowing your learning style make you a better student?	Discovering what type of learner you are can help you find out what strategies work best for you in reading and studying. It will also help you to recognize your limitations so that you can work on overcoming them.
What can you do to be sure that you understand your reading assignments?	First, you should pay attention to whether you sense positive or negative signals while reading. Next, if the signals are mostly negative, you should determine what is causing your poor comprehension—your concentration, the words, the ideas, or the organization. Finally, you should make changes in your reading methods to correct the problem.

Getting More Practice with . . .
Learning

WORKING TOGETHER

Directions: Bring to class a difficult paragraph or brief excerpt. Working in groups, each group member should read each piece and then together (1) discuss why the material was difficult and (2) compare negative and positive signals they received (refer to Table 1-2). Each student should then select strategies to overcome the difficulties.

GOING ONLINE

Internet Activities

1. Index of Learning Styles Questionnaire

   http://www.engr.ncsu.edu/learningstyles/ilsweb.html

   Try another learning style assessment at this site from North Carolina State University. Compare your results with those from the assessment in this book. How do online tests differ from those on paper? Which do you prefer? Is this a result of your learning style?

2. Improving Your Concentration

   http://www.k-state.edu/counseling/topics/career/concentr.html

   Kansas State University offers some interesting ideas for keeping your mind from wandering, being distracted, and much more! Try some of these techniques, and keep track of what works (and what does not) for you.

Companion Website

For additional readings, exercises, and Internet activities, visit this book's Companion Website at:

http://www.ablongman.com/mcwhorter

If you need a user name and password, please see your instructor.

My Reading Lab

For more practice on concentration, visit MyReadingLab, click on the Reading Skills tab, and then click on Memorization and Concentration—Mount Rushmore, South Dakota.

http://www.myreadinglab.com

TEST-TAKING TIPS

Starting with the Right Attitude

The attitude with which you approach a test is very important and can dramatically affect your performance. It is essential to think positively and approach the test actively. Use the following suggestions:

- Remind yourself that you have worked hard and deserve to pass.

- Think of the test as a chance to show what you have learned.

- Do not panic if you cannot answer a question. Make a guess and move on to items you can answer.

- If you do not immediately know an answer, *think!* You may be able to reason it out. This tip box in other chapters will offer suggestions.

Name _____

Section _____ Date _____

Number right _____ x 10 points = Score _____

ASSESSMENT READING SELECTION

This reading and the questions that follow are intended to help you assess your current level of skill. Read the article, and then answer the questions that measure your comprehension. You may refer back to the reading in order to answer them. Compute your score by filling in the scoring box above.

Primary Colors

Kim McLarin

This essay, originally published in the *New York Times Magazine,* describes a mother's response to her interracial child.

> **Vocabulary Preview**
>
> **retrospect** (par. 5) reviewing the past
>
> **eccentricities** (par. 6) oddities
>
> **abduction** (par. 9) kidnapping
>
> **disconcerting** (par. 10) upsetting
>
> **condemnation** (par. 13) strong criticism or disapproval
>
> **allegiances** (par. 13) loyalties
>
> **denounce** (par. 13) to criticize openly
>
> **align** (par. 14) join with others

1   A few weeks after my daughter was born, I took her to a new pediatrician for an exam. The doctor took one look at Samantha and exclaimed: "Wow! She's so light!" I explained that my husband is white, but it didn't seem to help. The doctor commented on Sam's skin color so often that I finally asked what was on her mind.

2   "I'm thinking albino*," she said.

3   The doctor, who is white, claimed she had seen the offspring of many interracial couples, but never a child this fair. "They're usually a darker, coffee-with-cream color. Some of them are this light at birth, but by 72 hours you can tell they have a black parent."

4   To prove her point, she held her arm next to Samantha's stomach. "I mean, this could be my child!"

---

*person lacking skin pigmentation resulting in abnormally white hair or skin

5   It's funny now, in retrospect. But at the time, with my hormones still raging from childbirth, the incident sent me into a panic. Any fool could see that Samantha wasn't an albino—she had black hair and dark blue eyes. It must be a trick. The doctor, who had left the room, probably suspected me of kidnapping this "white" child and was outside calling the police. By the time she returned I was ready to fight.

Children of different racial backgrounds

6   Fortunately, her partner dismissed the albino theory, and we escaped and found a new pediatrician, one who knows a little more about genetic eccentricities. But the incident stayed with me because, in the months since, other white people have assumed Samantha is not my child. This is curious to me, this inability to connect across skin tones, especially since Samantha has my full lips and broad nose. I'll admit that I myself didn't expect Sam to be quite so pale, so much closer to her father's Nordic‡ coloring than my own umber tones. My husband is a blue-eyed strawberry blond; I figured that my genes would take his genes in the first round.

7   Wrong.

8   Needless to say, I love Sam just as she is. She is amazingly, heartbreakingly beautiful to me in the way that babies are to their parents. She sweeps me away with her mischievous grin and her belly laugh, with the coy way she tilts her head after flinging the cup from her highchair. When we are alone and I look at Samantha, I see Samantha, not the color of her skin.

9   And yet I admit that I wouldn't mind if she were darker, dark enough so that white people would know she was mine and black people wouldn't give her a hard time. I know a black guy who, while crossing into Canada, was suspected of having kidnapped his fair-skinned son. So far no one has accused me of child abduction, but I have been mistaken for Samantha's nanny. It has happened so often that I've considered going into business as a nanny spy. I could sit in the park and take notes on your child-care worker. Better than hiding a video camera in the living room.

10   In a way it's disconcerting, my being mistaken for a nanny. Because, to be blunt, I don't like seeing black women caring for white children. It may be because I grew up in the South, where black women once had no choice but to leave their own children and suckle the offspring of others. The weight of that past, the whiff of a power imbalance, still stains such pairings for me. That's unfair, I know, to the professional, hard-working (mostly Caribbean) black nannies of New York. But there you are.

---

‡characteristic of Scandinavian people: light-skinned, blond-haired people

11   On the flip side, I think being darker wouldn't hurt Samantha with black people, either. A few weeks ago, in my beauty shop, I overheard a woman trashing a friend for "slathering" his light-skinned children with sunscreen during the summer.

12   "Maybe he doesn't want them getting skin cancer," suggested the listener. But my girl was having none of that.

13   "He doesn't want them getting black!" she said, as full of righteous condemnation as only a black woman in a beauty shop can be. Now, maybe the woman was right about her friend's motivation. Or maybe she was 100 percent wrong. Maybe because she herself is the color of butterscotch she felt she had to declare her allegiances loudly, had to place herself prominently high on the unofficial black scale and denounce anyone caught not doing the same. Either way, I know it means grief for Sam.

14   I think that as time goes on my daughter will probably align with black people anyway, regardless of the relative fairness of her skin. My husband is fine with that, as long as it doesn't mean denying him or his family.

15   The bottom line is that society has a deep need to categorize people, to classify and, yes, to stereotype. Race is still the easiest, most convenient way of doing so. That race tells you, in the end, little or nothing about a person is beside the point. We still feel safer believing that we can sum up one another at a glance.

CHECKING YOUR COMPREHENSION

Directions: Select the best answer for each of the following questions.

_____ 1. The main point of this selection is that
   a. people classify others on the basis of skin color because it is what they notice first.
   b. being the mother of an interracial child has more negative than positive moments.
   c. having an interracial child is easier in the North than in the South.
   d. although people are still aware of race, most people realize that race is not important.

_____ 2. The main idea of paragraph 9 is that
   a. having people think she is not the mother has several advantages.
   b. people usually think a dark-skinned adult is not the parent of a light-skinned child.
   c. white people have more difficulty than black people in accepting skin tone differences in a parent and child.
   d. having a light-skinned child is easier for the author than having a dark-skinned child.

_____ 3. The main idea of paragraph 10 is that
   a. the author has negative feelings about black women caring for white children.
   b. black women have always cared for white children.
   c. Caribbean nannies are hardworking professionals.
   d. because the author grew up in the South, she is used to seeing nannies.

_____ 4. Samantha has
   a. blond hair.
   b. brown eyes.
   c. coffee-with-cream skin coloring.
   d. full lips.

_____ 5. One reason the author wishes her daughter were darker is that she
   a. wants Sam to identify more with her father's family.
   b. does not want Sam to have to use sunscreen.
   c. wants to travel to Canada with Sam.
   d. does not want black people to criticize Sam.

_____ 6. The term "retrospect" in paragraph 5 means
   a. analysis.
   b. looking back.
   c. expectation.
   d. commentary.

_____ 7. The incident at the pediatrician's office upset the author because she was afraid that
   a. her daughter might have a serious disease.
   b. the doctor thought Samantha was not her child.
   c. her child might have been switched at birth.
   d. the doctor would harm Samantha.

_____ 8. The main idea of paragraph 8 is that
   a. Sam is a beautiful, teasing child.
   b. the author is most aware of Sam's skin tone when she is with other people.
   c. skin color does not come between the author and Sam.
   d. the author feels guilty for wishing Sam were darker.

_____ 9. The author finds a new pediatrician because the first one
   a. calls in her partner to help her.
   b. has never examined an interracial child.
   c. offended her and seemed to have incorrect ideas about genetics.
   d. accuses the author of kidnapping a child.

_____ 10. The term "slathering" in paragraph 11 means
   a. rubbing in thoroughly.
   b. artificially coloring.
   c. insisting on applying.
   d. covering thickly.

> For more practice, ask your instructor for an opportunity to work on the mastery tests that appear in the Test Bank.

Chapter
2

Using Context Clues

**THIS CHAPTER
WILL SHOW YOU
HOW TO**

**1 Figure out the
meanings of words
from their use in a
sentence**

**2 Use five types of
context clues**

Getting Started with . . .
Context Clues

A portion of the photograph is blocked out. Can you guess what is
missing from the photograph? The photograph shows a soccer
player kicking the ball. You used the existing information shown in
the photograph to reason out what was missing. In much the
same way as you figured out what was missing from the photograph, you can also figure out a word that you do not know
within a sentence. By using the words around a word you do not
know, you can figure out its meaning. This chapter shows you
how to use context, the words around a given word, to determine
meaning.

WHAT IS CONTEXT?

Try to figure out what is missing in the following brief paragraph. Write the missing words in the blanks provided.

Most Americans can speak only one _____. Europeans, however,

_____ several. As a result, Europeans think _____

are unfriendly and unwilling to communicate with them.

Did you insert the word *language* in the first blank, *speak* or *know* in the second blank, and *Americans* in the third blank? Most likely, you correctly identified all three missing words. You could tell from the sentence which word to put in. The words around the missing words—the sentence context— gave you clues as to which word would fit and make sense. Such clues are called **context clues.**

While you probably will not find missing words on a printed page, you will often find words that you do not know. Context clues can help you to figure out the meanings of unfamiliar words.

Example:

Phobias, such as fear of heights, water, or confined spaces, are difficult to eliminate.

From the sentence, you can tell that *phobia* means "fear of specific objects or situations."

Here is another example:

The couple finally **secured** a table at the popular, crowded restaurant.

You can figure out that *secured* means "got" or "took ownership of" the table.

TYPES OF CONTEXT CLUES

There are five types of context clues to look for: (1) definition, (2) synonym, (3) example, (4) contrast, and (5) inference.

Definition Clues

Many times a writer defines a word immediately following its use. The writer may directly define a word by giving a brief definition or a synonym (a word that has the same meaning). Such words and phrases as *means, is, refers to,* and *can be defined as* are often used. Here are some examples:

> **Corona** refers to the outermost part of the sun's atmosphere.
>
> A **soliloquy** is a speech made by a character in a play that reveals his or her thoughts to the audience.

At other times, rather than formally define the word, a writer may provide clues or synonyms. Punctuation is often used to signal that a definition clue to a word's meaning is to follow. Punctuation also separates the meaning clue from the rest of the sentence. Three types of punctuation are used in this way. In the examples below, notice that the meaning clue is separated from the rest of the sentence by punctuation.

1. Commas

   An **oligopoly,** *control of a product by a small number of companies,* exists in the long-distance phone market.

   Equity, *general principles of fairness and justice,* is used in law when existing laws do not apply or are inadequate.

2. Parentheses

   A leading cause of heart disease is a diet with too much **cholesterol** (*a fatty substance made of carbon, hydrogen, and oxygen*).

3. Dashes

   Ancient Egyptians wrote in **hieroglyphics**—*pictures used to represent words.*

   Facets—*small flat surfaces at different angles*—bring out the beauty of a diamond.

EXERCISE 2-1

Directions: Read each sentence, and write a definition or synonym for each boldfaced word or phrase. Use the definition context clue to help you determine word meaning.

1. **Glog,** a Swedish hot punch, is often served at holiday parties.

   _____

2. The judge's **candor**—his sharp, open frankness—shocked the jury.

   _____

3. A **chemical bond** is a strong attractive force that holds two or more atoms together.

_____

4. **Lithium** (an alkali metal) is so soft it can be cut with a knife.

_____

5. Hearing, technically known as **audition,** begins when a sound wave reaches the outer ear.

_____

6. Five-line rhyming poems, or **limericks,** are among the simplest forms of poetry.

_____

7. Our country's **gross national product**—the total market value of its national output of goods and services—is increasing steadily.

_____

8. A **species** is a group of animals or plants that share similar characteristics and are able to interbreed.

_____

9. Broad, flat noodles that are served covered with sauce or butter are called **fettuccine.**

_____

10. Many diseases have **latent periods,** periods of time between the infection and the first appearance of a symptom.

_____

Synonym Clues

At other times, rather than formally define the word, a writer may provide a synonym—a word or brief phrase that is close in meaning. The synonym may appear in the same sentence as the unknown word.

The author purposely left the ending of his novel **ambiguous,** or _unclear,_ so readers would have to decide for themselves what happened.

Other times, it may appear anywhere in the passage, in an earlier or later sentence.

After the soccer match, a **melee** broke out in the parking lot. Three people were injured in the *brawl,* and several others were arrested.

EXERCISE 2-2   **Directions:** Read each sentence and write a definition or synonym for each boldfaced word or phrase. Use the synonym context clue to help you determine word meaning.

1. The mayor's assistant was accused of **malfeasance,** although he denied any wrongdoing.

   _____

2. The words of the president seemed to excite and **galvanize** the American troops, who cheered enthusiastically throughout the speech.

   _____

3. Mia Hamm's superior ability and **prowess** on the soccer field have inspired many girls to become athletes.

   _____

4. Many gardeners improve the quality of their soil by **amending** it with organic compost.

   _____

5. Eliminating salt from the diet is a **prudent,** sensible decision for people with high blood pressure.

   _____

6. The **cadence,** or rhythm, of the Dixieland band had many people tapping their feet along with the music.

   _____

7. Edgar Allan Poe is best known for his **macabre** short stories and poems. His eerie tale "The Fall of the House of Usher" was later made into a horror movie starring Vincent Price.

   _____

8. While she was out of the country, Greta authorized me to act as her **proxy,** or agent, in matters having to do with her business and her personal bank accounts.

    _____

9. The **arsenal** of a baseball pitcher ideally includes several different kinds of pitches. From this supply of pitches, he or she needs to have at least one that can fool the batter.

    _____

10. A **coalition** of neighborhood representatives formed to fight a proposed highway through the area. The group also had the support of several local businesses.

    _____

Example Clues

Writers often include examples that help to explain or clarify a word. Suppose you do not know the meaning of the word *toxic,* and you find it used in the following sentence:

> **Toxic** materials, such as arsenic, asbestos, pesticides, and lead, can cause bodily damage.

This sentence gives four examples of toxic materials. From the examples given, which are all poisonous substances, you could conclude that *toxic* means "poisonous."

Examples:

Forest floors are frequently covered with **fungi**—molds, mushrooms, and mildews.

Legumes, such as peas and beans, produce pods.

Arachnids, including tarantulas, black widow spiders, and ticks, often have segmented bodies.

Newsmagazines, like *Time* or *Newsweek,* provide more details about news events than newspapers because they focus on only a few stories.

Directions: Read each sentence and write a definition or synonym for each boldfaced word or phrase. Use the example context clue to help you determine meaning.

1. Many **pharmaceuticals,** including morphine and penicillin, are not readily available in some countries.

   _____

2. The child was **reticent** in every respect; she would not speak, refused to answer questions, and avoided looking at anyone.

   _____

3. Most **condiments,** such as pepper, mustard, and catsup, are used to improve the flavor of foods.

   _____

4. Instructors provide their students with **feedback** through test grades and comments on papers.

   _____

5. **Physiological needs**—hunger, thirst, and sex—promote survival of the human species.

   _____

6. Clothing is available in a variety of **fabrics,** including cotton, wool, polyester, and linen.

   _____

7. In the past month, we have had almost every type of **precipitation**—rain, snow, sleet, and hail.

   _____

8. **Involuntary reflexes,** like breathing and beating of the heart, are easily measured.

   _____

9. The student had a difficult time distinguishing between **homonyms**—words such as *see* and *sea, wore* and *war,* and *deer* and *dear.*

   _____

10. Abstract paintings often include such **geometrics** as squares, cubes, and triangles.

_____

Contrast Clues

It is sometimes possible to determine the meaning of an unknown word from a word or phrase in the context that has an opposite meaning. If a single word provides a clue, it is often an **antonym**—a word opposite in meaning to the unknown word. Notice, in the following sentence, how a word opposite in meaning to the boldfaced word provides a clue to its meaning:

> One of the dinner guests **succumbed** to the temptation to have a second piece of cake, but the others resisted.

Although you may not know the meaning of *succumbed,* you know that the one guest who succumbed was different from the others who resisted. The word *but* suggests this. Since the others resisted a second dessert, you can tell that one guest gave in and had a piece. Thus, *succumbed* means the opposite of *resist;* that is, to give in to.

Examples:

The professor **advocates** testing on animals, *but* many of her students feel it is cruel.

Most of the graduates were **elated,** *though* a few felt sad and depressed.

The old man acted **morose,** *whereas* his grandson was very lively.

The gentleman was quite **portly,** *but* his wife was thin.

EXERCISE 2-4   **Directions:** Read each sentence and write a definition or synonym for each boldfaced word. Use the contrast clue to help you determine meaning.

1. Some city dwellers are **affluent;** others live in or near poverty.

_____

2. I am certain that the hotel will hold our reservation; however, if you are **dubious,** call to make sure.

_____

3. Although most experts **concurred** with the research findings, several strongly disagreed.

_____

4. The speaker **denounced** certain legal changes while praising other reforms.

_____

5. The woman's parents **thwarted** her marriage plans though they liked her fiancé.

_____

6. In medieval Europe, **peasants** led difficult lives, whereas the wealthy landowners lived in luxury.

_____

7. When the couple moved into their new home they **revamped** the kitchen and bathroom but did not change the rest of the rooms.

_____

8. The young nurse was **bewildered** by the patient's symptoms, but the doctor realized she was suffering from a rare form of leukemia.

_____

9. Despite my husband's **pessimism** about my chances of winning the lottery, I was certain I would win.

_____

10. The mayoral candidate praised the town council, while the mayor **deprecated** it.

_____

Inference Clues

Many times you can figure out the meaning of an unknown word by using logic and reasoning skills. For instance, look at the following sentence:

> Bob is quite **versatile;** he is a good student, a top athlete, an excellent car mechanic, and a gourmet cook.

You can see that Bob is successful at many different types of activities, and you could reason that *versatile* means "capable of doing many things competently."

Examples:

When the customer tried to pay with Mexican **pesos,** the clerk explained that the store accepted only U.S. dollars.

The potato salad looked so plain that I decided to **garnish** it with parsley and paprika to give it some color.

We had to leave the car and walk up because the **incline** was too steep to drive.

Since Reginald was nervous, he brought his rabbit's foot **talisman** with him to the exam.

EXERCISE 2-5 **Directions:** Read each sentence and write a definition or synonym for each boldfaced word. Try to reason out the meaning of each word using information provided in the context.

1. The **wallabies** at the zoo looked like kangaroos.

   _____

2. The foreign students quickly **assimilated** many aspects of American culture.

   _____

3. On hot, humid summer afternoons, I often feel **languid.**

   _____

4. Some physical fitness experts recommend jogging or weight lifting to overcome the effects of a **sedentary** job.

   _____

5. The legal aid clinic was **subsidized** by city and county funds.

   _____

6. When the bank robber reached his **haven,** he breathed a sigh of relief and began to count his money.

   _____

7. The teenager was **intimidated** by the presence of a police officer walking the beat and decided not to spray-paint the school wall.

_____

8. The vase must have been **jostled** in shipment because it arrived with several chips in it.

_____

9. Although she had visited the fortune-teller several times, she was not sure she believed in the **occult.**

_____

10. If the plan did not work, the colonel had a **contingency** plan ready.

_____

EXERCISE 2-6

Directions: Read each sentence and write a definition or synonym for each boldfaced word. Use the context clue to help you determine meaning.

1. The economy was in a state of continual **flux;** inflation increased one month and decreased the next.

_____

2. The grand jury **exonerated** the police officer of any possible misconduct or involvement in illegal activity.

_____

3. Art is always talkative, but Ed is usually **taciturn.**

_____

4. Many **debilities** of old age, including poor eyesight and loss of hearing, can be treated medically.

_____

5. Police **interrogation,** or questioning, can be a frightening experience.

_____

6. The soap opera contained numerous **morbid** events: the death of a young child, the suicide of her father, and the murder of his older brother.

_____

7. After long hours of practice, Peter finally learned to type; Sam's efforts, however, were **futile.**

_____

8. Although the farm appeared **derelict,** we discovered that an elderly man lived there.

_____

9. The newspaper's error was **inadvertent;** the editor did not intend to include the victim's name.

_____

10. To save money, we have decided to **curtail** the number of DVDs we buy each month.

_____

11. Steam from the hot radiator **scalded** the mechanic's hand.

_____

12. The businesswoman's **itinerary** outlined her trip and listed Cleveland as her next stop.

_____

13. **Theologies,** such as Catholicism, Buddhism, and Hinduism, are discussed at great length in the class.

_____

14. Steven had very good **rapport** with his father but was unable to get along well with his mother.

_____

15. The duchess had a way of **flaunting** her jewels so that everyone could see and envy them.

_____

Directions: Read each of the following passages and use context clues to figure out the meaning of each boldfaced word or phrase. Write a synonym or brief definition for each in the space provided.

A. Can looking at a color affect your behavior or **alter** your mood? Some researchers are **skeptical,** but others believe color can influence how you act and feel. A number of experiments have been conducted that **demonstrate** the effects of color. In 1979 a psychologist named Schauss **evaluated** the effect of the color pink. He found that the color relaxed the subjects so much that they could not perform simple strength tests as well as they did when looking at other **hues.** The officer in charge of a U.S. Navy **brig** in Washington noticed Schauss's findings and allowed Schauss to test his calm-color **hypothesis** on inmates. Today, many **institutions,** such as jails, juvenile correction facilities, and holding centers, put individuals in pink rooms when their tempers **flare.**

No one is certain how color affects behavior. Schauss **conjectures** that a person's response to color is determined in the brain's **reticular formation,** a relay station for millions of the body's nerve impulses. Another researcher **speculates** that **perception** of color by the eye **spurs** the release of important chemicals in the body.

—Geiwitz, *Psychology,* p. 189.

1. alter

   _____

2. skeptical

   _____

3. demonstrate

   _____

4. evaluated

   _____

5. hues

   _____

6. brig

   _____

7. hypothesis

   _____

8. institutions

_____

9. flare

_____

10. conjectures

_____

11. reticular formation

_____

12. speculates

_____

13. perception

_____

14. spurs

_____

B. The most important set of symbols is language. **Language,** among humans, refers to the systemized use of speech and hearing to convey or express feelings and ideas. It is through language that our ideas, values, beliefs, and knowledge are **transmitted,** expressed, and shared. Other **media** such as music, art, and dance are also important means of communication, but language is uniquely flexible and precise. It permits us to share our experiences in the past and present, to **convey** our hopes for the future, and to describe dreams and fantasies that may bear little **resemblance** to reality. Some scientists have questioned whether thought is even possible without language. Although language can be used **imprecisely** and may seem hard to understand, it is the chief factor in our ability to transmit culture.

—Eschelman, et al., *Sociology,* p. 93.

1. language

_____

2. transmitted

_____

3. media

_____

4. convey

_____

5. resemblance

_____

6. imprecisely

_____

C. Social norms are another element of culture. **Norms** are rules of conduct or social expectations for behavior. These rules and social expectations **specify** how people should and should not behave in various social situations. They are both **prescriptive** (they tell people what they should do) and **proscriptive** (they tell people what they should not do) . . . .

An early American sociologist, William G. Sumner (1840–1910), identified two types of norms, which he labeled "folkways" and "mores." They are **distinguished** not by their content, but by the degree to which group members are **compelled** to conform to them, by their degree of importance, by the **severity** of punishment if they are violated, or by the intensity of feeling associated with adherence to them. Folkways are customs or conventions. They are norms in that they provide rules for conduct, but **violations** of folkways bring only mild censure.

—Eschelman, et al., *Sociology,* pp. 98–99.

1. norms

_____

2. specify

_____

3. prescriptive

_____

4. proscriptive

_____

5. distinguished

_____

6. compelled

_____

7. severity

_____

8. violations

_____

THE LIMITATIONS OF CONTEXT CLUES

There are two limitations to the use of context clues. First, context clues seldom lead to a complete definition. Second, sometimes a sentence does not contain clues to a word's meaning. In these cases you will need to draw on other vocabulary skills. Chapters 3 and 4 will help you with these skills.

LEARNING STYLE TIPS

If you tend to be a(n) . . .	Then use context by . . .
Auditory learner	Reading the context aloud
Visual learner	Visualizing the context

SELF-TEST SUMMARY

What are context clues used for?	They are used to figure out the meaning of an unknown word used in a sentence or paragraph.
What are the five types of context clues?	The five types of context clues are: • Definition—a brief definition of or synonym for a word • Synonym—a word or phrase that is similar in meaning to the unknown word • Example—specific instances or examples that clarify a word's meaning • Contrast—a word or phrase of opposite meaning • Inference—the use of reasoning skills to figure out word meanings

Getting More Practice with . . .
Context Clues

WORKING TOGETHER

Directions: Bring a brief textbook excerpt, editorial, or magazine article that contains difficult vocabulary to class. Working with another student, locate and underline at least three words in your article that your partner can define by using context clues. Work together in reasoning out each word, checking a dictionary to verify meanings.

GOING ONLINE

Internet Activities

1. Using Context Clues

   http://www.nj.devry.edu/esc/vocab.htm

   Review the types of context clues for learning the meanings of unfamiliar words. Write your own sentence for each type of clue.

2. Using Context Clues

   http://www.csupomona.edu/~lrc/crsp/handouts/context_clues.html

   This site also reviews the ways to use context clues. Read this over carefully, and then complete the exercise at the bottom of the page.

Companion Website

For additional readings, exercises, and Internet activities, visit this book's Companion Website at:

http://www.ablongman.com/mcwhorter

If you need a user name and password, please see your instructor.

My Reading Lab

For more practice on vocabulary, visit MyReadingLab, click on the Reading Skills tab, and then click on Vocabulary—The Library of Congress, Washington, D.C.

http://www.myreadinglab.com

Using Context

When answering questions about the meaning of a word in a sentence or paragraph, use the following suggestions:

• Test writers do not ask questions that students are unable to answer. So, if you are being asked the meaning of a particular word, there is probably a way to figure it out.

• Read beyond the word in question. Look beyond the word to find a clue to its meaning. Sometimes the context clue appears after the unknown word, either in the same sentence or in a later sentence.

Example: The economy was in a constant state of *flux.* One month inflation increased; the next month it decreased.

In this example, the clue to the meaning of *flux* appears in the sentence following the one in which the word is used.

• When you are unsure about your answer in a multiple choice question about the meaning of a word in a sentence or paragraph, first try to eliminate one or more choices. Then substitute the choice(s) you are considering for the unknown word in the sentence in which it appears. Choose the choice that makes the most sense and seems to fit.

Example: After the shopper *succumbed* to the temptation of buying an expensive new dress, she was filled with regret.

a. gave in

b. resisted

c. alerted

d. ridiculed

Choice a is correct. Choice b, *resisted,* does not fit because the shopper would not be filled with regret if she had resisted. Choice c, *alerted,* does not make sense—temptation is not usually alerted. Choice d does not make sense because temptation is usually not ridiculed.

Name _____

Section _____ Date _____

Number right _____ x 10 points = Score _____

Directions: Each of the following sentences contains a word whose meaning can be determined from context. Select the choice that most nearly states the meaning of the underlined word as it is used in the sentence.

_____ 1. The new zoo project will be underlined subsidized by city, county, state, and federal funds.
   a. prevented
   b. forgotten
   c. replaced
   d. financed

_____ 2. The burglar was so intimidated by the bright lights and barking dogs that he left hastily.
   a. frightened
   b. assisted
   c. excited
   d. encouraged

_____ 3. I explained to him that I would take care of his problem later, but he was not appeased.
   a. satisfied
   b. angry
   c. present
   d. frightened

_____ 4. Embassies typically follow well-established protocols, or accepted procedures, for seating guests at a government dinner.
   a. sets of rules
   b. scientific plans
   c. lists of invitations
   d. preferences of leaders

_____ 5. He seemed quite free and easy with a few friends, but at large parties he was quite inhibited.
   a. occupied
   b. controlled
   c. breathless
   d. expressive

_____ 6. He was prone to taking a nap in the afternoon as he had done every day for most of his life.
   a. not going
   b. trying
   c. likely
   d. anxious

_____ 7. Cracking passwords is the most prevalent method of illicit entry to computer systems.
   a. illegal
   b. permitted
   c. regular
   d. senseless

_____ 8. She disrupted the entire performance by coughing during the most important part.
   a. showed she appreciated
   b. participated in
   c. enjoyed
   d. upset

_____ 9. You can <u>confirm</u> that your test results are correct by checking the answer key.
   a. not know
   b. make sure
   c. apply
   d. guess

_____ 10. Rather than staying together, the group <u>dispersed</u>, and many became lost.
   a. sat down
   b. laughed
   c. scattered
   d. arranged itself

Name _____

Section _____ Date _____

Number right _____ x 20 points = Score _____

Directions: For each of the following statements, select the answer that correctly defines the underlined word.

_____ 1. In the past two hundred years, many species of whales have been hunted almost to the point of extinction. In response to worldwide concern over whales, the International Whaling Commission (IWC) declared a <u>moratorium</u> on commercial whaling in 1986.
   a. promotion
   b. proposition
   c. stopping of activity
   d. competition

_____ 2. Despite the example of athletic, attractive young women such as soccer star Mia Hamm, many teenage girls believe "the thinner the better." Fashion magazines featuring rail-thin models only <u>perpetuate</u> this belief, leading some teenagers to develop unrealistic and often unhealthy perceptions about their bodies.
   a. continue
   b. distort
   c. prevent
   d. correct

_____ 3. Although Lillian was 94 years old, she was healthy and mentally sharp. As she had done for most of her life, she insisted on living in her own apartment, buying her own groceries and paying her own bills, taking care of herself and making her own decisions—it was clear that she valued her <u>autonomy</u> above all else.
   a. social life
   b. family support
   c. loneliness
   d. independence

_____ 4. Our idea of the perfect vacation includes first-class airline tickets, a deluxe hotel room, and 24-hour room service, whereas Anne and Neil prefer something much more <u>rustic</u>. The last place they stayed didn't even have indoor plumbing!
   a. elegant
   b. simple
   c. comfortable
   d. active

_____ 5. The third-grade teacher marveled at the physical <u>disparities</u> among her students. Some were the size of kindergartners while others were almost as tall as she was.
   a. dislikes
   b. attitudes
   c. differences
   d. appearances

Name _____

Section _____ Date _____

Number right _____ x 20 points = Score _____

Directions: Read the following passage and choose the answer that best defines each boldfaced word from the passage.

Worms and *viruses* are rather unpleasant terms that have entered the **jargon** of the computer industry to describe some of the ways that computer systems can be invaded.

A worm can be defined as a program that transfers itself from computer to computer over a network and plants itself as a separate file on the target computer's disks. One worm was **injected** into an electronic mail network where it multiplied uncontrollably and clogged the memories of thousands of computers until they could no longer function.

A virus is a set of illicit instructions that passes itself on to other programs or documents with which it comes in contact. It can change or delete files, display words or obscene messages, or produce bizarre screen effects. In its most **vindictive** form, a virus can slowly **sabotage** a computer system and remain undetected for months, contaminating data or wiping out an entire hard drive. A virus can be dealt with using a vaccine, or antivirus, which is a computer program that stops the virus from spreading and often **eradicates** it.

—Capron, *Computers*, p. 233.

_____ 1. jargon
    a. language
    b. system
    c. confusion
    d. security

_____ 2. injected
    a. avoided
    b. introduced
    c. removed
    d. discussed

_____ 3. vindictive
    a. creative
    b. simple
    c. harmful
    d. typical

_____ 4. sabotage
    a. prevent
    b. destroy
    c. transfer
    d. produce

_____ 5. eradicates
    a. eliminates
    b. allows
    c. repeats
    d. produces

Chapter 2
Mastery Test 4
Reading Selection

Name _____

Section _____ Date _____

Number right* _____ x 10 points = Score _____

My Life as an Illegal

John Spong

This essay, taken from the periodical *Read*, which focuses on classic and contemporary issues, describes one man's life as an illegal immigrant in the United States. Read it to find out the problems he faces and how his life is affected by his illegal status.

> **Vocabulary Preview**
>
> **legal card** (par. 10) photograph identification given to noncitizens who are legal permanent residents of the United States
>
> **MoneyGram** (par. 12) a process for sending cash electronically

1   I've been here for sixteen years now, since I was sixteen years old, and I have been illegal the whole time. It has helped that I speak good English. When I got here, I knew words like "table" and "chicken," stuff like that, but when there was no chicken on the table, I was in trouble. You have to learn English if you want to communicate, to earn more money. I went to school, but not to learn English. Maybe I learned it watching TV, reading newspapers. My wife is illegal, too, and we have been living in Austin for thirteen years. She thinks I'm okay here because I look white, but she gets scared that she might get sent back. She's got darker skin, and her English is not as good, and she's afraid the migra are going to catch her. We have three kids who were all born here, who are all American citizens. Even if my wife and I are illegal, they have a right to be here. But if she gets thrown out, who's going to be with the kids? Who's going to be with me?

2   I pay Social Security tax every week, and I pay income tax every year. I have a driver's license, and I always drive with insurance, inspection, and registration. I don't want to do anything but to become legal and to work and to stay here with my kids. So I do everything right. That's all I want.

Crossing the Border

3   I was just a kid the first time I used one of my nephews' birth certificates to get across the border, so they didn't ask me any questions or anything. They just said, "Come on." I went to junior high in Los Angeles for a year or a year and a half, but things weren't really good. There were family problems, like always. I was not getting along with my brothers, and there were hard times. So I went back to Mexico, and

---

*To calculate the number right, use items 1–10 under "Mastery Test Skills Check."

that's when I hung out there for five years. When you're in Mexico like I was, it's always nice when you hear about somebody here. You always want to be here. You hear that you make money, that you wear nice clothes, have nice shoes. Back there, there's nothing.

4   So I came back when I was sixteen to work. I had been living with my parents and depending on them, and I was ready not to depend on anyone anymore. At that time, what you did was ride a bus to Tijuana, and once you were there, you would ask around for a coyote. Everybody knows a coyote, somebody who can get people across. But you have got to know the right guy, because there are some coyotes that can screw you. They take your money and don't pick you up, or they leave you someplace bad. I paid $300 to a guy to show me where to go.

5   I was with a group of men, and for us, there was no river or anything. We just jumped a six-foot-tall fence and ran across a big field. Then we hid under the trees for, like, ten minutes until somebody said run again. Then we crossed a highway, twelve lanes, and after that, somebody else picked us up and took us to a house somewhere in San Diego. They kept us there in the house for, like, a day. That night there were at least fifty of us, all over the house. We were from all over Mexico or South America. Those people were all strangers, but none of them worried me, because I knew everybody in there had family over here waiting for them and that we all just wanted to make it across and start working.

6   A van came and got some of us a little bit at a time. We all had to hide in the van. You have to sit on the floor in a line so your back is against the chest of the guy behind you, and somebody else's back is against your chest in front of you. And you have your legs bent so that your knees are by the shoulders of the guy in front of you. You sit like that from San Diego all the way to L.A., so once you get to L.A., your legs are numb. You can barely move. That's where they catch people, because they can't run. . . .

Making Ends Meet

7   I had one sister living in Austin, and she asked me to move here. She said to try Texas. I liked it here and stayed.

8   I was working in restaurants as a busboy, a food prep, a cook, and then a manager, at an Indian food place, a hamburger place, a barbecue place, and then a big restaurant, where I ran everything. I made the food orders and the work schedules. I always had two jobs at a time, eight hours in the day at one and then five more hours at night at another, almost every day. It was hard, but you have to work if you want to pay the rent. I was only twenty years old, but I had to pay $600 a month for our apartment and $200 a month for our car. And I always send $100 a month home to my parents.

9   But I needed a job that gave me better money and more time with my wife and kids. I had always been like a handyman, done a little bit of everything, and I started doing work for somebody here in town that needed a handyman. He referred me to the guy I work for now, Brian, and I started doing electrical work. That was eight

years ago. I'd changed a switch before, but never big jobs like wiring a whole house myself. But I picked it up real fast, in, like, six months, and in about one year of working with Brian, I was also doing side jobs on my own. Somebody would ask me to do something for them, and I would do it.

10   We're always aware that we don't have a legal card, so we stay out of trouble and try to lead a normal life. We take the kids to church every Sunday, because that's the way we grew up. The kids like school, and we go with them when they are in a show or make a presentation. We just try to live normal.

11   I went back to visit my little town in Mexico more often when I was single. But since I got married I have only been twice. The last time I went was the winter before 9/11 happened. It was easy then. When I was coming back, I just walked across the border and said I was a U.S. citizen, and they let me back in. But I decided it's not a good idea for me to go anymore. Basically, I am the support of my family, and I need to work and pay bills, and I am afraid maybe I couldn't get back across, or I could be put in jail.

12   We don't really have a plan if one of us gets deported except to come back as quick as we can. When I lived with my sister, I saw other illegals leave money with somebody they knew well, like a cousin or a friend, somebody who you know is not going to spend it. Leave, like, $1,000 or $2,000 and say, "If something happens, just send this down to me in Mexico." Then the friend would send a MoneyGram from the Money Box store, and sometimes it would go to a bank or sometimes you would pick it up. And then you would be back here in a week.

13   My wife and I have each other for that. And I tell her to keep some money in her wallet to get a hotel or to eat in case she gets thrown out, and then just try to get back. If she cannot, I'll send the kids to her and stay here and work. But we don't want to do that. That's something we don't like to think about, really. It's depressing.

Secrets, Hopes, and Dreams

14   My kids don't know we are illegal. Sometimes kids talk to other kids at school, and the other kids talk to their parents. We try not to tell everybody that we're not legal because you never know. Like my neighbor here, he doesn't know. He always talks about wetbacks, and he doesn't know he's got one next door.

15   I want to start by being a legal resident, and then I'd like to be a U.S. citizen. They could change the law like that. You start with a permit to work, and then if you don't get in any trouble, they give you the citizenship to stay here and go in and out of America legally. Maybe after eighteen years of the permit, you could get citizenship.

16   I know they have a test you take now. You have to learn to read and write English good to pass the test. Some guys tell me it's hard, but sometimes they just don't know much. One guy told me that they ask how many states America has and what are the colors of the flag. And they ask you to write something in English. That guy failed the test because he couldn't write the word "yellow," which is funny, because he is a painter.

17   There's a lot of people that don't like us to be here, but the thing is, we are here.

18   I want to be legal. I want to buy a house, like a bigger house with more rooms. But because we are illegal, they would ask for too much interest on it. And I would like to be able to take my kids home to see where I grew up and maybe see my old friends. We are not far from Guadalajara. It is only a sixteen-hour drive. I would like to be able to get in our own car and drive there for a couple weeks and then come back.

19   I guess there's hope when my son turns 21. Then he can apply for citizenship for me. It's too late for me to do like some guys who get married to a U.S. citizen, because I'm already married. Who knows, maybe I'll win the lottery. I bet they would give me citizenship then.

20   But until then we will just keep doing everything right and waiting.

MASTERY TEST SKILLS CHECK

Checking Your Comprehension

Directions: Select the best answer for each of the following questions.

_____ 1. The purpose of the selection is to
   a. compare life in Mexico to life in the United States.
   b. tell how immigration officials make life hard for illegal aliens.
   c. describe one person's experience as an illegal alien living in the United States.
   d. argue that immigration laws in the United States should be reformed.

_____ 2. Paragraph 5 is primarily about
   a. why the author decided to come to the United States.
   b. how the author came across the border.
   c. the difficulties the author and his family face as illegal aliens.
   d. the people who helped the author cross the border.

_____ 3. Which of the following best expresses the main point of paragraph 8?
   a. The author is a hard worker.
   b. The author hates his job.
   c. Most places will not hire illegal aliens.
   d. Texas offers better opportunities than California.

_____ 4. The author does not cross the border into Mexico anymore because
   a. his parents no longer live there.
   b. he doesn't like to visit his home town.
   c. he doesn't want to take time off from work.
   d. his family depends on him, and he doesn't want to risk being caught.

Applying Your Skills

_____ 5. In paragraph 1, the word "communicate" means
   a. travel.
   b. interact with others.
   c. work.
   d. settle.

_____ 6. In paragraph 1, the word "migra" refers to
   a. wild animals.
   b. immigration officials.
   c. people paid to smuggle immigrants across the border.
   d. children born to illegal immigrant parents.

_____ 7. In paragraph 12, the word "deported" means
   a. sent back to one's own country.
   b. taken prisoner for being illegal.
   c. taught how to act as a citizen.
   d. given citizenship in the United States.

_____ 8. In paragraph 13, the word "depressing" means
   a. slowing down.
   b. encouraging.
   c. sad.
   d. relaxing.

_____ 9. In paragraph 14, the word "wetbacks" refers to
   a. Mexican immigrants, in a derogatory way.
   b. restaurant workers, in a derogatory way.
   c. the payment made to smugglers.
   d. Mexican money used for smuggling.

_____ 10. In the sentence "Everybody knows a coyote, somebody who can get people across," the meaning of the word "coyote" is indicated by which of the following types of context clues?
   a. synonym
   b. definition
   c. contrast
   d. inference

> For more practice, ask your instructor for an opportunity to work on the mastery tests that appear in the Test Bank.

Chapter 3

Learning Word Parts

THIS CHAPTER WILL SHOW YOU HOW TO

1 **Figure out the meaning of unfamiliar words**

2 **Use prefixes, roots, and suffixes**

Getting Started with. . .
Word Parts

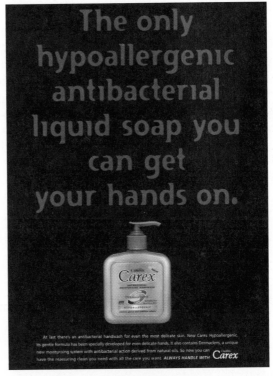

The only hypoallergenic antibacterial liquid soap you can get your hands on.

At last there's an antibacterial handwash for even the most delicate skin. New Carex Hypoallergenic. Its gentle formula has been specially developed for even delicate hands. It also contains Dermaclens, a unique new moisturising system with antibacterial action derived from natural oils. So now you can have the reassuring clean you need with all the care you want. *ALWAYS HANDLE WITH* *Carex*

The advertising copy in the photograph shows just one of millions of words that are made up of word parts—beginnings, middles, or endings of words. The word *hypoallergenic* is made up of a root that refers to allergy. It also has a prefix "hypo-" which means below or beneath. The word ends with the suffix "-genic" which means producing or generating. So you can figure out that *hypoallergenic* soap is one that has a lower tendency to produce an allergic reaction. Similarly, the word *antibacterial* is made up of a prefix "anti-" which means against, a root refering to bacteria, and a suffix "-al" (relating to). *Antibacterial* soap, then, is one that works against or fights bacteria. This chapter shows you how to use your knowledge of word parts to figure out the meanings of words you do not know.

59

Many students build their vocabulary word by word: if they study ten new words, then they have learned ten new words. If they study 30 words, they can recall 30 meanings. Would you like a better and faster way to build your vocabulary?

By learning the meaning of the parts that make up a word, you will be able to figure out the meanings of many more words. For example, if you learn that *pre-* means *before,* then you can begin to figure out hundreds of words that begin with *pre* (premarital, premix, preemployment).

In this chapter you will learn about compound words and about the beginnings, middles, and endings of words called prefixes, roots, and suffixes.

FINDING MEANINGS IN COMPOUND WORDS

A new word formed by two words that are put together is called a compound word. For example, the word *paperwork* is formed from the words *paper* and *work.* The meanings of the two words will lead you to the meaning of the compound word: *work done on paper.* Following are a few more examples of compound words:

waterproof	water + proof
horseshoe	horse + shoe
endpoint	end + point
checklist	check + list
outcome	out + come

Some words appear frequently in compound words. The word *under,* for example, is common:

undertow

underage

underachiever

undergo

undercover

A first step, then, when you meet an unfamiliar word, is to look for words you recognize within it. *Underachiever,* for example, means someone who achieves or performs under or below average.

EXERCISE 3-1   **Directions:** Select five additional compound words and show your understanding of them by writing a sentence using each word.

LEARNING PREFIXES, ROOTS, AND SUFFIXES

Suppose that you came across the following sentence in a human anatomy textbook:

> Trichromatic plates are used frequently in the text to illustrate the position of body organs.

If you did not know the meaning of *trichromatic,* how could you determine it? There are no clues in the sentence context. One solution is to look up the word in a dictionary. An easier and faster way is to break the word into parts and analyze the meaning of each part. Many words in the English language are made up of word parts called **prefixes, roots,** and **suffixes.** These word parts have specific meanings that, when added together, can help you determine the meaning of the word as a whole.

The word *trichromatic* can be divided into three parts: its prefix, root, and suffix.

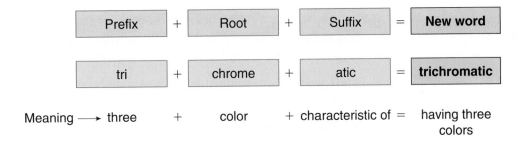

You can see from this analysis that *trichromatic* means "having three colors."

Here are a few other examples of words that you can figure out by using prefixes, roots, and suffixes:

> The parents thought the child was **unteachable.**
>
> un- = not
>
> teach = help someone learn
>
> -able = able to do something
>
> unteachable = not able to be taught

The student was a **nonconformist.**

non- = not

conform = go along with others

-ist = one who does something

nonconformist = someone who does not go along with others

The first step in using the prefix-root-suffix method is to become familiar with the most commonly used word parts. The prefixes and roots listed in Tables 3-1 and 3-2 (pages 64–70) will give you a good start in determining the meanings of thousands of words without looking them up in the dictionary. For instance, more than ten thousand words can begin with the prefix *non-*. Not all these words are listed in a collegiate dictionary, but they would appear in an unabridged dictionary (see Chapter 4). Another common prefix, *pseudo-*, is used in more than four hundred words. A small amount of time spent learning word parts can yield a large payoff in new words learned.

Before you begin to use word parts to figure out new words, there are a few things you need to know:

1. In most cases, a word is built upon at least one root.
2. Words can have more than one prefix, root, or suffix.
    a. Words can be made up of two or more roots (geo/logy).
    b. Some words have two prefixes (in/sub/ordination).
    c. Some words have two suffixes (beauti/ful/ly).
3. Words do not always have a prefix and a suffix.
    a. Some words have neither a prefix nor a suffix (read).
    b. Others have a suffix but no prefix (read/ing).
    c. Others have a prefix but no suffix (pre/read).
4. The spelling of roots may change as they are combined with suffixes. Some common variations are included in Table 3-2.
5. Different prefixes, roots, or suffixes may have the same meaning. For example, the prefixes *bi-*, *di-*, and *duo-* all mean "two."
6. Sometimes you may identify a group of letters as a prefix or root but find that it does not carry the meaning of that prefix or root. For example, the letters *mis* in the word *missile* are part of the root and are not the prefix *mis-*, which means "wrong; bad."

PREFIXES

Prefixes appear at the beginnings of many English words. They alter the meaning of the root to which they are connected. For example, if you add the prefix *re-* to the word *read,* the word *reread* is formed, meaning "to read again." If *pre-* is added to the word *reading,* the word *prereading* is formed, meaning "before reading." If the prefix *post-* is added, the word *postreading* is formed, meaning "after reading." In Table 3-1 (p. 64), more than 40 common prefixes are grouped according to meaning.

EXERCISE 3-2

Directions: Using the list of common prefixes in Table 3-1, match each word in Column A with its meaning in Column B. Write the letter of your choice in the space provided.

Column A	Column B
_____ 1. misplaced	a. half of a circle
_____ 2. postgraduate	b. build again
_____ 3. dehumidify	c. tiny duplicate of printed material
_____ 4. semicircle	d. continuing studies past graduation
_____ 5. nonprofit	e. not fully developed
_____ 6. reconstruct	f. put in the wrong position
_____ 7. triathlete	g. build up electrical power again
_____ 8. microcopy	h. not for making money
_____ 9. recharge	i. to remove moisture from
_____ 10. immature	j. one who participates in three-part sporting events

TABLE 3-1 Common Prefixes

Prefix	Meaning	Sample Word
Prefixes referring to amount or number		
mono/uni	one	monocle/unicycle
bi/di/du	two	bimonthly/divorce/duet
tri	three	triangle
quad	four	quadrant
quint/pent	five	quintet/pentagon
deci	ten	decimal
centi	hundred	centigrade
milli	thousand	milligram
micro	small	microscope
multi/poly	many	multipurpose/polygon
semi	half	semicircle
equi	equal	equidistant
Prefixes meaning "not" (negative)		
a	not	asymmetrical
anti	against	antiwar
contra	against, opposite	contradict
dis	apart, away, not	disagree
in/il/ir/im	not	incorrect/illogical/irreversible/impossible
mis	wrongly	misunderstand
non	not	nonfiction
pseudo	false	pseudoscientific
un	not	unpopular
Prefixes giving direction, location, or placement		
ab	away	absent
ad	toward	adhesive
ante/pre	before	antecedent/premarital
circum/peri	around	circumference/perimeter
com/col/con	with, together	compile/collide/convene
de	away, from	depart
dia	through	diameter
ex/extra	from, out of, former	ex-wife/extramarital
hyper	over, excessive	hyperactive
inter	between	interpersonal
intro/intra	within, into, in	introduction/intramural
post	after	posttest
re	back, again	review
retro	backward	retrospect
sub	under, below	submarine
super	above, extra	supercharge
tele	far	telescope
trans	across, over	transcontinental

EXERCISE 3-3

Directions: Use the list of common prefixes in Table 3-1 to determine the meaning of each of the following words. Write a brief definition or synonym for each. If you are unfamiliar with the root, you may need to check a dictionary.

1. interoffice

   _____

2. supernatural

   _____

3. nonsense

   _____

4. introspection

   _____

5. prearrange

   _____

6. reset

   _____

7. subtopic

   _____

8. transmit

   _____

9. multidimensional

   _____

10. imperfect

   _____

Directions: Write a synonym for each word in boldface type.

1. an **atypical** child

   _____

2. to **hyperventilate**

   _____

3. an **extraordinary** request

   _____

4. **semisoft** cheese

   _____

5. **antisocial** behavior

   _____

6. to **circumnavigate** the globe

   _____

7. a **triweekly** publication

   _____

8. an **uneventful** weekend

   _____

9. a **disfigured** face

   _____

10. to **exhale** smoke

   _____

EXERCISE 3-5

Directions: Read each of the following sentences. Use your knowledge of prefixes to fill in the blank and complete the word.

1. A person who speaks two languages is _____ **lingual.**

2. A letter or number written beneath a line of print is called a

   _____ **script.**

3. The new sweater had a snag, and I returned it to the store because it was

   _____ **perfect.**

4. The flood damage was permanent and _____ **reversible.**

5. I was not given the correct date and time; I was _____
   informed.

6. People who speak several different languages are _____

   lingual.

7. A musical _____ **lude** was played between the events in the

   ceremony.

8. I decided the magazine was uninteresting, so I _____

   continued my subscription.

9. Merchandise that does not pass factory inspection is considered

   _____ **standard** and sold at a discount.

10. The tuition refund policy approved this week will apply to last year's tuition as well;

    the policy will be _____ **active** to January 1 of last year.

11. The elements were _____ **acting** with each other when they

    began to bubble and their temperature rose.

12. _____ **ceptives** are widely used to prevent unwanted

    pregnancies.

13. All of the waitresses were required to wear the restaurant's

    _____ **form.**

14. The _____ **viewer** asked the presidential candidates unexpected questions about important issues.

15. The draperies were _____ **colored** from long exposure to the sun.

Directions: Use your knowledge of prefixes to supply the missing word in each sentence. Write the word in the space provided.

1. Our house is a duplex. The one next door with three apartments is a

   _____.

2. A preparation applied to the skin to reduce or prevent perspiration is called an

   _____.

3. A person who cannot read or write is _____.

4. I did not use my real name; instead I gave a _____.

5. If someone seems to have greater powers than do normal humans, he or she might be called _____.

6. A friend who criticizes you too often is _____.

7. If you plan to continue to take college courses after you graduate, you will be taking _____ courses.

8. Substances that fight bacteria are known as _____ drugs.

9. The branch of biology that deals with very small living organisms is

   _____.

10. In the metric system _____ a is one one-hundredth of a meter.

11. One one-thousandth of a second is called a _____.

12. The tape showed an instant _____ of the touchdown.

13. A disabling physical handicap is often called a _____.

EXERCISE 3-7 **Directions:** Working with a classmate, list as many words as you can think of for two of the following prefixes: multi-, mis-, trans-, com-, inter-. Then share your lists with the class.

ROOTS

Roots carry the basic or core meaning of a word. Hundreds of root words are used to build words in the English language. More than thirty of the most common and most useful are listed in Table 3-2 on p. 70. Knowledge of the meanings of these roots will enable you to unlock the meanings of many words. For example, if you know that the root *dic/dict* means "tell or say," then you would have a clue to the meanings of such words as *dictate* (to speak for someone to write down), *diction* (wording or manner of speaking), or *dictionary* (book that "tells" what words mean).

EXERCISE 3-8 **Directions:** Using the list of common roots in Table 3-2, match each word in Column A with its meaning in Column B. Write the letter of your choice in the space provided.

Column A

_____ 1. benediction

_____ 2. audible

_____ 3. missive

_____ 4. telecommunicate

_____ 5. mortician

_____ 6. intervene

_____ 7. reverted

_____ 8. aqueduct

_____ 9. photoactive

_____ 10. vocalize

Column B

a. undertaker

b. went back

c. able to respond to light

d. come between two things

e. channel or pipe that brings water from a distance

f. use the voice

g. blessing

h. letter or message

i. can be heard

j. send and receive messages over long distances

TABLE 3-2   Common Roots

Common Root	Meaning	Sample Word
aster/astro	star	astronaut
aud/audit	hear	audible
bene	good, well	benefit
bio	life	biology
cap	take, seize	captive
chron/chrono	time	chronology
cog	to learn	cognitive
corp	body	corpse
cred	believe	incredible
dict/dic	tell, say	predict
duc/duct	lead	introduce
fact/fac	make, do	factory
geo	earth	geophysics
graph	write	telegraph
log/logo/logy	study, thought	psychology
mit/miss	send	permit/dismiss
mort/mor	die, death	immortal
path	feeling	sympathy
phono	sound, voice	telephone
photo	light	photosensitive
port	carry	transport
scop	seeing	microscope
scrib/script	write	inscription
sen/sent	feel	insensitive
spec/spic/spect	look, see	retrospect
tend/tens/tent	stretch or strain	tension
terr/terre	land, earth	territory
theo	god	theology
ven/vent	come	convention
vert/vers	turn	invert
vis/vid	see	invisible/video
voc	call	vocation

EXERCISE 3-9

Directions: Use the list of common roots in Table 3-2 to determine the meanings of the following words. Write a brief definition or synonym for each, checking a dictionary if necessary.

1. dictaphone

   _____

2. biomedicine

   _____

3. photocopy

   _____

4. porter

   _____

5. visibility

   _____

6. credentials

   _____

7. speculate

   _____

8. terrain

   _____

9. audition

   _____

10. sentiment

   _____

11. astrophysics

_____

12. capacity

_____

13. chronicle

_____

14. corporation

_____

15. facile

_____

16. autograph

_____

17. sociology

_____

18. phonometer

_____

19. sensation

_____

20. vocal

_____

EXERCISE 3-10

Directions: Complete each of the following sentences with one of the words listed below.

apathetic	dictated	graphic	scriptures	tendon
captivated	extensive	phonics	spectators	verdict
deduce	extraterrestrial	prescribed	synchronized	visualize

1. The jury brought in its _____ after one hour of deliberation.

2. Religious or holy writings are called _____.

3. She closed her eyes and tried to _____ the license plate number.

4. The _____ watching the football game were tense.

5. The doctor _____ two types of medication.

6. The list of toys the child wanted for his birthday was _____.

7. The criminal appeared _____ when the judge pronounced the sentence.

8. The runners _____ their watches before beginning the race.

9. The textbook contained numerous _____ aids, including maps, charts, and diagrams.

10. The study of the way different parts of words sound is called _____.

11. The athlete strained a(n) _____ and was unable to continue training.

12. The movie was about a(n) _____, a creature not from earth.

13. The district manager _____ a letter to her secretary, who then typed it.

14. Through his attention-grabbing performance, he _____ the audience.

15. By putting together the clues, the detective was finally able to _____ who committed the crime.

EXERCISE 3-11   **Directions:** List two words for each of the following roots: dict/dic, spec/spic/spect, fact/fac, phono, scrib/script.

SUFFIXES

Suffixes are word endings that often change the part of speech of a word. For example, adding the suffix -y to the noun *cloud* forms the adjective *cloudy*. Accompanying the change in part of speech is a shift in meaning (*cloudy* means "resembling clouds; overcast with clouds; dimmed or dulled as if by clouds").

Often, several different words can be formed from a single root word by adding different suffixes.

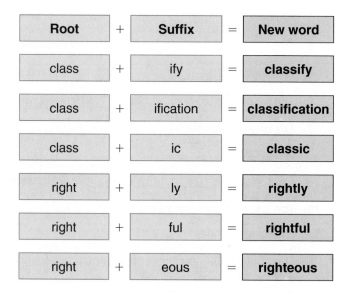

Root	+	Suffix	=	New word
class	+	ify	=	classify
class	+	ification	=	classification
class	+	ic	=	classic
right	+	ly	=	rightly
right	+	ful	=	rightful
right	+	eous	=	righteous

If you know the meaning of the root word and the ways in which different suffixes affect the meaning of the root word, you will be able to figure out a word's meaning when a suffix is added. A list of common suffixes and their meanings appears in Table 3-3.

You can expand your vocabulary by learning the variations in meaning that occur when suffixes are added to words you already know. When you find a word that you do not know, look for the root. Then, using the sentence the word is in (its context; see Chapter 2), figure out what the word means with the suffix added. Occasionally you may find that the spelling of the root word has been changed. For instance, a final *e* may be dropped, a final consonant may be doubled, or a final *y* may be changed to *i*. Consider the possibility of such changes when trying to identify the root word.

Examples:

The article was a **compilation** of facts.

root + suffix

compil(e) + -ation = something that has been compiled, or put together into an orderly form

We were concerned with the **legality** of our decision to change addresses.

root + suffix

legal + -ity = pertaining to legal matters

Our college is one of the most **prestigious** in the state.

root + suffix

prestig(e) + -ious = having prestige or distinction

TABLE 3-3   Common Suffixes

Suffix	Sample Word
Suffixes that refer to a state, condition, or quality	
able	touchable
ance	assistance
ation	confrontation
ence	reference
ible	tangible
ion	discussion
ity	superiority
ive	permissive
ment	amazement
ness	kindness
ous	jealous
ty	loyalty
y	creamy
Suffixes that mean "one who"	
an	Italian
ant	participant
ee	referee
eer	engineer
ent	resident
er	teacher
ist	activist
or	advisor

continued

TABLE 3-3   Common Suffixes

Suffix	Sample Word
Suffixes that mean "pertaining to or referring to"	
al	autumnal
ship	friendship
hood	brotherhood
ward	homeward

EXERCISE 3-12

Directions: For each suffix shown in Table 3-3, write another example of a word you know that has that suffix.

EXERCISE 3-13

Directions: For each of the words listed, add a suffix so that the word will complete the sentence. Write the new word in the space provided. Check a dictionary if you are unsure of the spelling.

1. converse

    Our phone _____ lasted ten minutes.

2. assist

    The medical _____ labeled the patient's blood samples.

3. qualify

    The job applicant outlined his _____ to the interviewer.

4. intern

    The doctor completed her _____ at Memorial Medical Center.

5. eat

    We did not realize that the blossoms of the plant could be _____.

6. audio

    She spoke so softly that her voice was not _____.

7. season

    It is usually very dry in July, but this year it has rained constantly. The weather is not very _____.

8. permit

The professor granted her _____ to miss class.

9. instruct

The lecture on Freud was very _____.

10. remember

The wealthy businessman donated the building in _____ of his deceased father.

11. mortal

The _____ rate in Ethiopia is very high.

12. president

The _____ race held many surprises.

13. feminine

She called herself a _____, although she never actively supported the movement for equal rights for women.

14. hazard

The presence of toxic waste in the lake is _____ to health.

15. destine

The young man felt it was his _____ to become a priest.

EXERCISE 3-14 **Directions:** For each word listed below, write as many new words as you can create by adding suffixes.

1. compare

_____

2. adapt

_____

3. right

_____

4. identify

_____

5. will

_____

6. prefer

_____

7. notice

_____

8. like

_____

9. pay

_____

10. promote

_____

HOW TO USE WORD PARTS

Think of roots as being at the root or core of a word's meaning. There are many more roots than are listed in Table 3-2. You already know many of these, because they are used in everyday speech. Think of prefixes as word parts that are added before the root to qualify or change its meaning. Think of suffixes as add-ons that make the word fit grammatically into the sentence in which it is used.

When you come upon a word you do not know, keep the following pointers in mind:

1. **First, look for the root.** Think of this as looking for a word inside a larger word. Often a letter or two will be missing.

Examples:

un/utter/able   defens/ible

inter/colleg/iate   re/popular/ize

post/operat/ive   non/adapt/able

im/measur/ability non/commit/tal

2. **If you do not recognize the root, then you will probably not be able to figure out the word.** The next step is to check its meaning in a dictionary. For tips on locating words in a dictionary rapidly and easily, see Chapter 4.

3. **If you did recognize the root word, look for a prefix.** If there is one, determine how it changes the meaning of the word.

Examples:

un/utterable   un- = not

post/operative   post- = after

4. **Locate the suffix.** Determine how it further adds to or changes the meaning of the root word.

Examples:

unutter/able   -able = able to

postoperat/ive   -ive = state or condition

5. **Next, try out the meaning in the sentence in which the word was used.** Substitute your meaning for the word, and see whether the sentence makes sense.

Examples:

Some of the victim's thoughts were **unutterable** at the time of the crime.

unutterable = cannot be spoken

My sister was worried about the cost of **postoperative** care.

postoperative = describing state or condition after an operation

EXERCISE 3-15 **Directions:** Use the steps listed previously to determine the meaning of each boldfaced word. Underline the root in each word, and then write a brief definition of the word that fits its use in the sentence.

1. The doctor felt the results of the X-rays were **indisputable**

   _____

2. The **dissimilarity** among the three brothers was surprising.

   _____

3. The **extortionist** demanded two payments of $10,000 each.

   _____

4. It is **permissible** to camp in most state parks.

   _____

5. The student had **retentive** abilities.

   _____

6. The **traumatic** event changed the child's attitude toward animals.

   _____

7. We were surprised by her **insincerity**.

   _____

8. The child's **hypersensitivity** worried his parents.

   _____

9. The English instructor told Peter that he had written a **creditable** paper.

   _____

10. The rock group's agent hoped to **repopularize** their first hit song.

   _____

11. The gambler was filled with **uncertainty** about the horse race.

   _____

12. The **nonenforcement** of the speed limit led to many deaths.

_____

13. The effects of the disease were **irreversible**.

_____

14. The mysterious music seemed to **foretell** the murder of the movie's heroine.

_____

15. The **polyphony** filled the concert hall.

_____

16. Sailors used to think the North Sea **unnavigable**.

_____

17. She received a **dishonorable** discharge from the Marines.

_____

18. The criminal was **unapologetic** to the judge about the crimes he had committed.

_____

19. A systems analysis revealed that the factory was **underproductive**.

_____

20. He rotated the dial **counterclockwise**.

_____

EXERCISE 3-16

Directions: Read each of the following paragraphs and determine the meaning of each boldfaced word. Write a brief definition for each in the space provided.

A. Exercising in hot weather can create stress on the circulatory system due to the high **production** of body heat. In hot weather the **distention** of blood vessels in the skin **diverts** increased quantities of blood to the body surfaces, where heat is released. As the body heats, skin heat evaporates the sweat, cooling the skin and the blood **circulating** near the skin.

—Byer and Shainberg, *Living Well,* p 360.

1. production

_____

2. distention

_____

3. diverts

_____

4. circulating

_____

B. In addition to being **irreversible,** interpersonal communication is also **unrepeatable.** The reason is simple: Everyone and everything are constantly changing. As a result, you can never **recapture** the exact same situation, frame of mind, or relationship that defined a previous interpersonal act. For example, you can never repeat meeting someone for the first time, comforting a grieving friend, or resolving a specific conflict.

—DeVito, *Messages,* pp. 22–23.

1. irreversible

_____

2. unrepeatable

_____

3. recapture

_____

C. People with positive emotional **wellness** can function **independently.** They can think for themselves, make decisions, plan their lives, and follow through with their plans. **Conversely,** people who have difficulty making decisions are often immature and **insecure.** They are afraid to face the consequences of the decisions they make, so they make as few decisions as possible. Growth involves making **mistakes** as well as achieving success. Our mistakes are best viewed as learning experiences. We must take some risks in order to live our lives most fully.

—Byer and Shainberg, *Living Well,* p. 67.

1. wellness

_____

2. independently

_____

3. conversely

_____

4. insecure

_____

5. mistakes

_____

D. We could probably greatly reduce the risks associated with nuclear power by simply exercising more care and common sense. There are a **multitude** of published accounts that attest to our carelessness, however. For example, it has been revealed that the Diablo Canyon nuclear power plant in California was built on an earthquake fault line. Of course it was girded for that risk. **Incredibly,** however, the blueprints were somehow **reversed,** and the earthquake supports were put in backward. Furthermore, the mistake was not noticed for four years. At the Comanche Peak Plant in Texas, supports were **constructed** 45 degrees out of line. At the Marble Hill in Indiana, the concrete surrounding the core was found to be full of air bubbles. At the WNP-2 plant in Washington state, the concrete contained air bubbles and pockets of water as well as shields that had been **incorrectly** welded. At the San Onofre plant in California, a 420-ton reactor vessel was installed backward, and the error was not detected for months.

—Wallace, *Biology*, p. 834.

1. multitude

_____

2. incredibly

_____

3. reversed

_____

4. constructed

_____

5. incorrectly

_____

If you tend to be a(n) . . .	Then learn word parts by . . .
Social learner	Studying with a group of classmates
Independent learner	Making up review tests, or asking a friend to do so, and practice taking the tests

SELF-TEST SUMMARY

When you cannot figure out an unknown word by using context clues, what should you do?	Break the word into word parts and use your knowledge of prefixes, roots, and suffixes to figure out the word.
What are prefixes, roots, and suffixes?	Prefixes are beginnings of words, roots are middles of words, and suffixes are endings of words.
Why is it useful to learn prefixes, roots, and suffixes?	They unlock the meanings of thousands of English words.

Getting More Practice with . . .
Word Parts

WORKING TOGETHER

Directions: Your instructor will choose a reading selection from Part Five and form groups. Locate and underline at least five words in the selection not included in its Vocabulary Preview or Words in Context that other group members can define by analyzing word parts. Work together with group members to determine the meaning of each word, checking a dictionary to verify meanings.

GOING ONLINE

Internet Activities

1. Take Our Word for It

   http://www.takeourword.com/theory.html

   Learn about the different ways words have come into our language. Come up with an example of each method that is listed.

2. Word Families

   http://www.rit.edu/~seawww/wordknowledge/wordkn06guided_6.html

   Complete this exercise that shows how roots combine with various prefixes and suffixes to form different parts of speech.

Companion Website

For additional readings, exercises, and Internet activities, visit this book's Companion Website at:

http://www.ablongman.com/mcwhorter

If you need a user name and password, please see your instructor.

My Reading Lab

For more practice on vocabulary, visit MyReadingLab, click on the Reading Skills tab, and then click on Vocabulary—The Library of Congress, Washington, D.C.

http://www.myreadinglab.com

TEST-TAKING TIPS

Using Word Parts

Use your knowledge of word parts to help you figure out the meaning of vocabulary test items. Here are some specific suggestions:

- Pronounce the word in question to yourself. By saying the word, you may hear a part (prefix, root, or suffix) that is familiar.

  Example: *Configuration* means

  a. detail.

  b. distance.

  c. shape.

  d. reason.

  If you hear the word *figure* in the word *configuration,* then you may be able to reason that *configuration* means shape (choice c) or outline.

- If you do not recognize the root of a word, concentrate on the prefix, if there is one. Often, knowing the meaning of the prefix can help you figure out the right answer, or at least help you identify one or more choices as wrong.

  Example: A *monologue* is

  a. a debate among politicians.

  b. secrets shared by friends.

  c. an intimate conversation.

  d. a long, uninterrupted speech.

  If you know that *mono-* means "one," then you can figure out that the right answer is choice d, because choices a, b, and c each involve two or more people.

- Pay attention to suffixes. Like prefixes, they can help you figure out a word, even if you do not know the root.

  Example: Someone who believes in positive outcomes is a(n)

  a. isogenic.

  b. micelle.

  c. feticide.

  d. optimist.

  If you know that the suffix *-ist* means "someone who," then choice d is a reasonable choice.

Name _____

Section _____ Date _____

Number right _____ x 10 points = Score _____

Directions: Each of the following words contains a root and a prefix and/or suffix. Select the answer that correctly divides the word into its parts.

Example: bo/tan/i/cal

_____ 1. teleconference
   a. tel/e/con/ference
   b. te/le/con/fer/ence
   c. tele/confer/ence
   d. tele/conference

_____ 2. intangible
   a. in/tan/gi/ble
   b. in/tang/ible
   c. in/ta/ngi/ble
   d. in/tangi/ble

_____ 3. avocation
   a. a/voc/ation
   b. avo/ca/tion
   c. av/o/cation
   d. a/vo/cation

_____ 4. biographer
   a. bio/graph/er
   b. bi/og/ra/pher
   c. bio/grapher
   d. bi/ograph/er

Directions: Each of the following underlined words contains a root and a prefix and/or suffix. Using your knowledge of roots, prefixes, and suffixes, select the best definition for each word.

_____ 5. The <u>antiwar</u> movement of the 1960s helped bring about United States withdrawal from Vietnam.
   a. before war
   b. against war
   c. in favor of war
   d. during war

_____ 6. If you use spaces instead of tabs in your computer document, your columns will <u>misalign.</u>
   a. be against one line
   b. skip a line
   c. form a small line
   d. line up wrong

_____ 7. The coroner prepared a <u>postmortem</u> report on the drowning victim.
   a. before life
   b. after death
   c. written again
   d. confused

_____ 8. The Supreme Court's decisions are <u>irreversible.</u>
   a. capable of great injury
   b. not able to be turned around
   c. unacceptable
   d. flawless

_____ 9. The congressman pledged to put an end to <u>substandard</u> wages in his district.
  a. illegal
  b. under investigation
  c. below normal
  d. dishonest

_____ 10. The <u>economist</u> predicted that unemployment will increase.
  a. person who studies economics
  b. theories of economics
  c. former studies of the economy
  d. the quality of the economy

Name _____

Section _____ Date _____

Number right _____ x 20 points = Score _____

Chapter 3
Mastery Test 2
Vocabulary Skills

Directions: For each of the following statements, select the answer that provides the correct prefix, root, or suffix that makes sense in the blank next to the boldfaced word.

_____ 1. Students who attend ethnically diverse schools are often exposed to a variety of foreign languages. One suburban Atlanta elementary school, for instance, has students whose native languages are Spanish, Vietnamese, Romanian, and Sudanese. Parents and school administrators in this school speak in glowing terms about their _____**lingual** student population.
   a. mono
   b. tri
   c. multi
   d. semi

_____ 2. Samuel L. Clemens was born in 1835 in Hannibal, Missouri. Using the _____**nym** Mark Twain, he drew upon his childhood experiences along the Mississippi River to write *Tom Sawyer* and *The Adventures of Huckleberry Finn.*
   a. anti
   b. pseudo
   c. poly
   d. retro

_____ 3. Melanie's father and grandfather are both police officers, so it was not surprising that she decided to pursue a career in law enforcement. She has already enrolled at the community college where she plans to major in criminal justice and take classes in **crimino**_____ in order to learn more about crime, criminals, and criminal behavior.
   a. graphy
   b. scopy
   c. pathy
   d. logy

_____ 4. The portion of the earth that is inhabited by living things is known as the earth's _____**sphere**. It includes the atmosphere and the oceans to specified heights and depths, as well as lakes and rivers.
   a. bio
   b. astro
   c. geo
   d. chrono

_____ 5. Our composition instructor always asked us to exchange our essays with each other in class in order to get another person's feedback on our work. He allowed us to give only **construct**_____ criticism, encouraging us to keep in mind how we would want our own work to be reviewed.
   a. ent
   b. ible
   c. ive
   d. or

Name _____

Section _____ Date _____

Number right _____ x 20 points = Score _____

Directions: Using your knowledge of roots, pre-fixes, and suffixes, choose the correct definition for each of the boldfaced words from the following passage.

Concerns about being overweight are based on more than vanity. Too much weight is harmful to your health and may significantly increase your risk for **hypertension**, cancer, stroke, heart disease, and adult-onset diabetes.

There is also a **relationship** between weight and the length of a hospital stay. Researchers have found that extremely overweight patients had average hospital stays 35 percent longer than patients of normal weight. One possible reason that obese patients stay in the hospital longer is an increased incidence of **postoperative** wound infections.

In many respects, underweight represents as serious a health threat as **obesity**. Even thin men and women who are well have higher **mortality** rates than do well men and women of average weight.

—Pruitt and Stein, *Health Styles*, pp. 127–31.

_____ 1. hypertension
   a. low blood pressure
   b. high blood pressure
   c. normal blood pressure
   d. absence of blood pressure

_____ 2. relationship
   a. difference
   b. connection
   c. cause
   d. performance

_____ 3. postoperative
   a. before a surgical operation
   b. during a surgical operation
   c. after a surgical operation
   d. between surgical operations

_____ 4. obesity
   a. one who is obese
   b. the condition of being obese
   c. not obese
   d. unrelated to obesity

_____ 5. mortality
   a. sickness
   b. health
   c. death
   d. body

Name _____

Section _____ Date _____

Number right* _____ x 10 points = Score _____

Trouble at Home

Catharine Skipp and Dan Ephron

This reading first appeared in an October 2006 issue of *Newsweek* magazine. As you read it, discover what problems military families are facing when a family member is deployed to Iraq.

> **Vocabulary Preview**
> **grunts** (par. 2) low-ranking soldiers
> **IEDs** (par. 6) improvised explosive devices, usually roadside bombs

1   The first year of the deployment was bearable, at least. Jodi Velotta got by on the daily phone calls and e-mail exchanges she had with her husband, Brad, in Iraq. She sent photos of their fast-growing brood, while Brad, a 29-year-old Army captain, focused on keeping his men alive. But since August, when Brad's Blackhawk Company and the rest of the 4-23 unit of the 172nd Stryker Brigade were redeployed to the heart of Baghdad, the couple has grown more distant, like two planets spinning farther away from each other. "This is just starting to get old for all of us. The phone calls are getting stale," Jodi, 31, told *Newsweek*. "Everything is getting frustrating; you don't know if you are saying the right things." They love each other deeply, but Jodi says her husband doesn't understand how the family has changed, how the two babies he remembers aren't babies anymore. "He doesn't know them as growing children. He hasn't experienced what is going on here."

2   In Vietnam and Korea, the average soldier spent less than a year overseas, and most of the troops were young conscripts. The grunts who fought in the 1991 Gulf War rejoined their families after a few months in the desert. In Iraq, much of the burden has fallen on older reservists and National Guardsmen, many of whom have gone back for second and third tours. The toll on family life is still being calculated. Divorces in the military doubled in 2004, according to the Pentagon, and though they dropped the following year, many experts believe the real impact can be assessed only over a longer period. "The question is not whether it affects the marriage," says Dorothy Ogilvy-Lee, who served as chief of family programs for the National Guard until 2004. "It's more a matter of how bad the impact [on marriage] gets."

3   For the Velottas, who have spent just two weeks together in the past 14 months, the struggle ebbs and flows. Though the Velottas' marriage is clearly strong, what emerges from conversations with both and e-mail exchanges they shared with

*To calculate the number right, use items 1–10 under "Mastery Test Skills Check."

Newsweek is a painful picture of longing and bitterness; little misunderstandings and larger anxieties about the distance and about their future together. "I'm seeing another side of you, and I'm not quite sure what to make of it," Brad writes Jodi after one heated exchange. "When we get to talk, I feel like we are still carrying frustrations from the last call and the call before that," says Jodi from her home in Plaucheville, LA.

4   Raising two kids alone—3-1/2-year-old Sophia and 2-year-old Hudson—is hard enough on Jodi, who also volunteers at Sophia's school. What drives her nuts, she says, is when Brad tries to control the parenting from afar. Recently she told him about Sophia's shenanigans in preschool. For the first week, Sophia refused to nap, crying and disturbing the other children. The preschool teacher let her sit at a desk and color, until one day she put her head on the table and fell asleep. Now she's allowed to take a blanket to the desk and sleep there regularly, Jodi told Brad. "His first reaction is, 'Yeah, that's my girl,' but then he starts saying that she needs to listen to her teachers and she needs to lie down with the other children. I thought it was funny and now he is turning it around on me. I give up. He can't come over and talk to the teachers."

5   Brad does his best to stay engaged, but he is often exhausted by the time he gets to the phone or the computer on base after dodging gunfire all day. Reading news from home about his children's longings drains him. "Hudson saw a plane today while he was riding his Big Wheel on the sidewalk and he was telling you hello," Jodi wrote Brad recently. "The plane went behind the clouds and he got upset that he couldn't see it anymore. He asked where is DaDa with tears in his eyes, then threw himself on the ground."

6   Brad—who keeps pictures of his family in the military notebook he carries with him on missions, hunting bad guys and scouring Baghdad for IEDs—agonizes over the milestones he's missed. "My son speaks and runs whereas he didn't walk/talk when I left. I try to keep him engaged with sounds and various questions about trucks, his favorite topic. He lasts 20 seconds and then he's off to play," Brad wrote *Newsweek* in an e-mail. "My daughter speaks to me in organized, coherent, and logical conversations about her daily tasks. . . . All I wanted to do is hear her little voice. She is so assertive. This is where and when I feel stress."

7   In another e-mail, Jodi reproached Brad for not being there when she needed him. Brad wrote back: "I'm upset that you . . . and I can't seem to get along. I don't want to re-deploy and go home to this type of a relationship. I'm sure you don't want to either. . . . Life is too short." He added: "I have changed since I left. I know what I want. I don't want strife and preconceived ill feelings about how I feel toward the No. 1 person in my life."

8   There are other exchanges as well: tender messages and loving phone calls. Ogilvy-Lee, the former family-programs chief, says in some cases the distance makes couples realize what they have and actually brings them closer. The Army in recent years has spent millions on programs aimed at doing just that. But the programs, even when they work, are only stopgap measures. "This needs to come to an end because it's tearing families apart," says Jodi Velotta. At a military base in Baghdad, where soldiers hope to be home by Christmas, Brad would surely agree.

MASTERY TEST SKILLS CHECK

Checking Your Comprehension

Directions: Select the best answer for each of the following questions.

_____ 1. The main point of this selection is that
   a. most military families are opposed to the war in Iraq.
   b. today's military force includes more reservists and National Guardsmen than in the past.
   c. extended deployments in the Iraq war have put a strain on relationships between soldiers and their families.
   d. the Army has programs to help military families cope with the stress of separation.

_____ 2. Paragraph 2 is primarily about
   a. differences between the wars in Vietnam, Korea, and Iraq.
   b. family programs for the National Guard.
   c. divorces in the military.
   d. the impact of the Iraq war on military families.

_____ 3. Which of the following best expresses the main point of paragraph 4?
   a. Despite the strain of separation, the Velottas have a strong marriage.
   b. The long deployment has been hardest on the Velottas' daughter.
   c. Parenting apart has been a challenge for both Jodi and Brad.
   d. The Velottas have completely different parenting styles.

_____ 4. According to the passage, Hudson is
   a. a member of Brad's unit in Iraq.
   b. Brad and Jodi's young son.
   c. Jodi's maiden name.
   d. the Velottas' hometown.

_____ 5. The Army's family programs are described as "stopgap measures" because they
   a. are temporary solutions.
   b. do not work at all.
   c. often make problems worse.
   d. are available only for certain branches of the military.

Applying Your Skills

Directions: Using your knowledge of roots, prefixes, and suffixes, as well as context, choose the correct definition for each of the following words from the passage.

_____ 6. redeployed (par. 1)
   a. not deployed
   b. wrongly deployed
   c. deployed again
   d. deployed with

_____ 7. assessed (par. 2)
   a. measured
   b. conflicted
   c. agreed
   d. arranged

_____ 8. misunderstandings (par. 3)
   a. poor communications
   b. incorrect understandings
   c. corrections
   d. approvals

_____ 9. engaged (par. 5)
  a. promised
  b. tired
  c. upset
  d. involved

_____ 10. preconceived (par. 7)
  a. formed beforehand
  b. taken away
  c. made again
  d. overly done

Studying Words

_____ 11. In paragraph 1, the word "deployment" means
  a. one who deploys.
  b. deploying together.
  c. a state of being deployed.
  d. deploying again.

_____ 12. In paragraph 2, the root of the word "conscripts" means
  a. write.
  b. carry.
  c. against.
  d. time.

_____ 13. In paragraph 2, the suffix of the word "reservists" means
  a. again.
  b. one who.
  c. hundred.
  d. out of.

_____ 14. In the sentences following this one in paragraph 4, "Recently she told him about Sophia's shenanigans in pre-school," the word "shenanigans" can be understood using which of the following types of context clue?
  a. synonym
  b. definition
  c. contrast
  d. example

_____ 15. In the sentence "My daughter speaks to me in organized, coherent, and logical conversations about her daily tasks," (paragraph 6) the word "coherent" can be understood using which of the following types of context clue?
  a. synonym
  b. definition
  c. contrast
  d. example

For more practice, ask your instructor for an opportunity to work on the mastery tests that appear in the Test Bank.

Chapter 4

Learning New Words

THIS CHAPTER WILL SHOW YOU HOW TO

1 Use the dictionary and the thesaurus

2 Pronounce unfamiliar words

3 Develop a system for learning new words

Getting Started with . . .
Learning New Words

What one word with two different meanings do the photographs illustrate? Can you think of other meanings of this word? Learning the various meanings of a word is one way to expand your vocabulary. This chapter focuses on a variety of techniques to improve your vocabulary.

Most people think they have just one level of vocabulary and that this can be characterized as large or small, strong or weak. Actually, everyone has at least four levels of vocabulary, and each varies in strength:

1. Words you use in everyday speech or writing

    Examples: decide, death, daughter, damp, date

2. Words you know but seldom or never use in your own speech or writing

    Examples: document, disregard, destination, demon, dense

3. Words you have heard or seen before but cannot fully define

    Examples: denounce, deficit, decadent, deductive, decisive

4. Words you have never heard or seen before

    Examples: doggerel, dogma, denigrate, deleterious, diatropism

In the spaces provided, list five words that fall under each of these four categories. It will be easy to think of words for Category 1. Words for Categories 2–4 may be taken from the following list:

contort	connive	fraught
continuous	congruent	gastronome
credible	demean	havoc
activate	liberate	impertinent
deletion	heroic	delicacy
focus	voluntary	impartial
manual	resistance	delve
garbanzo	alien	attentive
logic	meditate	osmosis

Category 1	Category 2	Category 3	Category 4
_____	_____	_____	_____
_____	_____	_____	_____
_____	_____	_____	_____
_____	_____	_____	_____
_____	_____	_____	_____

To build your vocabulary, try to shift as many words as possible from a less familiar to a more familiar category. This task is not easy. You start by noticing words. Then you question, check, and remember their meanings. Finally, and most important, you use these new words often in your speech and writing.

This chapter will help you improve your word awareness by (1) discussing the use of reference sources, (2) showing you how to pronounce difficult words, and (3) presenting an index card system for learning new words.

WORD INFORMATION SOURCES

Three written sources are most useful in improving one's vocabulary: (1) the dictionary, (2) subject area dictionaries, and (3) the thesaurus.

The Dictionary

The Collegiate Dictionary   The dictionary is an essential tool. If you do not already own a collegiate dictionary, buy one as soon as possible. You will need it to complete the exercises in this chapter.

Inexpensive paperback editions of the collegiate dictionary are available and recommended. Do not buy a condensed pocket dictionary. These do not contain enough words and will not give you enough information to suit your needs. Most college bookstores stock several collegiate dictionaries. Among the most widely used are *The American Heritage Dictionary of the English Language, Webster's New Collegiate Dictionary,* and *Webster's New World Dictionary of the American Language.*

The Unabridged Dictionary   Libraries own large, complete dictionaries, called *unabridged dictionaries.* These often have thousands of pages. They contain much more information about each word than collegiate dictionaries. You may need to refer to an unabridged dictionary to find an unusual word, to find an unusual meaning of a word, or to check the various prefixes or suffixes that can be used with a particular word.

The Online Dictionary   Many dictionaries of different types are available on the World Wide Web. Two of the most widely used English print dictionaries are:

- Merriam-Webster http://www.m-w.com
- American Heritage http://www.yourdictionary.com

Online dictionaries are particularly helpful if you are not sure of the exact spelling of a word or if you mistype the word. In m-w.com, if you type in a word with the incorrect spelling, several suggested words will be returned:

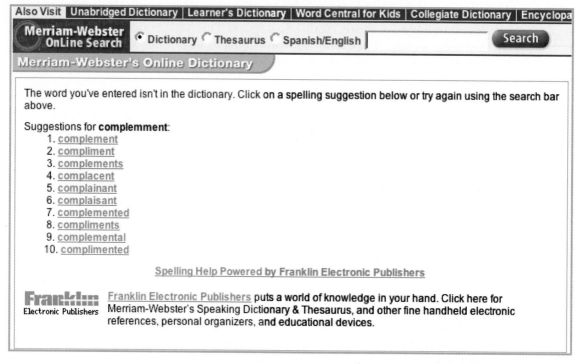

—By permission. From *Merriam-Webster Online ©2007* by Merriam-Webster, Incorporated (www.Merriam-Webster.com).

Both online dictionaries mentioned above feature an audio component that allows you to hear how a word is pronounced. When you hear the word, write it the way it sounds, so you can remember its pronunciation.

These sites are useful for both quick lookups and also in-depth assistance. For example, while you are completing a reading assignment for class, keep an online dictionary open on your computer. Use it to find definitions for new words or to clarify unfamiliar shades of meaning. When writing a paper, use an online dictionary to help with spelling and proper usage. If there is a thesaurus (dictionary of synonyms) feature, use it to find more descriptive or more accurate words for your essays. (See p. 100 for more information about using a thesaurus.) The thesaurus feature at m-w.com gives synonyms, related words, and near antonyms:

Also Visit | Unabridged Dictionary | Learner's Dictionary | Word Central for Kids | Collegiate Dictionary | Encyclopædia Britannica

Merriam-Webster OnLine Search   ○ Dictionary ● Thesaurus ○ Spanish/English ○ Medical | **Search**

Merriam-Webster's Online Thesaurus

congratulate

One entry found for **congratulate**.

Entry Word: **congratulate**
Function: *verb*
Text: to express to (someone) admiration for his or her success or good fortune <let me be the first to *congratulate* you on winning the award>
Synonyms compliment, felicitate
Related Words applaud, cheer, commend, hail; extol (*also* extoll), glorify, laud, praise
Near Antonyms bad-mouth, belittle, decry, disparage, put down; jeer, mock, ridicule, taunt, tease

—By permission. From *Merriam-Webster Online ©2007* by Merriam-Webster, Incorporated (www.Merriam-Webster.com).

You can also use an online dictionary as a vocabulary building tool. Explore the English language by following links that connect related words. The Merriam Webster online dictionary has a word-of-the-day feature. You can sign up to have this word sent to your computer daily. Think of this feature as a daily, quick word study lesson. Be careful when clicking around the site to avoid getting distracted by ads and other unrelated material. Remember, do not take definitions word for word from an online dictionary and use them as your own. Be sure to paraphrase or quote and use proper citations to avoid plagiarism.

In addition to the standard English language dictionaries, there are specialized dictionaries in all fields available online. From medical terminology to foreign languages, web searchers can find vocabulary and spelling help for almost all their needs. For example, go to http://www.law.com to see a legal dictionary.

Subject Area Dictionaries

Many subject areas have specialized dictionaries that list most of the important words used in that field. These dictionaries give specialized meanings for words and suggest how and when to use them. For the field of nursing, for instance, there is *Taber's Cyclopedic Medical Dictionary*. Other subject area dictionaries include *A Dictionary of Anthropology, The New Grove Dictionary of Music and Musicians,* and *A Dictionary of Economics*.

Find out whether there are subject area dictionaries for the subjects you are studying. Most such dictionaries are available only in hardback and are likely to be expensive. However, many students find them worth the initial investment. You might find less expensive copies on sale at a used-book store. Most libraries have copies of specialized dictionaries in the reference section. Many are also available online.

Directions: Find the name of a subject area dictionary for each of the fields listed below.

1. psychology

   _____

2. law

   _____

3. statistics

   _____

The Thesaurus

A thesaurus is a dictionary of synonyms. It groups words with similar meanings together. A thesaurus is particularly useful when you want to do the following:

- locate the precise term to fit a particular situation
- find an appropriate descriptive word
- replace an overused or unclear word
- convey a more specific shade of meaning

Suppose you are looking for a more precise word for the expression *tell us about* in the following sentence:

In class today, our chemistry instructor will **tell us about** our next assignment.

A thesaurus lists the following synonyms for "tell–explain":

10 explain, explicate, expound, exposit; give the meaning, tell the meaning of; spell out, unfold; account for, give reason for; clarify, elucidate, clear up; make clear, make plain; simplify, popularize; illuminate, enlighten, shed *or* throw light upon;

rationalize, euhemerize, demythologize, allegorize; tell *or* show how, show the way; demonstrate, show, illustrate, exemplify; decipher, crack, unlock, find the key to, unravel, solve; explain oneself; explain away.

11 comment upon, commentate, remark upon; annotate, gloss; edit, make an edition.

12 translate, render, transcribe, transliterate, put *or* turn into, transfuse the sense of; construe; English.

13 paraphrase, rephrase, reword, restate, rehash; give a free *or* loose translation.

Read the above entry and underline words or phrases that you think would be more descriptive than *tell about.* You might underline words and phrases such as *comment upon, illustrate, demonstrate,* and *spell out.*

The most widely used thesaurus is *Roget's Thesaurus.* Inexpensive paperback editions are available in most bookstores.

When you first consult a thesaurus, you will need to familiarize yourself with its format and learn how to use it. The following is a step-by-step approach:

1. **Start with the extensive index in the back to locate the word you are trying to replace.** Following the word, you will find the number(s) of the section(s) in the main part of the thesaurus that list the synonyms of that word.

2. **Turn to those sections, scanning each list and jotting down all the words you think might work.**

3. **Test each of the words you selected in the sentence in which you will use it.** The word should fit the context of the sentence.

4. **Select the word that best expresses what you are trying to say.**

5. **Choose only words whose shades of meaning you know.** Check unfamiliar words in a dictionary before using them. Remember, misusing a word is often a more serious error than choosing an overused or general one.

EXERCISE 4-2

Directions: Using a thesaurus, replace the boldfaced word or phrase in each sentence with a more precise or descriptive word. Write the word in the space provided. Rephrase the sentence, if necessary.

1. Although the movie was **good,** it lasted only an hour.

_____

2. The judge **looked at** the criminal as she pronounced the sentence.

_____

3. The accident victim was awarded a **big** cash settlement.

_____

4. The lottery winner was **happy** to win the $100,000 prize, but he was surprised to learn that a sizable portion had already been deducted for taxes.

_____

5. On the first day of class, the instructor **talked to** the class about course requirements.

_____

USING YOUR DICTIONARY

The first step in using your dictionary is to become familiar with the kinds of information it provides. In the sample entry below, each kind of information is marked:

Pronunciation

Parts of speech

Meanings

Restrictive meanings

Etymology

Spelling of other forms
of the entry word

curve (kùrv) *n.* **1a.** A line that deviates from straightness in a smooth, continuous fashion. **b.** A surface that deviates from planarity in a smooth, continuous fashion. **c.** Something characterized by such a line or surface, especially a rounded line or contour of the human body. **2.** A relatively smooth bend in a road or other course. **3a.** A line representing data on a graph. **b.** A trend derived from or as if from such a graph: *"Once again, the politicians are behind the curve"* (Ted Kennedy). **4.** A graphic representation showing the relative performance of individuals as measured by each other, used especially as a method of grading students in which the assignment of grades is based on predetermined proportions of student. **5.** *Mathematics* **a.** The graph of a function on a coordinate plane. **b.** The intersection of two surfaces in three dimensions. **c.** The graph of the solutions to any equation of two variables. **6.** *Baseball* A curve ball. **7.** *Slang* Something that is unexpected or designed to trick or deceive. ❖*v.* **curved, curv•ing, curves** —*intr.* To move in or take the shape of a curve: *The path curves around the lake.* —*tr.* **1.** To cause to curve. See synonyms at **bend**[1]. **2.** *Baseball* To pitch a curve ball to. **3.** To grade (students, for example) on a curve. [From Middle English, *curved*, from Latin *curvus*; see **sker-**[2] in Appendix I. N., sense 6, short for CURVE BALL.] —**curv′ed•ness** *n.* —**curv′y** *adj.*

—"Curve," *American Heritage Dictionary of the English Language*, p. 447.

You can see that a dictionary entry provides much more than the definition of a word. Information about the word's pronunciation, part of speech, history, and special uses can also be found.

Directions: Use the sample dictionary entry above to complete the following items.

1. Find three meanings for *curve* and write a sentence using each.

   _____

2. Explain what *curve* means when used in baseball.

   _____

3. Explain how the meaning of *curve* differs from the meaning of the word *bend*.

   _____

Directions: Find each of the following words in your dictionary, and in the space provided list all the different parts of speech it can be.

1. that

   _____

2. except

   _____

3. clear

   _____

4. fancy

   _____

5. record

   _____

In the past, you may have found parts of the dictionary confusing or difficult to use. Many students complain about the numerous symbols and abbreviations. Actually, once you are familiar with its format, you will see that the dictionary is systematic and highly organized. It provides a great deal of information about each word. The following is a brief review of the parts of a dictionary entry most often found confusing.

Abbreviations

All dictionaries provide a key to abbreviations used in the entry itself as well as some commonly used in other printed material. Most often this key appears on the inside front cover or on the first few pages of the dictionary.

EXERCISE 4-5   **Directions:** Find the meaning of each of the following symbols and abbreviations in a dictionary and write it in the space provided.

1. v.t. _____

2. < _____

3. c. _____

4. Obs. _____

5. Fr. _____

6. pl. _____

Word Pronunciation

After each word entry, the pronunciation of the word is given in parentheses.

Examples:

helmet (hĕl′mĭt)   connection (kə-nek′shən)
apologize (ə-pŏl′ə-jīz)   orchestra (ôr′kĭ-strə)

This part of the entry shows how to pronounce a word by spelling it the way it sounds. Different symbols are used to indicate certain sounds. Until you become familiar with this symbol system, you will need to refer to the pronunciation key. Most dictionaries include a pronunciation key at the bottom of every or every other page. Here is a sample key from the *American Heritage Dictionary*:

ă pat/ā pay/â care/ä father/b bib/ch church/d deed/ĕ pet/ē be/f fife/g gag/ h hat/hw which/ĭ pit/i pie/îr pier/j judge/k kick/l lid, needle/m mum/n no, sudden/ng thing/ŏ not/ō toe/ô paw, for/oi noise/ou out/ŏŏ took/ōō boot/ p pop/r roar/s sauce/sh ship, dish/t tight/th thin, path/*th* this, bathe/ŭ cut/ ûr urge/v valve/w with/y yes/z zebra, size/zh vision/ə about, item, edible, gallop, circus/

—"Pronunciation Key," *American Heritage Dictionary.*

The key shows the sound the symbol stands for in a word you already know how to pronounce. For example, suppose you are trying to pronounce the word *helix* (hē'lĭks). The key shows that the letter *e* in the first part of the word sounds the same as the *e* in the word *be*. The *i* in *helix* is pronounced the same way as the *i* in *pit*. To pronounce a word correctly, you must also accent (or put stress on) the appropriate part of the word. In a dictionary respelling, an accent mark (') usually follows the syllable, or part of the word, that is stressed most heavily.

Examples:

audience	ō'de-əns
football	fŏŏt'bôl
literacy	lĭt'ər-ə-sē
juror	jŏŏr'ər
immediate	ĭ-mē'dē-ĭt

Some words have two accents—a primary stress and a secondary stress. The primary one is stressed more heavily and is printed in darker type than the secondary accent.

Examples:

interstate	in'ter-stāt'
homicide	hôm'i-sīd'

Try to pronounce each of the following dictionary respellings, using the pronunciation key:

dĭ-vûr'sə-fī'	bŏŏsh'əl
chăl'ənj	bär'bĭ-kyōō'

Directions: Use the pronunciation key above to sound out each of the following words. Write the word, spelled correctly, in the space provided.

1. kə-mĭt _____

2. kăp′chər _____

3. bə-rŏm′ĭ-tər _____

4. skĕj′o͞ol _____

5. ī-den′te-fĭ-kā′shən _____

6. ĭn-dĭf′ər-əns _____

7. lûr′nĭd _____

8. lĭk′wĭd _____

9. no͞o′səns _____

10. fär′mə-sē _____

Etymology

Many dictionaries include information on each word's **etymology**—its origin and development. A word's etymology is its history, traced back as far as possible to its earliest use, often in another language. The sample dictionary entry on p. 102 shows that the word *curve* was derived from the Latin word *curvus* and the Greek word *koronos*.

Directions: Find the origin of each of the following words in a dictionary and write it in the space provided.

1. ginger _____

_____

_____

2. tint _____

3. calculate _____

4. fantastic _____

_____

5. authentic _____

_____

_____

Restrictive Meanings

Many dictionaries include restrictive meanings of words. These are definitions that apply only when the word is being used with respect to a specific topic or field of study. The sample entry on p. 102 gives two restrictive meanings for the word *curve*—one for baseball and another for math.

EXERCISE 4-8   **Directions:** Locate the following words in your dictionary and find the restrictive meaning for the field of study given in parentheses beside each word. Write the definitions in the spaces provided.

1. trust (law)

_____

_____

2. induction (logic)

_____

_____

3. compound (chemistry)

_____

_____

4. primary (government)

_____

_____

5. journal (accounting)

_____

_____

_____

Multiple Meanings

Most words have more than one meaning. When you look up the meaning of a new word, you must choose the meaning that fits the way the word is used in the sentence context. On the next page, the sample entry for the word *green* contains many meanings for the word.

The meanings are grouped by part of speech and are numbered consecutively in each group. Generally, the most common meanings of the word are listed first, with more specialized, less-common meanings appearing toward the end of the entry. Now find the meaning that fits the use of the word *green* in the following sentence:

The local veterans' organization held its annual fund-raising picnic on the village **green.**

In this sentence, *green* refers to "an area of grass used for special purposes." Since this is a specialized meaning of the word, it appears toward the end of the entry.

Pronunciation

Restrictive meaning

Parts of speech

Meanings

green (grēn) *n*. **1.** The hue of that portion of the visible spectrum lying between yellow and blue, evoked in the human observer by radiant energy with wavelengths of approximately 490 to 570 nanometers; any of a group of colors that may vary in lightness and saturation and whose hue is that of the emerald or somewhat less yellow that that of growing grass; one of the additive or light primaries; one of the psychological primary hues. **2.** Something green in color. **3. greens** Green growth or foliage, especially: **a.** The branches and leaves of plants used for decoration. **b.** Leafy plants or plant parts eaten as vegetables. **4.** A grassy lawn or plot, especially: **a.** A grassy area located usually at the center of a city or town and set aside for common use; a common. **b.** *Sports* A putting green. **5. greens** A green uniform: "A young…sergeant in dress greens" (Nelson DeMille). **6.** *Slang* Money. **7. Green** A supporter of a social and political movement that espouses global environmental protection, bioregionalism, social responsibility, and nonviolence. ❖*adj*. **green•er, green•est 1.** Of the color green. **2.** Abounding in or covered with green growth or foliage: *the green woods*. **3.** Made with green or leafy vegetables: *a green salad*. **4.** Characterized by mild or temperate weather: *a green climate*. **5.** Youthful; vigorous: *at the green age of 18*. **6.** Not mature or ripe; young: *green tomatoes*. **7.** Brand-new; fresh. **8.** Not yet fully processed, especially: **a.** Not aged: *green wood*. **b.** Not cured or tanned: *green pelts*. **9.** Lacking training or experience. See synonyms at **young. 10a.** Lacking sophistication or worldly experience; naive. **b.** Easily duped or deceived; gullible. **11.** Having a sickly or unhealthy pallor indicative of nausea or jealousy, for example. **12a.** Beneficial to the environment: *green recycling policies*. **b.** Favoring or supporting environmentalism: *green legislators who strengthened pollution controls*. ❖*tr. & intr. v.* **greened, green•ing, greens** To make or become green.
—**idiom: green around** (or **about**) **the gills** Pale or sickly in appearance. [Middle English *grene*, from Old English *grēne*, see **ghrē-** in Appendix I. N., sense 7, translation of German *(die) Grünen*, (the) Greens, from *grün*, green.] —**green′ly** *adv.* —**green′ness** *n.*

Etymology

Spelling of other forms
of the entry word

—"Green," *American Heritage Dictionary of the English Language*, p. 770.

Here are a few suggestions for choosing the correct meaning from among those listed in an entry:

1. **If you are familiar with the parts of speech, try to use these to locate the correct meaning.** For instance, if you are looking up the meaning of a word that names a person, place, or thing, you can save time by reading only those entries given after *n* (noun).

2. **For most types of college reading, you can skip definitions that give slang and colloquial (abbreviated *colloq.*) meanings.** Colloquial meanings refer to informal or spoken language.

3. **If you are not sure of the part of speech, read each meaning until you find a definition that seems correct.** Skip over restrictive meanings that are inappropriate.

4. **Test your choice by substituting the meaning in the sentence with which you are working.** Substitute the definition for the word and see whether it makes sense in the context (see Chapter 2).

Suppose you are looking up the word *oblique* to find its meaning in this sentence:

My sister's **oblique** answers to my questions made me suspicious.

Oblique is used in the above sentence as an adjective. Looking at the entries listed after *adj.* (adjective), you can skip over the definition under the heading *Geometry,* as it would not apply here. Definition 4a (indirect, evasive) best fits the way *oblique* is used in the sentence.

Pronunciation

Restrictive meanings

Meanings

Parts of speech

Etymology

Spelling of other forms of the entry word

o•blique (ō-blēk′, ə-blēk′) *adj.* **1a.** Having a slanting or sloping direction, course or position; inclined. **b.** *Mathematics* Designating geometric lines or planes that are neither parallel nor perpendicular. **2.** *Botany* Having sides of unequal length or form: *an oblique leaf.* **3.** *Anatomy* Situated in a slanting position; not transverse or longitudinal: *oblique muscles or ligaments.* **4a.** Indirect or evasive: *oblique political maneuvers.* **b.** Devious, misleading, or dishonest: *gave oblique answers to the questions.* **5.** Not direct in descent; collateral. **6.** *Grammar* Designating any noun case except the nominative or the vocative. ❖*n.* **1.** An oblique thing, such as a line, direction, or muscle. **2.** *Nautical* The act of changing course by less than 90°. ❖*adv.* (ō-blĭk′, ə-blĭk′) At an angle of 45°. [Middle English, from Old French, from Latin *oblīquus.*] **—o•blique′ly** *adv.* **—o•blique′ness** *n.*

—"Oblique," *American Heritage Dictionary of the English Language.*

EXERCISE 4-9

Directions: The following words have two or more meanings. Look them up in your dictionary, and write two sentences with different meanings for each word.

1. culture

_____

_____

2. perch

_____

_____

3. surge

_____

_____

4. apron

_____

_____

5. irregular

_____

_____

EXERCISE 4-10

Directions: Use the dictionary to help you find an appropriate meaning for the boldfaced word in each of the following sentences.

1. The last contestant did not have a **ghost** of a chance.

_____

2. The race car driver won the first **heat.**

_____

3. The police took all possible **measures** to protect the witness.

_____

4. The orchestra played the first **movement** of the symphony.

_____

5. The plane stalled on the **apron.**

_____

Spelling

The dictionary entry gives the correct spelling of a word. It also shows how the spelling changes when a word is made plural or endings (suffixes—see Chapter 3) are added, as in the following examples.

Word	Word + Ending
budget	budgetary
	budgeter
exhibit	exhibitor
	exhibition
fancy	fancily
	fanciness
	fancier

Entries may also include alternative spellings of words when there are two acceptable ways to spell the word. If you see the word *also* or *or* following the entry word, you will know that either is acceptable:

medieval also **mediaeval**

archaeology or **archeology**

Each entry shows how the word is divided into syllables, so you know how to hyphenate a word when it appears at the end of a line of print (hyphens are placed only between syllables).

per-cen-tile   mil-li-me-ter   ob-li-ga-tion

For verbs, each entry contains the verb's principal parts: past tense, past participle, present participle (if different from the past), and third person singular present tense.

go   went, gone, going, goes

feed   fed, feeding, feeds

Copyright © 2009 by Kathleen T. McWhorter

EXERCISE 4-11

Directions: Use your dictionary to answer the following questions. Write your answers in the spaces provided.

1. What is the plural form of *crisis*?

   _____

2. What is the alternate spelling of *judgment*?

   _____

3. If you had to hyphenate *surprise* at the end of a line, where would you divide it?

   _____

4. What is the past form of *burst*?

   _____

5. What is the adverb form of *criminal*?

   _____

Usage Notes

Collegiate dictionaries contain a Usage Note or Synonym section of the definition for words that are close in meaning to others. For example, a usage note for the word *indifferent* may explain how it differs in meaning from *unconcerned, detached,* and *uninterested.*

EXERCISE 4-12

Directions: Use your dictionary to find the differences in meaning between the following pairs of words. Write your explanations in the spaces provided.

1. petite, diminutive

   _____

   _____

   _____

2. careless, thoughtless

   _____

   _____

   _____

3. odor, aroma

_____

_____

_____

4. grin, smirk

_____

_____

_____

5. hurt, damage

_____

_____

_____

Idioms

An idiom is a phrase that has a meaning other than what the common meanings of the words in the phrase mean. For example, the phrase "wipe the slate clean" is not about slates. It means "to start over." Most idiomatic expressions are not used in academic writing because they are trite or overused.

EXERCISE 4-13   **Directions:** Use your dictionary to help you explain the meanings of the following underlined idiomatic expressions. Write your explanations in the spaces provided.

1. One thousand dollars is nothing to <u>sneeze at</u>.

_____

2. The home team <u>kicked off</u> the season with an easy win.

_____

3. I intend to <u>turn over a new leaf</u> and work harder next semester.

_____

4. The lake is two miles from here <u>as the crow flies</u>.

_____

5. The owner's incompetent nephew was <u>kicked upstairs</u> rather than fired.

_____

Other Aids

Many dictionaries (especially hardback editions) also contain numerous useful lists and tables. These are usually printed at the back of the dictionary. Frequently included are tables of weights and measures and of periodic elements in chemistry, biographical listings of famous people, a pronouncing gazetteer (a geographical dictionary), and lists of standard abbreviations, colleges, and signs and symbols.

EXERCISE 4-14   **Directions:** Use a dictionary to answer each of the following questions. Write your answer in the space provided.

1. What parts of speech can the word *interior* be used as?

_____

2. How is the word *exacerbate* pronounced? Record its phonetic spelling.

_____

3. Which part of the word *opinion* is stressed (accented)?

_____

4. How many different meanings can you think of for the word *pitch*? Write as many as you can think of. Then check to see how many meanings are given in the dictionary.

_____

Locating Words Rapidly

Most dictionaries include guide words to help you locate words rapidly. At the top of each dictionary page are two words in bold print, one in the left corner and one in the right. The guide word on the left is the first entry on that page. The right-hand guide word is the last entry. All the words on that page come between the two guide words in alphabetical order.

To check quickly whether a word is on a certain page, look at the guide words. If the word you are looking for falls alphabetically between the two guide words on the page, scan that page until you find the word. If the word does not come between those guide words, you need not look at that page at all.

Suppose you are looking up the word *loathsome*. The guide words on a particular page are *livid* and *lobster*. You know that the word *loathsome* will be on that page because, alphabetically, *loathsome* comes after *livid* and before *lobster*.

EXERCISE 4-15

Directions: Read each entry word and the pair of guide words that follows it. Decide whether the entry word would be found on the dictionary page with those guide words. Write *yes* or *no* in the space provided.

Entry Word	Guide Words	
1. grotesque	gritty–ground	_____
2. stargaze	standard–starfish	_____
3. ridicule	ridgepole–rigid	_____
4. exponent	expletive–express	_____
5. dissident	displease–dissidence	_____

PRONOUNCING UNFAMILIAR WORDS

At one time or another, each of us comes across words that we are unable to pronounce. To pronounce an unfamiliar word, sound it out syllable by syllable. Here are a few simple rules for dividing words into syllables:

1. **Divide compound words between the individual words that form the compound word.**

   Examples:

   house/broken   house/hold   space/craft

   green/house   news/paper   sword/fish

2. **Divide words between prefixes (word beginnings) and roots (base words) and/or between roots and suffixes (word endings).**

   Examples:

   Prefix + Root

   pre/read   post/pone   anti/war

Root + Suffix

sex/ist   agree/ment   list/ing

(For a more complete discussion of prefixes, roots, and suffixes, see Chapter 3.)

3. **Each syllable is a separate, distinct speech sound.** Pronounce the following words and try to hear the number of syllables in each.

Examples:

expensive	ex/pen/sive = 3 syllables
recognize	rec/og/nize = 3 syllables
punctuate	punc/tu/ate = 3 syllables
complicated	com/pli/cat/ed = 4 syllables

4. **Each syllable has at least one vowel and usually one or more consonants.** (The letters *a, e, i, o, u,* and sometimes *y* are vowels. All other letters are consonants.)

Examples:

as/sign   re/act   cou/pon   gen/er/al

5. **Divide words before a single consonant, unless the consonant is the letter *r*.**

Examples:

hu/mid   re/tail   fa/vor   mor/on

6. **Divide words between two consonants appearing together.**

Examples:

pen/cil   lit/ter   lum/ber   sur/vive

7. **Divide words between two vowel sounds that appear together.**

Examples:

te/di/ous   ex/tra/ne/ous

These rules will prove helpful but, as you no doubt already know, there will always be exceptions.

Directions: Use vertical marks (|) to divide each of the following words into syllables.

1. polka

2. pollute

3. ordinal

4. hallow

5. judicature

6. innovative

7. obtuse

8. germicide

9. futile

10. extol

11. tangelo

12. symmetry

13. telepathy

14. organic

15. hideous

16. tenacity

17. mesmerize

18. intrusive

19. infallible

20. fanaticism

USING WORD MAPPING TO EXPAND YOUR VOCABULARY

Word mapping is a visual method of expanding your vocabulary. It involves examining a word in detail by considering its meanings, synonyms (words similar in meaning), antonyms (words opposite in meaning), part(s) of speech, word parts, and usages. A word map is a form of word study. By the time you have completed the map, you will find that you have learned the word and are ready to use it in your speech and writing. On the next page is a sample map for the word *compound*.

Word Map

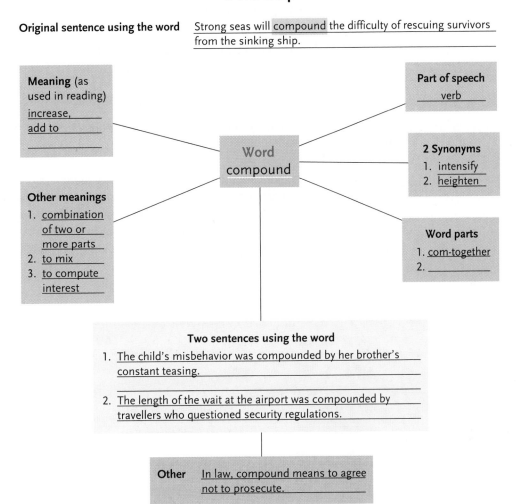

Original sentence using the word   Strong seas will compound the difficulty of rescuing survivors from the sinking ship.

Meaning (as used in reading)
increase, add to

Part of speech
verb

Word compound

2 Synonyms
1. intensify
2. heighten

Other meanings
1. combination of two or more parts
2. to mix
3. to compute interest

Word parts
1. com-together
2. _____

Two sentences using the word
1. The child's misbehavior was compounded by her brother's constant teasing.
2. The length of the wait at the airport was compounded by travellers who questioned security regulations.

Other   In law, compound means to agree not to prosecute.

Use the following steps in completing a word map:

1. **When you find a word you don't know, locate the entry for the word in a dictionary.** Write the sentence in which the word appeared at the top of the map. Figure out which meaning fits the context and write it in the box labeled "Meaning (as used in the reading)." Fill in the word's part of speech based on how it is used in context.

2. **Study the dictionary entry to discover other meanings of the word.** Put them in the map in the box labeled "Other meanings."

3. **Find or think of two synonyms (words similar in meaning).** You might need to use a thesaurus for this.

4. **Write two sentences using the word.**

5. **Analyze the word's parts. Identify any prefixes, roots, and suffixes.** Write the word part and its meaning in the space provided.

6. **In the box labeled "Other" include any other interesting information about the word.** You might include antonyms, restrictive meanings, or word history.

EXERCISE 4-17 **Directions:** Using a dictionary, complete a word map for one of the underlined words in the paragraph below.

Did you know that color can <u>alter</u> your mood? Some researchers believe that color can change how you act and feel. Numerous experiments demonstrate that certain colors are <u>associated</u> with certain moods. Blues and pinks are soothing and relaxing. Orange and red are <u>stimulating</u>. Whether you are choosing paint for a wall or a shirt to wear, consider the reaction the color may create in those who see it.

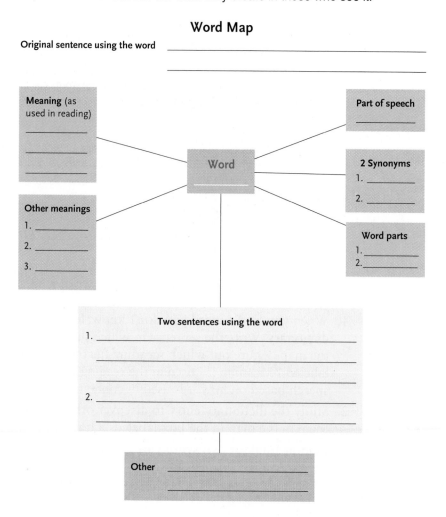

Word Map

Original sentence using the word _____

_____

Meaning (as used in reading)
_____
_____
_____

Other meanings
1. _____
2. _____
3. _____

Word
_____

Part of speech
_____

2 Synonyms
1. _____
2. _____

Word parts
1. _____
2. _____

Two sentences using the word
1. _____
_____
_____
2. _____
_____

Other _____
_____

A SYSTEM FOR LEARNING NEW WORDS

As you read textbook assignments and reference sources and while listening to your instructors' class presentations, you are constantly exposed to new words. Unless you make a deliberate effort to remember and use these words, many of them will probably fade from your memory. One of the most practical and easy-to-use systems for expanding your vocabulary is the index card system. It works like this:

1. **Whenever you hear or read a new word that you intend to learn, jot it down in the margin of your notes or mark it some way in the material you are reading.**

2. **Later, write the word on the front of an index card.** Then look up its meaning and write it on the back of the card. Also, record a phonetic key for the word's pronunciation, its part of speech, other forms the word may take, and a sample sentence or example of how the word is used. Your cards should look like the one in Figure 4-1.

3. **Once a day, take a few minutes to go through your pack of index cards.** For each card, look at the word on the front and try to recall its meaning on the back. Then check the back of the card to see whether you were correct. If you were unable to recall the meaning or if you confused the word with another word, retest yourself. Shuffle the cards after each use.

4. **After you have gone through your pack of cards several times, sort the cards into two piles—words you know and words you have not learned.** Then, putting the known words aside, concentrate on the words still to be learned.

5. **Once you have learned the entire pack of words, review them often to refresh your memory.**

ostracize

(ŏs' trə sīz)

Front

to banish from social
or political favor

Ex.: A street gang will
ostracize a member who
refuses to wear the gang emblem.

Back

Figure 4-1   Sample Index Card

This index card system is effective for several reasons. First, it can be reviewed in the spare time that is often wasted waiting for a class to begin, riding a bus, and so on. Second, the system enables you to spend time learning what you do *not* know rather than wasting time studying what you already know. Finally, the system overcomes a major problem that exists in learning information that appears in list form. If the material to be learned is presented in a fixed order, you tend to learn it in that order and may be unable to recall individual items when they appear alone or out of order. By shuffling the cards, you scramble the order of the words and thus avoid this problem.

EXERCISE 4-18

Directions: Make a set of at least 20 word cards, choosing words from one of your textbooks or from one of the reading selections in Part Five of this book. Then study the cards using the method described in this chapter.

LEARNING STYLE TIPS

If you tend to be a . . .	Then strengthen your vocabulary by . . .
Creative learner	Experimenting with new words in both speech and writing
Pragmatic learner	Creating lists or computer files of words you need to learn and use

SELF-TEST SUMMARY

What reference sources are useful in building a strong vocabulary?	Collegiate and unabridged dictionaries, online dictionaries, subject area dictionaries, and the thesaurus are all useful.
How do you pronounce unfamiliar words?	To pronounce unfamiliar words, use the pronunciation key in the dictionary and apply the seven rules listed in this chapter.
Explain the index card system.	The index card system is a method of learning vocabulary. Write a word on the front of an index card and its meaning on the back. Study the cards by sorting them into two piles—known and unknown words.

Getting More Practice with . . .
Learning New Words

WORKING TOGETHER

Directions: Locate ten words that you find difficult to pronounce. Sources may be a dictionary, a textbook, or one of the reading selections in Part Six of this book. Write each of the ten words on a separate index card, and then establish a list of the words and how they are pronounced. Your instructor will form groups. Pass the cards around the group. Each student should attempt a pronunciation. The student who pronounces the word correctly keeps the card. Make a note of words that you were unable to pronounce; check their pronunciation in your dictionary.

GOING ONLINE

Internet Activities

1. Learn a Word a Day
   http://www.wordsmith.org/awad/index.html
   Sign up to receive a word a day in your e-mail or read a newsletter about words at this interesting language lovers' site. Use the new words in your writing and speech.

2. Vocabulary Learning Resources
   http://www.m-w.com
   Explore the Merriam-Webster Website. Look up some words in the dictionary section and then in the thesaurus. How useful do you think this feature is?

Companion Website

For additional readings, exercises, and Internet activities, visit this book's Companion Website at:
http://www.ablongman.com/mcwhorter
If you need a user name and password, please see your instructor.

My Reading Lab

For more practice on vocabulary, visit MyReadingLab, click on the Reading Skills tab, and then click on Vocabulary—Library of Congress, Washington, D.C.
http://www.ablongman.com/myreadinglab

Taking Vocabulary Tests

Many vocabulary test items consist of a word and four or five choices for its meaning. The word whose meaning is being tested often stands alone—it does not appear in the context of a sentence. Use the following suggestions for approaching this type of vocabulary test:

• Try pronouncing the word to yourself. "Hearing" the word may just make it more familiar.

• Read all the choices before you select and mark an answer. Usually the directions tell you to choose the *best* answer. So while choice b may be somewhat close to the meaning or seem right at first, choice d may be a more exact and precise answer, as in the following example:

Example: 1. seniority

a. degrees held

b. age

c. importance

d. length of service

While you may see the word *senior* in the word *seniority* and think of age (choice b), as in *senior citizen,* and think that those who have seniority are usually older, the correct answer is choice d.

• Many vocabulary tests are timed, and your score is based on the number of right answers. If you work too slowly, you will not have attempted enough items to get a high score. So be sure to work at a steady, efficient pace.

• Find out if there is a penalty for guessing (some tests subtract a percentage of a point for wrong answers but do not do so for those left blank). If there is no penalty for guessing, be sure to guess at items you are not sure of. For an item containing four choices, you have a 25 percent chance of guessing correctly. For every four items you guess, you are likely to get one correct.

Directions: Use the dictionary entry below to answer the following questions.

ar•tic•u•late (är-tĭk′yə-lĭt) *adj.* **1.** Endowed with the power of speech. **2.** Composed of distinct, meaningful syllables or words, as human speech. **3.** Expressing oneself easily in clear and effective language: *an articulate speaker.* **4.** Characterized by the use of clear, expressive language: *an articulate essay.* **5.** *Anatomy* Consisting of sections united by joints; jointed. ❖ *v.* (-lāt′) **-lat•ed, -lat•ing, -lates**—*tr.* **1.** To pronounce distinctly and carefully; enunciate. **2.** To utter (a speech sound) by making the necessary movements of the speech organs. **3.** To express in coherent verbal form; give words to: *couldn't articulate my fears.* **4.** To fit together into a coherent whole; unify: *a plan to articulate nursing programs throughout the state.* **5.** *Anatomy* To unite by forming a joint or joints. **6.** *Architecture* To give visible or concrete expression to (the composition of structural elements): *a spare design in which windows and doors are barely articulated.* —*intr.* **1.** To speak clearly and distinctly. **2.** To utter a speech sound. **3.** *Anatomy* To form a joint; be jointed: *The thighbone articulates with the bones of the hip.* [Latin *articulātus,* past participle of *articulāre,* to divide into joints, utter distinctly, from *articulus,* small joint. See ARTICLE.] —**ar•tic′u•late•ly** *adv.* —**ar•tic′u•late•ness, ar•tic′u•la•cy**(-lə-sē) *n.*

—"Articulate," *American Heritage Dictionary of the English Language,* p. 102.

_____ 1. The origin of **articulate** is
    a. Middle English.
    b. Latin.
    c. French.
    d. Greek.

_____ 2. For the adjective form of **articulate,** the dictionary provides
    a. 4 meanings.
    b. 5 meanings.
    c. 10 meanings.
    d. 13 meanings.

_____ 3. For the verb form of **articulate,** the most accurate phonetic spelling is
    a. are tick you lit.
    b. are tick uh lit.
    c. are tick you late.
    d. are tick uh late.

_____ 4. One restrictive meaning for **articulate** refers to the field of
    a. law.
    b. music.
    c. computer science.
    d. anatomy.

_____ 5. The adverb form of **articulate** is
    a. articulately.
    b. articulated.
    c. articulateness.
    d. articulacy.

Name _____

Section _____ Date _____

Number right _____ x 20 points = Score _____

Directions: Each numbered sentence below is followed by a dictionary entry for the boldfaced word. Use this entry to select the choice that best fits the meaning of the word as it is used in the sentence.

_____ 1. At the entrance to the international exhibition hall, visitors are greeted by a **panoply** of flags representing every nation in the world.

pan•o•ply (păn′ə-plē) *n., pl.* **-plies 1.** A splendid or striking array: *a panoply of colorful flags.* See synonyms at **display. 2.** Ceremonial attire with all accessories: *a portrait of the general in full panoply.* **3.** Something that covers and protects: *a porcupine's panoply of quills.* **4.** The complete arms and armor of a warrior. [Greek *panopliā: pan-,* pan- + *hopla,* arms, armor, pl. of *hoplon,* weapon.]
— "Panoply," *American Heritage Dictionary of the English Language,* p. 1270.

   a. the complete arms and armor of a warrior
   b. ceremonial attire with all accessories
   c. something that covers and protects
   d. a splendid and striking array

_____ 2. At the town meeting, several citizens **ventilated** their concerns about the proposed increase in property taxes.

ven•ti•late (věn′tl-āt′) *tr.v.* **-lat•ed, -lat•ing, -lates 1.** To admit fresh air into (a mine, for example) to replace stale or noxious air. **2.** To circulate through and freshen: *A sea breeze ventilated the rooms.* **3.** To provide with a vent, as for airing. **4.** To expose (a substance) to the circulation of fresh air, as to retard spoilage. **5.** To expose to public discussion or examination: *The students ventilated their grievances.* **6.** To aerate or oxygenate (blood). [Middle English *ventilaten,* to blow away, from Latin *ventilāre, ventilāt-,* to fan, from *ventulus,* diminutive of *ventus,* wind. See **wē-** in Appendix I.]
— "Ventilate," *American Heritage Dictionary of the English Language,* p. 1909.

   a. to admit fresh air in order to replace stale or noxious air
   b. to circulate through and freshen
   c. to expose to the circulation of fresh air, as to retard spoilage
   d. to expose to public discussion or examination

_____ 3. Many people with coronary artery disease do not **manifest** symptoms until they have their first heart attack.

man•i•fest (măn′ə-fĕst′) *adj.* Clearly apparent to the sight or understanding; obvious. See synonyms at **apparent.** ❖ *tr.v.* **-fest•ed, -fest•ing, -fests 1.** To show or demonstrate plainly; reveal: *"Mercedes . . . manifested the chaotic abandonment of hysteria"* (Jack London). **2.** To be evidence of; prove. **3a.** To record in a ship's manifest. **b.** To display or present a manifest of (cargo). ❖ *n.* **1.** A list of cargo or passengers carried on a ship or plane. **2.** An invoice of goods carried on a truck or train. **3.** A list of railroad cars according to owner and location. [Middle English *manifeste,* from Old French, from Latin *manufestus, manifestsus,* caught in the act, blatant, obvious. See **gʷhedh-** in Appendix I.] —**man′i•fest′ly** *adv.*

—"Manifest," *American Heritage Dictionary of the English Language,* p. 1064.

a. clearly apparent to the sight or understanding; obvious
b. to show or demonstrate plainly; reveal
c. to be evidence of; prove
d. to record in a ship's manifest

_____ 4. After moving halfway across the country for his new job, Kerry was **besieged** by rumors that the company was going out of business.

be•siege (bĭ-sēj′) *tr.v.* -**sieged, -sieg•ing, -sieg•es** **1.** To surround with hostile forces. **2.** To crowd around; hem in. **3.** To harass or importune, as with requests: *Reporters besieged the winner for interviews.* **4.** To cause to feel distressed or worried: *She was besieged by problems.* [Middle English *besegen,* probably *assegen,* from Old French *assegier,* from Vulgar Latin* *assedicāre:* Latin *ad-,* ad- + Vulgar Latin* *sedicāre,* to sit; see SIEGE.] —**be•siege′ment;** *n.*—**be•sieg′er** *n.*

—"Besiege," *American Heritage Dictionary of the English Language,* p. 172.

Synonyms **besiege, beleaguer, blockade, invest, siege.** These verbs mean to surround with hostile forces: *besiege a walled city; the enemy beleaguered the enclave; blockaded the harbor; investing a fortress; a castle sieged by invaders.*

a. to cause to feel distressed or worried
b. to crowd around; hem in
c. to harass or importune, as with requests
d. to surround with hostile forces

_____ 5. The student task force obviously did not spend much time considering the problem of the limited number of parking spaces on campus; its facile solution to the problem disappointed all of us.

fac•ile (făs′əl) *adj.* **1.** Done or achieved with little effort or difficulty; easy. See Synonyms at **easy. 2.** Working, acting, or speaking with effortless ease and fluency. **3.** Arrived at without due care, effort, or examination; superficial: *proposed a facile solution to a complex problem.* **4.** Readily manifested, together with an aura of insincerity and lack of depth: *a facile slogan devised by politicans.* **5.** *Archaic* Pleasingly mild, as in disposition or manner. [Middle English, from Old French, from Latin *facilis.* See **dhe-** in Appendix I.] —**fac′ile•ly** *adv.* —**fac′ile•ness** *n.*

—"Facile," *American Heritage Dictionary of the English Language,* p. 633.

a. done or achieved with little effort or difficulty; easy
b. working, acting, or speaking with effortless ease and fluency
c. arrived at without due care, effort, or examination; superficial
d. pleasingly mild, as in disposition or manner

Name _____

Section _____ Date _____

Number right _____ x 10 points = Score _____

Directions: Use a dictionary to select the best answer for each of the following questions.

_____ 1. The definition of the word "ligature" is
    a. legal suit
    b. relief
    c. coal
    d. bond

_____ 2. The most accurate phonetic spelling for the word "neuropathy" is
    a. nyu ro path e
    b. nyur o path e
    c. nyu rop a the
    d. nyu rop a te

_____ 3. What part of speech is the word "tole"?
    a. noun
    b. verb
    c. adjective
    d. adverb

_____ 4. What is the origin of the word "hirsute"?
    a. French
    b. German
    c. Latin
    d. Middle English

_____ 5. The noun form of the word "infallible" is
    a. infallibility
    b. infallibly
    c. infallibleness
    d. infallible

_____ 6. The correct syllabication of the word "marsupial" is
    a. mar sup i al
    b. mar su pi al
    c. mars up ial
    d. mar su pial

_____ 7. What syllable or part of the word "developer" is stressed?
    a. de
    b. vel
    c. op
    d. er

Directions: Use *Roget's Thesaurus* to select the best answer for each of the following questions.

_____ 8. Which of the following is a synonym for "gross"?
    a. net
    b. chasete
    c. total
    d. fumble

_____ 9. Which of the following is a synonym for "droll"?
    a. boring
    b. eccentric
    c. elf
    d. confused

_____ 10. Which of the following is a synonym for "grip"?
    a. suitcase
    b. lost
    c. repel
    d. protest

Name _____

Section _____ Date _____

Number right* _____ x 10 points = Score _____

Spare Parts for Human Bodies

Teresa Audesirk, Gerald Audesirk, and Bruce E. Byers

This reading, taken from the biology textbook *Life on Earth*, explores an important new area of research. Read the selection to find out what this new field of research is, what it involves, and why it is controversial.

Vocabulary Review

bioengineering (par. 1) the application of engineering principles to the fields of biology and medicine, often concerned with the development of aids or replacements of body organs

cadavers (par. 2) corpses; dead bodies

scaffolds (par. 3) temporary frameworks or platforms used by researchers for growing artificial skin

cartilage (par. 7) strong elastic body tissue

incubating (par. 7) providing conditions that allow growth and development

collagen (par. 8) a fibrous protein found in skin, bone, cartilage

1 "I don't think I've ever screamed so loud in my life"—a mother looks back on the terrible day when bubbling oil from a deep-fat fryer spilled from the stove onto her 10-month-old baby, burning over 70% of his body. "The 911 operator said to get his clothes off, but they'd melted onto him. I pulled his socks off and the skin came right with them." A few decades ago, this child's burns would have been fatal. Now, the only evidence of the burn on his chest is slightly crinkled skin. Zachary was saved by the bioengineering marvel of artificial skin.

2 Skin consists of several specialized cell types with complex interactions. The outer (epithelial) cells of skin are masters of multiplication, so minor burns heal without a trace. However, if the deeper (dermal) layers of the skin are completely destroyed, healing occurs only very slowly, from the edges of the burn. Deep burns are often treated by grafting skin, including some dermis taken from other sites on the body; but for extensive burns, the lack of healthy skin makes this approach impossible. Until recently, the only alternative was to use skin from human cadavers or pigs. At best, these tissues serve as temporary "biological bandages" because the victim's body eventually rejects both of them. Extensive and disfiguring scars are a common legacy.

*To calculate the number right, use items 1–10 under "Mastery Test Skills Check."

3   The availability of bioengineered skin has radically changed the prognosis for burn victims. The child [described in this reading's first paragraph] . . . was treated with a bioengineered skin that contains living skin cells. The cells are obtained from the donated foreskins of infants who were circumcised at birth. After being cultured in the laboratory, a single square inch of tissue can provide enough cells to produce 250,000 square feet of artificial skin. The cells are grown under exacting conditions and seeded onto sponge-like, degradable polyester scaffolds. When complete, the artificial skin is frozen at $-94°F$ ($-70°C$), a temperature that allows cells to survive. The skin is shipped in dry ice to hospitals treating burn patients.

4   The living cells in bioengineered skin produce a variety of proteins, including fibrous proteins that form outside the cells in normal deep layers of skin, and protein growth factors that stimulate regeneration of deeper tissue layers and encourage growth of new blood vessels to nourish the tissue. As new tissue forms within the scaffold, the polyester breaks down into carbon dioxide, oxygen, and water.

5   Creation of artificial skin demonstrates our increasing power to manipulate cells, the fundamental units of life. All living things are constructed of cells, including tissues and organs that can be damaged by injury or disease. If scientists can shape cells into artificial, but living, skin, might they someday be able to sculpt cells into working bones, livers, kidneys, and lungs?

6   Bioengineering tissues and organs such as skin requires the coordinated efforts of biochemists, biomedical engineers, cell biologists, and physicians. To heal broken bones, teams of researchers are working to use degradable plastics, incorporating protein growth factors into the material. These growth factors would encourage nearby bone cells and tiny blood vessels to invade the plastic as it breaks down, eventually replacing it with the patient's own bone.

7   In laboratories across the world, teams of scientists are working to grow not only skin and bone but cartilage, heart valves, bladders, and breast tissue on plastic scaffolds, and they are implanting some of these artificial tissues into experimental animals. The mouse shown in Figure A is incubating an ear-shaped scaffold seeded with human cartilage cells (cartilage supports the natural ear). In the future, artificial ears might be grown directly on people with missing or deformed ears.

8   Researchers continue to refine tissue-culturing techniques and to develop better scaffolding materials with the goal of duplicating entire organs. Bioartificial bladders have been created using muscle and bladder-lining cells from patients with improperly functioning bladders. The cells were seeded onto a bladder-shaped scaffold composed of collagen and transplanted into the patients. Seven recipients of these engineered bladders continued to report improved bladder function after about four years.

9   A major challenge in growing new organs is that, unlike the bladder, most organs are relatively thick, and it's difficult to deliver nutrients to the innermost cells. To solve this problem, Dr. Joseph Vacanti of Massachusetts General Hospital in Boston has teamed up with a microengineering expert to devise a bioengineered liver with its own blood supply. The team created a plastic cast of a liver's blood vessels by injecting liquid plastic into the vessels and (after the plastic hardened) dissolving away the surrounding tissue. They then

produced a three-dimensional computer image of the plastic blood vessel network and used it to create a mold for scaffolding material. This material will be seeded with at least seven different types of cells that form the bulk of the liver. The network of blood vessels is represented by channels of varying size penetrating the scaffold framework. The researchers will inject these channels with blood vessel cells, which will hopefully line the channels and eventually form new vessels. Since the complexity of the project is staggering, it is unlikely that any of the over 17,000 people currently awaiting liver transplants in the United States will benefit from this research. In the future, however, bioengineered organs could save hundreds of thousands of livers worldwide each year.

Figure A   Ear-shaped scaffold under the skin of a mouse

10   The mouse photo [shown in Figure A] . . . anger[ed] some individuals who believe that this was an inappropriate use of laboratory animals. But virtually all modern medicinal drugs and medical procedures were developed using animal research. Do you believe that using certain types of animals or performing some types of animal experimentation is unethical and should be prohibited? If you oppose all use of any animals in research, what techniques do you believe medical researchers should use to develop better treatments for human health problems?

MASTERY TEST SKILLS CHECK

Checking Your Comprehension

Directions: Select the best answer for each of the following questions.

_____ 1. The main point of this selection is that
   a. household accidents can have terrible consequences for children.
   b. using animals for medical research is unethical and should be prohibited.
   c. bioengineering offers real and potential benefits for people with damaged tissues or organs.

   d. researchers from many fields must work together to create breakthroughs in treatment for human health problems.

_____ 2. The main idea of paragraph 2 is that
   a. minor burns heal quickly and easily.
   b. the skin is made up of different cell types.
   c. skin grafts are created using skin from pigs.
   d. deep or extensive burns are difficult to treat successfully.

_____ 3. The focus of paragraph 6 is on the efforts of researchers to heal
   a. heart valves.
   b. burn-damaged skin.
   c. broken bones.
   d. improperly functioning bladders.

_____ 4. The mouse is included in the selection to illustrate the
   a. technique of implanting artificial tissues into experimental animals.
   b. harmful effects of medical research on laboratory animals.
   c. types of deformities that can be treated with bioengineering.
   d. use of three-dimensional computer imaging to create a mold.

_____ 5. In paragraph 9, the authors' main purpose is to
   a. defend the use of laboratory animals to develop lifesaving drugs and medical procedures.
   b. describe how scientists are attempting to deliver nutrients to an organ's innermost cells.
   c. suggest new techniques for medical researchers to use to develop better treatments.
   d. explain why bioartificial bladders are easier to create than most other organs.

Applying Your Skills

_____ 6. What is the correct pronunciation of the word "cadavers" (paragraph 2)?
   a. kuh DAV erz
   b. KAD uh verz
   c. KADE uh verz
   d. kuh DAVE erz

_____ 7. What is the best definition for the word "legacy" as it is used in paragraph 2?
   a. a gift of personal property by will
   b. a student attending a school that was attended by his or her parents
   c. pertaining to outdated computer hardware, software, or data that does not work well with up-to-date systems
   d. something inherited or left over from the past

_____ 8. The word "prognosis" (paragraph 3) originated from which of the following languages?
   a. German
   b. French
   c. Latin
   d. English

_____ 9. What is the best definition for the word "bulk" as it is used in paragraph 9?
   a. the greater portion
   b. a massive size or quantity
   c. the body of a living creature
   d. goods or cargo not in packages or boxes

_____ 10. What is the best synonym for the word "staggering" as it is used in paragraph 9?
   a. stumbling
   b. overwhelming
   c. alternating
   d. wavering

Studying Words

Directions: Use a dictionary to answer the following questions.

_____11. The prefix in the word "microengineering" (paragraph 9) means
   a. outside.
   b. small.
   c. unimportant.
   d. valuable.

_____12. In paragraph 3, the word "degradable" means
   a. having been dishonored or disgraced.
   b. capable of being decomposed or broken down.
   c. a decline in worth or value.
   d. worn away by erosion or weather.

_____13. The word "regeneration" is used in paragraph 4 to mean
   a. the activity of spiritual or moral renewal.
   b. the process of making lost or destroyed tissue grow again.
   c. a process in which energy from an amplifier is fed back to an electrical grid circuit.
   d. the act of giving new life or allowing rebirth.

_____14. The root of the word "incorporating" (paragraph 6) means
   a. within.
   b. study.
   c. body.
   d. light.

_____15. The word "collagen" (paragraph 8) originated from which of the following languages?
   a. Greek
   b. Latin
   c. French
   d. Spanish

> For more practice, ask your instructor for an opportunity to work on the mastery tests that appear in the Test Bank.

Chapter
5

Reading as Thinking

**THIS CHAPTER
WILL SHOW YOU
HOW TO**

1 Preview before
reading

2 Develop questions
to guide your
reading

3 Review after you
read

Getting Started with . . .
Reading as Thinking

How are the basketball players in the photograph preparing for their next play? They may be in a huddle during a time out to discuss plans for running the next play or strategies for defending against specific players on the opposing team. In much the same way as basketball players plan their upcoming plays, you should think ahead before you begin to read a textbook chapter.

Rhonda is taking an anatomy and physiology course, one required in nursing. She reads all the assignments and spends long hours studying. She rereads the assignments, and rereads them before each quiz. When the instructor returns the weekly quiz, Rhonda is always surprised and disappointed. She thinks she has done well, but receives a failing grade. She cannot understand why she fails the quizzes, since she has read the material.

Rhonda decides to visit the college's learning center. The first thing the instructor asks her to do is to locate the correct answer to each quiz item in her textbook. When Rhonda has difficulty doing this, the instructor questions her on portions of the textbook. The instructor realizes that Rhonda has not thought about what she read, so he asks Rhonda several questions about how she read the chapters and discovers that she simply reads and rereads. Rhonda did nothing before beginning to read a chapter to sharpen her mind and make reading easier. She read mechanically, from beginning to end, and she did not check her understanding of the material. She did not realize her comprehension was poor or incomplete, and she did not review what she had read. She was reading, but she was not thinking about what she was reading. The instructor then suggests five strategies to help Rhonda get involved with what she is reading, and shows her how to keep track of her level of comprehension.

In this chapter you will learn to approach reading as a thinking process. You will learn five strategies that, when combined, lead to a systematic, effective method of reading called SQ3R. You will also learn how to keep track of your level of understanding and what to do if it is poor or incomplete.

PREVIEW

Would you cross a city street without checking for traffic first? Would you pay to see a movie you had never heard of and knew nothing about? Would you buy a car without test-driving it or checking its mechanical condition?

Most likely you answered "no" to each of these questions. Now answer a related question, one that applies to reading: Should you read an article or textbook chapter without knowing what it is about or how it is organized? You can probably guess that the answer is "no." This section explains a technique called previewing.

Previewing is a way of quickly familiarizing yourself with the organization and content of written material *before* beginning to read it. It is an easy method to use and will make a dramatic difference in how effectively you read.

How to Preview

When you preview, try to (1) find only the most important ideas in the material, and (2) note how they are organized. To do this, look only at the parts that state these important ideas and skip the rest. Previewing is a fairly rapid technique.

Take only a few minutes to preview a 15- to 20-page textbook chapter. The parts to look at in previewing a textbook chapter are listed here:

1. **The Title and Subtitle** The title is a label that tells what the chapter is about. The subtitle, if there is one, suggests how the author approaches the subject. For example, an article titled "Brazil" might be subtitled "The World's Next Superpower." In this instance, the subtitle tells which aspects of Brazil the article discusses.

2. **Chapter Introduction** Read the entire chapter introduction if it is brief. If it is lengthy, read only the first few paragraphs.

3. **The First Paragraph** The first paragraph, or introduction, of each section of the chapter may provide an overview of the section and/or offer clues about its organization.

4. **Boldfaced Headings** Headings, like titles, serve as labels and identify the topic of the material. By reading each heading, you will be reading a list of the important topics the chapter covers. Together, the headings form a minioutline of the chapter.

5. **The First Sentence under Each Heading** The first sentence following the heading often further explains the heading. It may also state the central thought of the entire selection. If the first sentence is purely introductory, read the second as well.

6. **Typographical Aids** Typographical aids are those features of a page that help to highlight and organize information. These include *italics*, **boldfaced type**, marginal notes, colored ink, <u>underlining</u>, and enumeration (listing). A writer frequently uses typographical aids to call attention to important key words, definitions, and facts.

7. **Graphs, Charts, and Pictures** Graphs, charts, and pictures will point you toward the most important information. Glance at these to determine quickly what information is being emphasized or clarified.

8. **The Final Paragraph or Summary** The final paragraph or summary will give a condensed view of the chapter and help you identify key ideas. Often, a summary outlines the key points of the chapter.

9. **End-of-Chapter Material** Glance through any study or discussion questions, vocabulary lists, or outlines that appear at the end of the chapter. These will help you decide what in the chapter is important.

Demonstration of Previewing

The following article was taken from a chapter of a communications textbook on nonverbal messages. It discusses four major functions of eye communication and has been included to demonstrate previewing. Everything that you should look at or read has been shaded. Preview this excerpt now, reading only the shaded portions.

Functions of Eye Communication

From Ben Jonson's poetic observation "Drink to me only with thine eyes, and I will pledge with mine" to the scientific observations of contemporary researchers, the eyes are regarded as the most important nonverbal message system. Researchers note four major functions of eye communication.

To Seek Feedback

You frequently use your eyes to seek feedback from others. In talking with someone, you look at her or him intently,* as if to say, "Well, what do you think?" As you might predict, listeners gaze at speakers more than speakers gaze at listeners. Research shows that the percentage of interaction time spent gazing while listening was between 62 and 75 percent. However, the percentage of time spent gazing while talking was between 38 and 41 percent.

Women make eye contact more and maintain it longer (both in speaking and in listening) than do men. This holds true whether the woman is interacting with other women or with men. This difference in eye behavior may result from women's tendency to display their emotions more than men; eye contact is one of the most effective ways of communicating emotions. Another possible explanation is that women have been conditioned more than men to seek positive feedback from others. Women may thus use eye contact in seeking this visual feedback.

To Regulate the Conversation

A second function of eye contact is to regulate the conversation and particularly to pass the speaking turn from one person to another. You use eye contact, for example, to tell the listener that you are finished with your thought and that you would now like to assume the role of listener and hear what the other person has to say. Or, by maintaining a steady eye contact while you plan your next sentence, you tell the other person that although you are now silent, you don't want to give up your speaking turn. You also see this in the college classroom when the instructor asks a question and then locks eyes with a student—without saying anything, the instructor clearly communicates the desire for that student to say something.

To Signal the Nature of the Relationship

Eye contact is also used to signal the nature of the relationship between two people— for example, a focused attentive glance indicates a positive relationship, but avoiding eye contact shows one of negative regard. You may also signal status relationships with your eyes. This is particularly interesting because the same movements of the eyes

*Boxed words appear in the Mastering Vocabulary exercise on p. 150.

may signal either subordination or superiority. The superior individual, for example, may stare at the subordinate or may glance away. Similarly, the subordinate may look directly at the superior or perhaps at the floor.

Eye movements may also signal whether the relationship between two people is amorous, hostile, or indifferent. Because some of the eye movements expressing these different relationships are so similar, you often use information from other areas, particularly the rest of the face, to decode the message before making any final judgments.

To Compensate for Increased Physical Distance

Last, eye movements may compensate for increased physical distance. By making eye contact you overcome psychologically the physical distance between you and the other individual. When you catch someone's eye at a party, for example, you become psychologically close even though separated by a large physical distance. Not surprisingly, eye contact and other expressions of psychological closeness, such as self-disclosure, are positively related; as one increases, so does the other.

—Devito, "Functions of Eye Communication," *Messages,* p. 146.

Although you may not realize it, you have gained a substantial amount of information from the minute or so that you spent previewing. You have become familiar with the key ideas in this section. To demonstrate, read each of the following statements and mark them *T* for "true" or *F* for "false" based on what you learned by previewing.

_____ 1. The most important nonverbal message system involves the eyes.

_____ 2. We can obtain feedback from others by using just our eyes.

_____ 3. Eye movements cannot compensate for physical distances.

_____ 4. The relationship between two people can be signaled through eye contact.

_____ 5. Eye contact regulates conversations.

This quiz tested your recall of some of the more important ideas in the article. Check your answers by referring back to the article. Did you get most or all of the above items correct? You can see, then, that previewing acquaints you with the major ideas contained in the material before you read it.

EXERCISE 5-1

Directions: Preview Chapter 6 in this book. After you have previewed it, complete the items below.

1. What is the subject of Chapter 6?

   _____

2. List the three major topics Chapter 6 covers.

   a. _____

   b. _____

   c. _____

EXERCISE 5-2

Directions: Preview a chapter from one of your other textbooks. After you have previewed it, complete the items below.

1. What is the chapter title?

   _____

2. What subject does the chapter cover?

   _____

3. List some of the major topics covered.

   _____

Previewing Articles and Essays

Previewing works on articles and essays, as well as textbook chapters. However, you may have to make a few changes in the steps listed on page 136. Here are some guidelines:

1. **Check the author's name.** If you recognize the author's name, you may have an idea of what to expect in the article or essay. For example, you would expect humor from an article by Dave Barry but more serious material from an article written by the governor of your state.

2. **Check the source of the article.** Where was it originally published? The source may suggest something about the content or slant of the article. (For more about sources see Chapter 13.)

3. **If there are no headings, read the first sentence of a few paragraphs throughout the essay.** These sentences will usually give you a sense of what the paragraph is about.

EXERCISE 5-3

Directions: Preview the article that appears at the end of this chapter, "Body Piercing and Tattooing." Then answer the following questions.

1. What is the purpose of the article?

_____

2. The article offers advice to those considering tattoos or body piercing. Which can you recall?

_____

LEARNING STYLE TIPS

If you tend to be a(n) . . .	Then strengthen your prereading skills by . . .
Auditory learner	Asking and answering guide questions aloud or tape-recording them
Visual learner	Writing guide questions and their answers

Discover What You Already Know

After you have previewed an assignment, take a moment to discover what you already know about the topic. Regardless of the topic, you probably know *something* about it. We will call this your **background knowledge.** Here is an example.

A student was about to read an article titled "Growing Urban Problems" for a sociology class. At first she thought she knew very little about urban problems since she lived in a small town. Then she began thinking about her recent trip to a nearby city. She remembered seeing homeless people and over-crowded housing. Then she recalled reading about drug problems, drive-by shootings, and muggings.

Now let us take a sample chapter from a business textbook titled *Small Business Management.* The headings are listed below. Spend a moment thinking about each one; then make a list of things you already know about each.

- Characteristics of Small Businesses
- Small-Business Administration

- Advantages and Disadvantages of Small Businesses
- Problems of Small Businesses

Discovering what you already know is useful for three important reasons. First, it makes reading easier because you have already thought about the topic. Second, the material is easier to remember because you can connect the new information with what you already know. Third, topics become more interesting if you can link them to your own experiences. You can discover what you know by using one or more of the following techniques:

1. **Ask questions and try to answer them.** For the above business textbook headings, you might ask and try to answer questions such as: Would I want to own a small business or not? What problems could I expect?

2. **Draw upon your own experience.** For example, if a chapter in your business textbook is titled "Advertising: Its Purpose and Design," you might think of several ads you have seen on television, in magazines, and in newspapers and analyze the purpose of each and how it was constructed.

3. **Brainstorm.** On a scrap sheet of paper, jot down everything that comes to mind about the topic. For example, suppose you are about to read a chapter on domestic violence in your sociology textbook. You might list types of violence—child abuse, rape, and so on. You could write questions such as: "What causes child abuse?" or "How can it be prevented?" Or you might list incidents of domestic violence you have heard or read about. Any of these approaches will help to make the topic interesting.

EXERCISE 5-4

Directions: Assume you have just previewed a chapter in your American government text on freedom of speech. Discover what you already know about freedom of speech by using each of the techniques suggested above. Then answer the questions below.

1. Did you discover you knew more about freedom of speech than you initially thought?

_____

2. Which technique worked best? Why?

_____

EXERCISE 5-5

Directions: Preview the essay "Body Piercing and Tattooing" at the end of the chapter, and discover what you already know about the health risks of tattooing or body piercing by using one of three techniques described in this section.

DEVELOP QUESTIONS TO GUIDE YOUR READING

Did you ever read an entire page or more and not remember anything you read? Have you found yourself going from paragraph to paragraph without really thinking about what the writer is saying? Most likely you are not looking for anything in particular as you read. As a result, you do not notice or remember anything specific, either. The solution is a relatively simple technique that takes just a few seconds: develop questions that will guide your reading and hold your attention.

How to Ask Guide Questions

Here are a few useful suggestions to help you form questions to guide your reading:

1. **Preview before you try to ask questions.** Previewing will give you an idea of what is important and indicate which questions you should ask.
2. **Turn each major heading into a series of questions.** The questions should ask something that you feel is important to know.
3. **As you read the section, look for the answers to your questions.** Highlight the answers as you find them.
4. **When you finish reading a section, stop and check to see whether you can recall the answers.** Place check marks by those you cannot recall.
5. **Avoid asking questions that have one-word answers.** Questions that begin with *what, why,* or *how* are more useful.

Here are a few headings and some examples of questions you could ask:

Heading	Questions
1. Reducing Prejudice	1. How can prejudice be reduced? What type of prejudice is discussed?
2. The Deepening Recession	2. What is a recession? Why is it deepening?
3. Newton's First Law of Motion	3. Who is or was Newton? What is his First Law of Motion?

EXERCISE 5-6

Directions: Write at least one question for each of the following headings.

Heading

1. World War II and Black Protest

2. Foreign Policy Under Reagan

3. The Increase of Single-Parent Families

4. Changes in Optical Telescopes

5. Causes of Violent Behavior

Questions

1. _____
   _____

2. _____
   _____

3. _____
   _____

4. _____
   _____

5. _____
   _____

EXERCISE 5-7

Directions: Preview Chapter 8 of this book. Then write a question for each major heading.

1. _____

2. _____

3. _____

4. _____

5. _____

6. _____

EXERCISE 5-8

Directions: Turn back to the textbook excerpt on pp. 137–138. You have already previewed it. Without reading the article, write four important questions to be answered after finishing it. Then read the article and answer your questions.

1. _____

2. _____

3. _____

4. _____

EXERCISE 5-9 **Directions:** Select a textbook from one of your other courses. Preview a five-page portion of a chapter that you have not yet read. Then write questions for each heading.

_____

_____

_____

_____

READ FOR MEANING

Once you have previewed an assignment and written guide questions to focus your attention, you are ready to begin reading. Read to answer your guide questions. Each time you find an answer to one of your guide questions, highlight it. Also, highlight what is important in each paragraph. In Chapter 6 you will learn more about how to discover what is important in a paragraph; in Chapter 11 you will learn specific strategies for highlighting.

LEARNING STYLE TIPS

If you are a(n) . . .	Then improve your comprehension by . . .
Applied learner	Thinking of real-life situations that illustrate ideas in the passage
Conceptual learner	Asking questions

TEST YOUR RECALL AS YOU READ

Many students read an assignment from beginning to end without stopping. Usually, this is a mistake. Instead, it is best to stop frequently to test yourself to see if you are remembering what you are reading. You can do this easily by using your guide questions. If you write guide questions in the textbook margin next to the section to which they correspond, you can easily use them as test questions after you have read the section. Cover the textbook section and try to recall the answer. If you cannot, reread the section. You have not yet learned the material. Depending on your learning style, you might either repeat the answer aloud (auditory style) or write it (verbal style).

REVIEW AFTER YOU READ

Once you have finished reading, it is tempting to close the book, take a break, and move on to your next assignment. If you want to be sure that you remember what you have just read, take a few moments to go back through the material, looking things over one more time.

You can review using some or all of the same steps as you followed to preview (see page 135). Instead of viewing the assignment *before* reading, you are viewing it again *after* reading. Think of it as a "re-view." Review will help you pull ideas together as well as help you retain them for later use on a quiz or exam.

BUILDING A SYSTEM: SQ3R

Each of the five techniques presented in this chapter, (1) previewing, (2) asking guide questions, (3) reading for meaning, (4) testing yourself, and (5) reviewing will make a difference in how well you comprehend and remember what you read. While each of these makes a difference by itself, when you use all five together you will discover a much bigger difference. Because these five techniques do work together, numerous researchers and psychologists have put them together into a reading-learning system. One of the most popular systems is called SQ3R. The steps in the system are listed below. You will see that the steps are just other names for what you have already learned in this chapter.

SQ3R

S	Survey	(Preview)
Q	Question	(Ask Guide Questions)
R	Read	(Read for Meaning)
R	Recite	(Test Yourself)
R	Review	(Review After You Read)

Be sure to use SQ3R on all your textbook assignments. You will find that it makes an important difference in the amount of information you can learn and remember.

EXERCISE 5-10 **Directions:** Read the following excerpt from a chapter on digestion in a nutrition textbook (pp. 146–149), following the steps listed.

1. Preread the excerpt. Write a sentence describing what the excerpt will be about.

   _____

   _____

2. Form several questions that you want to answer as you read. Write them in the space provided.

   _____

   _____

3. Read the excerpt, and on a separate sheet, answer your guide questions.

4. Review the excerpt immediately after you finish reading.

What Happens to the Fats We Eat?

Because fats are not soluble in water, they cannot enter our bloodstream easily from the digestive tract. Thus, fats must be digested, absorbed, and transported within the body differently from carbohydrates and proteins, which are water **soluble**.

Foods containing fats, such as bread, can spoil quickly.

The digestion and absorbtion of fat is shown in Figure A. Dietary fats usually come mixed with other foods in our diet, which we chew and then swallow. Salivary enzymes have a limited role in the breakdown of fats, and so they reach the stomach intact (Figure A, step 1). The primary role of the stomach in fat digestion is to mix and break up the fat into droplets. Because they are not soluble in water, these fat droplets typically float on top of the watery digestive juices in the stomach until they are passed into the small intestine (Figure A, step 2).

The Gallbladder, Liver, and Pancreas Assist in Fat Breakdown

Because fat is not soluble in water, its digestion requires the help of digestive enzymes from the pancreas and mixing compounds from the gallbladder. Recall that the gallbladder is a sac attached to the underside of the liver, and the pancreas is an oblong-shaped organ sitting below the stomach. Both have a duct connecting them to the small intestine. As fat enters the small intestine from the stomach, the gallbladder contracts and releases a substance called bile (Figure A, step 3). Bile is produced in the liver from cholesterol and is stored in the gallbladder until needed. You can think of bile acting much like soap, breaking up the fat into smaller and smaller droplets. At the same time, lipid-digesting enzymes produced in the pancreas travel through the pancreatic duct into the small intestine. Once bile has broken the fat into small droplets, these pancreatic enzymes take over, breaking some of the fatty acids away from the glycerol backbone. Each triglyceride molecule is thus broken down into two free fatty acids and one *monoglyceride,* which is the glycerol backbone with one fatty acid still attached.

Most Fat Is Absorbed in the Small Intestine

The free fatty acids and monoglycerides next need to be transported to the cells that make up the wall of the small intestine (Figure A, step 4), so that they can be absorbed into the body. This trip requires the help *of micelles,* spheres of bile and phospholipids that surround the free fatty acids and monoglycerides and transport them to the intestinal cell wall. Once there, shorter fatty acids can pass directly across the intestinal cell membrane. Longer fatty acids first bind to a special carrier protein and then are absorbed.

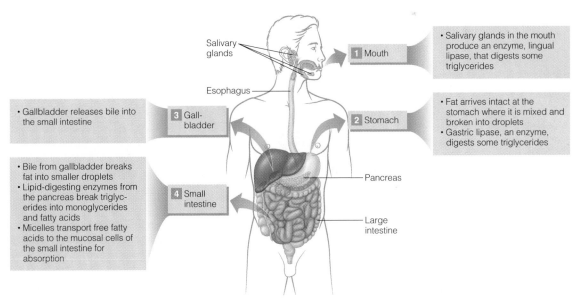

Figure A   The process of fat digestion.

lipoprotein
A spherical compound in which fat clusters in the center and phospholipids and proteins form the outside of the sphere.

chylomicron
A lipoprotein produced in the mucosal cell of the intestine; transports dietary fat out of the intestinal tract.

After absorption into the small intestine, the shortest fatty acids cross unassisted into the bloodstream and are then transported throughout the body. In contrast, the longer fatty acids and monoglycerides are reformulated back into triglycerides. As you know, triglyceride molecules don't mix with water, so they can't cross independently into the bloodstream. Once again, their movement requires special packaging, this time in the form of lipoproteins. A **lipoprotein** is a spherical compound in which triglycerides cluster deep in the center and phospholipids and proteins, which are water soluble, form the surface of the sphere (Figure B). The specific lipoprotein that transports fat from a meal is called a **chylomicron.** Packaged as chylomicrons, dietary fat finally arrives in your blood.

Fat Is Stored in Adipose Tissues for Later Use

The chylomicrons, which are filled with the fat you just ate, now begin to circulate through the blood looking for a place to unload. There are three primary fates of this dietary fat: (1) If your body needs the fat for energy, it will be quickly transported into your cells and used as fuel. (2) If the fat is not needed for immediate energy, it can be used to make lipid-containing compounds such as certain hormones and bile. (3) Alternatively, it can be stored in your muscles or adipose tissue for later use. If you are physically active, your body will preferentially store this extra fat in the muscle tissue first, so the next time you go out for a run, the fat is readily available for en-

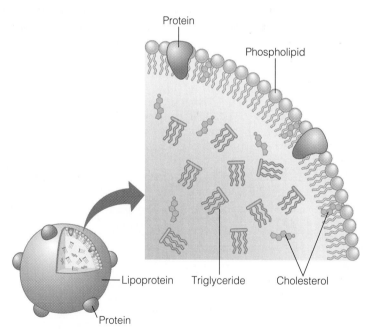

Figure B   Structure of a lipoprotein. Notice that the fat clusters in the center of the molecule and the phospholipids and proteins, which are water soluble, form the outside of the sphere. This enables lipoproteins to transport fats in the bloodstream.

ergy. That is why people who engage in regular physical activity are more likely to have extra fat stored in the muscle tissue and to have less adipose tissue—something many of us would prefer. Of course, fat stored in the adipose tissue can also be used for energy during exercise, but it must be broken down first and then transported to the muscle cells.

Recap: Fat digestion begins when fats are broken into droplets by bile. Enzymes from the pancreas subsequently digest the triglycerides into two free fatty acids and one monoglyceride. These end products of digestion are then transported to the intestinal cells with the help of micelles. Once inside the intestinal cells, triglycerides are reformed and packaged into lipoproteins called chylomicrons. Their outer layer is made up of proteins and phospholipids, which allows them to dissolve in the blood. Dietary fat is transported by the chylomicrons to cells within the body that need energy. Fat stored in the muscle tissue is used as a source of energy during physical activity. Excess fat is stored in the adipose tissue and can be used whenever the body needs energy.

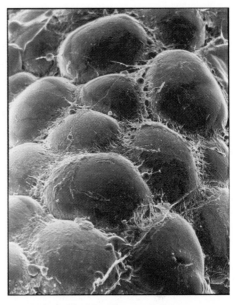

During times of weight gain, excess fat consumed in the diet is stored in adipose tissue.

EXERCISE 5-11

Directions: Choose a chapter from one of your textbooks, or use a later chapter in this book. Complete each of the following steps.

1. Preview the chapter. Write a sentence describing what the chapter will be about.

   _____

   _____

2. Form several questions that you want to answer as you read. Write them in the space provided.

   _____

   _____

3. Read the first section (major heading) of the chapter, and highlight the important information.

4. Review the section immediately after you finish reading and highlighting.

5. On a separate sheet, write a brief outline or draw a map of the major ideas in the section of the chapter that you read.

MASTERING VOCABULARY

Directions: Determine the meaning of each of the following words used in this chapter. Then insert each one in the sentence in which it makes the most sense.

intently (p. 137)

tendency (p. 137)

attentive (p. 137)

subordinate (p. 138)

hostile (p. 138)

transported (p. 146)

soluble (p. 146)

contracts (p. 147)

reformulated (p. 148)

excess (p. 149)

1. He has a _____ to snack too much.

2. The audience became loud and _____ when it was announced that the concert was being cancelled.

3. Salt is _____ in water.

4. Oral drugs are often _____ by the blood to needed areas of the body.

5. The children listened _____ to the story their teacher was reading.

6. When a muscle _____ it tightens or draws together.

7. They were very _____ to the guests at their party.

8. _____ fat can be stored in muscles or adipose tissues.

9. Some fatty acids and monoglycerides can be _____ into triglycerides.

10. The _____ member of the wolf pack ate only after more superior members had finished.

SELF-TEST SUMMARY

What techniques can you use *before* reading to read efficiently?	There are three techniques you can use *before* you even begin to read that will help you to read more efficiently. These three techniques are: 1. Preview. Become familiar with the material before you read it. 2. Activate your background knowledge. Bring to mind what you already know about the topic. 3. Use guide questions. Formulate a series of questions that you expect to answer as you read. These questions guide your reading and increase your recall.
How can you read for meaning?	Highlight answers to your guide questions. Also, highlight important information in each paragraph.
How can you test your recall as you read?	Cover the text and try to recall answers to each of your guide questions.
How can you review after you read?	Use the steps you followed to preview the assignment.
What is the SQ3R system?	SQ3R is a system that enables you to learn as you read (Survey, Question, Read, Recite, and Review).

Getting More Practice with . . .
Reading as Thinking

WORKING TOGETHER

Directions: Bring two brief magazine or newspaper articles or two 2-page textbook excerpts on interesting subjects to class. You should preview and then read both articles before class. Working in pairs with another student, exchange and preview each other's articles. Take turns predicting each article's content and organization. The student who has read the article verifies or rejects the predictions. Alternatively, the "reader" may ask the "previewer" about the article's content or organization. Then work together to generate a list of guide questions that could be used when reading the material.

GOING ONLINE

Internet Activities

1. Practice Reading Comprehension Test

   http://www.gsu.edu/~wwwrtp/pracread.htm

   Try this practice test from the Georgia State University Board of Regents. Questions are answered and scored online. You can even take an instructional version that explains the right and wrong answers.

2. Preview—Read—Recall

   http://www.utexas.edu/student/utlc/lrnres/handouts/1422.html

   Print out these tips for reading more effectively, and follow them while you read a short selection from a textbook, newspaper, or magazine. How effective are these suggestions?

Companion Website

For additional readings, exercises, and Internet activities, visit this book's Companion Website at:

http://www.ablongman.com/mcwhorter

If you need a user name and password, please see your instructor.

My Reading Lab

For more practice with active reading skills, visit MyReadingLab, click on the Reading Skills tab, and then click on Active Reading Strategies—New Orleans, LA.

http://www.ablongman.com/myreadinglab

Reading Comprehension Test Passages

Reading comprehension tests consist of passages to read and questions to answer based on each passage. Use the following suggestions for reading passages:

- Since many tests are timed, you cannot afford to take time to preview the passage, but you should assess the passage by quickly glancing through it. What is it about, and where might it have come from? Is it factual and textbooklike, or does it express a point of view on an issue? Having some idea of what you are about to read will help focus your attention, give you an idea of how to approach it, and improve your comprehension.

- The thinking process you use on reading comprehension tests is slightly different from what you use to read textbooks. Do *not* approach the passage as something you have to learn, as you would textbooks. Approach it as something you simply need to understand. Almost all tests allow you to look back to the passage to answer the questions. The test does not measure your recall, it measures your ability to locate, understand, and interpret information in the passage.

- As you read, do not try to remember all the facts and details. Instead, just try to remember what information is given. For example, if a passage gives the population of India, do not try to remember the exact number; instead, just note that the figure is given. If you need to answer a question about it, you can always look back and find the number.

- Since many tests are timed, it is important to work efficiently, not spending too much time on any one troublesome item.

Name _____

Section _____ Date _____

Number right _____ x 20 points = Score _____

Directions: For each of the following headings, choose the most effective guide question.

_____ 1. Stress and Disease (Psychology)
    a. Are stress and disease related?
    b. How are stress and disease related?
    c. Who first studied the connection between stress and disease?
    d. In what year was the connection between stress and disease first identified?

_____ 2. Human Digestive System (Biology)
    a. In what part of the body does digestion begin?
    b. Does most digestion take place in the stomach?
    c. How does the human digestive system work?
    d. Is the esophagus part of the digestive system?

_____ 3. Types of Visual Aids (Public Speaking)
    a. Are graphs considered visual aids?
    b. What are the various types of visual aids?
    c. Can you use more than one visual aid at a time?
    d. Should a visual aid be used every time you give a speech?

_____ 4. Internal Influences on Consumer Decisions (Marketing)
    a. Are consumers affected by internal influences?
    b. Is personality an internal influence on consumer decisions?
    c. Are consumer decisions influenced by external factors also?
    d. How do internal factors influence consumer decisions?

_____ 5. Internment of the Japanese (American History)
    a. When were Japanese-Americans interned?
    b. Why were Japanese-Americans interned?
    c. Where were the Japanese-American internment camps?
    d. Were German-Americans also sent to internment camps?

Name _____

Section _____ Date _____

Number right _____ x 20 points = Score _____

Indoor Air Pollution

1   Combating the problems associated with air pollution begins at home. Indoor air can be 10 to 40 times more hazardous than outdoor air. There are between 20 and 100 potentially dangerous chemical compounds in the average American home. Indoor air pollution comes primarily from six sources: woodstoves, furnaces, asbestos, formaldehyde, radon, and household chemicals.

Woodstove Smoke

2   Woodstoves emit significant levels of particulates and carbon monoxide in addition to other pollutants, such as sulfur dioxide. If you rely on wood for heating, you should make sure that your stove is properly installed, vented, and maintained. Burning properly seasoned wood reduces the amount of particulates released into the air.

Furnace Emissions

3   People who rely on oil- or gas-fired furnaces also need to make sure that these appliances are properly installed, ventilated, and maintained. Inadequate cleaning and maintenance can lead to a buildup of carbon monoxide in the home, which can be deadly.

Asbestos

4   **Asbestos** is another indoor air pollutant that poses serious threats to human health. Asbestos is a mineral that was commonly used in insulating materials in buildings constructed before 1970. When bonded to other materials, asbestos is relatively harmless, but if its tiny fibers become loosened and airborne, they can embed themselves in the lungs and cannot be expelled. Their presence leads to cancer of the lungs, stomach, and chest lining, and is the cause of a fatal lung disease called mesothelioma.

Formaldehyde

5   **Formaldehyde** is a colorless, strong-smelling gas present in some carpets, draperies, furniture, particle board, plywood, wood paneling, countertops, and many adhesives. It is released into the air in a process called *outgassing*. Outgassing is highest in new products, but the process can continue for many years.

6   Exposure to formaldehyde can cause respiratory problems, dizziness, fatigue, nausea, and rashes. Long-term exposure can lead to central nervous system disorders and cancer.

155

Radon

7   **Radon** is one of the most serious forms of indoor air pollution. This odorless, colorless gas is the natural by-product of the decay of uranium and radium in the soil. Radon penetrates homes through cracks, pipes, sump pits, and other openings in the foundation. An estimated 30,000 cancer deaths per year have been attributed to radon, making it second only to smoking as the leading cause of lung cancer.

Household Chemicals

8   When you use cleansers and other cleaning products, do so in a well-ventilated room, and be conservative in their use. All other caustic chemicals that zap mildew, grease, and other household annoyances cause a major risk to water and the environment. Avoid buildup. Regular cleanings will reduce the need to use potentially harmful substances. Cut down on dry cleaning, as the chemicals used by many cleaners can cause cancer. If your newly cleaned clothes smell of dry-cleaning chemicals, either return them to the cleaner or hang them in the open air until the smell is gone. Avoid the use of household air freshener products containing the carcinogenic agent *dichlorobenzene*.

—Donatelle and Davis, *Access to Health*, pp. 560–561.

Directions: Select the best answer for each of the following questions.

_____ 1. The typographical aids in this passage include
    a. boldfaced headings.
    b. italics.
    c. underlined phrases.
    d. a and b only.

_____ 2. The most useful guide question for the first heading would be
    a. How are woodstoves constructed?
    b. How do woodstoves contribute to indoor pollution?
    c. What types of wood produce the most heat?
    d. How is woodstove smoke different from furnace emissions?

_____ 3. The most useful guide question for the last heading would be
    a. Which household chemicals cause indoor pollution?

    b. Why do people use household chemicals?
    c. How are household chemicals manufactured?
    d. Which household chemicals are safest for children?

_____ 4. Which sentence in the first paragraph best describes what the remainder of the passage will discuss?
    a. Sentence 1
    b. Sentence 2
    c. Sentence 3
    d. Sentence 4

_____ 5. The best way to review this passage would be to
    a. brainstorm about the topic.
    b. reread the entire passage.
    c. reread the first and last paragraphs only.
    d. reread the headings.

Name _____

Section _____ Date _____

Number right _____ x 10 points = Score _____

The Real World: Bilingual Children

John J. Conger and Nancy L. Galambos

Directions: Preview the following article by reading only the title, first paragraph, headings, first sentence of each paragraph, and the last paragraph. Do not read the entire article.

1 What happens to children who are exposed to two or more languages from the beginning? How confusing is this for a child? And how can parents ease the process? At least two important practical questions surround this issue of bilingualism:

- Should parents who speak different native languages try to expose their children to both, or will that only confuse the child and make any kind of language learning harder? What's the best way to do this?
- If a child arrives at school age without speaking the dominant language of schooling, what is the best way for the child to acquire that second language?

Learning Two Languages at the Same Time

2 Parents should have no fears about exposing their child to two or more languages from the very beginning. Such simultaneous exposure does seem to result in slightly slower early steps in word learning and sentence construction, and the child will initially "mix" words or grammar from the two languages in individual sentences. But bilingual children catch up rapidly to their monolingual peers.

3 The experts agree that the best way to help a child to learn two languages fluently is to speak both languages to the child from the beginning, *especially* if the two languages come at the child from different sources. For example, if Mom's native language is English and Dad's is Italian, Mom should speak only English to the infant/toddler and Dad should speak only Italian. If both parents speak both languages to the child or mix them up in their own speech, this is a much more difficult situation for the child and language learning will be delayed. It will also work if one language is always spoken at home and the other is spoken in a day-care center, with playmates, or in some other outside situation.

Bilingual Education

4 For many children, the need to be bilingual does not begin in the home, but only at school age. In the United States today, there are 2.5 million school-age children for whom English is not the primary language of the home. Many of those children arrive at school with little or no facility in English. Educators have had to grapple with the task of teaching children a second language at the same time that they are trying to

157

teach them subject matter such as reading and mathematics. The problem for the schools has been to figure out the best way to do this. Should the child learn basic academic skills in his native language and only later learn English as a second language? Or will some combination of the two work?

5   The research findings are messy. Still, one thread does run through it all: Neither full immersion nor English-as-a-second-language programs are as effective as truly bilingual programs in which the child is given at least some of her basic instruction in subject matter in her native language in the first year or two of school but is also exposed to the second language in the same classroom. After several years of such combined instruction, the child makes a rapid transition to full use of the second language for all instruction. Interestingly, in her analysis of this research, Ann Willig has found that the ideal arrangement is very much like what works best at home with toddlers: If some subjects are always taught in one language and other subjects in the other language, children learn the second language most easily. But if each sentence is translated, children do not learn the new language as quickly or as well.

—Conger and Galambas, "The Real World:
Bilingual Children" from *The Developing Child*, p. 230.

Directions: Choose the best answer for each of the following questions.

_____ 1. The title of the article is
   a. "How to Teach Two Languages to Children"
   b. "Teaching Bilingual Children"
   c. "The Real World: Bilingual Children"
   d. "Children Who Learn Two Languages"

_____ 2. The article focuses *mostly* on what issue?
   a. The best way to teach two languages to children.
   b. Children who know several languages.
   c. Research findings on the academic performance of children.
   d. Whether parents should teach their children a foreign language.

_____ 3. What is the authors' view on whether parents should expose their children to two languages?
   a. It is better to teach a child only one language at a time.
   b. Children can be expected to learn a second language only after they have mastered the first.
   c. Teachers should teach a second language to a child if that language is spoken in the home.
   d. Parents should not be afraid to expose their children to two or more languages.

_____ 4. In the authors' view, the *best* way to help a child learn two languages fluently is to
   a. speak a second language to the child once she is fluent in the first.
   b. speak both languages to the child from the beginning.

c. speak both languages to a child but wait until the child is at least school age.

d. speak only one language to the child; otherwise confusion arises.

_____ 5. According to the article, the need to be bilingual (for many children) begins
a. at school age.
b. at home.
c. during the preschool years.
d. as soon as the child develops language.

_____ 6. According to the article, research findings on this topic are
a. in agreement.
b. plentiful.
c. messy.
d. rare.

_____ 7. Research shows that the best way to teach bilingual children is through
a. full immersion programs.
b. English as a second language (ESL) programs.
c. truly bilingual programs or combined instruction.
d. the same methods as monolingual children.

_____ 8. The best guide question for the heading that follows paragraph 1 is
a. What is learning two languages at the same time?
b. How should children learn two languages at the same time?
c. Can all students learn languages equally well?
d. What should be done about children who cannot learn two languages at the same time?

_____ 9. The best guide question for the heading that follows paragraph 3 is
a. What is bilingual education in the schools?
b. Who should teach bilingual students?
c. Should we eliminate bilingual education in the United States?
d. What is the best way for the schools to find out who is bilingual?

_____ 10. The authors' purpose in writing this article is to
a. criticize.
b. entertain.
c. persuade.
d. inform.

Chapter 5
Mastery Test 4
Reading Selection

Name _____

Section _____ Date _____

Number right* _____ x 10 points = Score _____

Body Piercing and Tattooing: Risks to Health

Rebecca J. Donatelle

Tattoos and body piercings are showing up almost everywhere these days. This selection discusses the growing popularity of "body art" as well as the health risks associated with it.

> **Vocabulary Review**
>
> **enclaves** (par. 1) distinct groups or communities
>
> **medium** (par. 2) a means of conveying something
>
> **elitism** (par. 2) a perceived superiority
>
> **transmitters** (par. 5) something that carries or spreads germs
>
> **exacerbates** (par. 6) makes worse
>
> **adverse** (par. 6) unfavorable

1   One look around college campuses and other enclaves for young people reveals a trend that, while not necessarily new, has been growing in recent years. We're talking, of course, about body piercing and tattooing, also referred to as "body art." For decades, tattoos appeared to be worn only by motorcyclists, military guys, and general roughnecks; and in many people's eyes, they represented the rougher, seedier part of society. Body piercing, on the other hand, was virtually nonexistent in our culture except for pierced ears, which didn't really appear until the latter part of the twentieth century. Even then, pierced ears were limited, for the most part, to women.

2   Various forms of body art, however, can be traced throughout human history when people "dressed themselves up" to attract attention or be viewed as acceptable by their peers. Examinations of cultures throughout the world, both historical and *contemporary,* provide evidence of the use of body art as a medium of self- and cultural expression. Ancient cultures often used body piercing as a mark of royalty or elitism. Egyptian pharaohs underwent rites of passage by piercing their navels. Roman soldiers demonstrated manhood by piercing their nipples.

The Popularity of Body Art

3   But why the surge in popularity of body art in current society, particularly among young people? Today, young and old alike are getting their ears and bodies pierced in record numbers, in such places as the eyebrows, tongues, lips, noses,

*To calculate the number right, use items 1–10 under "Mastery Test Skills Check."

navels, nipples, genitals, and just about any place possible. Many people view the trend as a fulfillment of a desire for self-expression, as this University of Wisconsin–Madison student points out:

The nipple [ring] was one of those things that I did as a kind of empowerment, claiming my body as my own and refuting the stereotypes that people have about me. . . . The tattoo was kind of a lark and came along the same lines and I like it too. . . . [T]hey both give me a secret smile.

4   Whatever the reason, tattoo artists are doing a booming business in both their traditional artistry of tattooing as well as in the "art" of body piercing. Amidst the "oohing" and "aahing" over the latest artistic additions, however, the concerns over health risks from these procedures have been largely ignored. Despite warnings from local health officials and federal agencies, the popularity of piercings and tattoos has grown.

Common Health Risks

5   The most common health-related problems associated with tattoos and body piercing include skin reactions, infections, and scarring. The average healing times for piercings depend on the size of the insert, location, and the person's overall health. Facial and tongue piercings tend to heal more quickly than piercings of areas not commonly exposed to open air or light and which are often teeming with bacteria, such as the genitals. Because the hands are great germ transmitters, "fingering" of pierced areas poses a significant risk for infection.

6   Of greater concern, however, is the potential transmission of dangerous pathogens that any puncture of the human body exacerbates. The use of unsterile needles—which can cause serious infections and can transmit

Body art in Thailand

HIV, hepatitis B and C, tetanus, and a host of other diseases—poses a very real risk. Body piercing and tattooing are performed by body artists, unlicensed "professionals" who generally have learned their trade from other body artists. Laws and policies regulating body piercing and tattooing vary greatly by state. While some states don't allow tattoo and body-piercing parlors, others may regulate them carefully, and still others provide few regulations and standards by which parlors have to abide. Standards for safety usually include minimum age of use, standards of sanitation, use of aseptic techniques, sterilization of equipment, informed risks, instructions for skin care, record keeping, and recommendations for dealing with adverse reactions. Because of this varying degree of standards regulating the business and the potential for transmission of dangerous pathogens, anyone who receives a tattoo, body piercing, or permanent makeup tattoo cannot donate blood for one year.

Important Advice

7   Anyone who does opt for tattooing or body piercing should remember the following points:

- Look for clean, well-lit work areas, and ask about sterilization procedures.
- Before having the work done, watch the artist at work. Tattoo removal is expensive and often undoable. Make sure the tattoo is one you can live with.
- Right before piercing or tattooing, the body area should be carefully sterilized and the artist should wear new latex gloves and touch nothing else while working.
- Packaged, sterilized needles should be used only once and then discarded. A piercing gun should not be used because it cannot be sterilized properly.
- Only jewelry made of noncorrosive metal, such as surgical stainless steel, niobium, or solid 14-karat gold, is safe for new piercing.
- Leftover tattoo ink should be discarded after each procedure.
- If any signs of pus, swelling, redness, or discoloration persist, remove the piercing object and contact a physician.

—Donatelle, "Body Piercing and Tattooing" from
Access to Health, pp. 470–471.

MASTERY TEST SKILLS CHECK

Directions: Choose the best answer for each of the following questions.

Checking Your Comprehension

_____ 1. The primary purpose of this selection is to
   a. discuss the use of body art throughout history.
   b. promote the use of body art as a form of self-expression.
   c. explain the popularity of body art.
   d. describe the health risks associated with body art.

_____ 2. The selection focuses on the trend in body piercing and tattooing among
   a. women.
   b. ancient cultures.
   c. young people.
   d. people in the military.

_____ 3. According to the selection, anyone who has received a tattoo or body piercing must wait a year before
   a. donating blood.
   b. getting another tattoo.
   c. getting another piercing.
   d. having a tattoo removed.

_____ 4. One of the greatest health risks from body piercing and tattooing results from
   a. leftover ink.
   b. unsterile needles.
   c. allergic reactions.
   d. overexposure to air or light.

_____ 5. The laws and policies regulating body piercing and tattooing can best be described as
   a. strict in every state.
   b. moderate in every state.
   c. completely nonexistent.
   d. varying from state to state.

_____ 6. In paragraph 3, which of the following sentences answers the question asked in the first sentence?
   a. second sentence
   b. third sentence
   c. fourth sentence
   d. fifth sentence

Applying Your Skills

_____ 7. The only typographical aid used in this selection is
   a. italics to emphasize key terms.
   b. boldfaced type to announce important ideas.
   c. listing of key points.
   d. underlining of key ideas.

_____ 8. The most useful guide question for this selection would be
   a. What does "body art" mean?
   b. What are the health risks of body piercing and tattooing?
   c. Which is more popular among young people, body piercing or tattooing?
   d. What is the average healing time for piercings?

_____ 9. Which of the following techniques would be most helpful in connecting the reading to your own experience?
   a. Reread the reading.
   b. Think of people you know who have tattoos or body piercing.
   c. Highlight key information in the reading.
   d. Locate and read another article on the same topic.

_____ 10. In previewing this article, you should read all of the following except
   a. the title.
   b. the first paragraph.
   c. the entire second paragraph.
   d. the first sentence of each paragraph.

Studying Words

_____ 11. In paragraph 1, the word "seedier" means
   a. healthier.
   b. stronger.
   c. shabbier.
   d. more remote.

_____ 12. The best synonym for the word "contemporary" (paragraph 2) is
   a. outdated.
   b. extraordinary.
   c. distant.
   d. modern.

_____ 13. What is the best definition of the word "teeming" as it is used in paragraph 5?
   a. filled with
   b. producing
   c. emptying or pouring out
   d. enriched by

_____ 14. What is the correct pronunciation of the word "exacerbates" (paragraph 6)?
   a. EX ace ur bates
   b. ex ACE ur bates
   c. ex ASS ur bates
   d. ex ACK ur bates

_____ 15. If "septic" means "containing germs that cause disease," then the word "aseptic" (paragraph 6) means
   a. not containing germs.
   b. containing thousands of germs.
   c. containing one type of germ.
   d. moving toward having germs.

For more practice, ask your instructor for an opportunity to work on the mastery tests that appear in the Test Bank.

Chapter 6

Understanding Paragraphs: Topics and Main Ideas

Getting Started with . . .
Topics and Main Ideas

What single overall feeling do you get from the photograph? Do you sense the woman's joy and happiness? Many photographs convey a single impression, as this one does. Paragraphs also convey a single impression—a single important idea that the paragraph develops and explains. This chapter focuses on finding main ideas in paragraphs.

Understanding a paragraph is a step-by-step process. The first thing you need to know is what the paragraph is about. Then you have to understand each of the sentences and what each one is saying. Next, you have to see how the sentences relate to one another. Finally, to understand the main point of the paragraph, you have to consider what all the sentences, taken together, mean.

The one subject the whole paragraph is about is called the **topic.** The point that the whole paragraph makes is called the **main idea.** The sentences that explain the main idea are called **details.** To connect their ideas, writers use words and phrases known as **transitions.**

A paragraph, then, is a group of related sentences about a single topic. It has four essential parts: (1) topic, (2) main idea, (3) details, and (4) transitions. To read paragraphs most efficiently, you will need to become familiar with each part of a paragraph and be able to identify and use these parts as you read.

This chapter concentrates on understanding main ideas, both stated and implied. The next chapter, Chapter 7, focuses on supporting details, transitions, and expressing paragraph ideas in your own words.

GENERAL AND SPECIFIC IDEAS

To identify topics and main ideas in paragraphs, it will help you to understand the difference between **general** and **specific.** A general idea is a broad idea that applies to a large number of individual items. The term *clothing* is general because it refers to a large collection of individual items—pants, suits, blouses, shirts, scarves, and so on. A specific idea or term is more detailed or particular. It refers to an individual item. The word *scarf,* for example, is a specific term. The phrase *red plaid scarf* is even more specific.

Examples:

General:	pies
Specific:	chocolate cream
	apple
	cherry
General:	countries
Specific:	Great Britain
	Finland
	Brazil

General: fruit

Specific: grapes

             lemons

             pineapples

General: types of context clues

Specific: definition

             example

             contrast

General: word parts

Specific: prefix

             root

             suffix

Directions: Read each of the following items and decide what term(s) will complete the group. Write the word(s) in the spaces provided.

1. General: college courses

   Specific: math

   _____

   _____

   _____

2. General: _____

   Specific: roses

              tulips

              narcissus

3. General: musical groups

   Specific: _____

   _____

   _____

4. General: art

   Specific: sculpture

   _____

   _____

5. General: types of movies

   Specific: comedies

   _____

   _____

EXERCISE 6-2   **Directions:** For each set of specifics, select the general idea that describes it.

_____ 1. Specific ideas: Martha Washington, Hillary Clinton, Jacqueline Kennedy
   a. famous twentieth-century women
   b. famous American parents
   c. wives of American presidents
   d. famous wives

_____ 2. Specific ideas: touchdown, home run, 3-pointer, 5 under par
   a. types of errors in sports
   b. types of activities
   c. types of scoring in sports
   d. types of sports

_____ 3. Specific ideas: for companionship, to play with, because you love animals
   a. reasons to visit the zoo
   b. reasons to feed your cat
   c. reasons to get a pet
   d. ways to solve problems

_____ 4. Specific ideas: taking a hot bath, going for a walk, watching a video, listening to music
   a. ways to relax
   b. ways to help others
   c. ways to listen
   d. ways to solve problems

_____ 5. Specific ideas: listen, be helpful, be generous, be forgiving
      a. ways to get a job
      b. ways to keep a friend
      c. ways to learn
      d. ways to appreciate a movie

EXERCISE 6-3   **Directions:** Underline the most general term in each group of words.

1. pounds, ounces, kilograms, weights

2. soda, coffee, beverage, wine

3. soap operas, news, TV programs, sports specials

4. home furnishings, carpeting, drapes, wall hangings

5. sociology, social sciences, anthropology, psychology

Applying General and Specific to Paragraphs

Now we will apply the idea of general and specific to paragraphs. The main idea is the most general statement the writer makes about the topic. Pick out the most general statement among the following sentences:

1. People differ according to height.
2. Hair color distinguishes some people from others.
3. People differ in a number of ways.
4. Each person has his or her own personality.

Did you choose item 3 as the most general statement? Now we will change this list into a paragraph by rearranging the sentences and adding a few facts.

People differ in a number of ways. They differ according to physical characteristics, such as height, weight, and hair color. They also differ in personality. Some people are friendly and easygoing. Others are more reserved and formal.

In this brief paragraph, the main idea is expressed in the first sentence. This sentence is the most general statement expressed in the paragraph. All the other statements are specific details that explain this main idea.

Directions: For each of the following groups of sentences, select the most general statement the writer makes about the topic.

_____ 1. a. Brightly colored annuals, such as pansies and petunias, are often used as seasonal accents in a garden.
     b. Most gardens feature a mix of perennials and annuals.
     c. Some perennials prefer shade, while others thrive in full sun.
     d. Butterfly bushes are a popular perennial.

_____ 2. a. Hiring a housepainter is not as simple as it sounds.
     b. You should try to obtain a cost estimate from at least three painters.
     c. Each painter should be able to provide reliable references from past painting jobs.
     d. The painter must be able to work within the time frame you desire.

_____ 3. a. Flaxseed is an herbal treatment for constipation.
     b. Some people use Kava to treat depression.
     c. Gingko biloba is a popular remedy for memory loss.
     d. A growing number of consumers are turning to herbal remedies to treat certain ailments.

_____ 4. a. Many students choose to live off-campus in apartments or rental houses.
     b. Most colleges and universities offer a variety of student housing options.
     c. Sororities and fraternities typically allow members to live in their organization's house.
     d. On-campus dormitories provide a convenient place for students to live.

_____ 5. a. Try to set exercise goals that are challenging but realistic.
     b. Increase the difficulty of your workout gradually.
     c. Several techniques contribute to success when beginning an exercise program.
     d. Reduce soreness by gently stretching your muscles before you exercise.

IDENTIFYING THE TOPIC

The **topic** is the subject of the entire paragraph. Every sentence in a paragraph in some way discusses or explains this topic. If you had to choose a title for a paragraph, the one or two words you would choose are the topic.

To find the topic of a paragraph, ask yourself: What is the one thing the author is discussing throughout the paragraph?

Now read the following paragraph with that question in mind:

Nutrition is the process of taking in and using food for growth, repair, and maintenance of the body. The science of nutrition is the study of foods and how the body uses them. Many North Americans define nutrition as eating a healthful diet. But what is healthful? Our food choices may be influenced by fads, advertising, or convenience. We may reflect on the meaning of nutrition while pushing a cart down a supermarket aisle, or while making a selection from a restaurant menu.

—Byer and Shainberg, *Living Well*, p. 256.

In this example, the author is discussing one topic—nutrition—throughout the paragraph. Notice that the word *nutrition* is used several times. Often the repeated use of a word can serve as a clue to the topic.

EXERCISE 6-5

Directions: Read each of the following paragraphs and then select the topic of the paragraph from the choices giver

_____ 1. Sometimes religious groups develop around a particular charismatic leader and have little or nothing in common with conventional religious traditions. These groups are called cults. Usually, cult members disavow the broader society because they view it as degenerate, and they further believe that each person must establish better relations with the spiritual. To accomplish these ends, cults sometimes require members to live together in group quarters or to move into communes.

—Curry et al., *Sociology for the 21st Century*, p. 356.

    a. religion
    b. spirituality
    c. cults
    d. communes

_____ 2. Solar energy—energy derived directly from the Sun—offers the best potential for providing the world's energy needs in future centuries. The Sun is a nonpolluting and virtually perpetual source of energy. At present, solar energy is used in two principal ways: thermal energy and photovoltaic electricity production. Solar thermal energy is heat collected from sunshine. Photovoltaic electric production is a direct conversion of solar energy to electricity. Solar energy is likely to become more attractive as other energy sources become more expensive.

—Bergman and Renwick,
Introduction to Geography, pp. 343–344.

   a. sources of energy
   b. solar energy
   c. thermal energy
   d. photovoltaic electricity

_____ 3. Because the mission of the Central Intelligence Agency (CIA) is to develop foreign intelligence and conduct counterintelligence activities to protect national security, it is not generally considered part of America's criminal justice system. However, it does engage in many of the same kinds of activities that are associated with domestic law enforcement, particularly the gathering of intelligence and the investigation of suspicious activities. The CIA employs thousands of people in a wide variety of jobs, from psychologists, engineers, computer scientists, and military analysts to statisticians, language instructors, attorneys, and theatrical effects specialists. Perhaps its most glamorous job is that of spy, referred to as the Clandestine Service.

—Barlow, *Criminal Justice in America*, p. 290

   a. the CIA
   b. national security
   c. America's criminal justice system
   d. domestic law enforcement

_____ 4. Daydreaming is a form of consciousness involving fantasy, occurring while you are awake. Almost all people daydream, although the frequency drops as we get older. Most daydreams are spontaneous images or thoughts that pop into our mind for a brief time and are then forgotten. We can, however, become adept at using daydreams to solve problems, to rehearse a sequence of events, or to find new ideas. Some daydreams are deliberate attempts to deal with situations like a boring job by providing some internal stimulation. Nevertheless, the content of most daydreams is related to such everyday events as paying bills or selecting clothes to wear.

—Davis and Palladino, *Psychology*, p. 190.

   a. consciousness
   b. fantasy
   c. internal stimulation
   d. daydreaming

_____ 5. The issue of inheritance is a controversial one in some families and should be resolved before the person dies in order to reduce both conflict and needless expense. Unfortunately, many people are so intimidated by the thought of making a will that they never do so and die intestate (without a will). This is tragic, especially because the procedure involved in establishing a legal will is relatively simple and inexpensive. In addition, if you don't make up a will before you die, the courts (as directed by state laws) will make up a will for you. Legal issues, rather than your wishes, will preside.

—Donatelle and Davis, *Access To Health,* p. 546.

a. death
b. inheritances
c. wills
d. state laws

EXERCISE 6-6

Directions: Read each of the following paragraphs and then write the topic of the paragraph in the space provided.

A. Discrimination doesn't go away: it just aims at whatever group appears to be out of fashion at any given moment. One expert feels that *age* is the major factor in employment discrimination today, although studies have shown older workers may be more reliable than young workers and just as productive. The Age Discrimination in Employment Act gives protection to the worker between forty and sixty-five. If you're in this age range, your employer must prove that you have performed unsatisfactorily before he can legally fire you. This act also prohibits* age discrimination in hiring, wages, and benefits. To report age discrimination, call your local office of the Wage and Hours Division of the U.S. Labor Department, or the Human Relations Commission in your state. If local offices are unable to help, try the national Equal Employment Opportunity Commission, Washington, D.C. 20460.

—George, *The New Consumer Survival Kit,* p. 212.

Topic: _____

B. Traditionally for men, and increasingly for women, one's job or career is tied in intimately with the way one regards oneself. Thus, loss of job becomes in part a loss of identity, and in part a seeming criticism of oneself as a total being, not merely as a worker. Even people who have lost jobs in mass layoffs through no fault of their own often feel guilty, especially if they are in the role of provider and no longer feel competent in fulfilling that role.

—Dorfman et al., *Well-Being,* p. 27.

Topic: _____

C. The words "effortless exercise" are a contradiction in terms. Muscles grow in strength only when subjected to overload. Flexibility is developed only by extending the normal range of body motion. Endurance is developed only through exercise

---

*Boxed words appear in the Mastering Vocabulary exercise on p. 198.

that raises the pulse rate enough to achieve a training effect on the heart, lungs, and circulatory system. In all cases, the benefits from exercise come from extending the body beyond its normal activity range. What this requires is, precisely, effort.

—Dorfman et al., *Well Being*, p. 263.

Topic: _____

D. Mental illness is usually diagnosed from abnormal behavior. A woman is asked the time of day, and she begins to rub her arms and recite the Apostles' Creed. A man is so convinced that someone is "out to get him" that he refuses to leave his apartment. Unusual behaviors like these are taken as evidence that the mental apparatus is not working quite right, and mental illness is proclaimed.

—Schaie and Geiwitz, *Adult Development and Aging*, pp. 371–372.

Topic: _____

E. How, exactly, does sleep replenish your body's fund of energy? Despite much interesting recent research on sleep, we still don't know. Certainly the metabolic rate slows during sleep (down to a level of about one met). Respiration, heartbeat, and other body functions slow down; muscular and digestive systems slow or cease their activity, allowing time for tissue repair. But the precise mechanisms by which sleep restores and refreshes us remain a mystery.

—Dorfman et al., *Well Being*, p. 263.

Topic: _____

FINDING THE STATED MAIN IDEA

The main idea of a paragraph is the most important idea; it is the idea that the whole paragraph explains or supports. Usually it is expressed in one sentence called the **topic sentence.** To find the main idea, use the following suggestions.

Locate the Topic

You have learned that the topic is the subject of a paragraph. The main idea is the most important thing the author wants you to know about the topic. To find the main idea, ask yourself, "What is the one most important thing to know about the topic?" Read the following paragraph and then answer this question.

The earth's water environments may be classified roughly as fresh water or marine, although not all bodies of water fall neatly into one category or the other. For example, Lake Pontchartrain, near New Orleans, is brackish, or a mixture of salt and freshwater. So are estuaries, the places where rivers flow into seas. Freshwater has about

0.1 percent salt; seawater has about 3.5 percent salt; and, as we will see, each has its importance in the earth's drama.

—Wallace, *Biology*, p. 497.

In this example, the topic is water classification. The most important point the author is making is that water can be classified as either fresh or marine, although exceptions do exist.

Locate the Most General Sentence

The most general sentence in the paragraph expresses the main idea. This sentence is called the topic sentence. This sentence must be broad enough to include or cover all the other ideas (details) in the paragraph. In the above paragraph, the first sentence makes a general statement about the earth's water—that most of it can be classified as fresh or marine. The rest of the sentences provide specifics about this classification.

Study the Rest of the Paragraph

The main idea must connect, draw together, and make meaningful the rest of the paragraph. You might think of the main idea as the one that all the details, taken together, add up to, explain, or support. In the above paragraph, sentences 2, 3, and 4 each give details about water classification. Sentences 2 and 3 give examples of exceptions to the fresh/marine categories. Sentence 4 defines the salt content of each category.

IDENTIFYING TOPIC SENTENCES

The topic sentence can be located anywhere in the paragraph. However, there are several positions where it is most likely to be found.

Topic Sentence First

Most often the topic sentence is placed first in the paragraph. In this type of paragraph, the author first states his or her main point and then explains it.

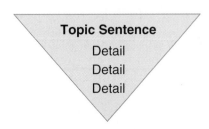

<u>D.W.Griffith, among the first "star" directors, paved the way for future filmmakers.</u> Griffith refined many of the narrative techniques that are still used, including varied camera distances, close-up shots, multiple story lines, fast-paced editing, and symbolic imagery. His major work, *The Birth of a Nation* (1915), was a controversial three-hour Civil War epic. Although considered a technical masterpiece, the film naively glorified the Ku Klux Klan and stereotyped southern blacks. It is nevertheless the movie that triggered Hollywood's eighty-year fascination with long narrative movies. By 1915, more than 20 percent of films were feature-length (around two hours), and *The Birth of a Nation,* which cost a filmgoer a record $2 admission to see, ran for a year on Broadway.

—Campbell, *Media and Culture,* p. 196.

Here the writer first states that D. W. Griffith paved the way for future filmmakers. The rest of the paragraph explains how he did this.

Topic Sentence Last

The second most likely place for a topic sentence to appear is last in the paragraph. When using this arrangement, a writer leads up to the main point and then directly states it at the end.

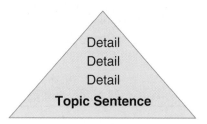

Detail
Detail
Detail
Topic Sentence

Fast foods tend to be short on fresh fruits and vegetables, and are low in calcium, although calcium can be obtained in shakes and milk. Pizza is a fast-food exception. It contains grains, meat, vegetables, and cheese, which represent four of the food groups. Pizza is often only about 25 percent fat, most of which comes from the crust. <u>Overall, studies have shown pizza to be highly nutritious.</u>

—Byer and Shainberg, *Living Well,* p. 289.

This paragraph first states what nutrients fast foods usually lack. Then it explains how pizza is an exception. The paragraph ends with a general statement about the contents of pizza—that studies have shown it to be highly nutritious.

Topic Sentence in the Middle

If it is placed neither first nor last, then the topic sentence appears somewhere in the middle of the paragraph. In this arrangement, the sentences before the topic sentence lead up to or introduce the main idea. Those that follow the main idea explain or describe it.

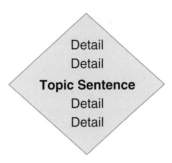

You could be the greatest mechanical genius since Thomas Edison, but if no one knows about your talent or is in a position to judge it, you're wasting your time. Being in the right field is important. But within that field, it's also a good idea to maintain a high degree of visibility. If you've got the potential to be a brilliant corporate strategist, you may be wasting your time working for a small company employing a dozen or so workers. You'd be better off working for a large corporation where you have the opportunity to take off in any number of directions, learn how the different departments interface, and thus have a larger arena to test your skills.

—Weinstein, *Jobs for the 21st Century,* p. 118.

In this paragraph, the writer begins with an example using Thomas Edison. He then states his main point and continues with examples that illustrate the importance of visibility in career advancement.

Topic Sentence First and Last

Occasionally the main idea will appear at the beginning of a paragraph and again at the end. Writers may use this organization to emphasize an important idea or to explain an idea that needs clarification.

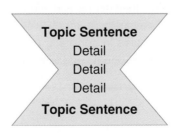

<u>Burger King Corporation offers both a service and a product to its customers</u>. Its service is the convenience it offers the consumer—the location of its restaurants and its fast food service—in catering to his or her lifestyle. Its product, in essence, is *the total Burger King experience,* which starts from the time you drive into the restaurant's parking lot and ends when you drive out. It includes the speed of service, the food you order, the price you pay, the friendliness and courtesy you are shown, the intangible feeling of satisfaction—in short, an experience. <u>Burger King, then, is marketing a positive experience, as promised by its advertising and promotional efforts and delivered by its product</u>.

—Fox and Wheatley, *Modern Marketing,* p. 142.

The first and last sentences both state, in slightly different ways, that Burger King provides a desirable product and service that result in a positive experience.

EXERCISE 6-7

Directions: Underline the topic sentence in each of the following paragraphs.

A. Leadership can assume any one of three basic styles: authoritarian, democratic, and laissez-faire. *Authoritarian* leaders give orders and direct activities with minimal input from followers. In extreme cases, they may be said to rule with an iron fist that crushes all dissent. In cultures where it is customary for authoritarian leaders to make decisions in both the political and domestic spheres, this leadership style may be preferred. In egalitarian societies, authoritarian leaders may be tolerated, but members of small groups typically prefer *democratic* leaders, who attempt to involve others in the decision-making process. *Laissez-faire* leaders take a "hands-off" approach; they neither set the agenda nor try to direct followers in any obvious way. Instead, they allow group members the freedom to choose whatever direction they think is best.

—Thompson and Hickey, *Society in Focus,* p. 156.

B. Dirty words are often used by teenagers in telling off-color stories and this can be considered part of their sex education. As their bodies grow and change, both boys and girls wonder and worry. To keep from being overwhelmed by these fears, they turn them into jokes or dirty-word stories. By telling and retelling off-color stories, they gain a little information, more misinformation, and a lot of reassurance. They learn that they aren't the only ones in the group disturbed about their future roles in courtship and marriage. Using dirty words and stories to laugh at sexual doubts and fears may diminish their importance and make them less frightening.

—Brothers, "What Dirty Words Really Mean," *Good Housekeeping.*

C. Deciding to buy a product or service takes preparation. Since time has already been spent to gather information and compare what is available, money managers should spend a little more time prior to arriving at a final decision. In this respect it is best if prospective buyers go home before making a selection. At home it is easier to evaluate all of the accumulated information while not under any sales or time pressure to make a purchase. In addition, at home it is possible to take a final look at financial plans to be sure the purchase will mesh with these plans.

—Weirich, *Personal Financial Management*, p. 155.

D. It is important to realize that the 1950s were to most Americans a time of great security. After World War II, the people prospered in ways they had never known before. Our involvement in the Korean War was thought to be successful from the point of view of national image. We saw ourselves as *the* world power, who had led the fight for democracy. When Dwight D. Eisenhower was elected president, we entered a period in American history where everything was all right, everyone was getting richer, and tomorrow would always be better than today.

—Weirich, *Personal Financial Management*, pp. 20–21.

E. The other day a good friend, senior executive of a large company and in his early forties, dropped by for a visit. He told me he had been thinking of divorce after sixteen years of marriage. The couple have a boy, twelve, and two girls, one of whom is ten, the other eight. "We've grown apart over the years, and we have nothing in common left anymore other than the children. There are at least twenty years of enjoying life still ahead of me. I was worried about the children until we discussed it with them. So many of their schoolmates have had divorced parents or parents who had remarried, they are accustomed to the idea. It's part of life. Of course, if the older ones need help, I want them to see a good psychiatrist while we go through with this. My wife is still a good-looking woman, younger than I, and probably will remarry. I'm not thinking of it now, but I'll probably remarry someday." This situation illustrates an attitude and the climate of the times. Divorce has become as much an institution as marriage.

—Smith and Liedlich, *From Thought to Theme*, pp. 281–82.

F. If you have ever seen someone hooked up to an oxygen tank and struggling to breathe while climbing a flight of stairs or listened to someone gasping for air for no apparent reason, you have probably witnessed an emphysemic episode. Emphysema involves the gradual destruction of the alveoli (tiny air sacs) of the lungs. As the alveoli are destroyed, the affected person finds it more and more difficult to exhale. The victim typically struggles to take in a fresh supply of air before the air held in the lungs has been expended. What we all take for granted—the

easy, rhythmic flow of air in and out of our lungs—becomes a continuous struggle for people with emphysema.

—Donatelle and Davis, *Access to Health,* p. 497.

G. Cultures can be classified in terms of their masculinity and femininity.
Masculine cultures emphasize success and socialize their people to be assertive, ambitious, and competitive. Members of masculine cultures are thus
more likely to confront conflicts directly and to competitively fight out any differences; they're more likely to emphasize win-lose conflict strategies. **Feminine
cultures** emphasize the quality of life and socialize their people to be modest
and to emphasize close interpersonal relationships. Members of feminine cultures are thus more likely to emphasize compromise and negotiation in resolving
conflicts; they're more likely to seek win-win solutions.

—DeVito, *The Interpersonal Communication Book,* p. 43.

H. Large collections of animals, which were originally called menageries, have
served as magnets for visitors since the times of the ancient Chinese, Egyptians,
Babylonians, and Aztecs. Modern zoos (sometimes called zoological parks) now
come in many sizes and can be found throughout the world. The Philadelphia
Zoo was the first (1859) location in the United States dedicated to the large-scale
collection and display of animals. While this facility is still of great importance, it
has been eclipsed by more spectacular zoos such as the Bronx Zoo and the San
Diego Zoo. Other notable zoos around the world can be found in Montreal, Van-
couver, Frankfurt, London, Paris, Moscow, New Delhi, Tokyo, and Sydney.

—Cook et al., *Tourism,* p. 151.

I. The lower courts are usually very busy places. If you visit one on a typical morning you will discover a crowded courtroom with all sorts of people milling around.
Some are lawyers, some are victims, a few are onlookers and relatives of defendants, and there may be a police officer or two. But most are defendants waiting for
their case to be called. At the front of the courtroom it is not uncommon to see the
judge engaged in three or four conversations at once. People come and go constantly, and there is a lot of talking going on around the room. A plea of "Order
in the court!" would probably be unheard, and court bailiffs have learned to overlook the apparent disorder so long as the day's business gets done.

—Barlow, *Criminal Justice in America,* pp. 422–23.

J. You will periodically see warnings on the Internet about e-mail messages carrying computer viruses. They typically tell you never to read anything with a specific subject header (like "Good Times" or "Pen Pal Greetings"), and then they tell
you to be sure to pass this warning along to everyone you know. These warnings
are all hoaxes. You cannot get a computer virus from reading a plain text mail

message. If you see such a virus warning and suspect that it's a hoax, you can visit the Computer Virus Myths Web site to see if it is a known hoax. Whatever you do, don't forward the message to all your friends and coworkers. If there is a real virus on the loose, leave it to the professionals in technical support to distribute appropriate warnings.

—Lehnert, *Light on the Internet*, p. 44.

LEARNING STYLE TIPS

If you tend to be a . . .	Then find topic sentences by . . .
Creative learner	Looking away from the paragraph and stating its main point in your own words. Find a sentence that matches your statement.
Pragmatic learner	Reading through the paragraph, sentence-by-sentence, evaluating each sentence.

IMPLIED MAIN IDEAS

When you imply something, you suggest an idea, but you do not state it outright. Study the cartoon below. The point the cartoonist is making is clear—relationships change quickly. Notice, however, that this point is not stated directly. To get the cartoonist's point, you had to study the details and read the signs in the cartoon, and then reason out what the cartoonist is trying to say. You need to use the same reasoning process when reading paragraphs that lack a topic sentence. You have to study the details and figure out what all the details mean when considered together. This chapter will show you how to figure out main ideas that are suggested (implied) but not directly stated in a paragraph.

What Does Implied Mean?

Suppose your favorite shirt is missing from your closet and you know that your roommate often borrows your clothes. You say to your roommate, "If that blue plaid shirt is back in my closet by noon, I'll forget that it was missing." Now, you did not directly accuse your roommate of borrowing your shirt, but your message was clear—return my shirt! Your statement implied or suggested that your roommate had borrowed it and should return it. Your roommate, if he understood your message, inferred (reasoned out) that you suspected that he had borrowed your shirt and that you want it back.

Speakers and writers imply ideas. Listeners and readers must make inferences in order to understand them. Here are two important terms you need to know:

Imply	means	**to suggest an idea but not state it directly.**
Infer	means	**to reason out something based on what has been said.**

Here is another statement; what is the writer implying?

I wouldn't feed that cake to my dog.

No doubt you inferred that the writer dislikes the cake and considers it inedible, but notice that the writer did not say that.

EXERCISE 6-8 **Directions:** For each of the following statements, indicate which choice best explains what the writer is implying but has not directly stated.

_____ 1. Jane's hair looks as if she just came out of a wind tunnel.
    a. Jane's hair needs rearranging.
    b. Jane's hair is messy.
    c. Jane's hair needs styling.
    d. Jane's hair needs coloring.

_____ 2. I would not recommend Professor Wright's class to my worst enemy.
    a. The writer likes Professor Wright's class.
    b. The writer dislikes Professor Wright's class.
    c. Professor Wright's class is popular.
    d. Professor Wright's class is unpopular.

_____ 3. The steak was overcooked and tough; the mashed potatoes were cold; the green beans were withered, and the chocolate pie was mushy.
    a. The dinner was tasty.
    b. The dinner was prepared poorly.
    c. The dinner was nutritious.
    d. The dinner was served carelessly.

_____ 4. Professor Rodriguez assigns three 5-page papers, gives weekly quizzes, and requires both a midterm and final exam. In addition to weekly assigned chapters in the text, we must read three to four journal articles each week. It is difficult to keep up.
    a. Professor Rodriguez's course is demanding.
    b. Professor Rodriguez is not a good teacher.
    c. Professor Rodriguez likes to give homework.
    d. Professor Rodriguez's course is unpopular.

_____ 5. It was my favorite time of year. The lilacs were blooming—finally!—and even though we still wore sweaters, the breeze held the promise of warm days to come.
    a. It was autumn.
    b. It was springtime.
    c. It was summertime.
    d. There was a storm coming.

_____ 6. When Alton got the estimate for repairing his car, he knew he had a tough decision to make.
   a. Alton was going to repair his own car.
   b. Alton would have to find another car repair shop.
   c. Alton's car repairs were going to be inexpensive.
   d. Alton would have to decide whether to repair the car or to buy a different one.

_____ 7. Charlie limped over to the couch and lay down. He put his foot up on a pillow and carefully placed the ice pack on his ankle.
   a. Charlie is getting ready to take a nap.
   b. Charlie has an injured ankle.
   c. Charlie has the flu.
   d. Charlie has been running.

_____ 8. After the girls' sleepover party last Saturday, it looked like a bomb had gone off in the basement.
   a. The sleepover party was too loud.
   b. The electricity went out during the sleepover party.
   c. There was an explosion in the basement after the sleepover party.
   d. The girls made a mess in the basement.

_____ 9. When it was Kei's turn to give her speech, her stomach did a flip, and her face felt as if it were on fire.
   a. Kei looked forward to giving her speech.
   b. Kei was experienced at giving speeches.
   c. Kei was nervous about giving her speech.
   d. Kei enjoyed giving speeches.

_____ 10. People filed out of the movie theater slowly and quietly; many of them wiped their eyes and noses with tissues as they walked to their cars.
   a. The movie was sad.
   b. The movie was funny.
   c. The theater was cold.
   d. The moviegoers were disappointed.

Figuring Out Implied Main Ideas

Implied main ideas, when they appear in paragraphs, are usually larger, more important ideas than the details. You might think of implied ideas as general ideas that are suggested by specifics.

What larger, more important idea do these details point to?

The wind was blowing at 35 mph.

The windchill was 5 degrees below zero.

Snow was falling at the rate of 3 inches per hour.

Together these three details suggests that a snowstorm or blizzard was occurring. You might visualize this as follows:

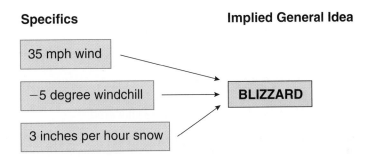

Now what idea does the following set of specifics suggest?

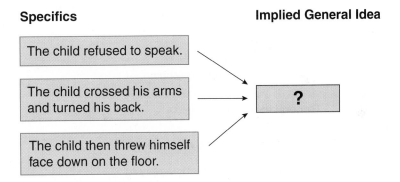

You probably determined that the child was angry or having a temper tantrum.

Copyright © 2009 by Kathleen T. McWhorter

EXERCISE 6-9

Directions: Find a word from the list below that describes the larger idea or situation each set of specifics suggests. Each will require you to infer a general idea.

tonsillitis	closed	dying	flu	accident
power outage	accident	a burglary	going too fast	

1. The child has a headache.

   The child has a queasy stomach.

   The child has a mild fever.

   General Idea: The child has the _____

2. The plant's leaves were withered.

   The blossoms had dropped.

   Its stem was drooping.

   General Idea: The plant was _____

3. The windshield of the car was shattered.

   The door panel was dented.

   The bumper was crumpled.

   General Idea: The car had been in a(n) _____

4. The lights went out.

   The clock radio flashed.

   The refrigerator stopped running.

   General Idea: There was a _____

5. The supermarket door was locked.

   The parking lot was nearly empty.

   A few remaining customers were checking out.

   General Idea: The supermarket was _____

Implied Ideas in Paragraphs

In paragraphs, writers sometimes leave their main idea unstated. The paragraph contains only details. It is up to you, the reader, to infer the writer's main point. You can visualize this type of paragraph as follows:

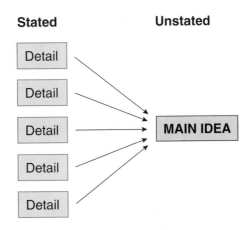

The details, when taken together, all point to a larger, more important idea. Think of the paragraph as a list of facts that you must add up or put together to determine the meaning of the paragraph as a whole. Use the following steps as a guide to find implied main ideas:

1. **Find the topic.** Ask yourself, "What is the one thing the author is discussing throughout the paragraph?"
2. **Decide what the writer wants you to know about that topic.** Look at each detail and decide what larger general idea each explains.
3. **Express this idea in your own words.** Make sure the main idea is a reasonable one. Ask yourself, "Does it apply to all the details in the paragraphs?"

Read the following paragraph; then follow the three steps listed above.

> Some advertisers rely on star power. Commercials may use celebrities to encourage consumers to purchase a product. Other commercials may use an "everyone's buying it" approach that argues that thousands of consumers could not possibly be wrong in their choice, so the product must be worthwhile. Still other commercials may use visual appeal to catch the consumers' interest and persuade them to make purchases.

The topic of this paragraph is commercials. More specifically it is about devices advertisers use to build commercials. Three details are given: use of star power, an everybody's-buying-it approach, and visual appeal. Each of the three details is a different persuasive device. The main point the writer is trying to make, then, is that commercials use various persuasive devices to appeal to consumers. Notice that no single sentence states this idea clearly.

You can visualize this paragraph as follows:

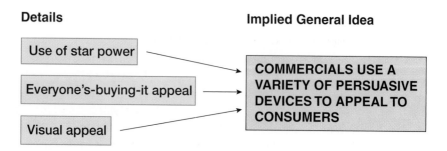

Here is another paragraph. Read it and then fill in the diagram that follows:

Yellow is a bright, cheery color; it is often associated with spring and hopefulness. Green, since it is a color that appears frequently in nature (trees, grass, plants), has come to suggest growth and rebirth. Blue, the color of the sky, may suggest eternity or endless beauty. Red, the color of both blood and fire, is often connected with strong feelings such as courage, lust, and rage.

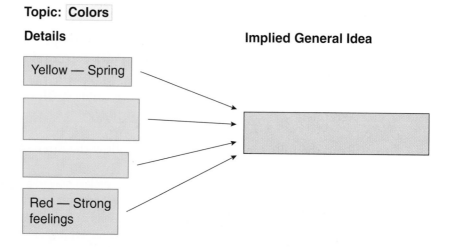

How to Know if You Have Made a Reasonable Inference

There is a test you can do to discover if you inferred a reasonable main idea. The idea you infer to be the main idea should be broad enough so that every sentence in the paragraph explains the idea you have chosen. Work through the paragraph, sentence by sentence. Check to see that each sentence explains or gives more information about the idea you have chosen. If some sentences do not explain your chosen idea, your main idea probably is not broad enough. Work on expanding your idea and making it more general.

EXERCISE 6-10

Directions: Read each of the following paragraphs and complete the diagram that follows

A. Workers in the **primary sector** of an economy extract resources directly from Earth. Most workers in this sector are usually in agriculture, but the sector also includes fishing, forestry, and mining. Workers in the **secondary sector** transform raw materials produced by the primary sector into manufactured goods. Construction is included in this sector. All other jobs in an economy are within the **tertiary sector,** sometimes called the **service sector.** The tertiary sector includes a great range of occupations, from a store clerk to a surgeon, from a movie ticket seller to a nuclear physicist, from a dancer to a political leader.

—Bergman and Renwick, *Introduction to Geography,* p. 365.

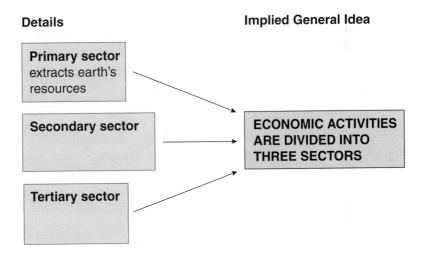

B. Among many other activities, urban gangs fight among themselves and prey on the weak and vulnerable. They delight in demonstrating ownership and control of their "turf," and they sometimes turn neighborhoods into war zones in defense of it. Once gangs form, their graffiti soon adorn buildings and alleyways, and membership is displayed through hand signs, clothing, and special colors. As a newly formed gang grows in reputation and confidence, it soon finds itself attracting those who would like to be members in order to reap the benefits: safety, or girlfriends, or a reputation for toughness.

—Barlow, *Criminal Justice in America,* p. 271.

Details   **Implied Main Idea**

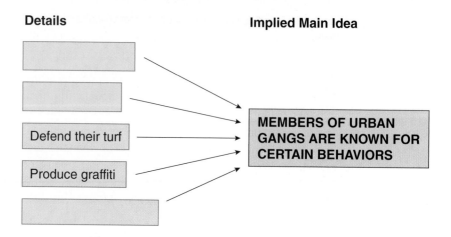

C. For many smokers, the road to quitting is too rough to travel alone. Some smokers turn to nontobacco products to help them quit; products such as nicotine chewing gum and the nicotine patch replace depleted levels of nicotine in the bloodstream and ease the process of quitting. Aversion therapy techniques attempt to reduce smoking by pairing the act of smoking with some sort of noxious stimulus so that smoking itself is perceived as unpleasant. For example, the technique of rapid smoking instructs patients to smoke rapidly and continuously until they exceed their tolerance for cigarette smoke, producing unpleasant sensations. Proponents of self-control strategies view smoking as a learned habit associated with specific situations. Therapy is aimed at identifying these situations and teaching smokers the skills necessary to resist smoking.

—Donatelle and Davis, *Access to Health,* pp. 285–86.

Details   **Implied Main Idea**

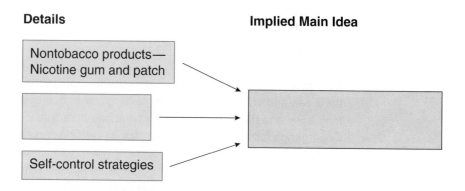

D. How should you present your speech? Let's consider your options. An **impromptu speech** is delivered on the spur of the moment, without preparation. The ability to speak off the cuff is useful in an emergency, but impromptu speeches produce unpredictable outcomes. It's certainly not a good idea to rely on impromptu speaking in place of solid preparation. Another option is a **memorized speech.** Speakers who use memorized presentations are usually most effective when they write their speeches to sound like informal and conversational speech rather than formal, written essays. A **manuscript speech** is written out beforehand and then read from a manuscript or TelePrompTer. When extremely careful wording is required (for example, when the president addresses Congress), the manuscript speech is appropriate. However, most speeches that you'll deliver will be extemporaneous. An **extemporaneous speech** is one that is prepared in advance and presented from abbreviated notes. Extemporaneous speeches are nearly as polished as memorized ones, but they are more vigorous, flexible, and spontaneous.

—German et al., *Principles of Public Speaking,* pp. 190–91.

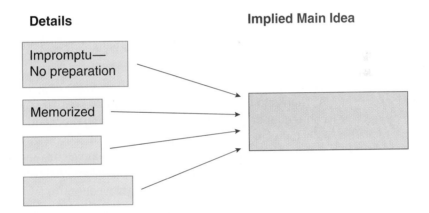

E. In order to measure social class standing, sociologists may use the *objective* method, which ranks individuals into classes on the basis of measures such as education, income, and occupational prestige. Sociologists may also use the *reputational* method, which places people into various social classes on the basis of reputation in the community (Warner 1960). A third method, *self-identification,* allows people to place themselves in a social class. Although people can readily place themselves in a class, the results are often difficult to interpret. People might be hesitant to call themselves upper-class for fear of appearing snobbish, but at the same time they might be reluctant to call themselves lower-class for fear of being stigmatized. The net result is that the method of self-identification substantially overestimates the middle portion of the class system.

—Curry et al., *Sociology for the 21st Century,* p. 138.

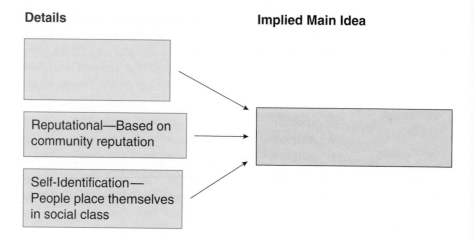

Details   **Implied Main Idea**

Reputational—Based on community reputation

Self-Identification— People place themselves in social class

Directions: Read each of the following paragraphs and answer the questions that follow.

A. Thanks to the Internet, you can shop 24 hours a day without leaving home, you can read today's newspaper without getting drenched picking up a hard copy in a rainstorm, and you don't have to wait for the 6:00 news to find out what the weather will be like tomorrow—at home or around the globe. And, with the increasing use of handheld devices and wireless communications, you can get that same information—from stock quotes to the weather—even when you're away from your computer.

—Solomon and Stuart, *The Brave New World of E-Commerce,* p. 13.

1. What is the topic? _____

2. What is the implied main idea? _____

_____

B. Watch a nursery school teacher talk to preschool children and you'll see how age gaps of twenty years or more can be overcome. Nursery school teachers know that they must adapt to their young listeners or risk chaos. They adapt partly by simplifying their vocabulary and shortening their sentences. If you've ever read a story to a child, you know another secret to engaging youngsters. If you talk like a wizard or a teapot or a mouse, you can see children's eyes widen.

—German et al., *Principles of Public Speaking,* p. 70.

1. What is the topic? _____

2. What is the implied main idea? _____

_____

C. The Federal Trade Commission has taken action against several infomercial producers when it decided their programs had the potential to be deceptive because viewers might believe the infomercial is a *bona fide* show. Some viewers have sued TV stations for losses when they were deceived by the advertisers. To avoid these problems, some infomercial producers and television stations voluntarily include a disclaimer to avoid lawsuits claiming deception or FTC actions. But because people tend to change channels frequently they may miss the disclaimer and thus be unaware of the true nature of the infomercial.

—Solomon, *Consumer Behavior,* p. 239.

1. What is the topic? _____

2. What is the implied main idea? _____

_____

D. Sleep conserves body energy so that we are rested and ready to perform during high-performance daylight hours. Sleep also restores the neurotransmitters that have been depleted during the waking hours. This process clears the brain of unimportant details as a means of preparing for a new day. Getting enough sleep to feel ready to meet daily challenges is a key factor in maintaining optimal physical and psychological status.

—Donatelle and Davis, *Access to Health,* p. 40.

1. What is the topic? _____

2. What is the implied main idea? _____

_____

E. Research suggests that women who are considered attractive are more effective in changing attitudes than are women thought to be less attractive. In addition, more attractive individuals are often considered to be more credible than less attractive people. They are also perceived to be happier, more popular, more sociable, and more successful than are those rated as being less attractive. With respect to shape and body size, people with fat, round silhouettes are consistently rated as older, more old-fashioned, less good-looking, more talkative, and more good-natured. Athletic, muscular people are rated as more mature, better looking, taller, and more adventurous. Tall and thin people are rated as more ambitious, more suspicious of others, more tense and nervous, more pessimistic, and quieter.

—Beebe and Masterson, *Communicating in Small Groups*, p. 150.

1. What is the topic? _____

2. What is the implied main idea? _____

_____

EXERCISE 6-12

Directions: None of the following paragraphs has a topic sentence. Read each paragraph and, in the space provided, write a sentence that expresses the main idea.

A. Immigration has contributed to the ⌐dramatic¬ population growth of the United States over the past 150 years. It has also contributed to the country's shift from a rural to an urban economy. Immigrants provided inexpensive labor which allowed industries to flourish. Native-born children of immigrants, benefitting from education, moved into professional and white collar jobs, creating a new middle class. Immigration also increased the U.S. mortality rate. Due to crowded housing and unhealthy living conditions, disease and fatal illness were common.

—Weinstein, *Jobs for the 21st Century,* pp. 110–11.

Implied Main Idea: _____

_____

B. Jack Schultz and Ian Baldwin found last summer that trees under attack by insects or animals will release an unidentified chemical into the air as a distress signal. Upon receiving the signal, nearby trees step up their production of tannin—a poison in the leaves that gives insects indigestion. The team learned, too, that production of the poison is in proportion to the ⌐duration¬ and intensity of the attack.

—"Trees Talk to One Another," *Science Digest,* p. 47.

Implied Main Idea: _____

_____

C. When President Lincoln was shot, the word was communicated by telegraph to most parts of the United States, but because we had no links to England, it was five days before London heard of the event. When President Reagan was shot, journalist Henry Fairlie, working at his typewriter within a block of the shooting, got word of it by telephone from his editor at the *Spectator* in London, who had seen a rerun of the assassination attempt on television shortly after it occurred.

—Naisbitt, *Megatrends,* p. 23.

Implied Main Idea: _____

_____

D. Suppose you wanted to teach your pet chimpanzee the English language. How would you go about it? Two psychologists raised Gua, a female chimpanzee, at home with their son, Donald. Both boy and chimp were encouraged to speak, but only Donald did. Gua indicated she could comprehend some language, for she could respond appropriately to about 60 different utterances, but she never *produced* a single word. A second attempt involved more intensive training in speech, and Viki, another chimpanzee, was eventually able to pronounce three recognizable words: "Mama," "Papa," and "cup."

—Geiwitz, *Psychology,* p. 276.

Implied Main Idea: _____

_____

E. Traffic is directed by color. Pilot instrument panels, landing strips, road and water crossings are regulated by many colored lights and signs. Factories use colors to distinguish between thoroughfares and work areas. Danger zones are painted in special colors. Lubrication points and removable parts are accentuated by color. Pipes for transporting water, steam, oil, chemicals, and compressed air are designated by different colors. Electrical wires and resistances are color coded.

—Gerritsen, *Theory and Practice of Color,* p. 9.

Implied Main Idea: _____

_____

F. The Grand Canyon and the Colorado River and its banks are deteriorating due to the ever-increasing numbers of visitors descending into the Canyon and the thousands each year who enjoy its river-rafting thrills. Likewise, Banff National Park, Canada's oldest national park, continues to suffer from the millions of visitors it receives annually. Many places in its tundra wilderness have been severely trampled by hikers. In Yosemite National Park, the increase in vehicle traffic through the park causes the very air pollution that visitors try to escape by fleeing to national parks.

—Cook et al., *Tourism,* pp. 246–47.

Implied Main Idea: _____

_____

G. As the effects of caffeine begin to wear off, users may feel let down, mentally or physically depressed, exhausted, and weak. To counteract these effects, people commonly choose to drink another cup of coffee. But before you say yes to another cup of coffee, consider this. Although you would have to drink between 66 and 100 cups of coffee in a day to produce a fatal overdose of caffeine, you may experience sensory disturbances after consuming only 10 cups of coffee within a 24-hour period. These symptoms include tinnitus (ringing in the ears), spots before the eyes, numbness in arms and legs, poor circulation, and visual hallucinations. Because 10 cups of coffee is not an extraordinary amount for many people to drink within a 24-hour period, caffeine use is clearly something to think about.

—Donatelle and Davis, *Access to Health,* pp. 289–90.

Implied Main Idea: _____

_____

H. In 1946, the Levitt Company was finishing up Levittown. Practically overnight, what was formerly a Long Island potato field 25 miles east of Manhattan became one of America's newest suburbs, changing the way homes were built. The land was bulldozed and the trees removed, and then trucks dropped building materials at precise 60-foot intervals. Construction was divided into 26 distinct steps. At the peak of production, the company constructed 30 new single-family homes each day.

—Bergman and Renwick, *Introduction to Geography,* pp. 384–85.

Implied Main Idea: _____

_____

I. Pathogens, also known as disease carrying agents, may be transmitted by direct contact between infected persons, such as sexual relations, kissing, or touching. Pathogens may also be spread by indirect contact, such as touching an object the infected person has had contact with. The hands are probably the greatest source of infectious disease transmission. For example, you may touch the handle of a drinking fountain that was just touched by a person whose hands were contaminated by a recent sneeze. You may also autoinoculate yourself, or transmit a pathogen from one part of your body to another. For example, you may touch a sore on your lip that is teeming with viral herpes and then transmit the virus to your eye when you subsequently scratch your itchy eyelid.

—Norstog and Meyerricks, *Biology,* p. 641.

Implied Main Idea: _____

_____

J. *Turn-requesting cues* tell the speaker that you, as a listener, would like to take a turn as speaker; you might transmit these cues by using some vocalized "er" or "um" that tells the speaker that you would now like to speak, by opening your eyes and mouth as if to say something, by beginning to gesture with a hand, or by leaning forward.

Through *turn-denying cues* you indicate your reluctance to assume the role of speaker by, for example, intoning a slurred "I don't know"; giving the speaker some brief grunt that signals you have nothing to say; avoiding eye contact with the speaker who wishes you now to take on the role of speaker; or engaging in some behavior that is incompatible with speaking—for example, coughing or blowing your nose.

Through *backchanneling cues* you communicate various meanings back to the speaker—but without assuming the role of the speaker. For example, you can indicate your *agreement* or *disagreement* with the speaker through smiles or frowns, nods of approval or disapproval; brief comments such as "right," "exactly," or "never"; or vocalizations such as "uh-huh" or "uh-uh."

—DeVito, *Messages*, pp. 224–25.

Implied Main Idea: _____

_____

MASTERING VOCABULARY

Directions: Select the answer that best provides the meaning of each word as it was used in this chapter. Use context clues, word parts, and a dictionary, if necessary.

_____ 1. prohibits (p. 173)
   a. recognizes
   b. forbids
   c. encourages
   d. identifies

_____ 2. proclaimed (p. 174)
   a. unstated
   b. ignored
   c. declared
   d. generated

_____ 3. precise (p. 174)
   a. exact
   b. speedy
   c. general
   d. slow

_____ 4. dissent (p. 178)
   a. crime
   b. disagreement
   c. people
   d. harmony

_____ 5. accumulated (p. 179)
   a. intellectual
   b. collected
   c. specific
   d. practical

_____ 6. prospered (p. 179)
   a. progressed
   b. worked
   c. communicated
   d. joked

_____ 7. dramatic (p. 194)
   a. limiting
   b. simultaneous
   c. impressive
   d. blunt

_____ 8. duration (p. 194)
   a. heaviness
   b. harshness
   c. difficulty
   d. length of time

_____ 9. intensive (p. 195)
   a. objective
   b. subtle
   c. simple
   d. concentrated

_____ 10. accentuated (p. 195)
   a. highlighted
   b. hidden
   c. negatively perceived
   d. made duller

SELF-TEST SUMMARY

Name and describe the four essential parts of a paragraph.	The four parts of a paragraph are: • **Topic.** The topic is the one thing the entire paragraph is about. • **Main idea.** The main idea is the most important idea the writer wants the reader to know about the topic. • **Details.** Details are facts and ideas that support the main idea. • **Transitions.** Transitions are words and phrases that lead the reader from one idea to another.
What sentence states the main idea of a paragraph?	The topic sentence states the main idea of a paragraph.
Where is the topic sentence located?	The topic sentence can be located anywhere in the paragraph. The most common positions are first or last, but the topic sentence can also appear in the middle, or first and last.
What are implied main ideas?	Implied main ideas are suggested but not directly stated in the paragraph.
How can one figure out implied main ideas?	To find implied main ideas: • find the topic • figure out what general ideas the paragraph explains • express the idea in your own words

Getting More Practice with . . .
Topics and Main Ideas

WORKING TOGETHER

Directions: Separate into groups. Using a reading selection from Part Six of this book, work with your group to identify and underline the topic sentence of each paragraph. If any of the main ideas are unstated, write a sentence that states the main idea. When all the groups have completed the task, the class should compare the findings of the various groups.

GOING ONLINE

Internet Activities

1. What Is a Topic Sentence?
   http://www.cerritos.edu/reading/topic1.html
   Review how to locate the topic sentence of a paragraph with these tips and exercises from Cerritos College.

2. Identifying Main Ideas in Paragraphs
   http://www.public.asu.edu/~ickpl/project/Main_Idea.htm
   Print out this worksheet and complete it using any article from a newspaper or magazine that interests you.

Companion Website

For additional readings, exercises, and Internet activities, visit this book's Companion Website at:
http://www.ablongman.com/mcwhorter
If you need a user name and password, please see your instructor.

My Reading Lab

For more practice on main ideas, visit MyReadingLab, click on the Reading Skills tab, and then click on Active Reading Strategies—Maine Woods.
http://www.ablongman.com/myreadinglab

Answering Questions on the Topic and Main Idea

Reading comprehension tests often include questions that ask you to identify the topic and main idea of a paragraph. Test writers do not always use the terms "topic" and "main idea." Once you understand what a test item is asking you to identify, you will probably be able to answer it.

Topic—Here are a few ways reading tests may ask you to identify the topic of a paragraph:

- This paragraph is primarily about . . .

- This paragraph concerns . . .

- This paragraph focuses on . . .

- The best title for the paragraph would be . . .

Main Idea—Here are a few words reading tests may use to mean main idea of a paragraph:

- Thesis

- Central point

- Central idea

- Controlling idea

- Most important idea

- Primary idea

So a question that asks "Which of the following statements expresses the central point of the paragraph?" is really asking you to identify the main idea.

Name _____

Section _____ Date _____

Number right _____ x 20 points = Score _____

Directions: For each of the following situations, indicate which choice best explains what the writer is implying.

_____ 1. Muttering angrily to himself, Edgar stomped into his office and packed all of his belongings in a cardboard box. Mrs. Chen, the personnel director, soon arrived at his door and escorted him out of the building.
   a. Edgar was going home sick.
   b. The building was being evacuated.
   c. Mrs. Chen wanted to talk to him about his job.
   d. Edgar had been fired.

_____ 2. We felt relaxed and happy. No telephone, no fax machine, no traffic jam at the end of the day. Just the wide open beach and all the seafood we could eat.
   a. The writer was on a business trip.
   b. The writer was on vacation.
   c. The writer was at a party.
   d. The writer was working at a restaurant.

_____ 3. The entire classroom was silent except for the sound of Professor Seiquist's footsteps as he walked up and down the aisles. Everywhere he looked, students were writing busily on the papers in front of them, some pausing briefly to look into space with expressions of intense concentration before continuing to write.
   a. Professor Seiquist's class was taking a test.
   b. Professor Seiquist was conducting an experiment.

   c. The class was writing an evaluation of Professor Seiquist.
   d. The class was taking a break from studying.

_____ 4. Even though it was just past noon, the sky was growing dark. Heavy clouds were moving along the horizon. The air felt thick, and all of the birds seemed to be holding their breath.
   a. It was summertime.
   b. A storm was coming.
   c. A solar eclipse was taking place.
   d. A storm had just passed.

_____ 5. Rosa stood up, wiping the dirt from her hands and the knees of her jeans before picking up the trowel and going inside. As she gulped a cold drink, she hoped that her hard work today would pay off later in the summer.
   a. Rosa was painting her house.
   b. Rosa was doing repairs around the house.
   c. Rosa was planting a garden.
   d. Rosa was helping a friend do yard work.

Name _____

Section _____ Date _____

Number right _____ x 20 points = Score _____

Directions: Read each of the following para-graphs, and select the answer that correctly identi-fies the paragraph's main idea.

_____ 1. Many "everyday" consumers have become entrepreneurs by participating in **virtual auctions.** Millions of con-sumers log on to eBay.com and other auction sites to bid on an enormous variety of new and used items offered by both businesses and individuals. From an economic standpoint, auctions offer savvy consumers the opportunity to buy overruns or excess inventories of new items at discounted prices much as they would in bricks-and-mortar dis-count stores. For many, however, the auctions also have become a form of entertainment. Players in the auction game spend hours a day on the auction sites, buying and selling collectibles or other items of (assumed?) value.

—Solomon and Stuart, *Brave New World of E-Commerce*, p. 16.

a. Millions of consumers use eBay.com to buy and sell a wide variety of items.

b. Virtual auctions offer consumers the chance to buy and sell items and to be entertained.

c. Virtual auctions provide the same service as traditional discount stores.

d. Most consumers view virtual auc-tions as a form of entertainment.

_____ 2. Pollutants have diverse sources. Some come from a *point source*—they enter a stream at a specific location, such as a wastewater discharge pipe. Others may come from a *nonpoint source*—they come from a large diffuse area, as happens when organic matter or fertil-izer washes from a field during a storm. Point-source pollutants are usually smaller in quantity and much easier to control. Nonpoint sources usually pollute in greater quantities and are much harder to control.

—Bergman and Renwick, *Introduction to Geography*, p. 348.

a. Point sources of pollution include wastewater discharge pipes.

b. Nonpoint sources of pollution are worse for the environment than point sources.

c. Nonpoint-source pollutants come from a widespread area, whereas point-source pollutants come from a specific location.

d. Pollutants can come from point or nonpoint sources.

_____ 3. Much as feedback contains informa-tion about messages already sent, **feedforward** is information about mes-sages before you send them. Opening comments such as "Wait until you hear this" or "Don't get me wrong, but . . ." are examples of feedforward. These messages tell the listener something about the messages to come or about the way you'd like the listener to respond. Nonverbally, feedforward is given by your facial expression, eye contact, and physical posture, for example; with these nonverbal messages you tell the other person something about the messages you'll be sending.

—DeVito, *Messages*, p. 140.

a. Feedback is the opposite of feedforward.
b. Feedforward consists primarily of nonverbal messages.
c. Feedforward describes information that comes before a message is sent.
d. Feedback and feedforward are both necessary to communication.

_____ 4. Support groups are an important part of stress management. Friends, family members, and co-workers can provide us with emotional and physical support. Although the ideal support group differs for each of us, you should have one or two close friends in whom you are able to confide and neighbors with whom you can trade favors. You should take the opportunity to participate in community activities at least once a week. A healthy, committed relationship can also provide vital support.

—Donatelle and Davis,
Access to Health, p. 78.

a. Support groups are important in managing stress.
b. Support groups consist of friends and family.

c. Participation in community activities is one way of managing stress.
d. The ideal support group is different for each person.

_____ 5. Nowhere in the world is the love affair with the automobile stronger than in North America. Much of the credit for this attraction goes to the pioneering genius of Henry Ford, who ushered in the age of mass automobile travel with his famous Model T. Between 1908 and 1923, 15 million of these affordable cars were produced. The car is now more than simply transportation for most Americans; it is a symbol of freedom and individualized lifestyles.

—Cook et al., *Tourism*, p. 86.

a. Henry Ford popularized mass automobile travel with his Model T.
b. Fifteen million Model T cars were produced between 1908 and 1923.
c. Americans love their cars.
d. Cars represent freedom and independence to Americans.

Name _____

Section _____ Date _____

Number right _____ x 10 points = Score _____

Directions: Read the following selection from a communications textbook and select the best answer for each of the following questions.

Eye Communication

1   The messages communicated by the eyes vary depending on the duration, direction, and quality of the eye behavior. In every culture, there are rather strict, though unstated, rules for the proper duration for eye contact. In much of England and the United States, for example, the average length of gaze is 2.95 seconds. The average length of mutual gaze (two persons gazing at each other) is 1.18 seconds. When eye contact falls short of this amount, you may think the person in uninterested, shy, or preoccupied. When the appropriate amount of time is exceeded, you may perceive this as showing high interest.

2   In much of the United States direct eye contact is considered an expression of honesty and forthrightness. But, the Japanese often view this as a lack of respect. The Japanese will glance at the other person's face rarely and then only for very short periods. In many Hispanic cultures direct eye contact signifies a certain equality and so should be avoided by, say, children when speaking to a person in authority. Try visualizing the potential misunderstandings that eye communication alone could create when people from Tokyo, San Francisco, and San Juan try to communicate.

3   The direction of the eye also communicates. Generally, in communicating with another person, you would glance alternately at the other person's face, then away, then again at the face, and so on. When these directional rules are broken, different meanings are communicated—abnormally high or low interest, self-consciousness, or nervousness over the interaction. The quality—how wide or how narrow your eyes get during interaction—also communicates meaning, especially interest level and such emotions as surprise, fear, and disgust.

4   On average we blink about 15 times a minute, in part to lubricate and protect the eye. You may increase blinking if you're uncomfortable or under lots of stress. For example, you would probably increase your blinking rate if you were being

Eye communication

interrogated by the police. Excess blinking is one of the cues people use to detect lying and so it may communicate a kind of nervousness over telling a lie. In actual fact, however, it may be due to dry eyes.

_____ 1. The topic of paragraph 1 is
   a. gazes.
   b. eye contact.
   c. cultures.
   d. time.

_____ 2. The topic sentence of paragraph 1 is expressed in the
   a. first sentence.
   b. second sentence.
   c. fifth sentence.
   d. sixth sentence.

_____ 3. Which of the following is the topic of paragraph 2?
   a. direct eye contact
   b. honesty
   c. correcting misunderstandings
   d. Hispanic cultures

_____ 4. Which of the following sentences in paragraph 2 does *not* add information on what different cultures think about eye contact?
   a. first
   b. second
   c. third
   d. fourth

_____ 5. Which of the following sentences best states the implied main idea of paragraph 2?
   a. Talking to a person from another culture is difficult.
   b. Different cultures have different rules about making direct eye contact.
   c. The Japanese have the most strict rules about eye contact.
   d. Direct eye contact should be avoided except in the United States.

_____ 6. The topic of paragraph 3 is expressed in the
   a. first sentence.
   b. second sentence.
   c. third sentence.
   d. last sentence.

_____ 7. The topic of paragraph 3 is
   a. glancing compared to staring.
   b. nervousness and fear.
   c. self-consciousness.
   d. the direction and quality of eye contact.

_____ 8. The topic of paragraph 4 is
   a. dry eyes.
   b. lubrication.
   c. detecting lying.
   d. blinking.

_____ 9. Which of the following sentences best expresses the implied main idea of paragraph 4?
   a. Nervous people have dry eyes.
   b. The primary purpose of blinking is to protect the eyes.
   c. Blinking a lot proves one is lying.
   d. Blinking increases under stress or discomfort.

_____ 10. The purpose of the last sentence in paragraph 4 is to show that
   a. blinking may not be a sign of lying.
   b. people get nervous when they have dry eyes.
   c. lying is due to dry eyes.
   d. blinking causes dry eyes.

Name _____

Section _____ Date _____

Number right* _____ x 10 points = Score _____

"Don't Ask"

Deborah Tannen

Men and women differ in many ways, including how they communicate. You will probably recognize some of the differences Tannen describes in this excerpt taken from her book *You Just Don't Understand*.

Vocabulary Review

asymmetries (par. 1) lack of harmony and balance

status (par. 1) position or rank; one's standing in relation to others

paradox (par. 4) a situation that may seem to be contradictory, but in fact is or may be true

metamessages (par. 4) meanings that appear beneath the surface; hidden meanings

framed (par. 5) placed within a context

implicit (par. 6) not directly stated

theoretically (par. 6) based on theory, hypothetical

1   Talking about troubles is just one of many conversational tasks that women and men view differently, and that consequently causes trouble in talk between them. Another is asking for information. And this difference too is traceable to the asymmetries of status and connection.

2   A man and a woman were standing beside the information booth at the Washington Folk Life Festival, a sprawling complex of booths and displays. "You ask," the man was saying to the woman. "I don't ask."

3   Sitting in the front seat of the car beside Harold, Sybil is fuming. They have been driving around for half an hour looking for a street he is sure is close by. Sybil is angry not because Harold does not know

A woman asking directions

*To calculate the number right, use items 1–10 under "Mastery Test Skills Check."

the way, but because he insists on trying to find it himself rather than stopping and asking someone. Her anger stems from viewing his behavior through the lens of her own: If she were driving, she would have asked directions as soon as she realized she didn't know which way to go, and they'd now be comfortably ensconced in their friends' living room instead of driving in circles, as the hour gets later and later. Since asking directions does not make Sybil uncomfortable, refusing to ask makes no sense to her. But in Harold's world, driving around until he finds his way is the reasonable thing to do, since asking for help makes him uncomfortable. He's avoiding that discomfort and trying to maintain his sense of himself as a self-sufficient person.

4   Why do many men resist asking for directions and other kinds of information? And, it is just as reasonable to ask, why is it that many women don't? By the paradox of independence and intimacy, there are two simultaneous and different metamessages implied in asking for and giving information. Many men tend to focus on one, many women on the other.

5   When you offer information, the information itself is the message. But the fact that you have the information, and the person you are speaking to doesn't, also sends a metamessage of superiority. If relations are inherently hierarchical, then the one who has more information is framed as higher up on the ladder, by virtue of being more knowledgeable and competent. From this perspective, finding one's own way is an essential part of the independence that men perceive to be a prerequisite for self-respect. If self-respect is bought at the cost of a few extra minutes of travel time, it is well worth the price.

6   Because they are implicit, metamessages are hard to talk about. When Sybil begs to know why Harold won't just ask someone for directions, he answers in terms of the message, the information: He says there's no point in asking, because anyone he asks may not know and may give him wrong directions. This is theoretically reasonable. There are many countries, such as, for example, Mexico, where it is standard procedure for people to make up directions rather than refuse to give requested information. But this explanation frustrates Sybil, because it doesn't make sense to her. Although she realizes that someone might give faulty directions, she believes this is relatively unlikely, and surely it cannot happen every time. Even if it did happen, they would be in no worse shape than they are in now anyway.

7   Part of the reason for their different approaches is that Sybil believes that a person who doesn't know the answer will say so, because it is easy to say, "I don't know." But Harold believes that saying "I don't know" is humiliating, so people might well take a wild guess. Because of their different assumptions, and the invisibility of framing, Harold and Sybil can never get to the bottom of this difference; they can only get more frustrated with each other. Keeping talk on the message level is common, because it is the level we are most clearly aware of. But it is unlikely to resolve confusion since our true motivations lie elsewhere.

8   To the extent that giving information, directions, or help is of use to another, it reinforces bonds between people. But to the extent that it is asymmetrical, it creates hierarchy: Insofar as giving information frames one as the expert, superior in

knowledge, and the other as uninformed, inferior in knowledge, it is a move in the negotiation of status.

9   It is easy to see that there are many situations where those who give information are higher in status. For example, parents explain things to children and answer their questions, just as teachers give information to students. An awareness of this dynamic underlies one requirement for proper behavior at Japanese dinner entertainment, according to anthropologist Harumi Befu. In order to help the highest-status member of the party to dominate the conversation, others at the dinner are expected to ask him questions that they know he can answer with authority.

10   Because of this potential for asymmetry, some men resist receiving information from others, especially women, and some women are cautious about stating information that they know, especially to men. For example, a man with whom I discussed these dynamics later told me that my perspective clarified a comment made by his wife. They had gotten into their car and were about to go to a destination that she knew well but he did not know at all. Consciously resisting an impulse to just drive off and find his own way, he began by asking his wife if she had any advice about the best way to get there. She told him the way, then added, "But I don't know. That's how I would go, but there might be a better way." Her comment was a move to redress the imbalance of power created by her knowing something he didn't know. She was also saving face in advance, in case he decided not to take her advice. Furthermore, she was reframing her directions as "just a suggestion" rather than "giving instructions."

MASTERY TEST SKILLS CHECK

Directions: Choose the best answer for each of the following questions.

Checking Your Comprehension

_____ 1. The main point of the passage is
   a. men and women differ on asking for information because of how they think about relationships.
   b. men and women ask for directions in different ways.
   c. women are willing to ask for help because they are bad at remembering directions.
   d. you should not give information to others because you will embarrass them.

_____ 2. The main idea of paragraph 5 is
   a. men have a fragile sense of self-respect.
   b. answers to questions are more important than the metamessages.
   c. men seem to need to retain their sense of superiority in relationships.
   d. because relations are based on gender, being competent is not important.

_____ 3. The main point of paragraph 6 is that
   a. information is more important than what motivates Harold and Sybil.
   b. Harold and Sybil have unspoken beliefs about what motivates people.
   c. Harold and Sybil know they have different approaches to asking for information.
   d. Harold and Sybil can never understand each other.

_____ 4. According to Harold's reasoning, when asked for directions, most people will
   a. try to embarrass him for having asked for help.
   b. be uncomfortable and avoid his question.
   c. lead him to his destination.
   d. give wrong directions rather than say "I don't know."

_____ 5. According to the passage, the wife said she was not sure her directions were the best because
   a. she has forgotten how to reach their destination.
   b. she was being considerate of how her husband would feel.
   c. she would prefer to ask for directions along the way.
   d. she wanted to confuse her husband with unclear advice.

_____ 6. The author uses the example of Sybil and Harold to
   a. interest both men and women.
   b. avoid appearing sexist.
   c. make her ideas real and understandable.
   d. show similarities between them.

Applying Your Skills

_____ 7. Which of the following sentences best states the implied main idea of paragraph 3?
   a. Sybil is angry.
   b. Harold is driving around in circles.
   c. Sybil does not understand Harold.
   d. Sybil is comfortable asking for directions, but Harold is uncomfortable.

_____ 8. Which sentence in paragraph 9 is the topic sentence?
   a. first sentence
   b. second sentence
   c. third sentence
   d. fourth sentence

_____ 9. Which of the following sentences best states the implied main idea of paragraph 8?
   a. Giving directions and information is helpful, but it also creates hierarchy.
   b. Negotiation of status depends on hierarchy.
   c. Direction-giving reinforces bonds between people.
   d. Giving directions creates a superior and an inferior position.

_____ 10. Which of the following sentences expresses the main idea of paragraph 10?
   a. first sentence
   b. second sentence
   c. fourth sentence
   d. last sentence

Studying Words

_____ 11. The word "status" (paragraph 1) originated from which of the following languages?
   a. German
   b. Latin
   c. English
   d. French

_____ 12. In paragraph 5, the word "hierarchical" means
   a. formal or stylized.
   b. powerless.
   c. arranged in a set order.
   d. not directly stated.

_____ 13. What is the correct pronunciation of
the word "prerequisite" (paragraph 5)?
   a. pre re QUIZ ite
   b. pre re QUIZ it
   c. pre REK wiz ite
   d. pre REK wiz it

_____ 14. The word "anthropologist" (paragraph 9) means
   a. the study of human beings.
   b. one who studies human beings.
   c. referring to human beings.
   d. one who writes about the earth.

_____ 15. The best synonym for the word
"redress" (paragraph 10) is
   a. arrange.
   b. correct.
   c. clothe.
   d. reimburse.

For more practice, ask
your instructor for an
opportunity to work on the mastery
tests that appear in the Test Bank.

Chapter 7

Understanding Paragraphs: Supporting Details and Transitions

Getting Started with . . .

Supporting Details and Transitions

What event do you think the people in the photograph are attending? How did you know? Most likely the details in the photograph—the painted faces, the colors being worn, the gestures, and so forth—reveal they are attending a sporting event. Details are important because they support and explain an idea. The details in this photograph explain how fans dress and act to support their team. In this chapter you will focus on details in paragraphs and discover how they support the main idea.

Suppose you read the following sentence in a communication textbook. It appears as the opening sentence of a paragraph.

Men and women communicate differently in their nonverbal messages.

After reading this sentence you are probably wondering how the nonverbal communication, also known as body language, differs between the sexes.

Only poor writers make statements without supporting them. So you expect, then, that in the remainder of the paragraph the author will support his statement about gender differences in nonverbal communication. Here is the full paragraph.

Men and women communicate differently in their nonverbal messages. You may have observed some or all of these differences in your daily interactions. Women smile more than men. Women stand closer to each other than men do. When they speak, both men and women look at men more than at women. Women both touch and are touched more than men. Men extend their bodies, taking up greater areas of space than women.   —DeVito, *Messages*, p. 150.

In this paragraph, the author explained his statement by giving examples of gender differences. The first sentence expresses the main idea; the remaining sentences are supporting details. You will recall from Chapter 6 that a paragraph has four essential elements.

- **Topic**—the one thing the whole paragraph is about
- **Main idea**—the broad, general idea the whole paragraph is concerned with
- **Supporting details**—the ideas that explain or support the main idea
- **Transitions**—the words or phrases that link ideas together

This chapter will focus on how to recognize supporting details and how to use transitions to guide your reading. You will also learn how to paraphrase paragraphs and longer pieces of writing.

RECOGNIZING SUPPORTING DETAILS

Supporting details are those facts and ideas that prove or explain the main idea of a paragraph. While all the details in a paragraph do support the main idea, not all details are equally important. As you read, try to identify and pay attention to the most important details. Pay less attention to details of lesser importance. The **key details** directly explain the main idea. Other **minor details**

may provide additional information, offer an example, or further explain one of the key details.

The diagram in Figure 7-1 shows how details relate to the main idea and how details range in degree of importance. In the diagram, less important details appear below the important details they explain.

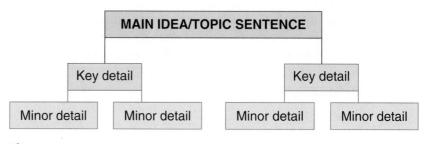

Figure 7-1

Read the following paragraph and study the diagram that follows.

The skin of the human body has several functions. First, it serves as a protective covering. In doing so, it accounts for 17 percent of the body weight. Skin also protects the organs within the body from damage or harm. The skin serves as a regulator of body functions. It controls body temperature and water loss. Finally, the skin serves as a receiver. It is sensitive to touch and temperature.

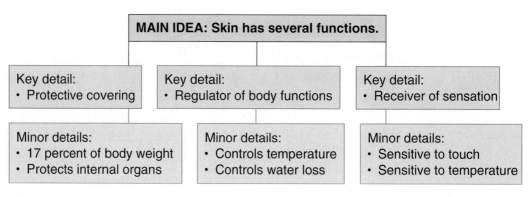

Figure 7-2

From the diagram in Figure 7-2 you can see that the details that state the three functions of skin are the key details. Other details, such as "protects internal organs," provide further information and are at a lower level of importance.

Read the following paragraph and try to pick out the more important details.

Communication occurs with words and gestures* but did you know it also occurs through the sense of smell? Odor can communicate at least four types of messages. First, odor can signal attraction. Animals give off scents to attract members of the opposite sex. Humans use fragrances to make themselves more appealing or attractive. Smell also communicates information about tastes. The smell of popcorn popping stimulates the appetite. If you smell a chicken roasting you can anticipate its taste. A third type of smell communication is through memory. A smell can help you recall an event that occurred months or even years ago, especially if the event was an emotional one. Finally, smell can communicate by creating an identity or image for a person or product. For example, a woman may wear only one brand of perfume. Or a brand of shaving cream may have a distinct fragrance, which allows users to recognize it.

—DeVito, *Messages*, p. 159.

This paragraph could be diagrammed as follows:

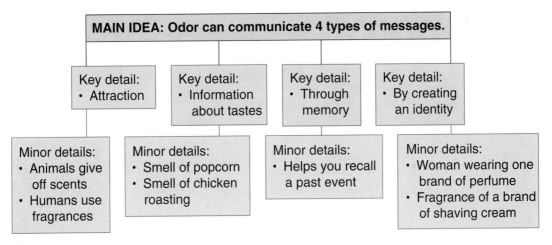

Figure 7-3

EXERCISE 7-1

Directions: Read each of the following paragraphs, and then answer the multiple-choice questions about the diagram that follows.

Paragraph 1
Don't be fooled by words that sound impressive but mean little. Doublespeak is language that fails to communicate; it comes in four basic forms. **Euphemisms** make the negative and unpleasant appear positive and appealing, for example, calling the firing of 200 workers "downsizing" or "reallocation of resources." **Jargon** is the specialized language of a professional class (for example, the computer language of the hacker); it becomes doublespeak when used to communicate with people who aren't members of the group and who don't know this specialized language. **Gobbledygook**

*Boxed words appear in the Mastering Vocabulary exercise on p. 236.

is overly complex language that overwhelms the listener instead of communicating meaning. **Inflated language** makes the mundane seem extraordinary, the common exotic ("take the vacation of a lifetime; explore unsurpassed vistas"). All four forms can be useful in some situations, but, when spoken or listened to mindlessly, they may obscure meaning and distort perceptions.   —DeVito, *Messages*, p. 130.

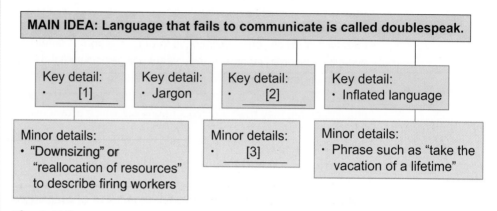

Figure 7-4

_____ 1. The correct word to fill in the blank labeled [1] is
　　　　　a. doublespeak.
　　　　　b. euphemisms.
　　　　　c. negative.
　　　　　d. positive.

_____ 2. The correct word or phrase to fill in the blank labeled [2] is
　　　　　a. complex language.
　　　　　b. specialized language.
　　　　　c. gobbledygook.
　　　　　d. mundane.

_____ 3. The correct phrase to fill in the blank labeled [3] is
　　　　　a. obscure meanings.
　　　　　b. distort perceptions.
　　　　　c. a professional class.
　　　　　d. the computer language of the hacker.

Paragraph 2

The risks associated with the consumption of alcohol are determined in part by how much an individual drinks. An **occasional drinker** is a person who drinks an alcoholic beverage once in a while. The occasional drinker seldom becomes intoxicated, and such drinking presents little or no threat to the health of the individual. A **social drinker** is someone who drinks regularly in social settings but seldom consumes enough alcohol to become intoxicated. Social drinking, like occasional drinking, does not necessarily increase health risks. **Binge drinking** is defined as having five drinks in a row for men or four in a row for women. Binge drinking can cause significant health and social problems. In comparison to nonbinge drinkers, binge drinkers are much more likely to have unprotected sex, to drive after drinking, and to fall behind in school.

—Pruitt and Stein, *Health Styles*, pp. 108, 110.

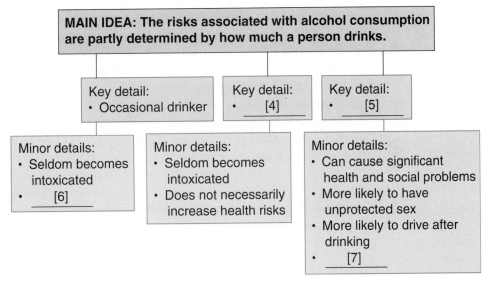

Figure 7-5

_____ 4. The correct phrase to fill in the blank labeled [4] is
   a. binge drinking.
   b. alcohol consumption.
   c. health risks.
   d. social drinker.

_____ 5. The correct phrase to fill in the blank labeled [5] is
   a. social drinker.
   b. binge drinking.
   c. health problems.
   d. social problems.

_____ 6. The correct phrase to fill in the blank labeled [6] is
   a. occasional drinker.
   b. social drinker.
   c. little or no health threat.
   d. drinks regularly in social settings.

_____ 7. The correct phrase to fill in the blank labeled [7] is
    a. more likely to fall behind in school.
    b. more likely to have health problems.
    c. little or no health threat.
    d. four or five drinks in a row.

Paragraph 3

There are four different dimensions of an arrest: legal, behavioral, subjective, and official (Erez, 1974; Walker, 1992). In **legal** terms, an arrest is made when someone lawfully deprives another person of liberty; in other words, that person is not free to go. The actual word *arrest* need not be uttered, but the other person must be brought under the control of the arresting individual. The **behavioral** element in arrests is often nothing more than the phrase "You're under arrest." However, that statement is usually backed up by a tight grip on the arm or collar, or the drawing of an officer's handgun, or the use of handcuffs. The **subjective** dimension of arrest refers to whenever people believe they are not free to leave; to all intents and purposes, they are under arrest. In any case, the arrest lasts only as long as the person is in custody, which might be a matter of a few minutes or many hours. Many people are briefly detained on the street and then released. **Official** arrests are those detentions that the police record in an administrative record. When a suspect is "booked" at the police station, a record is made of the arrest.

—Barlow, *Criminal Justice in America*, p. 238.

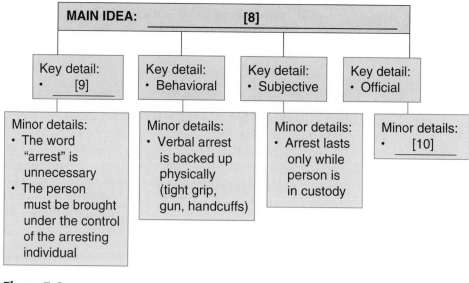

Figure 7-6

_____ 8. The correct sentence to fill in the blank labeled [8] is
   a. When a person is lawfully deprived of freedom, it is not necessary to use the word *arrest*.
   b. The four different dimensions of an arrest are legal, behavioral, subjective, and official.
   c. People can be subjectively under arrest even when they are not officially under arrest.
   d. The only official arrests are those that are recorded at the police station.

_____ 9. The correct word or phrase to fill in the blank labeled [9] is
   a. dimensions.
   b. liberty.
   c. not free to go.
   d. legal.

_____ 10. The correct word or phrase to fill in the blank labeled [10] is
   a. arrest is recorded at police station.
   b. detentions.
   c. briefly detained.
   d. booked.

EXERCISE 7-2

Directions: Each of the following topic sentences states the main idea of a paragraph. After each topic sentence are sentences containing details that may or may not support the topic sentence. Read each sentence and put a *K* beside those that contain **key details** that support the topic sentence.

1. *Topic sentence:* Many dramatic physical changes occur during adolescence between the ages of 13 and 15.

   Details:

   _____ a. Voice changes in boys begin to occur at age 13 or 14.

   _____ b. Facial proportions may change during adolescence.

   _____ c. Adolescents, especially boys, gain several inches in height.

   _____ d. Many teenagers do not know how to react to these changes.

   _____ e. Primary sex characteristics begin to develop for both boys and girls.

2. *Topic sentence:* The development of speech in infants follows a definite sequence or pattern of development.

   Details:

   _____ a. By the time an infant is six months old, he or she can make 12 different speech sounds.

   _____ b. Mindy, who is only three months old, is unable to produce any recognizable syllables.

   _____ c. During the first year, the number of vowel sounds a child can produce is greater than the number of consonant sounds he or she can make.

   _____ d. Between 6 and 12 months, the number of consonant sounds a child can produce continues to increase.

   _____ e. Parents often reward the first recognizable word a child produces by smiling or speaking to the child.

3. *Topic sentence:* The main motives for attending a play are the desire for recreation, the need for relaxation, and the desire for intellectual stimulation.

   Details:

   _____ a. By becoming involved with the actors and their problems, members of the audience temporarily forget about their personal cares and concerns and are able to relax.

   _____ b. In America today, the success of a play is judged by its ability to attract a large audience.

   _____ c. Almost everyone who attends a play expects to be entertained.

   _____ d. Even theater critics are often able to relax and enjoy a good play.

   _____ e. There is a smaller audience that looks to theater for intellectual stimulation.

4. *Topic sentence:* Licorice is used in tobacco products because it has specific characteristics that cannot be found in any other single ingredient.

   Details:

   _____ a. McAdams & Co. is the largest importer and processor of licorice root.

   _____ b. Licorice blends with tobacco and provides added mildness.

   _____ c. Licorice provides a unique flavor and sweetens many types of tobacco.

   _____ d. The extract of licorice is present in relatively small amounts in most types of pipe tobacco.

   _____ e. Licorice helps tobacco retain the correct amount of moisture during storage.

5. *Topic sentence:* An oligopoly is a market structure in which only a few companies sell a certain product.

   Details:

   _____ a. The automobile industry is a good example of an oligopoly, even though it gives the appearance of being highly competitive.

   _____ b. The breakfast cereal, soap, and cigarette industries, although basic to our economy, operate as oligopolies.

   _____ c. Monopolies refer to market structures in which only one industry produces a particular product.

   _____ d. Monopolies are able to exert more control and price fixing than oligopolies.

   _____ e. In the oil industry there are only a few producers, so each producer has a fairly large share of the sales.

EXERCISE 7-3

Directions: Read each of the following paragraphs and write the number of the sentences that contain only the most important key details.

Paragraph 1

Physical dependence is what was formerly called addiction. ²It is characterized by *tolerance* and *withdrawal.*³ *Tolerance* means that more and more of the drug must be taken to achieve the same effect, as use continues. ⁴*Withdrawal* means that if use is discontinued, the person experiences unpleasant symptoms. ⁵When I quit smoking cigarettes, for example, I went through about five days of irritability, depression, and restlessness. ⁶Withdrawal from heroin and other narcotics is much more painful, involving violent cramps, vomiting, diarrhea, and other symptoms that continue for at least two or three days. ⁷With some drugs, especially barbiturates, cold-turkey (sudden and total) quitting can result in death, so severe is the withdrawal.   —Geiwitz, *Psychology,* p. 512.

Key Details: _____

Paragraph 2

The two most common drugs that are legal and do not require a prescription are caffeine and nicotine. ²*Caffeine* is the active ingredient in coffee, tea, and many cola drinks. ³It stimulates the central nervous system and heart and therefore is often used to stay awake. ⁴Heavy use—say, seven to ten cups of coffee per day—has toxic effects, that is, it acts like a mild poison. ⁵Prolonged heavy use appears to be addicting. ⁶*Nicotine* is the active ingredient in tobacco. ⁷One of the most addicting of all drugs and one of the most dangerous, at least when obtained by smoking, it has been implicated in lung cancer, emphysema, and heart disease.

—Geiwitz, *Psychology,* p. 513.

Key Details: _____

Paragraph 3

Hypnosis today is used for a number of purposes, primarily in psychotherapy or to reduce pain, and it is an acceptable technique in both medicine and psychology. [2]In psychotherapy, it is most often used to eliminate bad habits and annoying symptoms. [3]Cigarette smoking can be treated, for example, by the suggestion that the person will feel nauseated whenever he or she thinks of smoking. [4]Sufferers of migraine headaches treated with hypnotic suggestions to relax showed a much greater tendency to improve than sufferers treated with drugs; 44 percent were headache-free after 12 months of treatment, compared to 12 percent of their drug-treated counterparts.

—Geiwitz, *Psychology,* p. 229.

Key Details: _____

Paragraph 4

There are four main types of sunglasses. [2]The traditional *absorptive* glasses soak up all the harmful sun rays. [3]*Polarizing* sunglasses account for half the market. [4]They're the best buy for knocking out glare, and reflections from snow and water, but they may admit more light rays than other sunglasses. [5]*Coated* sunglasses usually have a metallic covering that itself reflects light. [6]They are often quite absorptive, but a cheap pair of coated glasses may have an uneven or nondurable coating that could rub off after a short period of time. [7]New on the market are the somewhat more expensive *photochromatic* sunglasses. [8]Their chemical composition causes them to change color according to the brightness of the light: in the sun, they darken; in the shade, they lighten. [9]This type of sunglasses responds to ultraviolet light only, and will not screen out infrared rays, so they're not the best bet for continual exposure to bright sun.

—George, *The New Consumer Survival Kit,* p. 114.

Key Details: _____

Paragraph 5

How is a President chosen? [2]First, a candidate campaigns within his party for nomination at a national convention. [3]After the convention comes a period of competition with the nominee of the other major party and perhaps the nominees of minor parties. [4]The showdown arrives on Election Day; the candidate must win more votes than any other nominee in enough states and the District of Columbia to give him a majority of the electoral votes. [5]If he does all these things, he has won the right to the office of President of the United States.

—"ABCs of How a President is Chosen," *US News & World Report.*

Key Details: _____

TYPES OF SUPPORTING DETAILS

There are many types of details that a writer can use to explain or support a main idea. As you read, be sure you know *how* or what types of detail a writer uses to support his or her main idea. As you will see in later chapters, the way a writer explains and supports an idea may influence how readily you accept or agree with it. The most common types of supporting details are (1) examples, (2) facts or statistics, (3) reasons, (4) descriptions, and (5) steps or procedures. Each will be briefly discussed here.

Examples

One way a writer may support an idea is by using examples. Examples make ideas and concepts real and understandable. In the following paragraph, an example is used to explain instantaneous speed.

> The speed that a body has at any one instant is called instantaneous speed. It is the speed registered by the speedometer of a car. When we say that the speed of a car at some particular instant is 60 kilometers per hour, we are specifying its instantaneous speed, and we mean that if the car continued moving as fast for an hour, it would travel 60 kilometers. So the instantaneous speed, or speed at a particular instant, is often quite different from average speed.
>
> —Hewitt, *Conceptual Physics,* p. 15.

In this paragraph the author uses the speed of a car to explain instantaneous speed. As you read illustrations and examples, try to see the relationship between the example and the concept or idea it illustrates.

Facts and Statistics

Another way a writer supports an idea is by including facts and/or statistics. The facts and statistics may provide evidence that the main idea is correct. Or the facts may further explain the main idea. For example, to prove that the divorce rate is high, the author may give statistics about the divorce rate and percentage of the population that is divorced. Notice how, in the following paragraph, the main idea stated in the first sentence is explained using statistics.

The term **graying of America** refers to the increasing percentage of older people in the U.S. population. In 1900 only 4 percent of Americans were age 65 and older. Today almost 13 percent are. The average 65-year-old can expect to live another eighteen years. U.S. society has become so "gray" that the median age has doubled since 1850, and today there are seven million *more* elderly Americans than teenagers. Despite this change, on a global scale Americans rank fifteenth in life expectancy.

—Henslin, *Sociology*, p. 383.

In this paragraph, the main idea that the number of older Americans is increasing is supported using statistics.

Reasons

A writer may support an idea by giving reasons *why* a main idea is correct. A writer might explain *why* nuclear power is dangerous or give reasons *why* a new speed limit law should be passed by Congress. In the following paragraph, the author explains why warm air rises.

We all know that warm air rises. From our study of buoyancy we can understand why this is so. Warm air expands and becomes less dense than the surrounding air and is buoyed upward like a balloon. The buoyancy is in an upward direction because the air pressure below a region of warmed air is greater than the air pressure above. And the warmed air rises because the buoyant force is greater than its weight.

—Hewitt, *Conceptual Physics*, pp. 234–235.

Descriptions

When the topic of a paragraph is a person, object, place, or process, the writer may develop the paragraph by describing the object. Descriptions are details that help you create a mental picture of the object. In the following paragraph, the author describes a sacred book of the Islamic religion by telling what it contains.

The Koran is the sacred book of the Islamic religion. It was written during the lifetime of Mohammed (570–632) during the years in which he recorded divine revelations. The Koran includes rules for family relationships, including marriage and divorce. Rules for inheritance of wealth and property are specified. The status of women as subordinate to men is well defined.

Steps or Procedures

When a paragraph explains how to do something, the paragraph details are often lists of steps or procedures to be followed. For example, if the main idea of a paragraph is how to prepare an outline for a speech, then the details would list or explain the steps in preparing an outline. In the following paragraph the author explains how fog is produced.

> Warm breezes blow over the ocean. When the moist air moves from warmer to cooler waters or from warm water to cool land, it chills. As it chills, water vapor molecules begin coalescing rather than bouncing off one another upon glancing collisions. Condensation takes place, and we have fog.
>
> —Hewitt, *Conceptual Physics,* p. 259.

EXERCISE 7-4

Directions: Each topic sentence is followed by a list of possible details that could be used to support it. Label each detail as example, fact or statistic, reason, description, or step or procedure.

1. *Topic sentence:* People make inferences about you by the way you dress.

    _____ First, they size you up from head to toe.

    _____ College students assume casually dressed instructors are friendly and flexible.

    _____ Robert Molloy wrote a book called *Dress for Success* in which he discusses appropriate business attire.

2. *Topic sentence:* Many retailers with traditional stores have decided to market their products through Web sites as well.

    _____ The Gap promotes its Web site in its stores by displaying the slogan *surf.shop.ship* on cash registers and store windows.

    _____ Retailers are pushing e-commerce because the Internet can boost sales by luring nontraditional shoppers who don't usually visit their stores.

    _____ Between March 2003 and March 2004, the Gap reported a 13 percent increase in sales, some of which is attributable to increased Internet exposure.

    —Brown, "Gap Sales Up 13 Percent in February," *San Francisco Business Times*

3. *Topic sentence:* Every April 15th, millions of Americans make their way to the post office to mail their income tax forms.

    _____ Corporate taxes account for about 10 cents of every federal revenue dollar, compared with 47 cents from individual income taxes.

_____ This year, the Burnette family filed a return that entitles them to a substantial refund on their state income taxes.

_____ In order to submit an income tax return, you must first obtain the proper forms.

—Edwards III et al., *Government in America*, pp. 458–59.

4. *Topic sentence:* Schizophrenia is one of the most difficult psychological disorders to understand.

_____ Diagnosis is difficult due to the lack of physical tests for schizophrenia; researchers do not know if schizophrenia results from a single process or several processes.

_____ Although the rate of schizophrenia is approximately equal in men and women, it strikes men earlier and with greater severity.

_____ After spending time in mental hospitals and homeless shelters, Greg was finally diagnosed with schizophrenia; he has responded well to medication and now lives in a group home.

_____ Schizophrenia involves a range of symptoms, including disturbances in perception, language, thinking, and emotional expression.

—Davis and Palladino, *Psychology,* pp. 563, 564, 566.

5. *Topic sentence:* Many Americans are obsessed with losing weight.

_____ Weight loss obsession is often triggered by major events looming in the near future, such as a high school reunion or a "milestone" birthday.

_____ The two ways to lose weight are to lower caloric intake (through improved eating habits) and to increase exercise (expending more calories).

_____ Studies show that on any given day in America, nearly 40 percent of women and 24 percent of men over the age of 20 are trying to lose weight.

_____ Orlando, a college freshman from Raleigh, admits that he has been struggling with a weight problem since he reached puberty.

—Donatelle and Davis, *Access to Health*, pp. 358, 371.

6. *Topic sentence:* In the 1920s, many young American writers and artists left their country behind and became expatriates.

_____ One of the most talented of the expatriates was Ernest Hemingway.

_____ The expatriates flocked to Rome, Berlin, and Paris, in order to live cheaply and escape what seemed to them the "conspiracy against the individual" in America.

_____ Some earned a living as journalists, translators, and editors, or made a few dollars by selling a poem to an American magazine or a painting to a tourist.

—Garraty and Carnes, *The American Nation,* p. 706.

7. *Topic sentence:* Historical and cultural attractions can be found in a variety of shapes, sizes, and locations throughout the world.

_____ In Europe, for every museum that existed in 1950, there are now more than four.

_____ Living History Farms, located near Des Moines, Iowa, is an attraction that offers a "hands-on" experience for visitors.

_____ More and more communities and countries are taking action to preserve historical sites because they attract visitors and generate income for local residents.

—Cook et al., *Tourism,* pp. 150, 151.

8. *Topic sentence:* Knitting has become a popular hobby for many young career women.

_____ Typically, aspiring knitters begin by visiting a yarn shop and then enrolling in a knitting class.

_____ Knitting is popular because it provides a relaxing outlet and an opportunity to create something beautiful as well as useful.

_____ Far from the image of the grandmotherly knitter, today's devoted knitters include a wide range of women, from Wall Street stockbrokers to movie stars like Julia Roberts.

9. *Topic sentence:* Using a search engine is an effective, though not perfect, method of searching the Internet.

_____ Each time you begin a Web search, start with a simple query to see how many responses, or hits, you get.

_____ In May 1997, the largest search engines reportedly indexed no more than 140 million documents, or less than 75 percent of those on the Web.

_____ Used correctly, a search engine is efficient because it minimizes the time it takes to locate the information you're looking for.

—Lehnert, *Light on the Internet,* pp. 112, 131.

10. *Topic sentence:* The Anasazi Indians are best known for their artistic, architectural, and technological achievements.

_____ The Anasazi used all of the available materials to build their settlements; with wood, mud, and stone, they erected cliff dwellings and the equivalent of terraced apartment houses.

_____ The Anasazi built one structure with 500 living units; it was the largest residential building in North America until the completion of an apartment house in New York in 1772.

_____ One example of their technological genius was their use of irrigation: they constructed sand dunes at the base of hills to hold the runoff from the sometimes torrential rains.

_____ The Anasazi produced pottery that could rank in beauty with any in the world.

—Brummet et al., *Civilization,* p. 348.

EXERCISE 7-5

Directions: For each paragraph listed in Exercise 7-3 on pp. 221–223, identify the type or types of details used to support the main idea. Write your answers below.

1. Type(s) of details: _____

2. Type(s) of details: _____

3. Type(s) of details: _____

4. Type(s) of details: _____

5. Type(s) of details: _____

TRANSITIONS

Transitions are linking words or phrases used to lead the reader from one idea to another. If you get in the habit of recognizing transitions, you will see that they often guide you through a paragraph, helping you to read it more easily.

In the following paragraph, notice how the underlined transitions lead you from one important detail to the next.

> The principle of rhythm and line also contributes to the overall unity of the landscape design. This principle is responsible for the sense of continuity between different areas of the landscape. <u>One</u> way in which this continuity can be developed is by extending planting beds from one area to another. <u>For example</u>, shrub beds developed around the entrance to the house can be continued around the sides and into the backyard. Such an arrangement helps to tie the front and rear areas of the property together. <u>Another</u> means by which rhythm is given to a design is to repeat shapes, angles, or lines between various areas and elements of the design.
>
> —Reiley and Shry, *Introductory Horticulture,* p. 114.

Not all paragraphs contain such obvious transitions, and not all transitions serve as such clear markers of major details. Transitions may be used to alert you to what will come next in the paragraph. If you see the phrase *for instance* at the beginning of a sentence, then you know that an example will follow. When you see the phrase *on the other hand,* you can predict that a different, opposing idea will follow. Table 7-1 below lists some of the most common transitions used within a paragraph and indicates what they tell you.

TABLE 7-1   Common Transitions

Type of Transition	Example	What They Tell the Reader
Time/Sequence	first, later, next, finally	The author is arranging ideas in the order in which they happened.
Example	for example, for instance, to illustrate, such as	An example will follow.
Enumeration	first, second, third, last, one, another, next	The author is marking or identifying each major point (sometimes these may be used to suggest order of importance).
Continuation	also, in addition, and, further, another	The author is continuing with the same idea and is going to provide additional information.
Contrast	on the other hand, in contrast, however	The author is switching to a different, opposite, or contrasting idea from that previously discussed.
Comparison	like, likewise, similarly	The writer will show how the previous idea is similar to what follows.
Cause/Effect	because, thus, therefore, since, consequently	The writer will show a connection between two or more things, how one thing caused another, or how something happened as a result of something else.
Summation	to sum up, in conclusion	The writer will draw his or her ideas together.

Directions: Match each transition in Column A with a transition of similar meaning in Column B. Write the letter of your choice in the space provided.

Column A   **Column B**

_____ 1. Because   a. Therefore

_____ 2. In contrast   b. Also

_____ 3. For instance   c. Likewise

_____ 4. Thus   d. After that

_____ 5. First   e. Since

_____ 6. One way   f. In conclusion

_____ 7. Similarly   g. On the other hand

_____ 8. Next   h. One approach

_____ 9. In addition   i. In the beginning

_____ 10. To sum up   j. For example

Directions: Use the list below to identify the type of transition that appears in the following sentences. Note that b (Example) and e (Contrast) are each used twice.

a. Time/sequence   e. Contrast (2)

b. Example (2)   f. Comparison

c. Enumeration   g. Cause/effect

d. Continuation   h. Summation

_____ 1. The first step in the listening process involves receiving, or hearing, the message.

_____ 2. Some people consider computer games a purely passive activity. However, many games actually involve strategy, mathematical skills, and memorization.

_____ 3. On election day, several television stations reported a clear winner in the presidential race. Later, those stations were forced to retract their statements and wait—along with the rest of the nation—for a final tally.

_____ 4. In conclusion, proper soil preparation is essential to a successful garden.

_____ 5. There are many kinds of service dogs. For instance, there are dogs that are trained specifically to assist blind or deaf people as well as therapy dogs that are part of physical rehabilitation programs.

_____ 6. Always apply sunscreen before going out in the sun. In addition, a hat and protective clothing are recommended at high altitudes and near water.

_____ 7. In contrast to carnivores, _herbivores_ eat only plants.

_____ 8. Vegetarians typically do not have to worry about elevated cholesterol because cholesterol is found only in animal products.

_____ 9. Like Samuel Clemens, who became famous writing under the pen name Mark Twain, Mary Ann Evans found fame as the writer George Eliot.

_____ 10. In some communities, judges sentence offenders to community service programs instead of jail time. For example, in one Chicago program, offenders trade a "day for a day"—every day they would have spent in jail equals a day spent doing community service work.

EXERCISE 7-8

Directions: Read each of the following sentences. In each blank, choose a transitional word or phrase from the list below that makes sense in the sentence.

| next | however | for example | another | consequently |
| because | similarly | such as | to sum up | in addition |

1. After a heart attack, the heart muscle is permanently weakened;

_____ its ability to pump blood throughout the body may

be reduced.

2. Some metals, _____ gold and silver, are represented by

symbols derived from their Latin names.

3. In order to sight-read music, you should begin by scanning it.

_____, you should identify the key and tempo.

4. The *Oxford English Dictionary,* by giving all present and past definitions of words, shows how word definitions have changed with time. _____, it gives the date and written source where each word appears to have first been used.

5. Some scientists believe intelligence to be determined equally by heredity and environment. _____, other scientists believe heredity to account for about 60 percent of intelligence and environment for the other 40 percent.

6. Tigers tend to grow listless and unhappy in captivity. _____, pandas grow listless and have a difficult time reproducing in captivity.

7. _____, the most important ways to prevent heat stress are to (1) allow yourself time to get used to the heat, (2) wear the proper clothing, and (3) drink plenty of water.

8. Many people who are dissatisfied with the public school system send their children to private schools. _____ option that is gaining in popularity is homeschooling.

9. Studies have shown that it is important to "exercise" our brains as we age. _____, crossword puzzles are a good way to keep mentally fit.

10. Buying smaller-sized clothing generally will not give an overweight person the incentive to lose weight. People with weight problems tend to eat when they are upset or disturbed, and _____ wearing smaller clothing is frustrating and upsetting, overweight people will generally gain weight by doing so.

EXERCISE 7-9   **Directions:** Each of the following beginnings of paragraphs uses a transitional word or phrase to tell the reader what will follow in the paragraph. Read each, paying particular attention to the underlined word or phrase. Then, in the space provided, describe as specifically as you can what you would expect to find next in the paragraph.

1. Price is not the only factor to consider in choosing a pharmacy. Many provide valuable services that should be considered. <u>For instance</u>, . . .

_____

_____

2. There are a number of things you can do to prevent a home burglary. <u>First</u>, . . .

_____

_____

3. Most mail order businesses are reliable and honest. <u>However</u>, . . .

_____

_____

4. One advantage of a compact stereo system is that all the components are built into the unit. <u>Another</u> . . .

_____

_____

5. Taking medication can have an effect on your hormonal balance. <u>Consequently</u>, . . .

_____

_____

6. To select the presidential candidate you will vote for, you should examine his or her philosophy of government. <u>Next</u> . . .

_____

_____

7. Eating solely vegetables drastically reduces caloric and fat intake, two things on which most people overindulge. <u>On the other hand</u>, . . .

_____

_____

8. Asbestos, a common material found in many older buildings in which people have worked for decades, has been shown to cause cancer. <u>Consequently</u>, . . .

_____

_____

9. Cars and trucks are not designed randomly. They are designed individually for specific purposes. <u>For instance</u>, . . .

_____

_____

10. Jupiter is a planet surrounded by several moons. <u>Likewise</u>, . . .

_____

_____

EXERCISE 7-10   **Directions:** Turn back to Exercise 7-3 on pp. 221–223. Reread each paragraph and underline any transitions that you find.

PARAPHRASING PARAGRAPHS

Paraphrasing paragraphs is a useful technique for both building and checking your comprehension. By taking a paragraph apart sentence-by-sentence, you are forced to understand the meaning of each sentence and see how ideas relate to one another. Paraphrasing paragraphs is similar to paraphrasing sentences. It involves the same two steps:

1. Substituting synonyms
2. Rearranging sentence parts

Here are some guidelines for paraphrasing paragraphs.

1. Concentrate on maintaining the author's focus and emphasis. Ideas that seem most important in the paragraph should appear as most important in your paraphrase.
2. Work sentence-by-sentence, paraphrasing the ideas in the order in which they appear in the paragraph.

Here are two sample paraphrases of a paragraph. One is a good paraphrase; the other is poor and unacceptable.

Paragraph

For the most part, the American media share one overriding goal: to make a profit. But they are also the main instruments for manipulating public opinion. Politicians want to win our hearts and minds, and businesses want to win our dollars. Both use the media to try to gain mass support by manipulating public opinion. In other words, they generate **propaganda**—communication tailored to influence opinion. Propaganda may be true or false. What sets it apart from other communications is the intent to change opinion.   —Thio, *Sociology,* p. 374.

Good Paraphrase

American media (newspapers, TV, and radio) have one common purpose, which is to make money. Media are also vehicles for controlling how the public thinks. Politicians want us to like them; businesses want our money. Both use media to get support by controlling how people think. Both use propaganda. Propaganda is words and ideas that are used to affect how people think. Propaganda can be either true or false. It is different from other forms of communication because its purpose is to change how we think.

Poor and Unacceptable Paraphrase

In general, the media only wants to control people. But the media also manipulates public opinion. Both politicians and businesses want our money and they use the media to try to get it. To do that, they generate propaganda, which is communication tailored to influence opinion. What sets propaganda apart from other communications is whether it is true or false, and how well it changes people's opinions.

The above paraphrase is unacceptable because it is inaccurate and incomplete.

EXERCISE 7-11

Directions: Write a paraphrase of Paragraphs 1, 2, and 3 in Exercise 7-3 on pp. 221–223.

_____

_____

_____

_____

MASTERING VOCABULARY

Directions: Select the choice that best provides the meaning of each word as it is used in this chapter. Use context clues, word parts, and a dictionary, if necessary.

_____ 1. gestures (p. 215)
    a. comments
    b. movements
    c. emotions
    d. gifts

_____ 2. distinct (p. 215)
    a. similar
    b. mysterious
    c. unique
    d. powerful

_____ 3. mundane (p. 216)
    a. important
    b. proper
    c. ridiculous
    d. ordinary

_____ 4. depression (p. 221)
    a. gloominess
    b. concern
    c. weakness
    d. disagreement

_____ 5. toxic (p. 221)
    a. clean
    b. alcoholic
    c. distasteful
    d. poisonous

_____ 6. prolonged (p. 221)
    a. long-term
    b. brief
    c. temporary
    d. permanent

_____ 7. psychotherapy (p. 222)
    a. physical treatment
    b. physical disability
    c. mental treatment
    d. mental disability

_____ 8. nondurable (p. 222)
    a. inexpensive
    b. unsturdy
    c. flexible
    d. not returnable

_____ 9. subordinate (p. 224)
    a. greater
    b. powerful
    c. inferior
    d. equal

_____ 10. continuity (p. 229)
    a. separation
    b. connection
    c. difference
    d. change

SELF-TEST SUMMARY

Name and describe the four essential parts of a paragraph.	The four parts of a paragraph are: 1. **Topic.** The topic is the one thing the entire paragraph is about. 2. **Main idea.** The main idea is the most important idea the writer wants the reader to know about the topic. 3. **Details.** Details are facts and ideas that support the main idea. 4. **Transitions.** Transitions are words and phrases that lead the reader from one idea to another.
What is the difference between key details and minor details?	Key details directly explain the main idea; minor details provide additional information or further explain a key detail.
What are the five types of details used to support the main idea?	The types of details are examples, facts or statistics, reasons, descriptions, and steps or procedures.
What are transitions, and what information do they give the reader?	Transitions are linking words and phrases that lead the reader from one idea to another. They suggest time/sequence, exemplification, enumeration, continuation, contrast, comparison, cause/effect, and summation.
What two steps are involved in paraphrasing paragraphs?	Paraphrasing paragraphs involves: 1. substituting synonyms 2. rearranging sentence parts

Getting More Practice with . . .
Supporting Details and Transitions

WORKING TOGETHER

Directions: Separate into groups. Using a reading selection from Part Six of this book, work with your group to identify and underline the topic sentence of each paragraph. Try to identify key supporting details and/or type of supporting details. When all the groups have completed the task, the class should compare the findings of the various groups.

GOING ONLINE

Internet Activities

1. Building Paragraphs

   http://www.washburn.edu/services/zzcwwctr/paragraphs.txt

   Go through this site that reviews paragraph formation. Complete the exercises that are presented throughout the page.

2. Details in Paragraphs

   http://lrs.ed.uiuc.edu/students/fwalters/para.html#details

   Read about the importance of details in paragraphs at this site. After you have read and understood the information, follow the link to complete the exercise.

Companion Website

For additional readings, exercises, and Internet activities, visit this book's Companion Website at:

http://www.ablongman.com/mcwhorter

If you need a user name and password, please see your instructor.

My Reading Lab

For more practice on supporting details, visit MyReadingLab, click on the Reading Skills tab, and then click on Active Reading Strategies—The St. Louis Arch, Missouri.

http://www.ablongman.com/myreadinglab

TEST-TAKING TIPS

Answering Questions About Supporting Details

Reading comprehension tests often include questions about supporting details in the paragraph or passage. Test writers do not usually use the term "supporting details." Instead, they just ask questions that test your ability to understand the supporting details in a paragraph or passage. Use the following suggestions to answer questions about supporting details.

- Do not try to memorize factual information as you read the passage the first time. You are usually allowed to look back at the passage in order to answer questions based on it.

- As you read, pay attention to how the writer supports the main idea. You may discover the writer is giving a definition, or is making a comparison, or is offering an example.

- Do not trust your memory. If a question asks you for a fact, look back at the passage and find the answer. For example, if a question asks you to identify the date on which something happened or to identify the name of a person who performed an action, look back at the passage to find the date or name.

- It may be necessary to consider several details together in order to answer a question. For example, a passage may give the date of one event and state that a second event occurred ten years later (BuildingBlocks, Inc., was founded in 1991. . . . Ten years later the company began its first national advertising campaign.). The question may ask you to identify when the second event occurred (In what year did BuildingBlocks, Inc., begin its national advertising campaign?).

Name _____

Section _____ Date _____

Number right _____ x 20 points = Score _____

Directions: For each of the following sentences, choose the correct transition to fill in the blank.

_____ 1. College freshmen typically take a variety of courses their first semester. _____, freshman courses might include introductory biology, world history, sociology, English, and speech.
   a. In contrast
   b. For example
   c. Such as
   d. Similarly

_____ 2. Year-round schools offer the advantage of relatively uninterrupted learning throughout the year. _____, many teachers look forward to the traditional summer vacation as a time for traveling and studying.
   a. In addition
   b. Therefore
   c. On the other hand
   d. Second

_____ 3. It can be devastating to lose several hours of computer work because of a system failure. _____, be sure to save your documents frequently on a disk as well as on the hard drive.
   a. Another
   b. Next
   c. To illustrate
   d. Therefore

_____ 4. There are several points to consider when planting a tree in your yard. _____, select a site.
   a. First
   b. Further
   c. However
   d. Consequently

_____ 5. Most of the actors in community playhouses are employed in 9-to-5 jobs during the day. _____, the children who act in community playhouse productions are typically full-time students.
   a. For instance
   b. Likewise
   c. In conclusion
   d. Thus

Name _____

Section _____ Date _____

Number right _____ x 20 points = Score _____

Chapter 7
Mastery Test 2
Paragraph Skills

Directions: Read each of the following paragraphs; then choose the answer that correctly identifies the type of details used in the paragraph.

_____ 1. Many people do not know what to look for when considering the type of skin cancer called melanoma. A simple *ABCD* rule outlines the warning signals of melanoma: *A* is for asymmetry. One half of the mole does not match the other half. *B* is for border irregularity. The edges are ragged, notched, or blurred. *C* is for color. The pigmentation is not uniform. *D* is for diameter greater than 6 millimeters. Any or all of these symptoms should cause you to visit a physician.

—Donatelle and Davis,
Access to Health, pp. 446–47.

a. statistics
b. reasons
c. descriptions
d. procedures

_____ 2. In the second week of May 1940, the German armies overran neutral Holland, Belgium, and Luxembourg. The next week they went into northern France and to the English Channel. Designated as an open city by the French in order to spare its destruction, Paris fell on June 14. As the German advance continued, the members of the French government who wanted to continue resistance were voted down. Marshall Philippe Pétain, a 74-year-old World War I hero, became premier. He immediately asked Hitler for an armistice. On June 22, 1940, in the same dining car in which the French had imposed armistice terms on the Germans in 1917, the Nazis and French signed another peace agreement. The Germans had gained revenge for their shame in 1917.

—Brummet et al., *Civilization*,
p. 919.

a. facts
b. reasons
c. descriptions
d. examples

_____ 3. Ethnic minority group members in the United States have a much higher dropout rate for psychotherapy than do white clients. Among the reasons ethnic clients terminate treatment so early are a lack of bilingual therapists and therapists' stereotypes about ethnic clients. The single most important reason may be that therapists do not provide culturally responsive forms of therapy. They may be unaware of values and customs within a culture that would help in understanding and treating certain behaviors. Therapy should be undertaken with an understanding of cultural values.

—Davis and Palladino,
Psychology, p. 609.

a. steps
b. procedures
c. facts
d. reasons

_____ 4. Festivals celebrate a variety of special occasions and holidays. Some are derived from religious observances, such as New Orleans' or Rio de Janeiro's huge Mardi Gras festivals. Other festivals focus on activities as peaceful as ballooning (the Albuquerque Balloon Festival) or as terrifying as the running of the bulls in Pamplona, Spain. Often, festivals center on the cultural heritage of an area, such as the clan festivals that are prominent in the North Atlantic province of Nova Scotia. More recently, food has become the center of attention at locations such as the National Cherry Festival in Traverse City, Michigan, or the Garlic Festival in Gilroy, California.

—Cook et al., *Tourism*, p. 156.

a. statistics
b. examples
c. facts
d. procedures

_____ 5. The **dissolution** stage, in both friendship and romance, is the cutting of the bonds tying you together. At first it usually takes the form of *interpersonal separation*, in which you may not see each other anymore. If you live together, you move into separate apartments and begin to lead lives apart from each other. If this relationship is a marriage, you may seek a legal separation. If this separation period proves workable and if the original relationship is not repaired, you may enter the phase of *social* or *public separation*. If this is a marriage, this phase corresponds to divorce. Avoidance of each other and a return to being "single" are among the primary identifiable features of dissolution. In some cases, however, the former partners change the definition of their relationship; for example, ex-lovers become friends, or ex-friends become "just" business partners. This final, "goodbye," phase of dissolution is the point at which you become an ex-lover or ex-friend. In some cases this is a stage of relief and relaxation; finally it's over. In other cases this is a stage of anxiety and frustration, of guilt and regret, of resentment over time ill spent and now lost. In more materialistic terms, the goodbye phase is the stage when property is divided and when legal battles may ensue over who should get what.

—Devito, *Messages*, p. 284.

a. examples
b. reasons
c. descriptions
d. steps

Name _____

Section _____ Date _____

Number right _____ x 10 points = Score _____

Directions: Read the passage below and choose the best answer for each of the questions that follow.

1   A **punishment** is an unpleasant experience that occurs as a result of an undesirable behavior. Punishment is most effective if it has these three characteristics. First, punishment should be swift, occurring immediately after the undesired behavior. The old threat "Wait till you get home!" undermines the effectiveness of the punishment. Second, punishment must be consistent. The undesired behavior must be punished each and every time it occurs. Finally, the punishment should be sufficiently unpleasant without being overly unpleasant. For instance, if a child doesn't mind being alone in her room, then being sent there for pushing her brother won't be a very effective punishment.

2   Although punishment may decrease the frequency of a behavior, it doesn't eliminate the ability to perform that behavior. For example, your little sister may learn not to push you because your mother will punish her, but she may continue to push her classmates at school because the behavior has not been punished in that context. She may also figure out that if she hits you, but then apologizes, she will not get punished.

3   Furthermore, physical punishment, such as spanking, should be avoided. It may actually increase aggressive behavior in the person on the receiving end. In addition, the one being punished may come to live in fear of the one doing the punishing, even if the punishment is infrequent.

4   Overall, punishment alone hasn't been found to be an effective way of controlling behavior. This is because punishment doesn't convey information about what behavior should be exhibited in place of the undesired, punished behavior. That is, the person being punished knows what they should not do, but the person does not know what he or she should do.

—Kosslyn and Rosenberg, *Psychology*, pp. 180–81.

_____ 1. The primary purpose of the selection is to
   a. describe the concept of punishment.
   b. discourage the use of physical punishment.
   c. identify behaviors that require punishment.
   d. discuss alternative methods of discipline.

_____ 2. The main type of transition used in paragraph 1 is
   a. time/sequence.
   b. enumeration.
   c. continuation.
   d. summation.

_____ 3. The transition word or phrase in paragraph 1 that indicates an example will follow is
   a. first.
   b. second.
   c. finally.
   d. for instance.

_____ 4. The main idea of paragraph 1 is that
   a. punishment must be consistent.
   b. punishment must be unpleasant.
   c. punishment has three qualities.
   d. punishment is targeted toward undesired behavior.

_____ 5. The main idea of paragraph 2 is supported by
   a. examples.
   b. facts.
   c. reasons.
   d. description.

_____ 6. The main idea of paragraph 2 is that
   a. punishment decreases the frequency of a behavior.
   b. a behavior that is punished at home may not be punished elsewhere.
   c. punishment does not eliminate a person's ability to engage in a behavior.
   d. a child may learn to avoid punishment by apologizing for a behavior.

_____ 7. The transition words in paragraph 3 that indicate a continuation of the same idea are
   a. may actually.
   b. such as.
   c. even if.
   d. in addition.

_____ 8. A key detail in paragraph 3 that directly supports the main idea is
   a. spanking harms children.
   b. physical punishment may increase aggression in the person giving the punishment.
   c. physical punishment may increase aggression in the person receiving the punishment.
   d. physical punishment may become addictive.

_____ 9. The word or phrase that indicates a cause/effect transition in paragraph 4 is
   a. because.
   b. alone.
   c. in combination with.
   d. in place of.

_____ 10. The best paraphrase of paragraph 4 is
   a. Punishment alone is not an effective means of controlling behavior. Punishment does not convey information about what behavior should take the place of the undesired, punished behavior.
   b. Combining punishment and reinforcement is more effective than using punishment by itself. Punishment quickly lets people know what behaviors are not desirable.
   c. Punishment should never be used because it does not demonstrate desirable behavior.
   d. Punishment does not give information about what behavior should replace the undesired, punished behavior.

Name _____

Section _____ Date _____

Number right* _____ x 10 points = Score _____

The Beautiful Laughing Sisters—An Arrival Story

Mary Pipher

This reading is taken from Mary Pipher's book *The Middle of Everywhere*, which examines the plight of refugees who have fled to America from countries where they had been mistreated and abused. This selection tells the story of a courageous Kurdish family.

1   One of the best ways to understand the refugee experience is to befriend a family of new arrivals and observe their experiences in our country for the first year. That first year is the hardest. Everything is new and strange, and obstacles appear like the stars appear at dusk, in an uncountable array. This story is about a family I met during their first month in our country. I became their friend and **cultural broker** and in the process learned a great deal about the refugee experience, and about us Americans.

2   On a fall day I met Shireen and Meena, who had come to this country from Pakistan. The Kurdish sisters were slender young women with alert expressions. They wore blue jeans and clunky high-heeled shoes. Shireen was taller and bolder, Meena was smaller and more soft-spoken. Their English was limited and heavily accented. (I later learned it was their sixth language after Kurdish, Arabic, Farsi, Urdu, and Hindi.)† They communicated with each other via small quick gestures and eye movements. Although they laughed easily, they watched to see that the other was okay at all times.

3   Shireen was the youngest and the only one of the six sisters who was eligible for high school. Meena, who was twenty-one, had walked the ten blocks from their apartment to meet Shireen at school on a bitterly cold day. Shireen told the family story. Meena occasionally interrupted her answers with a reminder, an amendment, or laughter.

4   Shireen was born in Baghdad in 1979, the last of ten children. Their mother, Zeenat, had been a village girl who entered an arranged marriage at fourteen. Although their father had been well educated, Zeenat couldn't read or write in any language. The family was prosperous and "Europeanized," as Shireen put it. She said, "Before our father was in trouble, we lived just like you. Baghdad was a big city. In our group of friends, men and women were treated as equals. Our older sisters went to movies and read foreign newspapers. Our father went to cocktail parties at the embassies."

5   However, their father had opposed Saddam Hussein, and from the time of Shireen's birth, his life was in danger. After Hussein came to power, terrible things happened to families like theirs. One family of eleven was taken to jail by his security

---

cultural broker Someone who helps people from other countries learn the customs of the new country.

†These languages, in addition to many others, are spoken in the Middle Eastern countries of Iran, Iraq, India, and Pakistan.

*To calculate the number right, use items 1–10 under "Mastery Test Skills Check."

forces and tortured to death. Prisoners were often fed rice mixed with glass so that they would quietly bleed to death in their cells. Girls were raped and impregnated by the security police. Afterward, they were murdered or killed themselves.

6   It was a hideous time. Schoolteachers tried to get children to betray their parents. One night the police broke into the family's house. They tore up the beds, bookcases, and the kitchen, and they took their Western clothes and tapes. After that night, all of the family except for one married sister made a daring escape into Iran.

7   Meena said, "It was a long time ago but I can see everything today." There was no legal way to go north, so they walked through Kurdistan at night and slept under bushes in the day. They found a guide who made his living escorting **Kurds** over the mountains. Twice they crossed rivers near flood stage. Entire families had been swept away by the waters and one of the sisters almost drowned when she fell off her horse. The trails were steep and narrow and another sister fell and broke her leg. Meena was in a bag slung over the guide's horse for three days. She remembered how stiff she felt in the bag, and Shireen remembered screaming, "I want my mama."

8   This was in the 1980s. While this was happening I was a psychologist building my private practice and a young mother taking my kids to *Sesame Street Live* and **Vacation Village on Lake Okoboji.** I was dancing to the music of my husband's band, Sour Mash, listening to Van Morrison and Jackson Browne and reading P. D. James and Anne Tyler. Could my life have been happening on the same planet?

9   The family made it to a refugee camp in Iran. It was a miserable place with smelly tents and almost no supplies. Shireen said this was rough on her older siblings who had led lives of luxury. She and Meena adjusted more quickly. The sisters studied in an Iranian school for refugees.

10   They endured this makeshift camp for one very bad year. The Iranians insisted that all the women in the camp wear heavy scarves and robes and conform to strict rules. The soldiers in the camp shouted at them if they wore even a little lipstick. Shireen once saw a young girl wearing makeup stopped by a guard who rubbed it off her face. He had put ground glass in the tissue so that her cheeks bled afterward.

11   They decided to get out of Iran and traveled the only direction they could, east into Pakistan. They walked all the way with nothing to drink except salty water that made them even thirstier. I asked how long the trip took and Shireen said three days. Meena quickly corrected her: "Ten years."

12   Once in Pakistan they were settled by a relief agency in a border town called Quetta, where strangers were not welcome. The family lived in a small house with electricity that worked only sporadically. The stress of all the moves broke the family apart. The men left the women and the family has never reunited.

13   Single women in Quetta couldn't leave home unescorted and the sisters had no men to escort them. Only their mother, Zeenat, dared go out to look for food. As Meena put it, "She took good care of us and now we will take care of her."

Kurds A people of the Middle East whose homeland is in the mountainous regions of Iraq, Iran, and Turkey.
Vacation Village on Lake Okoboji A family resort in Northwestern Iowa.

14   The sisters almost never left the hut, but when they did, they wore robes as thick and heavy as black carpets. Meena demonstrated how hard it was to walk in these clothes and how she often fell down. Even properly dressed, they were chased by local men. When they rode the bus to buy vegetables, they were harassed.

15   Without their heroic mother, they couldn't have survived. For weeks at a time, the family was trapped inside the hut. At night the locals would break their windows with stones and taunt the sisters with threats of rape. Meena interrupted to say that every house in the village but theirs had weapons. Shireen said incredulously, "There were no laws in that place. Guns were laws."

16   One night some men broke into their hut and took what little money and jewelry they had left. They had been sleeping and woke to see guns flashing around them. The next day they reported the break-in to the police. Shireen said, "The police told us to get our own guns." Meena said, "We were nothing to them. The police slapped and pushed us. We were afraid to provoke them."

17   During the time they were there, the Pakistanis tested a nuclear bomb nearby and they all got sick. An older sister had seizures from the stress of their lives. Shireen said defiantly, "It was hard, but we got used to hard."

18   Still, the young women laughed as they told me about the black robes and the men with guns. Their laughter was a complicated mixture of anxiety, embarrassment, and relief that it was over. It was perhaps also an attempt to distance themselves from that time and place.

19   They'd studied English in the hut and made plans for their future in America or Europe. Shireen said, "I always knew that we would escape that place."

20   In Quetta the family waited ten years for papers that would allow them to immigrate. Shireen looked at me and said, "I lost my teenage years there—all my teenage years."

21   Finally, in frustration, the family went on a hunger strike. They told the relief workers they would not eat until they were allowed to leave Quetta. After a few days, the agency paperwork was delivered and the family was permitted to board a train for Islamabad.

22   In Islamabad they lived in a small apartment with no air conditioning. Every morning they would soak their curtains in water to try to cool their rooms. It was dusty and polluted and they got typhoid fever and heat sickness. They had a year of interviews and waiting before papers arrived that allowed them to leave for America. Still, it was a year of hope. Zeenat picked up cans along the roads to make money. One sister ran a beauty parlor from their home. They all watched American television, studied English, and dreamed of a good future.

23   Finally they flew to America—Islamabad to Karachi to Amsterdam to New York to St. Louis to Lincoln. Shireen said, "We came in at night. There were lights spread out over the dark land. Lincoln looked beautiful."

24   We talked about their adjustment to Lincoln. Five of the sisters had found work. They didn't have enough money though, and they didn't like the cold. Meena needed three root canals and Zeenat had many missing teeth and needed bridgework, false

teeth, everything really. Still, they were enjoying the sense of possibilities unfolding. Shireen put it this way, "In America, we have rights." She pronounced "rights" as if it were a sacred word.

25   Meena mentioned that traffic here was more orderly and less dangerous than in Pakistan. The girls loved American clothes and makeup. Two of their sisters wanted to design clothes. Another was already learning to do American hairstyles so that she could work in a beauty shop. Meena wanted to be a nurse and Shireen a model or flight attendant. She said, "I have traveled so much against my will. Now I would like to see the world in a good way."

26   Shireen said that it was scary to go to the high school. Fortunately, her study of English in Pakistan made it easy for her to learn Nebraska English. She liked her teachers but said the American students mostly ignored her, especially when they heard her thick accent.

27   I was struck by the resilience of these sisters. In all the awful places they had been, they'd found ways to survive and even joke about their troubles. These young women used their intelligence to survive. Had they lived different lives, they would probably have been doctors and astrophysicists. Since they'd been in Lincoln, they'd been happy. Shireen said, "Of course we have problems, but they are easy problems."

28   I gave the sisters a ride home in my old Honda. They invited me in for tea, but I didn't have time. Instead I wrote out my phone number and told them to call if I could help them in any way.

29   When I said good-bye, I had no idea how soon and how intensely I would become involved in the lives of this family. Two weeks later Shireen called to ask about an art course advertised on a book of matches. It promised a college degree for thirty-five dollars. I said, "Don't do it." A couple of weeks later she called again. This time she had seen an ad for models. She wondered if she should pay and enter the modeling contest. Again I advised, "Don't do it." I was embarrassed to tell her that we Americans lie to people to make money. Before I hung up, we chatted for a while.

30   I wanted to make sure they learned about the good things in our city. Advertisers would direct them to the bars, the malls, and anything that cost money. I told them about what I loved: the parks and prairies, the lakes and sunsets, the sculpture garden, and the free concerts. I lent them books with Georgia O'Keeffe paintings and pictures of our national parks.

31   For a while I was so involved with the lives of the sisters that Zeenat told me that her daughters were now my daughters. I was touched that she was willing to give her daughters away so that they could advance. I tactfully suggested we could share her daughters, but that she would always be the real mother.

MASTERY TEST SKILLS CHECK

Directions: Select the best answer for each of the following questions.

Checking Your Comprehension

_____ 1. The author's primary purpose in "Beautiful Laughing Sisters" is to
   a. examine the official channels people must go through to immigrate.
   b. comment on the racism that exists worldwide.
   c. encourage people to make friends with refugees.
   d. describe the experience of a refugee family.

_____ 2. In paragraphs 2–4, the author
   a. introduces all six sisters.
   b. provides background information on the family and their early life in Iraq.
   c. describes the childhood of the mother.
   d. sets out a plan for the rest of the article.

_____ 3. Which of the following questions is *not* answered in the paragraphs about the family's time in Quetta (paragraphs 12–16)?
   a. How did the local people treat refugees?
   b. What happened to the men of the family after they left?
   c. Which member of the family kept them going during this time?
   d. Why were these women so vulnerable?

_____ 4. The final three paragraphs (29–31) are included in order to
   a. describe the author's involvement in the family's life.
   b. criticize certain American businesses.
   c. draw conclusions about the girls' relationship with their mother.
   d. encourage the reader to learn more about the plight of refugees.

_____ 5. What finally made the family decide to escape from Iraq?
   a. the father's opposition to Hussein
   b. families being taken off to jail
   c. their own home being broken into
   d. the tactics of schoolteachers

_____ 6. According to the reading, who was responsible for the sisters' survival?
   a. their father
   b. the sisters themselves
   c. their mother
   d. their brothers

Applying Your Skills

_____ 7. All of the following types of supporting details are used in this selection *except*
   a. description of events.
   b. description of places.
   c. reasons.
   d. statistics.

_____ 8. In paragraph 7, which one of the following is a minor detail?
   a. There was no legal way to go north.
   b. Meena was in a bag slung over the guide's horse.
   c. The guide made his living escorting Kurds.
   d. They walked through Kurdistan.

_____ 9. Which one of the following is a major detail in paragraph 2?
   a. Their English was limited and heavily accented.
   b. The sisters wore clunky high-heeled shoes.
   c. The author met the sisters on a fall day.
   d. The sisters could speak Farsi.

_____ 10. A time/sequence transition is indicated in paragraph 5 by the word or phrase
   a. one family
   b. after
   c. however
   d. often

Studying Words

_____ 11. The suffix of the word "refugee" (paragraph 1) indicates that the word means
   a. the condition of seeking shelter.
   b. one who seeks shelter.
   c. pertaining to shelter.
   d. moving toward shelter.

_____ 12. What is the best definition of the word "array" as it is used in paragraph 1?
   a. to set out for display
   b. to dress in finery
   c. an impressively large number
   d. a rectangular arrangement of quantities in rows and columns

_____ 13. The best synonym for the word "hideous" as it is used in paragraph 6 is
   a. horrible.
   b. ugly.
   c. repulsive.
   d. repellent.

_____ 14. The root of the word "incredulously" (paragraph 15) means
   a. life.
   b. tell.
   c. see.
   d. believe.

_____ 15. What is the correct pronunciation of the word "resilience" (paragraph 27)?
   a. re ZILL yens
   b. re SILLY ens
   c. re ZYE lee ens
   d. re SILE ee ens

> For more practice, ask your instructor for an opportunity to work on the mastery tests that appear in the Test Bank.

Chapter 8

Following the Author's Thought Patterns

THIS CHAPTER WILL SHOW YOU HOW TO

1 **Improve your understanding and recall by recognizing thought patterns**

2 **Identify commonly used thought patterns**

3 **Learn transitional words and phrases that signal thought patterns**

Getting Started with . . .
Thought Patterns

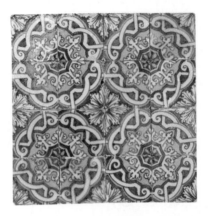

What do these three photographs have in common? Although the stadium seats, the flower, and the mosaic tile are very different in function, they are all symmetrical. That is, they follow a pattern. The stadium seats are arranged in a unique pattern, as are the petals of the flower and the individual tiles in the mosaic. Patterns appear in many places—in art, in nature, in buildings, etc. They are also used in writing. In this chapter you will see how writers use thought patterns to organize their writing.

251

As a way of beginning to think about authors' thought patterns, complete each of the following steps:

1. Study each of the drawings below for a few seconds (count to ten as you look at each one).
2. Cover up the drawings and try to draw each from memory.
3. Check to see how many you had exactly correct.

Most likely you drew all but the fourth correctly. Why did you get that one wrong? How does it differ from the others?

Drawings 1, 2, 3, and 5 have patterns. Drawing 4, however, has no pattern; it is just a group of randomly arranged lines.

From this experiment you can see that it is easier to remember drawings that have a pattern, some understandable form of organization. The same is true of written material. If you can see how a paragraph is organized, it will be easier to understand and remember. Writers often present their ideas in a recognizable order. Once you can recognize the organizational pattern, you will remember more of what you read.

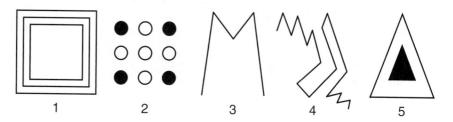

SIX COMMON THOUGHT PATTERNS

This chapter discusses six of the more common thought patterns that writers use and shows how to recognize them: (1) illustration/example, (2) definition, (3) comparison/contrast, (4) cause/effect, (5) classification, and (6) chronological order/process. A brief review of other useful patterns is provided in the section that follows.

Illustration/Example

One of the clearest, most practical, and most obvious ways to explain something is to give an example. Suppose you had to explain what anthropology is. You might give examples of the topics you study. By using examples, such as the study of apes and early humans, and the development of modern humans, you would give a fairly good idea of what anthropology is all about. When a subject is unfamiliar, an example often makes it easier to understand.

Usually a writer will state the idea first and then follow with examples. Several examples may be given in one paragraph, or a separate paragraph may be used for each example. It may help to visualize the illustration/example pattern this way:

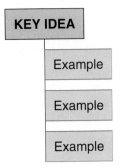

Notice how this thought pattern is developed in the following passage.

> Electricity is all around us. We see it in lightning. We receive electric shocks when we walk on a nylon rug on a dry day and then touch something (or someone). We can see sparks fly from a cat's fur when we pet it in the dark. We can rub a balloon on a sweater and make the balloon stick to the wall or the ceiling. Our clothes cling together when we take them from the dryer.
>
> These are all examples of *static electricity*. They happen because there is a buildup of one of the two kinds of electrical charge, either positive or negative. . . .
>
> —Newell, *Chemistry*, p. 11.

In the preceding passage, the concept of static electricity was explained through the use of everyday examples. You could visualize the selection as follows:

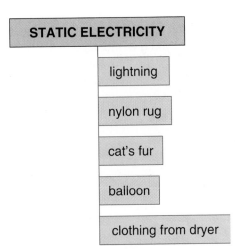

Here is another passage in which the main idea is explained through example:

It is a common observation that all bodies do not fall with equal accelerations. A leaf, a feather, or a sheet of paper, for example, may flutter to the ground slowly. That the air is the factor responsible for these different accelerations can be shown very nicely with a closed glass tube containing a light and heavy object, a feather and a coin, for example. In the presence of air, the feather and coin fall with quite unequal accelerations. But if the air in the tube is evacuated by means of a vacuum pump, and the tube is quickly inverted, the feather and coin fall with the same acceleration. . . . Although air resistance appreciably alters the motion of falling feathers and the like, the motion of heavier objects like stones and baseballs is not appreciably affected by the air. The relationships $v = gt$ and $d = 1/2\ gt^2$ can be used to a very good approximation for most objects falling in air.

—Hewitt, *Conceptual Physics*, p. 21.

The author explains that objects do not fall at equal rates by using the examples of a leaf, a feather, and a sheet of paper.

Paragraphs and passages organized using illustration/example often use transitional words and phrases to connect ideas. Examples of such words and phrases include:

for example	for instance	to illustrate

EXERCISE 8-1

Directions: For each of the following paragraphs, underline the topic sentence and list the examples used to explain it.

1. Perception is the process of gathering information and giving it meaning. You see a movie and you give meaning to it: "It's one of the best I've seen." You come away from class after the third week and you give meaning to it: "It finally makes sense." We gather information from what our senses see, hear, touch, taste, and smell, and we give meaning to that information. Although the information may come to us in a variety of forms, it is all processed, or *perceived,* in the mind.

—Weaver, *Understanding Interpersonal Communication*, p. 24.

Examples: _____

_____

2. The action and reaction forces make up a *pair* of forces. Forces always occur in pairs. There is never a single force in any situation. For example, in walking across the floor, we push against the floor, and the floor in turn pushes against us. Likewise, the tires of a car push against the pavement, and the pavement pushes back on the tires. When we swim, we push the water backward, and the water pushes us forward. The reaction forces, those acting in the direction of our resulting accelerations, are what account for our motion in these cases. These forces depend on friction; a person or car on ice, for example, may not be able to exert the action force to produce the needed reaction force by the ice.

—Hewitt, *Conceptual Physics*, p. 56.

Examples: _____

_____

3. Have you ever noticed that some foods remain hotter much longer than others? Boiled onions and squash on a hot dish, for example, are often too hot to eat when mashed potatoes may be eaten comfortably. The filling of hot apple pie can burn your tongue while the crust will not, even when the pie has just been taken out of the oven. And the aluminum covering on a frozen dinner can be peeled off with your bare fingers as soon as it is removed from the oven. A piece of toast may be comfortably eaten a few seconds after coming from the hot toaster, but we must wait several minutes before eating soup from a stove no hotter than the toaster. Evidently, different substances have different **capacities** for storing internal energy.

—Hewitt, *Conceptual Physics*, p. 224.

Examples: _____

_____

EXERCISE 8-2   **Directions:** Choose one of the following topics. On a separate sheet of paper, write a paragraph in which you use illustration/example to organize and express your ideas on the topic. Then draw a diagram showing the organization of your paragraph.

1. Parents or friends are helpful (or not helpful) in making decisions.

2. Attending college has (has not) made a major change in my life.

Definition

Another way to provide an explanation is to offer a definition. Let us say that you see an opossum while driving in the country. You mention this to a friend. Since your friend does not know what an opossum is, you have to give a definition. Your definition should describe an opossum's characteristics or features. The definition should have two parts: (1) tell what general group or class an opossum belongs to—in this case, animals; and (2) explain how an opossum is different or distinguishable from other items in the group. For the term *opossum*, you would need to describe features of an opossum that would help someone tell the difference between it and other animals, such as dogs, raccoons, and squirrels. Thus, you could define an opossum as follows:

> An opossum is an animal with a ratlike tail that lives in trees. It carries its young in a pouch. It is active at night and pretends to be dead when trapped.

This definition can be diagrammed as follows:

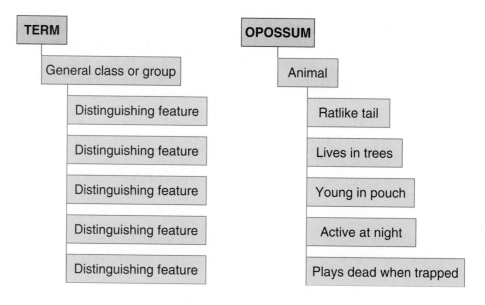

The following passage was written to define the term *ragtime music.*

> Ragtime music is a piano style that developed at the turn of the twentieth century. Ragtime music usually has four themes. The themes are divided into four musical sections of equal length. In playing ragtime music, the left hand plays chords and the right hand plays the melody. There is an uneven accenting between the two hands.

The thought pattern of this passage might be diagrammed as follows:

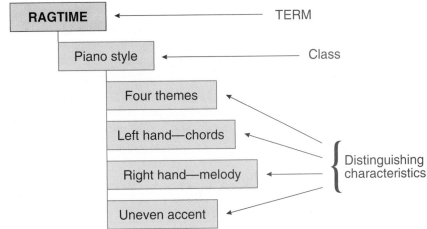

As you read passages that use the definition pattern, keep these questions in mind:

1. What is being defined?
2. What general group or class does it belong to?
3. What makes it different from others in the group?

Read the following passage and apply the above questions.

> Nez Perce Indians are a tribe that lives in north-central Idaho. The rich farmlands and forests in the area form the basis for the tribe's chief industries—agriculture and lumber.
>
> The name *Nez Perce* means *pierced nose,* but few of the Indians ever pierced their noses. In 1805, a French interpreter gave the name to the tribe after seeing some members wearing shells in their noses as decorations.
>
> The Nez Perce originally lived in the region where the borders of Idaho, Oregon, and Washington meet. Prospectors overran the Nez Perce reservation after discovering gold there in the 1860s.
>
> Part of the tribe resisted the efforts of the government to move them to a smaller reservation. In 1877, fighting broke out between the Nez Perce and U.S. troops. Joseph, a Nez Perce chief, tried to lead a band of the Indians into Canada. But he surrendered near the United States–Canadian border.
>
> —*The World Book Encyclopedia,* Vol. 14, p. 391.

This passage was written to define the Nez Perce. The general group or category is "Indian tribe." The distinguishing characteristics include the source of their name, their original location, and their fight against relocation.

EXERCISE 8-3   **Directions:** Read each of the following paragraphs. Then identify the term being defined, its general class, and its distinguishing features.

1. The partnership, like the sole proprietorship, is a form of ownership used primarily in small business firms. Two or more owners comprise a partnership. The structure of a partnership may be established with an almost endless variation of features. The partners establish the conditions of the partnership, contribution of each partner to the business, and division of profits. They also decide on the amount of authority, duties, and liability each will have.

—Pickle and Abrahamson, *Introduction to Business*, p. 40.

Term: _____

General class: _____

Distinguishing features: _____

_____

_____

_____

2. A language is a complex system of symbols with conventional meanings, used by members of a society for communication. The term *language* is often thought to include only the spoken word, but in its broadest sense language contains verbal, nonverbal * and written symbols. Whereas complex cultures employ all three kinds of symbols in communication, simple and preliterate cultures typically lack written symbols.

—Thompson and Hickey, *Society in Focus*, p. 70.

Term: _____

General class: _____

Distinguishing features: _____

_____

_____

_____

*Boxed words appear in the Mastering Vocabulary exercise on p. 287.

3. The Small Business Administration (SBA) is an independent agency of the federal government that was created by Congress when it passed the Small Business Act in 1853. Its administrator is appointed by and reports to the President. Purposes of the SBA are to assist people in getting into business, to help them stay in business, to help small firms win federal procurement contracts, and to act as a strong advocate for small business.

—Pickle and Abrahamson, *Introduction to Business*, p. 119.

Term: _____

General class: _____

Distinguishing features: _____

_____

_____

_____

Paragraphs and passages that are organized using definition often use transitional words and phrases to connect ideas. Examples of theses transitional words and phrases include:

can be defined as	consists of	involves
is	is called	is characterized by
means	refers to	

EXERCISE 8-4

Directions: Choose one of the topics listed below. On a separate sheet of paper, write a paragraph in which you define the topic. Be sure to include both the general group and what makes the item different from other items in the same group. Then draw a diagram showing the organization of your paragraph.

1. A type of music

2. Soap operas

3. Junk food

Comparison/Contrast

Often a writer will explain something by using **comparison** or **contrast**—that is, by showing how it is similar to or different from a familiar object or idea. Comparison treats similarities, while contrast emphasizes differences. For example, an article comparing two car models might mention these common, overlapping features: radial tires, clock, radio, power steering, and power brakes. The cars may differ in gas mileage, body shape, engine power, braking distance, and so forth. When comparing the two models, the writer would focus on shared features. When contrasting the two cars the writer would focus on individual differences. Such an article might be diagrammed as follows:

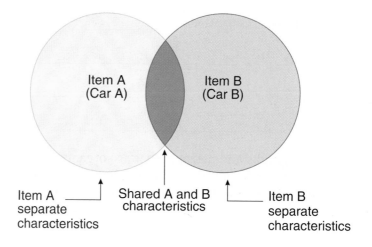

In this diagram, Items A and B are different except where they overlap and share the same characteristics.

In most articles that use the comparison/contrast method, you will find some passages that only compare, some that only contrast, and others that both compare and contrast. To read each type of passage effectively, you must follow the pattern of ideas. Passages that show comparison and/or contrast can be organized in a number of different ways. The organization depends on the author's purpose.

Comparison   If a writer is concerned only with similarities, he or she may identify the items to be compared and then list the ways in which they are alike. The following paragraph shows how chemistry and physics are similar.

Although physics and chemistry are considered separate fields of study, they have much in common. First, both are physical sciences and are concerned with studying and explaining physical occurrences. To study and record these occurrences, each field has developed a precise set of signs and symbols. These might be considered a specialized language. Finally, both fields are closely tied to the field of mathematics and use mathematics in predicting and explaining physical occurrences.

—Hewitt, *Conceptual Physics*, pp. 82–84.

Such a pattern can be diagrammed as follows:

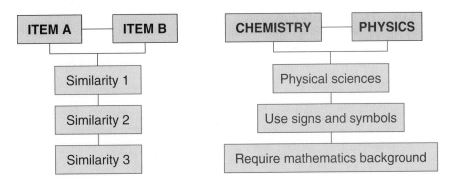

Contrast   A writer concerned only with the differences between sociology and psychology might write the following paragraph:

> Sociology and psychology, although both social sciences, are very different fields of study. Sociology is concerned with the structure, organization, and behavior of groups. Psychology, on the other hand, focuses on individual behavior. While a sociologist would study characteristics of groups of people, a psychologist would study the individual motivation and behavior of each group member. Psychology and sociology also differ in the manner in which research is conducted. Sociologists obtain data and information through observation and survey. Psychologists obtain data through carefully designed experimentation.

Such a pattern can be diagrammed as follows:

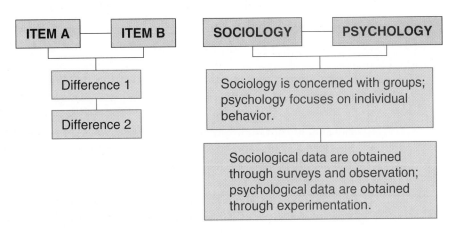

Comparison and Contrast In many passages, writers discuss both similarities and differences. Suppose you wanted to write a paragraph discussing the similarities and differences between sociology and psychology. You could organize the paragraph in several different ways.

1. You could list all the similarities and then all the differences, as shown in this diagram:

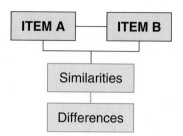

2. You could discuss Item A first, presenting both similarities and differences, and then do the same for Item B. Such a pattern would look like this:

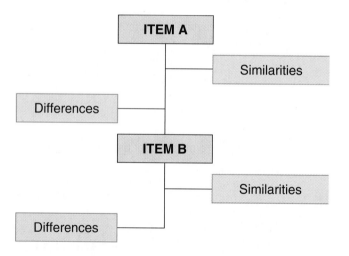

The following paragraph discusses housing in New York City. As you read it, try to visualize its pattern.

> Housing in New York City differs in several ways from that in most other cities of the United States. About 65 percent of New York's families live in apartment buildings or hotels. In other cities, most people live in one- or two-family houses. About 70 percent of the families in New York rent their homes. In other U.S. cities, most families own their homes. About half of the housing in New York City was built before 1840. Most other cities in the United States have a far larger percentage of newer housing.
>
> —*The World Book Encyclopedia*, Vol. 14, p. 332.

Did you visualize the pattern like this?

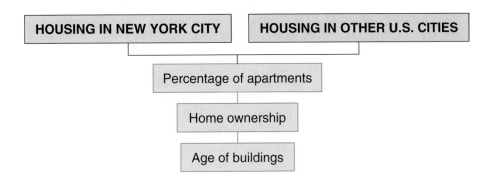

Now read the following passage and decide whether it discusses similarities, differences, or both.

> A program must be written in a form that a computer can understand. Every instruction must be prepared according to specific rules. The rules form a language that we use to instruct the computer. Humans use *natural languages* such as English and Spanish to communicate with each other. When we communicate with a computer, we use a *computer programming language.*
>
> To write a sentence in a natural human language, we form words and phrases from letters and other symbols. The construction of the sentence is determined by the grammar rules of the language. The meaning of the sentence depends on what words are used and how they are organized. A computer programming language also has rules that describe how to form valid instructions. These rules are called the *syntax* of the language. The meanings or effects of the instructions are called the *semantics* of the language.
>
> —Nickerson, *Fundamentals of Structured COBOL*, p. 2.

This passage *compares* natural language with computer programming language. Both are means of communication, and both are based on sets of rules.

Paragraphs and passages that use comparison/contrast often contain transitional words and phrases that guide readers through the material. These include:

Comparison	Contrast
both, in comparison, in the same way, likewise, similarly, to compare	as opposed to, differs from, however, in contrast, instead, on the other hand, unlike

EXERCISE 8-5

Directions: Read each of the following passages and identify the items being compared or contrasted. Then describe the author's approach to the items. Are they compared, contrasted, or both compared and contrasted?

1. Perhaps it will be easier to understand the nature and function of empathic listening if we contrast it to deliberative listening. When we make a definite "deliberate" attempt to hear information, analyze it, recall it at a later time and draw conclusions from it, we are listening deliberatively. This is the way most of us listen because this is the way we have been trained. This type of listening is appropriate in a lecture-based education system where the first priority is to critically analyze the speaker's content.

In empathic listening the objective is also understanding, but the first priority is different. Because empathic listening is transactional, the listener's first priority is to understand the communicator. We listen to what is being communicated not just by the words but by the other person's facial expressions, tone of voice, gestures, posture, and body motion.

—Weaver, *Understanding Interpersonal Communication*, p. 85.

Items compared or contrasted: _____

Approach: _____

2. The term *primary group*, coined by Charles H. Cooley (1808), is used to refer to small, informal groups who interact in a personal, direct and intimate way. . . . A secondary group is a group whose members interact in an impersonal manner, have few emotional ties, and come together for a specific purpose. Like primary groups, they are usually small and involve face-to-face contacts. Although the interactions may be cordial or friendly, they are more formal than primary group interactions. Sociologically, however, they are just as important. Most of our time is spent in secondary groups—committees, professional groups, sales-related groups, classroom groups, or neighborhood groups. The key difference between primary and secondary groups is in the quality of the relationships and the extent of personal intimacy and involvement. Primary groups are person-oriented, whereas secondary groups tend to be goal-oriented.

—Eshleman and Cashion, *Sociology*, pp. 109–11.

Items compared or contrasted: _____

Approach: _____

3. The differences in the lifestyles of the city and the suburbs should be thought of as differences of degree, not kind. Suburban residents tend to be more family-oriented and more concerned about the quality of education their children receive than city dwellers. On the other hand, because the suburbs consist largely of single-family homes, most young and single people prefer city life. Suburbanites are usually more affluent than city residents and more apt to have stable career or occupational patterns. As a result, they seem to be more hardworking and achievement-oriented than city residents. They may also seem to be unduly concerned with consumption, since they often buy goods and services that offer visible evidence of their financial success.

—Eshleman and Cashion, *Sociology*, p. 583.

Items compared or contrasted: _____

Approach: _____

EXERCISE 8-6

Directions: Choose one of the topics listed below. On a separate sheet of paper, write a paragraph in which you compare and/or contrast the two items. Then draw a diagram showing the organization of your paragraph.

1. Two restaurants

2. Two friends

3. Two musical groups

Cause/Effect

The **cause/effect** pattern is used to describe an event or action that is caused by another event or action. A cause/effect passage explains why or how something happened. For example, a description of an automobile accident would probably follow a cause/effect pattern. You would tell what caused the accident and what happened as a result. Basically, this pattern describes four types of relationships:

1. Single cause/single effect

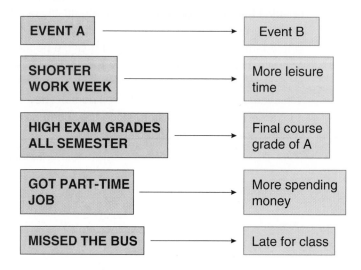

2. Single cause/multiple effects

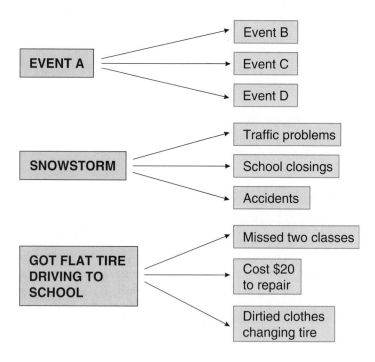

3. Multiple cause/single effect

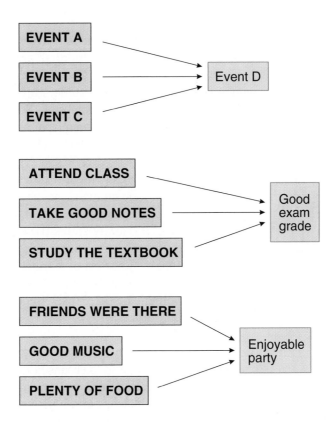

4. Multiple causes/multiple effects

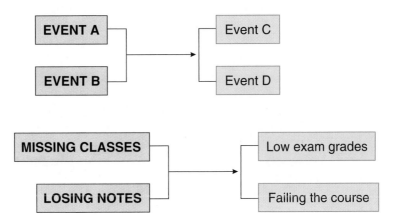

Read the following paragraph and determine which of the four relationships it describes.

> Research has shown that mental illnesses have various causes, but the causes are not fully understood. Some mental disorders are due to physical changes in the brain resulting from illness or injury. Chemical imbalances in the brain may cause other mental illnesses. Still other disorders are mainly due to conditions in the environment that affect a person's mental state. These conditions include unpleasant childhood experiences and severe emotional stress. In addition, many cases of mental illness probably result from a combination of two or more of these causes.

In this paragraph a single effect (mental illness) is stated as having multiple causes (chemical and metabolic changes, psychological problems).

To read paragraphs that explain cause/effect relationships, pay close attention to the topic sentence. It usually states the cause/effect relationship that is detailed in the remainder of the paragraph. Then look for connections between causes and effects. What event happened as the result of a previous action? How did one event cause the other to happen?

Look for the development of the cause/effect relationship in the following paragraph about racial conflict.

> Racial conflicts in New York City have had many causes. A major cause has been discrimination against blacks, Puerto Ricans, and other minority groups in jobs and housing. Many minority group members have had trouble obtaining well-paying jobs. Many also have had difficulty moving out of segregated neighborhoods and into neighborhoods where most of the people are white and of European ancestry. When members of a minority group have begun moving into such a neighborhood, the white residents often have begun moving out. In this way, segregated housing patterns have continued, and the chances for conflicts between the groups have increased.
>
> —*The World Book Encyclopedia*, Vol. 14, p. 271.

This paragraph explains why conflicts occur. It can be diagrammed as follows:

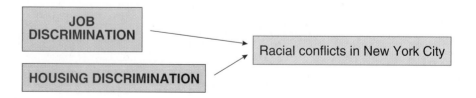

Within this paragraph, a second cause/effect relationship is introduced:

Paragraphs and passages that are organized using cause/effect often use transitional words and phrases to guide the reader. These include:

Cause	Effect
because, because of, for, since, stems from, one cause is, one reason is, for this reason, due to	consequently, one result is, as a result, therefore, thus, hence, results in

EXERCISE 8-7

Directions: Read each of the following paragraphs and describe the cause/effect relationship in each.

1. By far the major cause of all business failure is inadequate management. As the Dun & Bradstreet data show, nearly 82 percent of all business failures are attributed to this one cause. What contributes to inadequate management? We see that causes of inadequate management include a lack of experience, unbalanced business experience, and incompetence.

—Pickle and Abrahamson, *Introduction to Business*, p. 123.

Cause: _____

Effect: _____

2. If a light is directed into one eye, the pupils of both eyes normally constrict. The decrease in pupil size is caused by contraction of the sphincter muscles of the iris. Constriction of the pupil in the eye in which the light was directed is known as the direct light reflex. Constriction of the pupil in the other eye is called the consensual light reflex. Both light reflexes have the typical reflex components: a sensory pathway, a motor pathway, and a central nervous system integration center.

—Davis et al., *Conceptual Human Physiology*, p. 213.

Cause: _____

Effect: _____

3. Snow is a poor conductor and hence is popularly said to keep the earth warm. Its flakes are formed of crystals, which collect feathery masses, imprisoning air and thereby interfering with the escape of heat from the earth's surface. The winter dwellings of the Eskimos are shielded from the cold by their snow covering. Animals in the forest find shelter from the cold in snowbanks and in holes in the snow. The snow doesn't provide them with heat; it simply prevents the heat they generate from escaping.

—Hewitt, *Conceptual Physics*, p. 233.

Cause: _____

Effect: _____

EXERCISE 8-8 **Directions:** Choose one of the topics listed below. On a separate sheet of paper, write a paragraph using one of the four cause/effect patterns described above to explain the topic. Then draw a diagram showing the organization of your paragraph.

1. Why you are attending college

2. Why you chose the college you are attending

3. How a particularly frightening or tragic event happened

Classification

A common way to explain something is to divide the topic into parts and explain each part. For example, you might explain how a home computer works by describing what each major component does. You would explain the functions of the monitor (screen), the disc drives, and the central processing unit. Or you might explain the kinds of courses taken in college by dividing the courses into such categories as electives, required basic courses, courses required for a specific major, and so on, and then describing each category.

Textbook writers use the classification pattern to explain a topic that can easily be divided into parts. These parts are selected on the basis of common characteristics. For example, a psychology textbook writer might explain human needs by classifying them into two categories, primary and secondary. Or in a chemistry textbook, various compounds may be grouped or classified according to common characteristics, such as the presence of hydrogen or oxygen.

The following paragraph explains horticulture. As you read, try to identify the categories into which the topic of horticulture is divided.

Horticulture, the study and cultivation of garden plants, is a large industry. Recently it has become a popular area of study. The horticulture field consists of four major divisions. First, there is pomology, the science and practice of growing and handling fruit trees. Then there is olericulture, which is concerned with growing and storing vegetables. A third field, floriculture, is the science of growing, storing, and designing flowering plants. The last category, ornamental and landscape horticulture, is concerned with using grasses, plants, and shrubs in landscaping.

This paragraph approaches the topic of horticulture by describing its four areas or fields of study. You could diagram the paragraph as follows:

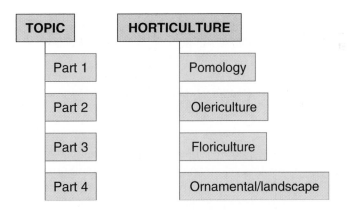

When reading textbook material that uses the classification pattern, be sure you understand *how* and *why* the topic was divided as it was. This technique will help you remember the most important parts of the topic.

Here is another example of the classification pattern:

A newspaper is published primarily to present current news and information. For large city newspapers, more than 2,000 people may be involved in the distribution of this information. The staff of large city papers, headed by a publisher, is organized into departments: editorial, business, and mechanical. The editorial department, headed by an editor-in-chief, is responsible for the collection of news and preparation of written copy. The business department, headed by a business manager, handles circulation, sales, and advertising. The mechanical department is run by a production manager. This department deals with the actual production of the paper, including typesetting, layout, and printing.

You could diagram this paragraph as follows:

LARGE CITY NEWSPAPERS

Editorial

Business

Mechanical

Paragraphs and passages that are organized using classification frequently use transitional words and phrases to guide the reader. These include:

another   another kind   classified as   include   is composed of   one   types of

EXERCISE 8-9

Directions: Read each of the following passages. Then identify the topic and the parts into which each passage is divided.

1. The peripheral nervous system is divided into two parts: the somatic (bodily) nervous system and the autonomic (self-governing) nervous system. The somatic nervous system, sometimes called the skeletal nervous system, controls the skeletal muscles of the body and permits voluntary action. When you turn off a light or write your name, your somatic system is active. The autonomic nervous system regulates blood vessels, glands, and internal (visceral) organs like the bladder, stomach, and heart. When you happen upon the secret object of your desire and your heart starts to pound, your hands get sweaty, and your cheeks feel hot, you can blame your autonomic nervous system.

—Wade and Tavris, *Psychology*, p. 77.

Topics: _____

Parts: _____

2. When we communicate with others we use either verbal messages, nonverbal messages, or a combination of the two. Verbal messages are either sent or not sent, just as a light switch is either on or off. They have an all-or-nothing feature built in. Nonverbal cues are not as clear-cut.

Nonverbal communication includes such behaviors as facial expressions, posture, gestures, voice inflection, and the sequence and rhythm of the words themselves. Just as a dimmer switch can be used to adjust a light, nonverbal cues often reveal shades or degrees of meaning. You may say, for example, "I am very upset" but *how* upset you are will be conveyed more by your facial expressions and gestures than by the actual words.

—Weaver, *Understanding Interpersonal Communication*, p. 24.

Topics: _____

Parts: _____

3. The word *script* is used in this concept to mean a habitual pattern of behavior. Thomas Harris defines scripts as decisions about how life should be lived. Muriel James and Dorothy Jongeward suggest that there are various levels of scripts: (1) cultural, which are dictated by society; (2) subcultural, defined by geographical location, ethnic background, religious beliefs, sex, education, age and other common bonds; (3) family, the identifiable traditions and expectations for family members; and (4) psychological, people's compulsion to perform in a certain way, to live up to a specific identity, or to fulfill a destiny.

—Weaver, *Understanding Interpersonal Communication*, p. 291.

Topics: _____

Parts: _____

EXERCISE 8-10 **Directions:** Choose one of the topics listed below. On a separate sheet of paper, write a paragraph explaining the topic, using the classification pattern. Then draw a diagram showing the organization of your paragraph.

1. Advertising

2. Colleges

3. Entertainment

Chronological Order/Process

The terms **chronological order** and **process** both refer to the order in which something is done. Chronological order, also called sequence of events, is one of the most obvious patterns. In a paragraph organized by chronology, the details are presented in the order in which they occur. That is, the event that happened first, or earliest in time, appears first in the paragraph, and so on. Process refers to the steps or stages in which something is done. You might expect to read a description of the events in a World War II battle presented in the order in which they happened—in chronological order. Similarly, in a computer programming manual, the steps to follow to locate an error in a computer program would be described in the order in which you should do them.

Both chronological order and process patterns can be diagrammed as follows:

EVENT OR PROCESS

1. Action or step

2. Action or step

3. Action or step

Read the following paragraph, paying particular attention to the order of the actions or steps.

> In the early 1830s, the newly established Federal Bureau of Narcotics took on a crucial role in the fight against marijuana. Under the directorship of Harry J. Anslinger, a rigorous campaign was waged against the drug and those using it. By 1837 many states had adopted a standard bill making marijuana illegal. In that same year, the federal government stepped in with the Marijuana Tax Act, a bill modeled after the Harrison "Narcotics" Act. Repressive legislation continued, and by the 1850s severe penalties were imposed on those convicted of possessing, buying, selling, or cultivating the drug.
>
> —Barlow, *Criminal Justice in America*, p. 332.

This paragraph traces the history of actions taken to limit the use of marijuana. These actions are described in chronological order, beginning with the earliest event and concluding with the most recent.

When reading text material that uses the chronological order/process pattern, pay particular attention to the order of the information presented. Both chronological order and process are concerned with the sequence of events in time.

Paragraphs and passages that use chronological order/process to organize ideas often contain transitional words and phrases to guide the reader. They include:

after	before	by the time	during	finally	first	later
meanwhile	on	second	then	until	when	while

EXERCISE 8-11   **Directions:** Read each of the following paragraphs. Identify the topic and write a list of the actions, steps, or events described in each paragraph.

1. These benefits of good listening occur only when the cues we give back to a speaker allow that person to know how we receive the message, permitting the speaker to adjust the message as needed. This important process is known as *feedback.* Feedback is not a simple, one-step process. First, it involves monitoring the impact or the influence of our messages on the other person. Second, it involves evaluating why the reaction or response occurred as it did. Third and finally, it involves adjustment or modification. The adjustment of our future messages reveals the process-oriented nature of communication, and, too, the impact the receiver has on the communication cycle. Feedback can provide reinforcement for the speaker if it shows if he or she is being clear, accepted, or understood.

—Weaver, *Understanding Interpersonal Communication*, p. 123.

Topic: _____

Steps: _____

_____

_____

2. A geyser is a periodically erupting pressure cooker. It consists of a long, narrow, vertical hole into which underground streams seep. The column of water is heated by volcanic heat below to temperatures exceeding 100°C. This is because the vertical column of water exerts pressure on the deeper water, thereby increasing the boiling point. The narrowness of the shaft shuts off convection currents, which allows the deeper portions to become considerably hotter than the water surface. Water at the surface, of course, will boil at 100°C. The water is heated from below, so a temperature high enough to permit boiling is reached near the bottom before it is at the top. Boiling therefore begins near the bottom, the rising bubbles push out the column of water above, and the eruption starts. As the water gushes out, the pressure of the remaining water is reduced. It then rapidly boils and erupts with great force.

—Hewitt, *Conceptual Physics*, p. 252.

Topic: _____

Steps: _____

_____

_____

_____

3. In spite of varied protests, the nineteenth century saw the admission of girls into elementary schools and eventually into secondary schools. In 1883, feminine education scored a victory when Oberlin College admitted women as well as men. In 1837, Mount Holyoke Seminary for Girls was established in Massachusetts, thanks to the pioneering efforts of Mary Lyon. Vassar College opened its doors in 1865, followed by Smith in 1871, Wellesley in 1877, and Bryn Mawr in 1880. The University of Michigan meanwhile had admitted women in 1870, and by the turn of the century coeducational colleges and universities were becoming commonplace. Today the great majority of the more than 2000 institutions of higher learning in the United States are coeducational, including practically all professional schools.

—Kephart and Jedlicka, *The Family, Society, and the Individual*, p. 332.

Topic: _____

Steps: _____

_____

_____

_____

EXERCISE 8-12   **Directions:** On a separate sheet of paper, write a paragraph explaining how to do something that you do well or often, such as cross-country ski, change a tire, or use a VCR to tape a TV show. Use the chronological order/process pattern. Then draw a diagram showing the organization of your paragraph.

EXERCISE 8-13   **Directions:** Read each of the following passages and identify the thought pattern used. Write the name of the pattern in the space provided. Choose from among these patterns: illustration/example, definition, comparison/contrast, cause/effect, classification, chronological order/process. Next, write a sentence explaining your choice. Then, on a separate sheet of paper, draw a diagram that shows the organization of each selection.

1. Many wedding customs have been popular since ancient times. For example, Roman brides probably wore veils more than 2,000 years ago. Bridal veils became popular in Britain and the New World during the late 1700s. The custom of giving a wedding ring dates back to the ancient Romans. The roundness of the ring probably represents eternity, and the presentation of wedding rings symbolizes that the man and woman are united forever. Wearing the wedding ring on the ring finger of the left hand is another old custom. People once thought that a vein or nerve ran directly

from this finger to the heart. An old superstition says that a bride can ensure good luck by wearing "something old, something new, something borrowed, and something blue." Another superstition is that it is bad luck for a bride and groom to see each other before the ceremony on their wedding day.

—*The World Book Encyclopedia*, Vol. 13, p. 221.

Pattern: _____

Reason: _____

2. Muscle is the tough, elastic tissue that makes body parts move. All animals except the simplest kinds have some type of muscle.

People use muscles to make various movements, such as walking, jumping, or throwing. Muscles also help in performing activities necessary for growth and for maintaining a strong, healthy body. For example, people use muscles in the jaw to chew food. Other muscles help move food through the stomach and intestines, and aid in digestion. Muscles in the heart and blood vessels force the blood to circulate. Muscles in the chest make breathing possible.

Muscles are found throughout the body. As a person grows, the muscles also get bigger. Muscle makes up nearly half the body weight of an adult.

—*The World Book Encyclopedia*, Vol. 13, p. 953.

Pattern: _____

Reason: _____

3. Unless they were employed as servants, colonial women had little occupational opportunity. Even during the early 1800s, after certain types of jobs had been opened to women, female wage earners continued to be stigmatized by inferior social status.

The first large-scale influx of female workers took place in the New England factories. Most of the workers were unmarried farm girls, some hardly more than children. They were welcomed, nevertheless, because they not only were conscientious employees but would work for low wages.

During the Civil War an increasing number of occupations were opened to women, a phenomenon that was to be repeated in the First and Second World Wars. During World War II, women were employed as welders, mechanics, machinists, taxi drivers, and streetcar operators; in fact, with the exception of heavy-duty laboring jobs, females could be found in virtually every branch of industry. Also, because of their excellent record, women were made a permanent part of the armed forces.

Today there are more than 52 million women in the work force. Of those not in the labor force, the great majority are retired or have home responsibilities. From the sociological perspective it is important to note that currently even mothers with small children are likely to be employed outside the home. "Regardless of marital status or the presence of young children, labor force participation has become the norm for women." Since 1986, more than half of all women with children under three years of age have been in the labor force.

—Kephart and Jedlicka, *The Family, Society, and the Individual*, pp. 332–33.

Pattern: _____

Reason: _____

4. Mimosa is the name of a group of trees, shrubs, and herbs that have featherlike leaves. Mimosas grow chiefly in warm and tropical regions. In the United States, they are found from Maryland to Florida and west to Texas. The seeds of mimosas grow in flat pods. The small flowers may be white, pink, lavender, or purple. The *silver wattle*, a shrub with silvery-gray leaves, is widely sold by florists as mimosa. It is closely related to mimosas.

—*The World Book Encyclopedia*, Vol. 13, p. 562.

Pattern: _____

Reason: _____

5. Morphine makes severe pain bearable and moderate pain disappear. The drug also stops coughing and diarrhea, checks bleeding, and may help bring sleep. Doctors give patients morphine only if other medicines fail. Besides being addictive, it interferes with breathing and heart action and may cause vomiting. Small doses of morphine leave the mind fairly clear. Larger doses cloud the mind and make the user feel extremely lazy. Most morphine users feel little hunger, anger, sadness, or worry, and their sex drive is greatly reduced. Most people with mental or social problems feel happy after using morphine, even though their problems have not really been solved.

—*The World Book Encyclopedia*, Vol. 13, p. 672.

Pattern: _____

Reason: _____

6. Personality disorders are characterized by behavioral traits that create significant difficulties in personal relationships. For example, antisocial personality disorder is characterized by aggressive and harmful behavior that first occurs before the early teens. Such behavior includes lying, stealing, fighting, and resisting authority. During adulthood, people with this disorder often have difficulty keeping a job or accepting responsibility.

People with *borderline personality disorder* often have unstable personal relationships, problems with self-identity, and very noticeable mood changes. They may also act impulsively in potentially self-damaging ways, such as shoplifting, drug use, or reckless driving.

Individuals who suffer from *paranoid personality disorder* are overly suspicious, cautious, and secretive. They may believe that people are watching them or talking about them. They often criticize others but have difficulty accepting criticism.

People with *obsessive-compulsive personality disorder* attach great importance to being organized. They strive for perfection and efficiency and may spend much time making lists and schedules. But they are indecisive, and their concern for details keeps them from accomplishing much outside of a narrow area of focus. They often make unreasonable demands on others and have difficulty expressing emotions.

—*The World Book Encyclopedia*, Vol. 13, pp. 795–96.

Pattern: _____

Reason: _____

7. Only female mosquitoes "bite," and only the females of a few species attack human beings and animals. They sip the victim's blood, which they need for the development of the eggs inside their bodies. Mosquitoes do not really bite because they cannot open their jaws. When a mosquito "bites," it stabs through the victim's skin with six needlelike parts called *stylets,* which form the center of the proboscis. The stylets are covered and protected by the insect's lower lip, called the *labium.* As the stylets enter the skin, the labium bends and slides upward out of the way. Then saliva flows into the wound through channels formed by the stylets. The mosquito can easily sip the blood because the saliva keeps it from clotting. Most persons are allergic to the saliva, and an itchy welt called a "mosquito bite" forms on the skin. After the mosquito has sipped enough blood, it slowly pulls the stylets out of the wound, and the labium slips into place over them. Then the insect flies away.

—*The World Book Encyclopedia*, Vol. 13, p. 832.

Pattern: _____

Reason: _____

8. To understand the organization of long-term memory, then, we need to understand what kinds of information can be stored there. Most theories distinguish skills or habits ("knowing how") from abstract or representational knowledge ("knowing that"). Procedural memories are memories of knowing how—for example, knowing how to comb your hair, use a pencil, or swim. Declarative memories are memories of "knowing that." Declarative memories, in turn, come in two varieties. Semantic memories are internal representations of the world, independent of any particular context. They include facts, rules, and concepts. On the basis of your semantic memory of the

concept *cat,* you can describe a cat as a small, furry mammal that typically spends its time eating, sleeping, and staring into space, even though a cat may not be present when you give this description and you probably won't know how or when you learned it. Episodic memories, on the other hand, are internal representations of personally experienced events. They allow you to "travel back" in time. When you remember how your furry feline once surprised you in the middle of the night by pouncing on your face as you slept, you are retrieving an episodic memory.

—Wade and Tavris, *Psychology,* p. 252.

Pattern: _____

Reason: _____

9. People turn to magic chiefly as a form of insurance—that is, they use it along with actions that actually bring results. For example, hunters may use a hunting charm. But they also use their hunting skills and knowledge of animals. The charm may give hunters the extra confidence they need to hunt even more successfully than they would without it. If they shoot a lot of game, they credit the charm for their success. Many events occur naturally without magic. Crops grow without it, and sick people get well without it. But if people use magic to bring a good harvest or to cure a patient, they may believe the magic was responsible. People also tend to forget magic's failures and to be impressed by its apparent successes. They may consider magic successful if it appears to work only 10 percent of the time. Even when magic fails, people often explain the failure without doubting the power of the magic. They may say that the magician made a mistake in reciting the spell or that another magician cast a more powerful spell against the magician.

Many anthropologists believe that people have faith in magic because they feel a need to believe in it. People may turn to magic to reduce their fear and uncertainty if they feel they have no control over the outcome of a situation. For example, farmers use knowledge and skill when they plant their fields. But they know that weather, insects, or diseases might ruin the crops. So farmers in some societies may also plant a charm or perform a magic rite to ensure a good harvest.

—*The World Book Encyclopedia,* Vol. 13, p. 46.

Pattern: _____

Reason: _____

10. Almost all companies realize the tremendous value of mathematics in research and planning. Many major industrial firms employ trained mathematicians. Mathematics has great importance in all engineering projects. For example, the design of a superhighway requires extensive use of mathematics. The construction of a giant dam would be impossible without first filling reams of paper with mathematical

formulas and calculations. The large number of courses an engineering student must take in mathematics shows the importance of mathematics in this field.

—*The World Book Encyclopedia*, Vol. 13, p. 238.

Pattern: _____

Reason: _____

OTHER USEFUL PATTERNS OF ORGANIZATION

The patterns presented in the preceding section are the most common. Table 8-1 (page 282) presents a brief review of those patterns and their corresponding transitional words. However, writers do not limit themselves to these six patterns. Especially in academic writing, you may find one or more of the patterns listed in Table 8-2 (page 283), as well.

Statement and Clarification

Many writers make a statement of fact and then proceed to clarify or explain that statement. For instance, a writer may open a paragraph by stating that "The best education for you may not be the best education for someone else." The remainder of the paragraph would then discuss that statement and make its meaning clear by explaining how educational needs are individual and based on one's talents, skills, and goals. Here is another example:

> In recent years, computer hackers have become a serious problem. It is very difficult to catch the culprits because the virus programs they introduce often affect a system afterwards. In fact, very few hacking incidents get reported and even fewer of the hackers get caught. According to the San Francisco–based Computer Security Institute (CSI), only about 17% of companies report hacking incidents because of the fear of adverse publicity, copycat hacking, and loss of customer confidence. Out of those reported cases, normally an infinitesimal number of those responsible are caught.
>
> —Bandyo-Padhyay, *Computing For Non-Specialists*, p. 260.

Transitional words associated with this pattern are listed in Table 8-2.

Summary

A summary is a condensed statement that provides the key points of a larger idea or piece of writing. The summaries at the end of each chapter of this text provide a quick review of the chapter's contents. Often writers summarize

TABLE 8-1   A Review of Patterns and Transitional Words

Pattern	Characteristics	Transitional Words
Illustration/Example	Organizes examples that illustrate an idea or concept	for example, for instance, such as, to illustrate
Definition	Explains the meaning of a word or phrase	are those that, can be defined as, consists of, corresponds to, entails, involves, is, is a term that, is called, is characterized by, is literally, means, occurs when, refers to
Comparison/Contrast	Discusses similarities and/or differences among ideas, theories, concepts, objects, or persons	*Similarities:* also, as well as, both, correspondingly, in comparison, in the same way, like, likewise, resembles, share, similarly, to compare, too *Differences:* as opposed to, despite, differs from, however, in contrast, in spite of, instead, nevertheless, on the other hand, unlike, whereas
Cause/Effect	Describes how one or more things cause or are related to another	*Causes:* because, because of, cause is, due to, for, for this reason, one cause is, one reason is, since, stems from *Effects:* as a result, consequently, hence, one result is, results in, therefore, thus
Classification	Divides a topic into parts based on shared characteristics	another, another kind, classified as, comprises, different groups that, different stages of, finally, first, include, is composed of, last, one, second, types of, varieties of
Chronological Order/ Process	Describes events, processes, procedures	after, as soon as, by the time, during, finally, first, following, in, last, later, meanwhile, next, on, second, then, until, when, while

what they have already said or what someone else has said. For example, in a psychology textbook you will find many summaries of research. Instead of asking you to read an entire research study, the textbook author will summarize the study's findings. Other times a writer may repeat in condensed form what he or she has already said as a means of emphasis or clarification. Here is a sample paragraph:

To sum up, the minimax strategy is a general principle of human behavior that suggests that humans try to minimize costs and maximize rewards. The fewer costs and the more rewards we anticipate from something, the more likely we are to do it. If we believe that others will approve an act, the likelihood increases that we will do it. In short, whether people are playing cards with a few friends or are part of a mob, the principles of human behavior remain the same.

—Henslin, *Sociology*, p. 637.

Transitional words associated with this pattern are listed in Table 8-2.

Addition

Writers often introduce an idea or make a statement and then supply additional information about that idea or statement. For instance, an education textbook may introduce the concept of homeschooling and then provide in-depth information about its benefits. This pattern is often used to expand, elaborate, or discuss an idea in greater detail. Here is an example:

Millions of people work at home on computers connected to an office, an arrangement known as **telecommuting**. Telecommuting eases the pressure on transport facilities, saves fuel, and reduces air pollution. Moreover, it has been shown to increase workers' productivity and reduce absenteeism. It also allows employers to accommodate employees who want flexible work arrangements, thus opening employment opportunity to more people, such as women who are still homemakers.

—Bergman and Renwick, *Introduction to Geography*, p. 410.

Transitional words associated with this pattern are listed in Table 8-2.

TABLE 8-2   A Review of Additional Patterns and Transitional Words

Pattern	Characteristics	Transitional Words
Statement and Clarification	Indicates that information explaining an idea or concept will follow	clearly, evidently, in fact, in other words, obviously
Summary	Indicates that a condensed review of an idea or piece of writing will follow	in brief, in conclusion, in short, in summary, on the whole, to sum up, to summarize
Addition	Indicates that additional information will follow	additionally, again, also, besides, further, furthermore, in addition, moreover
Spatial Order	Describes physical location or position in space	above, behind, below, beside, in front of, inside, nearby, next to, opposite, outside, within

Spatial Order

Spatial order is concerned with the physical location or position in space. Spatial order is used in disciplines in which physical descriptions are important. A photography textbook may use spatial order to describe the parts of a camera. An automotive technology textbook may use spatial order to describe disk brake operation. Here is a sample paragraph:

We can taste food because chemoreceptors in the mouth respond to certain chemicals in food. The chemoreceptors for taste are located in structures called **taste buds**, each of which contains 50–150 receptor cells and numerous support cells. At the top of each bud is a pore that allows receptor cells to be exposed to saliva and dissolved food molecules. Each person has over 10,000 taste buds, located primarily on the tongue and the roof of the mouth, but also located in the pharynx.

—Germann and Stanfield, *Principles of Human Physiology*, pp. 303–04.

Transitional words associated with this pattern are listed in Table 8-2.

EXERCISE 8-14   **Directions:** For each of the following statements, identify the pattern that is evident and indicate it in the space provided. Choose from among the following patterns:

a. statement and clarification
b. summary
c. addition
d. spatial order

_____ 1. Short fibers, dendrites, branch out around the cell body and a single long fiber, the axon, extends from the cell body.

_____ 2. Aspirin is not as harmless as people think. It may cause allergic reactions and stomach irritation. In addition, aspirin has been linked to an often fatal condition known as Reye's syndrome.

_____ 3. If our criminal justice system works, the recidivism rate—the percentage of people released from prison who return—should decrease. In other words, in a successful system, there should be a decrease in the number of criminals who are released from prison and then become repeat offenders.

_____ 4. Students who are informed about drugs tend to use them in greater moderation. Furthermore, they tend to help educate others.

_____ 5. To sum up, a successful drug addiction treatment program would offer free or very cheap drugs to addicts.

_____ 6. In conclusion, it is safe to say that crime by women is likely to increase as greater numbers of women assume roles traditionally held by men.

_____ 7. The pollutants we have just discussed all involve chemicals; we can conclude that they threaten our environment and our well-being.

_____ 8. A residual check valve that maintains slight pressure on the hydraulic system is located in the master cylinder at the outlet for the drum brakes.

_____ 9. Sociologists study how we are socialized into sex roles—the attitudes expected of males and females. Sex roles, in fact, identify some activities and behaviors as clearly male and others as clearly female.

_____ 10. The meninges are three membranes that lie just outside the organs of the central nervous system.

Using Transitional Words

As you learned earlier in the chapter, transitional words can help you identify organizational patterns. These words are called _transitional words_ because they help you make the transition or connection between ideas. They may also be called _clue words_ or _directional words_ because they provide readers with clues about what is to follow.

Transitional words are also helpful in discovering or clarifying relationships between and among ideas in any piece of writing. Specifically, transitional words help you grasp connections between and within sentences. Transitional words can help you predict what is to come next within a paragraph. For instance, if you are reading along and come upon the phrase _in conclusion,_ you know that the writer will soon present a summary. If you encounter the word _furthermore,_ you know that the writer is about to present additional information about the subject at hand. If you encounter the word _consequently_ in the middle of a sentence (The law was repealed; consequently, . . .), you know that the writer is about to explain what happened as a result of the repeal. Tables 8-1 and 8-2 on pages 282 and 283 list the directional words that correspond to the patterns discussed in this chapter.

EXERCISE 8-15

Directions: Each of the following beginnings of paragraphs uses a transitional word or phrase to tell the reader what will follow in the paragraph. Read each, paying particular attention to the underlined transitional word or phrase. Then, in the space provided, describe as specifically as you can what you would expect to find next in the paragraph.

1. Many Web sites on the Internet are reliable and trustworthy. <u>However,</u> . . .

2. One advantage of using a computer to take notes is that you can rearrange information easily. <u>Another</u> . . .

    _____

3. There are a number of ways to avoid catching the cold virus. <u>First of all</u>, . . .

    _____

4. Some pet owners care for their animals responsibly. <u>However</u>, others . . .

    _____

5. When planning a speech, you should choose a topic that is familiar or that you are knowledgeable about. <u>Next</u>, . . .

    _____

6. Following a high protein diet may be rewarding because it often produces quick weight loss. <u>On the other hand</u>, . . .

    _____

7. The iris is a doughnut-shaped portion of the eyeball. <u>In the center</u> . . .

    _____

8. Price is not the only factor consumers consider when making a major purchase. They <u>also</u> . . .

    _____

9. Cholesterol, commonly found in many fast foods, is associated with heart disease. <u>Consequently</u>, . . .

    _____

10. Many Web sites provide valuable links to related sites. <u>To illustrate</u>, visit . . .

    _____

LEARNING STYLE TIPS

If you tend to be a . . .	Then identify thought patterns by . . .
Spatial learner	Drawing a diagram of the ideas in the passage
Verbal learner	Outlining the passage

MASTERING VOCABULARY

Directions: Match each word in Column A with its meaning in Column B. Determine the meaning from its context in this chapter or its word parts, or use a dictionary, if necessary.

Column A

_____ 1. nonverbal (p. 258)

_____ 2. preliterate (p. 258)

_____ 3. interact (p. 264)

_____ 4. disorders (p. 268)

_____ 5. imbalances (p. 268)

_____ 6. erupting (p. 275)

_____ 7. coeducational (p. 276)

_____ 8. antisocial (p. 278)

_____ 9. uncertainty (p. 280)

_____ 10. superhighway (p. 280)

Column B

a. disparities

b. doubt

c. exploding

d. both sexes learning together

e. unspoken

f. communicate and cooperate

g. against what society expects

h. illnesses

i. before reading existed

j. broad, multilane highway

SELF-TEST SUMMARY

How can you better comprehend and recall paragraphs you read?	Recognizing the author's thought pattern will improve comprehension and recall.
What is a thought pattern?	A thought pattern is the way in which an author organizes ideas.
What are the six common thought patterns?	The six common thought patterns are: 1. Illustration/example—An idea is explained by providing specific instances or experiences that illustrate it. 2. Definition—An object or idea is explained by describing the general class or group to which it belongs and how the item differs from others in the same group (distinguishing features). 3. Comparison/contrast—A new or unfamiliar idea is explained by showing how it is similar to or different from a more familiar idea. 4. Cause/effect—Connections between events are explained by showing what caused an event or what happened as a result of a particular event. 5. Classification—An object or idea is explained by dividing it into parts and describing or explaining each. 6. Chronological order/process—Events or procedures are described in the order in which they occur in time.
What other thought patterns are used in academic writing?	1. Statement and clarification—An explanation will follow. 2. Summary—A condensed view of the subject will be presented. 3. Addition—Additional information will follow. 4. Spatial order—Physical location or position will be described.
How can transitional words and phrases help you understand thought patterns?	Transitional words and phrases emphasize the connection and relationship among ideas in a paragraph or passage.

Getting More Practice with . . .
Thought Patterns

WORKING TOGETHER

Directions: Locate and mark five paragraphs in one of your textbooks or in Part Six of this text that are clear examples of the thought patterns discussed in this chapter. Write the topic sentence of each paragraph on a separate index card. Once your instructor has formed small groups, choose a group "reader" who will collect all the cards and read each sentence aloud. Groups should discuss each and predict the pattern of the paragraph from which the sentence was taken. The "finder" of the topic sentence then confirms or rejects the choice, quoting sections of the paragraph if necessary.

GOING ONLINE

Internet Activities

1. Rhetorical Patterns for Organizing Documents
   http://www.ecf.utoronto.ca/~writing/handbook-rhetoric.html
   The University of Toronto presents this site that reviews the ways information is organized. Choose some objects and activities you experience in your daily life. Write about them according to the appropriate guidelines presented here.

2. Logic Patterns
   http://www.learner.org/teacherslab/math/patterns/logic.html#activities
   Try these online logic pattern activities from The Teachers' Lab, the Annenberg/CPB Math and Science Project. Observe patterns in your daily life. When do you find yourself sorting and classifying?

Companion Website

For additional readings, exercises, and Internet activities, visit this book's Companion Website at:
http://www.ablongman.com/mcwhorter
If you need a user name and password, please see your instructor.

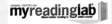

My Reading Lab

For more practice on thought patterns, visit MyReadingLab, click on the Reading Skills tab, and then click on Active Reading Strategies—New York Harbor.
http://www.ablongman.com/myreadinglab

TEST-TAKING TIPS

Answering Questions About Thought Patterns

Reading comprehension tests often contain questions about thought patterns and their transitions. Use the following suggestions to answer these questions correctly.

- If you are uncertain about the pattern of a particular paragraph, study the transitions. These may suggest the pattern.

- If you are having trouble identifying a pattern, ask yourself the following question: "How does the author explain his or her main idea?" You will hear yourself saying things such as "by giving examples" (the example pattern), "by explaining how it is done" (the process pattern), or "by telling what it is" (the definition pattern).

- A question may not use the term "pattern of organization," but it may be asking you to identify the pattern, as this example shows.

  Example: In the above paragraph, the writer supports her ideas by

  a. giving examples.

  b. listing information.

  c. offering definitions.

  d. explaining a process.

- The topic sentence of a paragraph often reveals or suggests the pattern to be used.

  Examples of Topic Sentences:

  1. The majority of Americans will be better off in the year 2050 than they are today. (contrast)

  2. Both Werner (2002) and Waible (2000) focus on genetic traces as a means of pinpointing cancer. (comparison)

  3. Computer users suffer in numerous ways when spam clogs their e-mail systems. (example)

  4. Acute stress may lead to the inability to think clearly and to make sensible decisions. (cause/effect)

Name _____

Section _____ Date _____

Number right _____ x 20 points = Score _____

Directions: For each of the following topic sentences, predict what pattern the paragraph is likely to follow.

_____ 1. Exposing children to music at an early age appears to have several positive effects.
   a. classification
   b. definition
   c. cause/effect
   d. comparison/contrast

_____ 2. Depending on how you plan to use the Internet at home, you may select either dial-up Internet service, cable modem service, or a digital subscriber line (DSL).
   a. definition
   b. summary
   c. chronological order
   d. comparison/contrast

_____ 3. Organisms can be grouped into three domains: Bacteria, Archaea, and Eukarya.
   a. classification
   b. cause/effect
   c. summary
   d. spatial order

_____ 4. According to psychiatrist Elisabeth Kübler-Ross, terminally ill patients go through five stages as they face death.
   a. comparison/contrast
   b. chronological order
   c. cause/effect
   d. spatial order

_____ 5. In conclusion, it is simply too soon to tell what President Clinton's legacy will be.
   a. enumeration
   b. summary
   c. comparison/contrast
   d. definition

Chapter 8
Mastery Test 2
Identifying Patterns

Name _____

Section _____ Date _____

Number right _____ x 10 points = Score _____

Directions: Read the passage below and then answer the questions that follow.

1   Companies need to be sensitive to the concerns of consumer groups. Building good relationships with these groups benefits an organization in two ways. First, by understanding the concerns of these groups, the firm is able to develop its own socially responsible programs and practices that will gain the favor of the groups and others in the community. Second, when problems arise, such as a potentially dangerous product design flaw, activist groups are more likely to work with the firm to make changes and less likely to organize some form of public protest against it.

2   Adolph Coors, the beer manufacturer, developed good relationships with several consumer groups when it promoted a romance novel as part of a $40 million, five-year marketing program against illiteracy. The book, titled *Perfect,* reached the *New York Times'* best-seller list. Coors's literacy program campaign drew thousands of inquiries, improved Coors's reputation in the community, and favorably influenced Coors's other important relationships with customers, employees, and shareholders.

3   To review, evaluating a firm's internal environment includes assessing corporate resources and competencies, understanding the corporate environment, and looking at the relationships a firm has with various groups. In this way the firm can identify the strengths and weaknesses that can create (or not create) both economic and social profit.

—Solomon and Stuart, *Marketing,* p. 71.

_____ 1. The pattern that the authors use to organize their ideas in the first paragraph is
a. definition.
b. comparison/contrast.
c. cause/effect.
d. enumeration.

_____ 2. The transitional words that signal the authors' thought pattern in the first paragraph are
a. "companies" and "consumer groups."
b. "programs" and "practices."
c. "first" and "second."
d. "more likely" and "less likely."

_____ 3. The pattern that the authors use to organize their ideas in the second paragraph is
a. chronological order.
b. illustration/example.
c. classification.
d. addition.

_____ 4. The pattern that the authors use to organize their ideas in the third paragraph is
a. comparison/contrast.
b. summary.
c. spatial order.
d. illustration/example.

_____ 5. The transitional words that signal the authors' thought pattern in the third paragraph are
a. "evaluating . . . includes."
b. "in this way."
c. "to review."
d. "strengths" and "weaknesses."

Name _____

Section _____ Date _____

Number right _____ x 10 points = Score _____

Chapter 8
Mastery Test 3
Identifying Patterns

Directions: Read each of the following paragraphs. In the blank provided, write the letter of the main thought pattern used.

a. definition
b. comparison/contrast
c. illustration/example
d. cause/effect
e. classification
f. chronological order/process

_____ 1. You need to take a few steps to prepare to become a better note-taker. First, get organized. It's easiest to take useful notes if you have a system. A loose-leaf notebook works best because you can add, rearrange, or remove notes for review. If you use spiral or other permanently bound notebooks, use a separate notebook for each subject to avoid confusion and to allow for expansion. Second, set aside a few minutes each day to review the syllabus for your course, to scan the assigned readings, and to review your notes from the previous class period. If you do this just before each lecture, you'll be ready to take notes and practice critical thinking. Finally, prepare your pages by drawing a line down the left margin approximately two inches from the edge of the paper. Leave this margin blank while you take notes so that later you can use it to practice critical thinking.

—Gronbeck, *Principles of Speech Communication*, pp. 32–33.

_____ 2. Genetics is the scientific study of heredity, the transmission of characteristics from parents to offspring. Genetics explains why offspring resemble their parents and also why they are not identical to them. Genetics is a subject that has considerable economic, medical, and social significance, and is partly the basis for the modern theory of evolution. Because of its importance, genetics has been a topic of central interest in the study of life for centuries. Modern concepts in genetics are fundamentally different, however, from earlier ones.

—Mix et al., *Biology*, p. 262.

_____ 3. Colors surely influence our perceptions and our behaviors. People's acceptance of a product, for example, is largely determined by its package. The very same coffee taken from a yellow can was described as weak, from a dark brown can too strong, from a red can rich, and from a blue can mild. Even our acceptance of a person may depend on the colors worn. Consider, for example, the comments of one color expert: "If you have to pick the wardrobe for your defense lawyer in court and choose anything but blue, you deserve to lose the case. . . ." Black is so powerful it could work against a lawyer with the jury. Brown lacks sufficient authority. Green would probably elicit a negative response.

—DeVito, *The Interpersonal Communication Book*, pp. 219–220.

_____ 4. France and the United States present an interesting contrast of cultural factors that affect the push-pull mix. U.S. homemakers spend more time watching television and reading magazines, and they rely more on friends and advertising before purchasing a new product. In contrast, French homemakers spend more time shopping, examining items on shelves, and listening to the opinions of retailers. Therefore, it has bee-neasier to presell U.S. homemakers, whereas in France discounts to distributors and point-of-purchase displays have been more effective.

—Daniels and Radebaugh, *International Business*, p. 679.

_____ 5. In 1980, the Asian children far outperformed the American children on a broad battery of mathematical tests. On computation and word problems, there was virtually no overlap between schools, with the lowest-scoring Beijing schools doing better than the highest-scoring Chicago schools. By 1980, the gap between the Asian and American children had grown ever greater. Only 4 percent of the Chinese children and 10 percent of the Japanese children had scores as low as those of the average American child. These differences could not be accounted for by educational resources: the Chinese had worse facilities and larger classes than the Americans. On the average, the

American children's parents were far better-off financially and were better educated than the parents of the Chinese children. Nor could the test differences be accounted for by differences in the children's fondness for math: 85 percent of the Chinese kids said they like math, but so did almost 75 percent of the American children. Nor did it have anything to do with intellectual ability in general, because the American children were just as knowledgeable and capable as the Asian children on tests of general information.

—Wade and Tavris, *Psychology*, pp. 327–28.

_____ 6. Convenience goods are products bought with a minimum of time and effort. Little forethought or planning occurs prior to the purchase of a convenience good. Convenience goods can be further categorized into three subtypes: staples, emergency goods, and impulse goods. Staples are convenience goods that consumers have purchased many times before. This means the consumer already has a high level of knowledge about the product and does not need to do a great deal of shopping. Emergency goods are convenience goods that consumers purchase with little forethought, planning, or effort because a situation arises that requires immediate possession of the item. If you are caught in a rainstorm while out of town you might purchase an umbrella even if you have one at home. Impulse goods are convenience goods that consumers purchase with no preplanning or thought. Seeing the item offered for sale is the stimulus that motivates the purchase. For example, have you ever stood in line at the checkout in a grocery store and added a candy bar, some gum, a magazine, or some batteries to your purchases? If so, you have bought impulse goods.

—Kinnear, *Principles of Marketing,*
pp. 283–84.

_____ 7. The next step is to install browser software on your computer. You can purchase a browser in your local software retail outlet or, if you have some other online access vehicle, possibly download it free from the browser vendor's Web site. As you are installing the browser, you will be asked for information about your ISP, for which your ISP will have prepared you. (An ISP typically furnishes several pages of detailed instructions.) Once you are set up, you invoke the browser as you would any software on your computer, and it will begin by dialing the Internet service provider for you. You are on your way to the Internet experience.

—Capron, *Computers,* p. 199.

_____ 8. The effects of alcohol on the fetus are different at different stages of pregnancy; the most dangerous stage is the first trimester (12 weeks), but a little alcohol later in pregnancy is sometimes recommended as a way to prevent premature contractions. In a longitudinal British study, the children of mothers who did not drink at all during pregnancy were not different from those of mothers who had had fewer than 10 drinks a week during pregnancy. In contrast, a similar American study, in which more than 500 children have been followed from birth to age 14, found small but significant differences in the children's intellectual performance when the mothers had a drink or two of alcohol per day during their pregnancies. So most American researchers conclude that the safest course of action for pregnant women is to abstain entirely.

—Wade and Tavris, *Psychology,* p. 494.

_____ 9. Pitch is the dimension of auditory experience related to the frequency of the sound wave and, to some extent, its intensity. Frequency refers to how rapidly the air (or other medium) vibrates—that is, the number of times per second the wave cycles through a peak and a low point. One cycle per second is known as 1 hertz (Hz). The healthy ear of a young person normally detects frequencies in the range of 16 Hz (the lowest note on a pipe organ) to 20,000 Hz (the scraping of a grasshopper's legs).

—Wade and Tavris, *Psychology,* p. 226.

_____ 10. Culture change can originate from two sources: innovation and borrowing. *Innovation* is the invention of new forms. It involves the recombination of what people already know into something different. For example, Canadian Joseph-Armand Bombardier became an innovator when he added tracks, designed to propel earth-moving equipment, to a small bus that originally ran on tires, producing the first snowmobile in the 1850s. Later the Skolt Lapps of Finland joined him as innovators when they adapted his now smaller, more refined snowmobile for herding reindeer in 1861. The Lapp innovation was not the vehicle itself. That was borrowed. What was new was the use of the vehicle in herding, something usually done by men on skis.

—Spradley and McCurdy, *Conformity and Conflict*, p. 349.

Name _____

Section _____ Date _____

Number right* _____ x 10 points = Score _____

Right Place, Wrong Face

Alton Fitzgerald White

In this selection, the author describes what it was like to be treated as a criminal on the basis of nothing more than having the "wrong face."

> **Vocabulary Preview**
>
> **ovation** (par. 3) enthusiastic, prolonged applause
>
> **overt** (par. 4) not secret, obvious
>
> **splurged** (par. 5) indulged in a luxury
>
> **vestibule** (par. 5) a small entrance hall or passage into the interior of a building
>
> **residue** (par. 9) something that remains after a substance is taken away
>
> **violation** (par. 14) the condition of being treated unfairly or offended

1   As the youngest of five girls and two boys growing up in Cincinnati, I was raised to believe that if I worked hard, was a good person, and always told the truth, the world would be my oyster. I was raised to be a gentleman and learned that these qualities would bring me respect.

2   While one has to earn respect, consideration is something owed to every human being. On Friday, June 16, 1999, when I was wrongfully arrested at my Harlem apartment building, my perception of everything I had learned as a young man was forever changed—not only because I wasn't given even a second to use the manners my parents taught me, but mostly because the police, whom I'd always naively thought were supposed to serve and protect me, were actually hunting me.

3   I had planned a pleasant day. The night before was payday, plus I had received a standing ovation after portraying the starring role of Coalhouse Walker Jr. in the Broadway musical *Ragtime*. It is a role that requires not only talent but also an honest emotional investment of the morals and lessons I learned as a child.

4   Coalhouse Walker Jr. is a victim (an often misused word, but in this case true) of overt racism. His story is every black man's nightmare. He is hardworking, successful, talented, charismatic, friendly, and polite. Perfect prey for someone with authority and not even a fraction of those qualities. On that Friday afternoon, I became a real-life Coalhouse Walker. Nothing could have prepared me for it. Not even stories told to me by other black men who had suffered similar injustices.

---

*To calculate the number right, use items 1–10 under "Mastery Test Skills Check."

5   Friday for me usually means a trip to the bank, errands, the gym, dinner, and then off to the theater. On this particular day, I decided to break my pattern of getting up and running right out of the house. Instead, I took my time, slowed my pace, and splurged by making strawberry pancakes. Before I knew it, it was 2:45; my bank closes at 3:30, leaving me less than 45 minutes to get to midtown Manhattan on the train. I was pressed for time but in a relaxed, blessed state of mind. When I walked through the lobby of my building, I noticed two light-skinned Hispanic men I'd never seen before. Not thinking much of it, I continued on to the vestibule, which is separated from the lobby by a locked door.

Alton Fitzgerald White

6   As I approached the exit, I saw people in uniforms rushing toward the door. I sped up to open it for them. I thought they might be paramedics, since many of the building's occupants are elderly. It wasn't until I had opened the door and greeted them that I recognized that they were police officers. Within seconds, I was told to "hold it"; they had received a call about young Hispanics with guns. I was told to get against the wall. I was searched, stripped of my backpack, put on my knees, handcuffed, and told to be quiet when I tried to ask questions.

7   With me were three other innocent black men who had been on their way to their U-Haul. They were moving into the apartment beneath mine, and I had just bragged to them about how safe the building was. One of these gentlemen got off his knees, still handcuffed, and unlocked the door for the officers to get into the lobby where the two strangers were standing. Instead of thanking or even acknowledging us, they led us out the door past our neighbors, who were all but begging the police in our defense.

8   The four of us were put into cars with the two strangers and taken to the precinct station at 165th and Amsterdam. The police automatically linked us, with no questions and no regard for our character or our lives. No consideration was given to where we were going or why. Suppose an ailing relative was waiting upstairs, while I ran out for her medication? Or young children, who'd been told that Daddy was running to the corner store for milk and would be right back? My new neighbors weren't even allowed to lock their apartment or check on the U-Haul.

9   After we were lined up in the station, the younger of the two Hispanic men was identified as an experienced criminal, and drug residue was found in a pocket of the other. I now realize how naive I was to think that the police would then uncuff me, apologize for their mistake, and let me go. Instead, they continued to search my backpack, questioned me, and put me in jail with the criminals.

10   The rest of the nearly five-hour ordeal was like a horrible dream. I was hand-cuffed, strip-searched, taken in and out for questioning. The officers told me that they knew exactly who I was, knew I was in *Ragtime,* and that in fact they already had the men they wanted.

11   How then could they keep me there, or have brought me there in the first place? I was told it was standard procedure. As if the average law-abiding citizen knows what that is and can dispute it. From what I now know, "standard procedure" is something that every citizen, black and white, needs to learn, and fast.

12   I felt completely powerless. Why, do you think? Here I was, young, pleasant, and successful, in good physical shape, dressed in clean athletic attire. I was carrying a backpack containing a substantial paycheck and a deposit slip, on my way to the bank. Yet after hours and hours I was sitting at a desk with two officers who not only couldn't tell me why I was there but seemed determined to find something on me, to the point of making me miss my performance.

13   It was because I am a black man!

14   I sat in that cell crying silent tears of disappointment and injustice with the realization of how many innocent black men are convicted for no reason. When I was handcuffed, my first instinct had been to pull away out of pure insult and violation as a human being. Thank God I was calm enough to do what they said. When I was thrown in jail with the criminals and strip-searched, I somehow knew to put my pride aside, be quiet, and do exactly what I was told, hating it but coming to terms with the fact that in this situation I was a victim. They had guns!

15   Before I was finally let go, exhausted, humiliated, embarrassed, and still in shock, I was led to a room and given a pseudo-apology. I was told that I was at the wrong place at the wrong time. My reply? "I was where I live."

16   Everything I learned growing up in Cincinnati has been shattered. Life will never be the same.

MASTERY TEST SKILLS CHECK

Directions: Choose the best answer for each of the following questions.

Checking Your Comprehension

_____ 1. The author's main purpose in this selection is to
   a. describe his recent experience with racism.
   b. discuss the effects of racism on young people.
   c. criticize the New York police department.
   d. contrast Cincinnati with New York.

_____ 2. Coalhouse Walker Jr. is the name of
   a. the author of the article.
   b. a black actor in New York.
   c. the main character in a Broadway play.
   d. a racist police officer.

_____ 3. The main idea of paragraph 5 is that the author
  a. had errands to take care of.
  b. was making strawberry pancakes.
  c. lives 45 minutes from midtown Manhattan.
  d. changed his routine and was enjoying a leisurely day.

_____ 4. The two strangers in the lobby of the building were
  a. friends of the author.
  b. new residents of the building.
  c. undercover police officers.
  d. suspected criminals.

_____ 5. After opening the door for the police, the author was
  a. thanked by the police and released to go.
  b. assaulted by criminals.
  c. handcuffed and taken away by the police.
  d. harassed by his neighbors.

_____ 6. "Life will never be the same" for the author because he
  a. can no longer trust in what he was raised to believe about manners and respect.
  b. was injured by the police.
  c. does not understand the criminal justice system.
  d. cannot face his neighbors.

Applying Your Skills

_____ 7. The main thought pattern used in this selection is
  a. definition.
  b. chronological order.
  c. enumeration.
  d. classification.

_____ 8. In paragraph 2, the transitional word or phrase that indicates the chronological order thought pattern is
  a. "while."
  b. "On Friday."
  c. "because."
  d. "but."

_____ 9. In paragraph 9, all of the following transitional words indicate the chronological order thought pattern *except*
  a. "after."
  b. "now."
  c. "instead."
  d. "then."

_____ 10. The main thought pattern used in paragraphs 12 and 13 is
  a. cause/effect.
  b. summary.
  c. enumeration.
  d. definition.

Studying Words

_____ 11. In paragraph 2, the word "naively" means
  a. innocently.
  b. negatively.
  c. purposely.
  d. unfortunately.

_____ 12. What is the correct pronunciation of the word "charismatic" (paragraph 4)?
  a. CHAIR iz mat ick
  b. chair IZ ma tick
  c. care iz MAT ick
  d. care IZ ma tick

_____ 13. The word "vestibule" (paragraph 5) originated from which of the following languages?
   a. Latin
   b. French
   c. German
   d. Greek

_____ 14. What is the best definition of the word "dispute" as it is used in paragraph 11?
   a. strive to win
   b. question the truth of
   c. quarrel angrily
   d. engage in discussion

_____ 15. The prefix of the word "pseudo-apology" (paragraph 15) indicates that the apology was
   a. excessive.
   b. false.
   c. written.
   d. small.

For more practice, ask your instructor for an opportunity to work on the mastery tests that appear in the Test Bank.

Chapter 9

Reading Textbook Chapters

THIS CHAPTER WILL SHOW YOU HOW TO

1 Use textbook learning aids

2 Follow the organization of textbook chapters

3 Approach textbooks in new fields of study

4 Read technical material

Getting Started with . . .
Reading Textbooks

CHAPTER 5

A firefly flashing for a mate

ENERGY AND THE CELL
5.1 Energy is the capacity to per fom work
5.2 Two laws govern energy transformations
5.3 Chemical r eactions either store or release energy
5.4 ATP shuttles chemical energy and drives cellular work

HOW ENZYMES FUNCTION
5.5 Enzymes speed up the cell's chemical reactions by lowering energy barriers
5.6 A specific enzyme catalyzes each cellular reaction
5.7 The cellular environment affects enzyme activity
5.8 Enzyme inhibitors block enzyme action
5.9 Many poisons, pesticides, and drugs are enzyme inhibitors

MEMBRANE STRUCTURE AND FUNCTION
5.10 Membranes or ganize the chemical activities of cells
5.11 Membrane phospholipids form a bilayer
5.12 The membrane is a fl uid mosaic of phospholipids and pr oteins
5.13 Proteins make the membrane a mosaic of function
5.14 Passive transport is diffusion across a membrane
5.15 Transport proteins may facilitate dif fusion acr oss membranes
5.16 Osmosis is the dif fusion of water across a membrane
5.17 Water balance between cells and their surroundings is crucial to organisms
5.18 Cells expend ener gy for active transport
5.19 Exocytosis and endocytosis transport large molecules
5.20 Faulty membranes can overload the blood with cholester ol
5.21 Chlor oplasts and mitochondria make energy available for cellular work

Cool "Fires" Attract Mates and Meals

BRIGHT YELLOW FLASHES in a dark field—we could be almost anywher ein the eastern or central United States. The light display comes from insects commonly known as fireflies or lightning bugs. Males on the wing do most of the flashing. The females are perched on leaves close to the ground.

Fireflies use light to send signals to potential mates, instead of using chemical signals like most other insects. When a female sees flashes of light from a male of her species, she reacts with flashes of her own. If the male sees her flashes, he automatically gives another display and flies in the female's direction. Members of both sexes are responding to particular patterns of light flashes characteristic of their species.

Each of the 2,000 or so species of fi reflies has its own way to signal a mate

Mating occurs after the female's display leads a male to her, and most females stop flashing after they mate. But in a few species, a mated female will continue to fl ash, using a patter that attracts males of *other* firefly species. A veritable *femme fatale*, she waits until the male gets close, then grabs him and eats him. In the photograph on the opposite page, the firefly clinging to the leaf is a female dining on a luckless male of another species.

Each of the 2,000 or so species of fireflies has its own way to signal a mate. Some fl ash more often than others or during

The page from a college biology text shown above is an example of the wide range of subjects college students study. It also demonstrates the kind of technical reading expected of college students. In this chapter you will learn numerous skills to help you cope with the demands of college textbook reading.

Did you know that nearly all textbook authors are college instructors? They work with students daily and understand students' difficulties. Therefore, they include in their textbooks numerous features or aids to make learning easier. They also organize chapters in ways that express their ideas as clearly as possible. This chapter will discuss textbook learning aids and the organization of textbook chapters. It will also suggest special approaches to use when reading technical material.

TEXTBOOK LEARNING AIDS

While textbooks may seem long, difficult, and impersonal, they do contain numerous features that are intended to help you learn. By taking advantage of these features, you can make textbook reading easier.

The Preface

The **preface** is the author's introduction to the text. The preface presents basic information about the text you should know before you begin reading. It may contain such information as:

- Why and for whom the author wrote the text
- How the text is organized
- Purpose of the text
- References and authorities consulted
- Major points of emphasis
- Learning aids included and how to use them
- Special features of the text

The following is an excerpt from the preface of a computer science text. Read the excerpt, noting the type of information it provides.

theme and purpose

Preface

Computers: Tools for an Information Age, Brief Edition, is up-to-date in every respect, from DVDs to MMX chips to cookies to push technology. The connectivity theme is integrated *into several aspects of the book. In particular, we make it easy for students to explore the Internet.

*Boxed words appear in the Mastering Vocabulary exercise on p. 326.

Focus on the Internet

The Internet is close to center stage here. Notable features are as follows:

primary
focus of
the text

- **Quick start in Chapter 1.** The Internet is introduced in Chapter 1, in a section that gives basic information about the Web, browsers, servers, and Internet protocol.
- **New Internet chapter.** Chapter 7, "The Internet: A Resource for All of Us," focuses on the important aspects of Internet technology, from URLs to links to search engines. This chapter may be used independently of other chapters if students want information early on. Chapter 7 begins on page 195.
- **Planet Internet.** In this edition, Planet Internet has been expanded to a two-page spread at the end of each chapter. Without being technically oriented, each introduces students to some aspect of the World Wide Web. Topics include places to start, global aspects of the Internet, FAQs, business, entrepreneurs, shopping, careers, entertainment, and resources. . . .

Organization of the Text

The text is divided into an introductory photo essay and three parts, followed by one appendix:

division of
text into
parts

- The opening Photo Essay gives students a feeling for the exciting world of computers and shows the diverse ways that people use them.
- Part 1, "An Overview of Computers," has two chapters, one to introduce hardware and another to introduce software, including home and business applications and brief coverage of operating systems.
- Part 2, "Hardware Tools," explores computer hardware including coverage of the central processing unit, input/output, and storage. . . .

Special Features

We have already described the new features called Getting Practical and New Directions, the two-page Planet Internet, and the Visual Internet gallery. In addition, the book offers:

features of
the text

- **Making the Right Connections.** Each chapter includes a feature article on linking people to computers. Topics range from the connectivity of workers in remote regions of Alaska (Chapter 2, page 56) to computers that can notify police if they are stolen (Chapter 4, page 96).
- **Margin notes.** To further engage the student, margin notes are placed throughout the text. The margin notes extend the text material by providing additional information and highlighting interesting applications of computers. . . .

In-Text Learning Aids

Each chapter includes the following pedagogical support:

learning
aids

- At the beginning of each chapter, **learning objectives** provide key concepts for students.
- **Key terms** are boldfaced throughout the text.
- A **Chapter Review** offers a summary of core concepts and boldfaced key terms.
- A **Quick Poll** offers ideas to generate class discussion. . . .

Service

Addison Wesley Longman is committed to providing you with service that is second to none. We would like to thank you for your interest in this textbook, and encourage you to contact us with your questions and comments. Please write to:

resources,
questions,
and
support

is@awl.com if the Information Systems team can be of assistance. We welcome any and all feedback about our company and products.

capron@awl.com if you have questions for the author about the material in this book.

—Capron, *Computers,* pp. xxiii, xxiv, xxv.

To the Student

Some textbooks contain a section titled "To the Student." This section is written specifically for you. It contains practical introductory information about the text. It may, for example, explain features of the book and how to use them, or it may offer suggestions for learning and studying the text. Often, a "To the Instructor" section precedes or follows "To the Student" and contains information useful to your instructor.

EXERCISE 9-1   **Directions:** Read the preface or "To the Student" section in a textbook from one of your other courses and answer the following questions.

1. What is the purpose of the text?

_____

_____

2. How is the textbook organized?

_____

_____

3. What learning aids does it contain? How useful have you found them to be?

_____

_____

Table of Contents

The **table of contents** is an outline of the text. It lists all the important topics and subtopics covered. Glancing through a table of contents will give you an overview of the text and suggest its organization.

Before beginning to read a particular chapter in a textbook, refer to the table of contents again. Although chapters are intended to be separate parts of a book, it is important to see how they fit together as parts of the whole—the textbook itself.

The Opening Chapter

The first chapter of a textbook is one of the most important. Here the author sets the stage for what is to follow. At first glance, the first chapter may not seem to say much, and you may be tempted to skip it. Actually, the opening chapter deserves close attention. More important, it introduces the important terminology used throughout the text.

Typically you can expect to find as many as 40 to 60 new words introduced and defined in the first chapter. These words are the language of the course, so to speak. To be successful in any new subject area, it is essential to learn to read and speak its language.

Typographical Aids

Textbooks contain various typographical aids (arrangements or types of print) that make it easy to pick out what is important to learn and remember. These include the following:

1. **Italic type** (slanted print) is often used to call attention to a particular word or phrase. Often new terms are printed in italics in the sentence in which they are defined.

    The term *drive* is used to refer to internal conditions that force an individual to work toward some goal.

2. **Enumeration** refers to the numbering or lettering of facts and ideas within a paragraph. It is used to emphasize key ideas and to make them easy to locate.

> Consumer behavior and the buying process involve five mental states: (1) awareness of the product, (2) interest in acquiring it, (3) desire or perceived need, (4) action, and (5) reaction or evaluation of the product.

3. **Headings and subheadings** divide the chapters into sections and label the major topic of each section. Basically, they tell in advance what each section will be about. When read in order, the headings and subheadings form a brief outline of the chapter.

4. **Colored print** is used in some texts to emphasize important ideas or definitions.

Chapter Questions

Many textbooks include discussion and/or review questions at the end of each chapter. Try to read these through when you preread the chapter (see Chapter 5). Then, after you have read the chapter, use the questions to review and test yourself. Since the review questions cover the factual content of the chapter, they can help you prepare for objective exams. Discussion questions often deal with interpretations or applications of the content. Use these in preparing for essay exams. Math, science, or technical courses may have problems instead of questions (see p. 322 of this chapter). Here are a few sample review and discussion questions taken from a business marketing textbook:

Review Questions

1. List some product characteristics that are of concern to marketers.
2. Distinguish between a trademark and a brand name.
3. What are some characteristics of good brand names?
4. Describe the three kinds of labels.

Discussion Questions

1. What do you think is the future of generic products?
2. Go to your local food store and look at the ways the products are packaged. Find three examples of packages that have value in themselves. Find three examples of packages that promote the products' effectiveness.
3. There is much controversy about the use of warning labels on products. Outline the pros and cons of this issue.
4. How would you go about developing a brand name for a new type of bread?

Did you notice that the review questions check your knowledge of factual information? These questions ask you to list, describe, or explain. To answer them, you have to recall the information contained in the chapter. The discussion questions, on the other hand, cannot be answered simply by looking up information in the text. Instead, you have to apply the information in the text to a practical situation or pull together and organize information.

Vocabulary List

Textbooks often contain a list of new terms introduced in the book. This list may appear at the beginning or end of individual chapters or at the back of the book. In some texts, new terms are printed in the margin next to the portion of the text in which the term is introduced. Regardless of where they appear, vocabulary lists are a valuable study and review aid. Many instructors include on exams items that test mastery of new terms. Here is a sample vocabulary list taken from a financial management textbook:

Key Terms

assets

budget

cash flow statement

fixed disbursements

liabilities

money market fund

net worth

net worth statement

occasional disbursements

Notice that the author identifies the terms but does not define them. In such cases, mark new terms as you come across them in a chapter. After you have finished the chapter, review each marked term and its definition. To learn the terms, use the index card system suggested in Chapter 4.

Glossary

A **glossary** is a minidictionary that lists alphabetically the important vocabulary used in a book. A glossary is faster and more convenient to use than a dictionary. It does not list all the common meanings of a word, as a dictionary does, but instead gives only the meaning used in the text. Here is an excerpt from the glossary of a health textbook:

continuum a progression of infinite degrees of some characteristic between two extremes

contraception the prevention of conception

contraceptive any technique, drug, or device that prevents conception

control in an experiment, the standard against which observations or conclusions must be checked in order to establish their validity; for example, a person who or animal that has not been exposed to the treatment or condition being studied in the other people or animals

convalescence the period of recovery after a disease

convulsion sudden and repeated involuntary contraction of all of the body's muscles.

—Byer and Shainberg, *Living Well*, p. 311.

Look at the entry for the word *control*. First, you can see that *control* is defined only as the term is used in the field of health science. The word *control* has many other meanings (see the section on multiple-meaning words in Chapter 4). Compare the glossary definition with the collegiate dictionary definition of the same word shown below.

Pronunciation

Meanings

Parts of speech

Etymology

Spelling of other forms
of the entry word

con•trol (kən•trōl′) *tr., v.* **-trolled, -trol•ling, -trols. 1.** To exercise authoritative influence over; direct. See synonyms at **conduct. 2.** To adjust to a requirement; regulate: *controlled trading on the stock market; controls the flow of water.* **3.** To hold in restraint; check: *struggled to control my temper.* **4.** To reduce or prevent the spread of: *control insects; controlled the fire by dousing it with water.* **5a.** To verify or regulate (a scientific experiment) by conducting a parallel experiment or by comparing with another standard. **b.** To verify (an account, for example) by using a duplicate register for comparison. ❖*n.* **1.** Authority or ability to manage or direct: *lost control of the skidding car; the leaders in control of the country.* **2a.** One that controls: a controlling agent, device or organization. **b.** An instrument or set of instruments used to operate, regulate, or guide a machine or vehicle. Often used in the plural. **3.** A restraining device, measure, or limit; a curb: *a control on prices; price controls.* **4a.** A standard of comparison for checking or verifying the results of an experiment. **b.** An individual or group used as a standard of comparison in a control experiment. **5.** An intelligence agent who supervises or instructs another agent. **6.** A spirit presumed to speak or act through a medium. [Middle English *controllen*; from Anglo-Norman *contreroller*, from Medieval Latin *contrārotulāre*, to check by duplicate register, from *contrārotulus*, duplicate register: Latin *contrā-*, contra- + Latin *rotulus*, roll, diminutive of *rota*, wheel; see **ret-** in Appendix I.] —**con•trol′la•bil′i•ty** *n.* —**con•trol′la•ble** *adj.* —**con•trol′la•bly** *adv.*

—*American Heritage Dictionary of the English Language*, p. 400.

Try to pick out the definition of *control* that is closest to the one given in the glossary. Did it take time to find the right definition? You can see that a glossary is a time-saving device.

At the end of a course, a glossary can serve as a useful study aid, since it lists the important terminology introduced throughout the text. Review the glossary and test your recall of the meaning of each entry.

EXERCISE 9-2 **Directions:** Choose a textbook from one of your other courses. (Do not choose a workbook or book of readings.) If you do not have a textbook, use a friend's or borrow one from the library. Answer each of the following questions by referring to the textbook.

Textbook title: _____

1. What learning aids does the book contain?

   _____

   _____

   _____

2. Of what importance is the information given in the preface?

   _____

   _____

3. Preread the opening chapter. What is its function?

   _____

   _____

4. Review the table of contents. How is the subject divided?

   _____

   _____

HOW TEXTBOOK CHAPTERS ARE ORGANIZED

Have you ever walked into an unfamiliar supermarket and felt lost and confused? You did not know where anything was located and thought you would never find the items you needed. How did you finally locate what you needed? You probably found that signs hanging over the aisles indicated the types of products shelved in each section, which enabled you to find the right aisle. Then you no doubt found that similar products were grouped together; for example, all the cereal was in one place, all the meat was in another, and so forth.

You can easily feel lost and confused when reading textbook chapters, too. A chapter can seem like a huge, disorganized collection of facts, ideas, numbers, dates, and events to be memorized. Actually, a textbook chapter is, in one respect, much like a large supermarket. It, too, has signs that identify what is located in each section. These signs are the headings that divide the chapter into topics. Underneath each heading, similar ideas are grouped together, just as similar products are grouped together in a supermarket. Sometimes a group of similar or related ideas is labeled by a subheading (usually set in smaller type than the heading and/or indented differently). In most cases, several paragraphs come under one heading. In this way chapters take a major idea, break it into its important parts, and then break those parts into smaller parts.

You could picture the organization of the present chapter as shown in the diagram below.

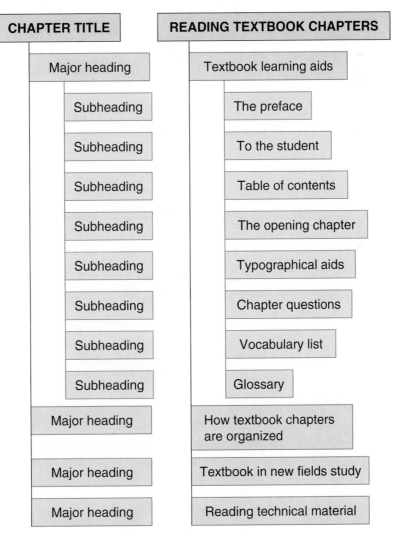

Notice that this chapter has four major headings and that the first major heading is divided into eight subheadings. Since the chapter is divided into four major headings, you know that it covers four major topics. You can also tell that the first major heading discusses eight types of textbook aids. Of course, the number of major headings, subheadings, and paragraphs under each will vary from chapter to chapter in a book.

When you know how a chapter is organized, you can use this knowledge to guide your reading. Once you are familiar with the structure, you will also begin to see how ideas are connected. The chapter will then seem orderly, moving from one idea to the next in a logical fashion.

Look at the following partial listing of headings and subheadings from a chapter of a sociology textbook.

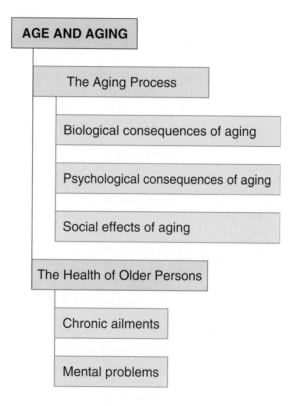

In this chapter on age and aging, "The Aging Process" and "The Health of Older Persons" are the first two major topics. The topic "The Aging Process" is broken into three parts: biological consequences, psychological consequences, and social effects. Although not shown on the diagram, each of these subtopics is further divided into paragraphs that list and describe, respectively, biological consequences, psychological consequences, and the social effects of aging. If there were four paragraphs under the subheading "Biological Consequences of Aging," it would be reasonable to expect that four main points will be presented about these consequences.

You are probably beginning to see that titles and headings, taken together, form a brief outline of a chapter. Later, in Chapter 11, you will see how these headings can help you make a more complete outline of a chapter. For now, think of headings as a guide to reading that directs you through a chapter point by point.

EXERCISE 9-3 **Directions:** On a separate sheet of paper, draw a diagram that shows the organization of Chapter 4 of this book.

EXERCISE 9-4 **Directions:** Choose one of the textbooks that you are using for another course. Select a chapter you have already read and, on a separate sheet of paper, draw an organizational diagram of its contents. Use the diagram on p. 311 as a guide.

APPROACHING TEXTBOOKS IN NEW FIELDS OF STUDY

Each academic discipline is a unique system of study; each takes a specialized approach to the study of the world around us. To illustrate, let us choose as an example a popular house pet—the dog—and consider how various disciplines might approach its study.

- An artist might consider the dog as an object of beauty and record its fluid, flexible muscular structure and meaningful facial expressions on canvas.
- A psychologist might study what human needs are fulfilled by owning a dog.
- The historian might research the historical importance of dogs—their use as guard dogs in warfare or their role in herding sheep.
- A zoologist might trace the evolution of the dog and identify its predecessors.
- A mathematician might treat the dog as a three-dimensional object comprising planes and angles.
- An economist might focus on the supply of and demand for dogs and the amount of business that they generate (kennels, supplies, dog food).
- A biologist would categorize the dog as *Canis familiaris.*
- A physiologist would be concerned with the animal's bodily functions (breathing, heart rate, temperature).

Each academic discipline, then, approaches a given object or event with a different focus or perspective. Each has its own special purposes and interests that define the scope of the discipline. You will find that each discipline has its own method of studying topics with which it is concerned. Because each discipline is unique, you have to read and study each somewhat differently.

In your first few years of college, you are likely to take courses in fields with which you have had no prior experience. Anthropology, political science, or organic chemistry may be new to you, for example. In the beginning, these new fields of study may seem unfamiliar, even foreign. To feel more comfortable with a new field of study, try the following:

Spend more time than usual reading and studying. You are doing more than reading and studying: you are learning how to learn as well.

Learn as much as possible until you discover more about what is expected. You will need as much information as is available to begin to fit information into patterns.

Since you do not know how you will eventually organize and use it, process the same information in several different ways. For example, in an anthropology course, you might learn events and discoveries chronologically (according to their occurrence in time) as well as comparatively (according to similarities and differences among various discoveries). In an accounting course, you might organize information by procedures as well as by important ideas.

Use several methods of learning. Since you are not sure which will be most effective for the types of learning and thinking that are required, try several methods at once. For example, you might highlight textbook information (to promote factual recall) as well as write outlines and summaries (to interpret and consolidate ideas). You might also draw diagrams that map the relations between concepts and ideas.

Ask questions. For example,
- How are the ideas arranged?
- Are there any cause and effect relationships operating?
- What are the practical applications of this information?

Look for similarities between the new subject matter and other academic fields that are familiar to you. If similarities exist, you may be able to modify or adapt existing learning approaches and strategies to fit your new field of study.

Establish an overview of the field. Spend time studying the table of contents of your textbook; it provides an outline of the course. Look for patterns, the progression of ideas, and recurring themes, approaches, or problems.

Obtain additional reference materials, if necessary. Some college texts delve into a subject immediately, providing only a brief introduction or overview in the first chapter. If your text does this, spend an hour or so in the library or online getting an overview of the field. You might locate two or three introductory texts in the field. Study the table of contents of each and skim the first chapter.

EXERCISE 9-5

Directions: List each course you are taking this semester in the space provided. For each course, describe what is unique or different about it and indicate how you have adapted or will adapt your study methods to suit the course.

Course	Unique Characteristics	Study Method Adaptation
1.		
2.		
3.		
4.		
5.		

READING TECHNICAL MATERIAL

If you are taking courses in the sciences, technologies, engineering, data processing, or health-related fields, you are working with a specialized type of textbook. This type of textbook is also used in courses that prepare students for specialized careers, such as food service, air conditioning and refrigeration repair, lab technology, and so forth.

In this section you will see how technical textbooks differ from those used in other classes. You will also learn several specific approaches to reading technical material.

Each of the following paragraphs describes a spice called nutmeg. Read each and decide how they differ.

Paragraph 1

Nutmeg is a spice derived by grating the kernel of the fruit produced by the nutmeg tree. This tree belongs to the nutmeg family, Myristicacae, genus *Myristica,* species *M. fragrans.* The tree grows to a height of seventy feet and is an evergreen. As the fruit of the tree ripens, it hardens and splits open at the top, showing a bright scarlet membrane. The spice called mace is made from this membrane.

Paragraph 2

Nutmeg is a pungent, aromatic spice often added to foods to give them a delicious tang and perfume. It adds a subtle spiciness to desserts and perks up the flavor of such bland dishes as potatoes. Nutmeg comes from a tree grown in warm climates. The nutmeg tree is tall and gracious, with long, pale leaves and beautiful yellow flowers.

Did you notice that the first paragraph presented only precise, factual information? The words used have exact meanings. Some words have technical meanings (*genus, species, Myristica*). Others are everyday words used in a special way (*evergreen, membrane*). An abbreviation, *M.*, was also used. Because of its language, the paragraph does not allow for interpretation or expression of opinion. In fact, you cannot tell whether the writer likes or has ever tasted nutmeg. The purpose of the paragraph is to give clear, detailed information about nutmeg.

The second paragraph is written quite differently. It presents fewer facts and more description. Many words—such as *delicious, beautiful, gracious,* and *subtle*—do not have a precise meaning. They allow room for interpretation and judgment. This paragraph is written to help you imagine how nutmeg tastes as well as to tell where it comes from.

The first paragraph is an example of technical writing. You can see that technical writing is a precise, exact, factual type of writing. This section will discuss particular features of technical writing and suggest approaches to reading technical material.

Fact Density

Technical writing is highly factual and dense (packed with ideas). A large number of facts are closely fitted together in each paragraph. Compared to other types of writing, technical writing may seem crowded with information and difficult to read. Here are a few suggestions on how to handle densely written material:

1. **Read technical material more slowly and carefully than other textbooks.** Allow more time for a technical reading assignment than for other assignments.

2. **Plan on reviewing various sections several times.** Sometimes it is useful to read a section once rather quickly to learn what key ideas it contains. Then read it a second time carefully, fitting together all the facts that explain the key ideas.

3. **Keep a notebook of important information.** In some textbooks, you can underline what is important to remember. (This method is discussed in Chapter 11.) However, since technical books are so highly factual, underlining may not work well—it may seem that everything is important, and you will end up with most of a page underlined. Instead, try using a notebook to

record information you need to remember. Writing information in your own words is a good way to check whether you really understand it.

Copyright © 2009 by Kathleen T. McWhorter

EXERCISE 9-6

Directions: Refer to the two paragraphs about nutmeg on pp. 315–316. Count how many facts (separate pieces of information) each paragraph contains. Write the number in the space provided. Then list several facts as examples.

	Paragraph 1	**Paragraph 2**
Number of facts:	_____	_____
Examples of facts:	1. _____	1. _____
	2. _____	2. _____
	3. _____	3. _____

The Vocabulary of Technical Writing

Reading a technical book is in some ways like visiting a foreign country where an unfamiliar language is spoken. You hear an occasional word you know, but, for the most part, the people are communicating in a way you cannot understand.

Technical writing is built upon a set of precise, exact word meanings in each subject area. Since each field has its own language, you must learn the language in order to understand the material. On the next page are a few sentences taken from several technical textbooks. As you read each sentence, note the large number of technical words used.

Engineering Materials

If the polymer is a mixture of polymers, the component homopolymers (polymers of a single monomer species) and their percentages should be stated.

—Budinski, *Engineering Matrials*, p. 15.

Auto Mechanics

Each free end of the three stator windings is connected to the leads of one negative diode and one positive diode.

—Ellinger, *Auto-Mechanics*, p. 183.

Data Processing

Another advantage of the PERFORM/VARYING statement is that the FROM value and the BY value may be any numeric value (except that the BY value may not be zero).

—Nickerson, *Fundamentals of Structures*, p. 271.

In the preceding examples, some words are familiar ones with new, unfamiliar meanings (*FROM, BY*). Others are words you may never have seen before (*monomer, stator*).

In technical writing, there are two types of specialized vocabulary: (1) familiar words with new technical meanings, and (2) specialized terms.

Examples of each are given in Table 9-1.

TABLE 9-1   Examples of Specialized Vocabulary in Technical Writing

Field	Word	Technical Meaning
Familiar words		
chemistry	base	a chemical compound that reacts with an acid to form a salt
electrical engineering	ground	a conductor that makes an electrical connection with the earth
nursing	murmur	an abnormal sound heard from a body organ (especially the heart)
Specialized terms		
computer science	modem	an interface (connector) that allows the computer to send and receive digital signals over telephone lines or through satellites
astronomy	magnetosphere	the magnetic field that surrounds the earth or another magnetized planet
biology	cocci	spherically shaped bacteria

Tips for Learning Technical Vocabulary

Many of the techniques you have already learned for developing your general vocabulary also work with technical vocabulary. Here are some ways to apply these techniques:

1. **Context clues (see Chapter 2) are commonly included in technical writing.** A definition clue is most frequently used when a word is introduced for the first time. As each new word is introduced, mark it in your text and later transfer it to your notebook. Organize this section of your notebook by chapter. Use the card system described in Chapter 4 to learn words you are having trouble remembering.

2. **Analyzing word parts (see Chapter 3) is a particularly useful approach for developing technical vocabulary.** The technical words in many fields are created from particular sets of prefixes, roots, and suffixes. Here are several examples from the field of medicine.

Prefix	Meaning	Example	Definition
cardi	heart	cardiogram	test that measures contractions of the heart
		cardiology	medical study of diseases and functioning of the heart
		cardiologist	physician who specializes in heart problems
hem/hema/hemo	blood	hematology	study of the blood
		hemophilia	disease in which blood fails to clot properly
		hemoglobin	protein contained in the red blood cells

Most technical fields have a core of commonly used prefixes, roots, and suffixes. As you read technical material, keep a list of common word parts in your notebook. Add to the list throughout the course. For those you have difficulty remembering, use a variation of the word card system suggested in Chapter 4. Write the word on the front and its meaning, its pronunciation, and a sample sentence on the back.

3. **Learn to pronounce each new term you come across.** Pronouncing a word is a good way to fix it in your memory and will also help you remember its spelling.

4. **Make use of the glossary in the back of the textbook, if it has one.** (See pp. 308–309 in this chapter for further information on using a glossary.)

5. **If you are majoring in a technical field, it may be worthwhile to buy a subject area dictionary (see Chapter 4).** Nursing students, for example, often buy a copy of Taber's *Cyclopedic Medical Dictionary*.

Abbreviations and Notations

In many technical fields, sets of abbreviations and notations (signs and symbols) provide shortcuts to writing out complete words or meanings.

Examples:

Field	Symbol	Meaning
Chemistry	Al	aluminum
	F	fluorine
	Fe	iron
Biology	X	crossed with
	Y	female organism
	0	male organism
Physics	M	mass
Astronomy	D	diameter
	D	distance

To understand technical material, you must learn the abbreviations and notation systems that are used in a specific field. Check to see whether lists of abbreviations and symbols are included in the appendix (reference section) in the back of the textbook. Make a list in your notebook of those you need to learn. Make a point of using these symbols in your class notes whenever possible. Putting them to use regularly is an excellent way to learn them.

Graphic Aids

Most technical books contain numerous drawings, charts, tables, and diagrams. These may make the text look difficult and complicated, but such graphic aids actually help explain and make the text easier to understand. Illustrations, for example, give a visual picture of the idea or process being explained. An example of a diagram taken from a computer programming text appears in Figure 9-1. The text to which the diagram refers is included on the next page. Would you find the text easy to understand without the diagram?

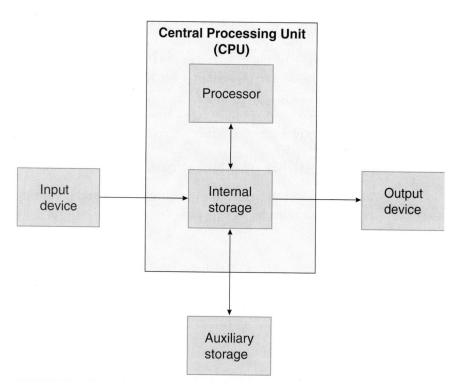

Figure 9-1   The Organization of a Computer

An *input device* is a mechanism that accepts data from outside the computer and converts it into an electronic form understandable to the computer. The data that is accepted is called *input data,* or simply *input.* For example, one common way of entering input into a computer is to type it with a typewriter-like *keyboard.*

An *output device* performs the opposite function of an input device. An output device converts data from its electronic form inside the computer to a form that can be used outside. The converted data is called *output data,* or simply *output.* . . .

Between the input devices and the output devices is the component of the computer that does the actual computing or processing. This is the *central processing unit,* or CPU. Input data is converted into an electronic form by an input device and sent to the central processing unit where the data is stored. In the CPU the data is used in calculations or other types of processing to produce the solution to the desired problem. The central processing unit contains two basic units: the internal storage and the processor. The *internal storage* is the "memory" of the computer. The *processor* is the unit that executes instructions to the program. Among other things, the processor contains electronic circuits that do arithmetic and perform logical operations. The final component of a computer is the auxiliary storage. This component stores data that is not currently being processed by the computer and programs that are not currently in use.

—Nickerson, *Fundamentals of Structured COBOL,* p. 2.

Here are a few suggestions on how to use illustrations:

1. **Go back and forth between the text and the illustrations.** Illustrations are intended to be used together with the paragraphs that refer to them. You may have to stop reading several times to refer to an illustration. For example, when *input device* is mentioned in the preceding example, stop reading and find where the input device is located on the diagram. You may also have to reread parts of the explanation several times.

2. **Study each illustration carefully.** First, read the title or caption. These tell what the illustration is intended to show. Then look at each part of the illustration and try to see how they are connected. Notice any abbreviations, symbols, arrows, or labels. In the example given, the arrows are important. They suggest the direction or order in which the parts of the computer operate.

3. **Test your understanding of illustrations by drawing and labeling an illustration of your own without looking at the one in the text.** Then compare your drawing with the text. Notice whether anything is left out. If so, continue drawing and checking until your drawing is complete and correct. Include these drawings in your notebook, and use them for review and study.

Examples and Sample Problems

Technical books include numerous examples and sample problems. Use the following suggestions when working with these:

1. **Pay more attention to examples than you normally do in other textbooks.** Examples and sample problems will often help you understand how rules, principles, theories, or formulas are actually used. Think of examples as connections between ideas on paper and practical, everyday use of those ideas.

2. **Be sure to work through sample problems.** Make sure you understand what was done in each step and why. For particularly difficult problems, try writing in your notebook a step-by-step list of how to solve that type of problem. Refer to sample problems as guides or models when doing problems at the end of the chapter or others assigned by the instructor.

3. **Use the problems at the end of the chapter as a self-test.** As you work through each problem, keep track of rules and formulas that you did not know and had to look up. Make note of the types of problems you could not solve without referring to the sample problems. You will need to do more work with each of these types.

EXERCISE 9-7   **Directions:** Read the following excerpt from a textbook chapter titled "Mechanics" and answer the questions that follow.

Mechanics

Potential Energy

An object may store energy by virtue of its position. Such stored energy is called *potential energy,* for in the stored state an object has the potential for doing work. A stretched or compressed spring, for example, has potential energy. When a BB gun is cocked, energy is stored in the spring. A stretched rubber band has potential energy because of its position, for if it is part of a slingshot it is capable of doing work.

The chemical energy in fuels is potential energy, for it is actually energy of position when looked at from a microscopic point of view. This energy is available when the positions of electrical charges within and between molecules are altered , that is, when a chemical change takes place. Potential energy is possessed by any substance that can do work through chemical action. The energy of coal, gas, electric batteries, and foods is potential energy. Potential energy may be due to an elevated position of a body. Water in an elevated reservoir and the heavy ram of a pile driver when lifted have energy because of position. The energy of elevated positions is usually called *gravitational potential energy.*

The measure of the gravitational potential energy that an elevated body has is the work done against gravity in lifting it. The upward force required is equal to the weight of the body W, and the work done in lifting it through a height h is given by the product Wh; so we say

$$\text{Gravitational potential energy} = Wh$$

The potential energy of an elevated body depends only on its weight and vertical displacement h and is independent of the path taken to raise it (Figure A).

Kinetic Energy

If we push on an object, we can set it in motion. More specifically, if we do work on an object, we can change the energy of motion of that object. If an object is in motion, by virtue of that motion it is capable of doing work. We call energy of motion *kinetic energy* (Figure B, next page). The kinetic energy of an object is equal to half its mass [m] multiplied by its velocity [v] squared.

$$\text{Kinetic energy} = \tfrac{1}{2}mv^2$$

It can be shown that the kinetic energy of a moving body is equal to the work it can do in being brought to rest.*

$$\text{Net force } [F] \times \text{distance } [d] = \text{kinetic energy}$$

or, in shorthand notation,

$$Fd = \tfrac{1}{2}mv^2$$

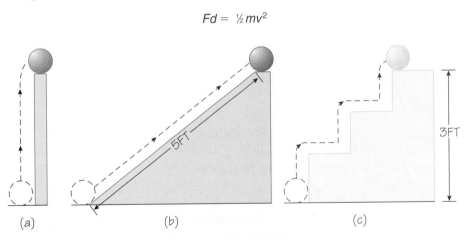

(a)   (b)   (c)

Figure A   The potential energy of the 9-lb ball is the same in each case because the work done in elevating its 3 feet is the same whether it is (a) lifted with 9 lb of force, or (b) pushed with 6 lb of force up the 5-foot incline, or (c) lifted with 9 lb up each 1-foot stair—no work is done in moving it horizontally (neglecting friction).

*If we multiply both sides of $F = ma$ (Newton's second law) by d, we get $Fd = mad$; since $d = \tfrac{1}{2}at^2$, we can say $Fd = ma \, (\tfrac{1}{2}at^2) = \tfrac{1}{2}m(at)^2$; and substituting $v = at$, we get $Fd = \tfrac{1}{2}mv^2$.

Accident investigators are well aware that an automobile traveling at 60 miles per hour has four times as much kinetic energy as an automobile traveling 30 miles per hour. This means that a car traveling at 60 miles per hour will skid four times as far when its brakes are locked as a car traveling 30 miles per hour. This is because the velocity is squared for kinetic energy.

Question

When the brakes of a car traveling at 90 miles per hour are locked, how much farther will the car skid compared to locking the brakes at 30 miles per hour?

—Hewitt, *Conceptual Physics*, pp. 54–56.

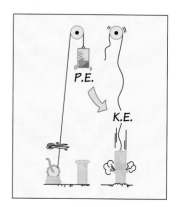

Figure B   The potential energy of the elevated ram is converted to kinetic energy when released.

1. Underline the sentences that best define the terms *potential energy* and *kinetic energy*.

2. List the technical or specialized terms used in this selection. Define as many as possible.

3. List the abbreviations (notations) used in the article and give their meanings.

_____

_____

4. The writer uses examples as a means of explaining various ideas. List four of these examples and tell what each explains.

    a. _____

    b. _____

    c. _____

    d. _____

5. This excerpt contains two illustrations (Figures A and B). The author does not discuss either in the text itself. Their use is left up to the reader. Describe when and how often you referred to each diagram.

_____

_____

6. What is Figure A intended to show?

_____

_____

7. What is Figure B intended to show?

_____

_____

8. What is the purpose of the question at the end of the article? To what type of energy does this question refer?

_____

_____

9. In your own words, explain the difference between potential energy and kinetic energy.

_____

_____

_____

LEARNING STYLE TIPS

If you tend to be a(n) . . .	Then grasp textbook organization by . . .
Applied learner	Writing a list of what you expect to learn from the chapter in the order in which you expect it to be presented
Conceptual learner	Studying the headings in the table of contents and discovering how they fit together

MASTERING VOCABULARY

Directions: Determine the meaning of each of the following words used in this chapter. Then insert each one in the sentence in which it makes most sense.

integrated (p. 303)   converts (p. 321)

global (p. 304)   component (p. 321)

diverse (p. 304)   executes (p. 321)

derived (p. 315)   auxiliary (p. 321)

subtle (p. 316)   altered (p. 322)

1. A generator _____ mechanical power into electrical power.

2. Congress makes laws and the president _____ them.

3. The committee _____ integrated many different ideas into its final plan.

4. By examining it closely, they determined that the document had been _____ .

5. She _____ great pleasure from her walk in the park.

6. The use of satellites has made instantaneous _____ communication possible.

7. To upgrade your stereo system, first you will need to install a new amplifier _____ .

8. The town meeting provided an opportunity for _____ ideas to be expressed.

9. It is wise to have _____ engines on a sailboat.

10. A _____ joke may be hard to understand at first.

SELF-TEST SUMMARY

What types of learning aids do textbooks contain?	At the beginning of a textbook, the table of contents and opening chapter provide information on the scope and focus of the book. Within each chapter, typographical aids—italic type, enumeration, headings and subheadings, and colored print—call attention to key information. At the end of each chapter, discussion questions and vocabulary lists provide an outline of important information and key words presented in the chapter. At the end of the textbook, the glossary provides a quick reference for important vocabulary presented in the book.
How are textbooks organized?	Textbooks are also organized to express ideas as clearly as possible. Through the use of headings and subheadings, chapters are divided into a number of sections that deal with different aspects of the subject covered in the chapter.
How can I adapt to new fields of study?	Techniques include: spend more time, overlearn, process information in several ways, use several methods of learning, ask questions, look for similarities, get an overview, and obtain reference materials.
What features distinguish technical material?	The distinguishing features of technical material include fact density, specialized vocabulary, abbreviations and notations, drawings and illustrations, and examples and sample problems.

Getting More Practice with . . .
Reading Textbooks

WORKING TOGETHER

Directions: Bring one of your textbooks to class. You may bring a textbook from another course or obtain one from the library. After your instructor forms groups, exchange texts with group members and review the learning aids in each text. Each student should evaluate the learning aids in each. Then, through discussion, make a list of the learning aids contained in each text and select the textbook that provides the "best" learning assistance. Groups may compare "winning" textbooks and choose an overall winner. Class members or the instructor may notify the course instructor(s) using the winning textbook that theirs was chosen.

GOING ONLINE

Internet Activities

1. Academic Success: Reading Textbooks

   http://www.dartmouth.edu/~acskills/success/reading.html

   Dartmouth College offers several online handouts designed to help students read textbooks more effectively and efficiently. Two featured documents are "Six Reading Myths" and "Harvard Report on Reading." Read them over and discuss with your classmates how these documents apply to your current experiences. Offer each other suggestions for improving your reading skills.

2. 'Twas the Night Before Christmas

   http://xmasfun.com/Stories/NightB4/Default.htm

   http://xmasfun.com/Stories/NightBeforeTechnical.asp

   Compare these two versions of this classic holiday poem. The one written in technical language is meant to be humorous, of course, but note how it illustrates the characteristics of technical writing. Try writing a technical version of how you spent your day. Give it to some friends and see if they can figure out what you did.

Companion Website

For additional readings, exercises, and Internet activities, visit this book's Companion Website at:

http://www.ablongman.com/mcwhorter

If you need a user name and password, please see your instructor.

My Reading Lab

For more practice with reading textbooks, visit MyReadingLab, click on the Reading Skills tab, and then click on Reading Textbooks—Grand Canyon, Arizona.

http://www.ablongman.com/myreadinglab

TEST-TAKING TIPS

Studying for Exams in Your Other Courses

Exams in your courses, other than this one, are based on textbook and lecture content. Use the following suggestions to improve your ability to prepare for tests in your other college courses.

- **Review textbook chapters.** Reread your highlighting and marking. Usually you will not have time to reread entire chapters, especially for exams covering multiple chapters. Review chapter summaries and outlines, notes, summaries, or maps you have prepared.

- **Review lecture notes.** Reread your notes and highlight important information.

- **Test yourself.** Rereading highlighting by itself is not enough. Everything looks familiar when you reread. You must find out what you have learned and what you still need to learn. Construct tests for yourself or study with a classmate, quizzing each other on chapter and lecture content.

- **Review previous exams and quizzes.** Review exams and quizzes you have already taken in the course. Mark items you missed and look for a pattern of error. Is there a particular type of question you miss? Are you weak in particular topics? If you need help, be sure to talk to your instructor for advice.

Chapter 9
Mastery Test 1
Textbook Skills

Name _____

Section _____ Date _____

Number right _____ x 20 points = Score _____

_____ 1. Light energy that has traveled millions of miles from the sun is captured by the chloroplasts of plant cells and converted into chemical energy. Of the following words from this sentence, the one that is an example of specialized vocabulary is
   a. "light."
   b. "millions."
   c. "chloroplasts."
   d. "converted."

_____ 2. When an endotherm goes into the state of reduced activity known as torpor, its metabolic rate, body temperature, heart rate, and respiration rate decrease, thereby reducing its consumption of energy. Of the following words from this sentence, the only one that can be defined using context clues is
   a. "endotherm."
   b. "torpor."
   c. "metabolic."
   d. "respiration."

_____ 3. Over 30 different substances enhance the clotting of blood, also known as coagulation; numerous factors can contribute to anticoagulation, some of them producing life-threatening effects. Of the following words from this sentence, the only one that can be defined by analyzing word parts is
   a. "substance."
   b. "anticoagulation."
   c. "enhance."
   d. "clotting."

_____ 4. Of the following sentences, choose the one that is most factually dense.
   a. In the world of biology, it is typical for plants to obtain most of the nitrogen they require from various nitrates that have been dissolved in water in the soil.
   b. Not to be confused with meiosis, the remarkably accurate mechanism known as mitosis consists of a multistage process of cell division in plants and animals.
   c. Bacteria and other prokaryotes reproduce most commonly by a specific type of cell division called binary fission, meaning "dividing in half" or "splitting."
   d. When a semipermeable membrane, such as a cell wall, divides two levels of a solvent, the molecules from the greater concentration of solvent will pass through the membrane until equilibrium is reached.

_____ 5. Of the following sentences, choose the one that contains notations that would be most important to learn in a chemistry course.
   a. Sodium (Na) and chlorine (Cl) can be combined to form salt.
   b. The Perseids meteor shower is typically most visible between 1 and 4 a.m. EDT (Eastern Daylight Time).
   c. Nitrogen makes up over 78 percent of the earth's atmosphere.
   d. X-rays are electromagnetic waves that can penetrate thick materials.

Name _____

Section _____ Date _____

Number right _____ x 20 points = Score _____

Directions: For questions 1–3 below, use the portion of the table of contents from an economics textbook shown here.

_____ 1. To find out what the term "logrolling" means, you should look under the heading
   a. "Government Spending."
   b. "Taxation."
   c. "The Federal Budget."
   d. "Summary."

_____ 2. The heading "The Federal Budget" includes all of the following subtopics except
   a. Majority Rule: The Power of the Median Voter.
   b. Deficits and Debt.
   c. Problems of Deficit Reduction.
   d. The Case for a Balanced Budget.

_____ 3. The textbook learning aids featured in the table of contents include
   a. examples and figures.
   b. a vocabulary list.
   c. chapter questions.
   d. all of the above.

Directions: For questions 4 and 5, refer to the following excerpt from the preface of a health textbook.

As we enter a new millennium, health challenges once considered unimaginable have emerged. Needless to say, writing an introductory health text presents an interesting challenge. As quickly as the last words are written for one edition, a new discovery is announced that probably should have been included in the book. So today's text has gone high tech, linking you to the latest developments in disease prevention, health promotion, and policy change through the *Access to Health* companion Web site at www.abacon.com and the interactive CD-ROM you received along with this text.

Access to Health is designed not just to help teach you health facts, but to help you think of health as a broader concept. Many chapters include special feature boxes designed to help you build health behavior skills as well as think about and apply the concepts: **"Reality Check"** boxes focus attention on potential risks and safety issues, often as they relate to college-age students; **"Health in a Diverse World"** boxes promote acceptance of diversity on college campuses and assist you in adjusting to an increasingly diverse world; **"Consumer Health"** boxes focus on health issues as they relate to consumer skills; and, **"Assess Yourself"** boxes allow you the chance to examine your behaviors and determine ways to improve your health.

—Donatelle and Davis, *Access to Health*, pp. xix–xxi.

_____ 4. According to the preface, this textbook provides access to the latest health information through
    a. its companion Web site.
    b. "Assess Yourself" boxes.
    c. including new discoveries in each new edition.
    d. "Reality Check" boxes.

_____ 5. The special feature box intended to help you find ways to improve your own health is called
    a. "Reality Check."
    b. "Health in a Diverse World."
    c. "Consumer Health."
    d. "Assess Yourself."

Name _____

Section _____ Date _____

Number right _____ x 20 points = Score _____

Directions: Read the selection and answer the questions that follow.

The Physiology of Stress

In his 1956 book *The Stress of Life,* Canadian physician Hans Selye (1907–1982) greatly advanced the study of stress. Selye noted that many environmental factors—heat, cold, pain, toxins, viruses, and so on—can throw the body out of balance. These factors, called *stressors,* force the body to respond by mobilizing its resources and preparing the individual to fight or flee. Using data from many animal studies, Selye concluded that "stress" consists of a series of physiological reactions that occur in three phases:

1. *The alarm phase,* in which the organism mobilizes to meet the threat with a package of biological responses that allow the person or animal to escape from danger no matter what the stressor is: crossing a busy street or having deadline pressures at work.

2. *The resistance phase,* in which the organism attempts to resist or cope with a threat that cannot be avoided. During this phase, the body's physiological responses are in high gear—a response to the original stressor—but this very mechanism makes the body more susceptible to other stressors. For example, when your body has mobilized to fight off the flu, you may find that you are more easily annoyed by minor frustrations. In most cases, the body will eventually adapt to the stressor and return to normal.

3. *The exhaustion phase,* which occurs if the stressor persists. Over time, the body's resources may be overwhelmed. Depleted of energy, the body becomes vulnerable to fatigue, physical problems, and eventually illness.

Not all stress is bad, however. Some stress, which Selye called *eustress* (YOO-stress), is positive and feels good, even if it also requires the body to produce short-term energy: competing in an athletic event, falling in love, working hard on a project you enjoy. Selye did not believe that all stress could be avoided or that people should aim for a stress-free life, which is an impossible goal anyway. The goal is to minimize wear and tear on the system.

Selye recognized that psychological stressors, such as fighting with a loved one or grief over loss, can have as great an impact on health as do physical stressors, such as heat, crowds, or noise. He also observed that some factors *mediate,* or act as buffers, between the stressor and the stress. A comfortable climate or a nutritious diet, for example, can soften the impact of an environmental stressor such as pollution. Conversely, a harsh climate or a poor diet can make such stressors worse. But by and large, Selye concentrated on the biological responses that result from a person's or animal's attempt to adapt to environmental demands. A diagram of his view would look like this:

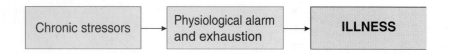

Health psychologists have since expanded on Selye's model of stressors and illness, hoping to find out why individuals differ so much in their susceptibility to stress and vulnerability to disease. They want to know why, of two people who are exposed to a flu virus, one is sick all winter and the other doesn't even get the sniffles; or why, of two people who have high-pressure jobs, one gets heart disease and the other doesn't. They want to know how external stressors "get under the skin" and make trouble for some people but not others.

One of the most intensively studied bodily systems in relation to stress is the immune system. In the 1980s, scientists created an interdisciplinary field with the cumbersome name **psychoneuroimmunology**, or *PNI* for short: "psycho" for psychological processes such as emotions and perceptions, "neuro" for the nervous and endocrine systems, and "immunology" for the immune system. The white blood cells of the immune system are designed to do two things: (1) recognize foreign substances (antigens), such as flu viruses, bacteria, and tumor cells; and (2) destroy or deactivate them. When an antigen invades the body, white blood cells called *phagocytes* are dispatched to ingest and eliminate the intruder. If this effort is unsuccessful, other white blood cells, called *lymphocytes,* and other processes of the immune system are summoned. To defend the body against antigens, the immune system deploys different cells as weapons, depending on the nature of the enemy.

Prolonged stress can suppress some or many of these cells that fight disease and infection. For instance, in one study 420 people heroically volunteered to fight in the war against the common cold. Some were given nose drops containing viruses known to cause a cold's miserable symptoms and others received uncontaminated nose drops. Everyone was then quarantined for a week. The results: contaminated people who were under high stress, who felt their lives were "unpredictable, uncontrollable, and overwhelming," were twice as likely to develop colds as those reporting low levels of stress.

A second approach to studying individual vulnerability to stress focuses on *psychological factors*, such as personality traits, perceptions, and emotions. An event that is stressful or enraging for one person may be challenging for another and boring for a third. Likewise, losing a job, traveling to China, or having "too much" work is stressful to some people and not to others.

A third approach focuses on *how the individual behaves when under stress* and how he or she manages it. Not all individuals who are under stress behave in the same way. Some drink too much, drive recklessly, or fail to take care of themselves, all of which increases their risk of illness or accident. Others, in contrast, cope constructively and thereby reduce the effects of stress.

Thus, unlike Selye, who defined stress narrowly as the body's response to any environmental threat, health psychologists now define stress to include qualities of the individual (e.g., how the person perceives the stressor) and whether the individual feels able to cope with the stressor.

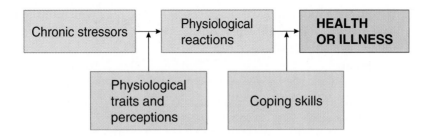

Psychological stress is caused by an interaction of the person and the environment, in which the person believes that the situation strains or overwhelms his or her resources and is endangering his or her ability to cope.

_____ 1. Which of the following is the best definition of the word "stressors" as it is used in the selection?
   a. psychological reactions to the world
   b. how an individual copes with the environment
   c. germs or bacteria which cause illness
   d. environmental factors that throw the body out of balance

_____ 2. The abbreviation "PNI" stands for which of the following?
   a. psychoneuroimmunology
   b. physiology and neurological institute
   c. the three phases of stress
   d. psychological factors

_____ 3. Selye defined "eustress" as stress that
   a. keeps one from acting.
   b. lasts a long time.
   c. is helpful.
   d. someone else has.

_____ 4. The selection uses _all_ of the following learning aids _except_
   a. boldface.
   b. diagrams.
   c. enumeration.
   d. marginal notations.

_____ 5. Which of the following is a type of white blood cell mentioned in the selection?
   a. phagocytes
   b. antigens
   c. bacteria
   d. viruses

_____ 6. The experiment with the common cold was done to show the relationship between
   a. loneliness and tension.
   b. stress and physical illness.
   c. quarantine and stress.
   d. coping skills and emotions.

_____ 7. If you are easily annoyed when you have the flu, you are in which of the following phases of stress?
   a. chronic
   b. resistance
   c. alarm
   d. exhaustion

_____ 8. Health psychologists recently have added which of the following to Selye's model of stressors and illness?
   a. illness
   b. stressors
   c. individual differences in response to stressors
   d. physiological alarm

_____ 9. Which of the following best describes the purpose of the diagrams?
   a. to analyze a debate
   b. to outline a problem
   c. to classify an example
   d. to show a process

_____ 10. The selection would best fit as part of which of the following larger textbook sections?
   a. Stress and the Body
   b. Avoiding Illnesses
   c. Coping with Stress
   d. The Sense of Control

Name _____

Section _____ Date _____

Number right* _____ x 10 points = Score _____

Legible Clothing

Joseph A. DeVito

What do the clothes you wear reveal about you? In this article, taken from a book titled *Human Communication,* the author discusses the messages that clothing sends about the wearer.

Vocabulary Preview

status (par. 1) social standing or position

paraphrase (par. 3) explain in other words

affiliation (par. 4) association or connection with a group

metaphorical (par. 4) one thing representing another

satirizing (par. 4) making fun of

insignia (par. 5) a distinguishing sign

1   Legible clothing is anything that you wear which contains some verbal message; such clothing can literally be read. In some instances it says status; it tells others that you are, for example, rich or stylish or youthful. The Gucci or Louis Vuitton logos on your luggage communicate your status and financial position. In a similar way your sweatshirt saying Bulls or Pirates communicates your interest in sports and perhaps your favorite team.

2   John Molloy, in *Molloy's Live for Success,* advises you to avoid legible clothing except the kind that says rich. Legible clothing, argues Molloy, communicates lower status and lack of power. Humorist Fran Lebowitz says that legible clothes "are an unpleasant indication of the general state of things. I mean, be realistic. If people don't want to listen to you, what makes you think they want to hear from your sweater?"

3   Yet legible clothing is being bought and worn in record numbers. Many designers and manufacturers have their names integrated into the design of the clothing: DKNY, Calvin Klein, L.L. Bean, and Levi's are just a few examples. At the same time that you are paying extra to buy the brand name, you also provide free advertising for the designer and manufacturer. To paraphrase Vidal Sassoon, "As long as you look good, so does the advertiser. And, when you look bad, the advertiser looks bad." Imitators—the cheap knock-offs you see on the street—are resisted by the

*To calculate the number right, use items 1–10 under "Mastery Test Skills Check."

original manufacturers not only because these impact on their own sales. In fact, the impact is probably minimal since the person who would pay $6,000 for a Rolex would not buy a $9 imitation on the street. Rather, such knock-offs are resisted because they are perceived to be worn by the wrong people—people who would destroy the image the manufacturer wishes to communicate.

An example of legible clothing

4   T-shirts and sweatshirts are especially popular as message senders. In one study, the types of T-shirt messages were classified into four main categories. The order in which these are presented reflects the shirts the subjects (600 male and female college students) considered their favorites. Thirty-three percent, for example, considered affiliation message shirts their favorites while 17 percent considered those with personal messages their favorites. The order from most favorite down was:

1. Affiliation messages, for example, a club or school name. It communicates that you are a part of a larger group.

2. Trophy, for example, a shirt from a high-status event such as a concert or perhaps a ski lodge. This is a way of saying that the wearer was in the right place.

3. Metaphorical expressions, for example, pictures of rock groups or famous athletes.

4. Personal messages, for example, "beliefs, philosophies, and causes, as well as satirizing current events."

5   Another important dimension of clothing, currently being debated in educational and legal circles, is the use of gang clothing. Some argue that gang clothing and gang colors contribute to violence in the schools and should therefore be prohibited. Others argue that gang clothing—or any clothing—is covered by the first amendment to the Constitution. Consider a specific case. In Harvard, Illinois, you can be arrested for wearing a Star of David in public—not because it's a religious symbol, but because certain gangs use it as a gang symbol. In 1993, Harvard passed a law that makes it illegal "for any person within the city to knowingly use, display, or wear

colors, emblems, or insignia" that would communicate their membership in (or sympathy for) gangs.

6   Consider your own use of legible clothing. Do you wear legible clothing? What messages do you wish to communicate? Are you successful in communicating the messages you want? Do labels influence your perceptions of others? How do you feel about the law in Harvard, Illinois? Would you support such a law in your own community?

MASTERY TEST SKILLS CHECK

Directions: Choose the best answer for each of the following questions.

Checking Your Comprehension

_____ 1. The main point of the reading is that legible clothing
   a. is only worn by members of the lower class.
   b. has a negative effect on sales of higher-priced clothing.
   c. says something about the wearer.
   d. is often banned in high schools.

_____ 2. The main idea of paragraph 4 is that
   a. many people wear personal messages on shirts.
   b. college students are the most likely group to wear legible clothing.
   c. sports sweatshirts indicate your favorite team.
   d. messages on shirts fit into four categories.

_____ 3. Which of the following statements best summarizes the main point of paragraph 5?
   a. Legible clothing is a form of free speech protected by the U.S. Constitution.
   b. The role of gang-related clothing is being discussed by both lawyers and teachers.
   c. The Star of David has become a gang symbol in Illinois.
   d. Gang violence in schools is increasing.

_____ 4. According to the passage, manufacturers are mainly against brand-name knock-offs because
   a. knock-offs destroy the image the manufacturer wants to communicate.
   b. the profits of the manufacturers are effectively cut in half by knock-offs.
   c. knock-offs do not provide free advertising for the manufacturers.
   d. the brand-name products generally cost more than the knock-offs.

_____ 5. According to the passage, which of the following examples of T-shirt messages is in the most popular category for wearers?
   a. Rolling Stones Spring 1995 tour
   b. a Michael Jordan picture
   c. "Life, liberty, and the pursuit of chocolate"
   d. Howard University

_____ 6. Which of the following is an example of an affiliation message?
   a. a photo of an NFL footbal player
   b. a logo on a T-shirt opposing the testing of cosmetics on animals
   c. a pair of Levi jeans
   d. a ball cap with a sports team emblem

Applying Your Skills

_____ 7. The learning aid contained in this selection is
   a. enumeration.
   b. subheadings.
   c. italics.
   d. vocabulary lists.

_____ 8. The main purpose of the questions at the end of this selection is to
   a. review the main points.
   b. emphasize technical vocabulary.
   c. make you think about yourself.
   d. solve problems.

_____ 9. In paragraph 4, "affiliation" is used to mean
   a. dependent.
   b. connection.
   c. personal.
   d. negative.

_____ 10. The dictionary defines "legible" as "able to be read." As used in the selection, "legible" includes all of the following *except*
   a. pictures.
   b. words and numbers.
   c. shape of a shirt.
   d. logos and labels.

Studying Words

_____ 11. In paragraph 1, the word "status" is best defined as
   a. situation.
   b. legal condition.
   c. powerlessness.
   d. rank or position.

_____ 12. What is the best definition of the word "integrated" as it is used in paragraph 3?
   a. open to all people without restriction
   b. made of something
   c. calculated the integer of
   d. acceptance as part of a group

_____ 13. What part of speech is the word "metaphorical" (paragraph 4)?
   a. adjective
   b. adverb
   c. noun
   d. verb

_____ 14. The best synonym for the word "prohibited" as it is used in paragraph 5 is
   a. withheld.
   b. hindered.
   c. forbidden.
   d. disqualified.

_____15. What is the correct pronunciation of
the word "insignia" (paragraph 5)?

a. in SINE ee uh

b. in SIG nee uh

c. in sig NEE uh

d. in sine EE uh

> For more practice, ask your instructor
> for an opportunity to work on
> the mastery tests that appear in the
> Test Bank.

Chapter 10

Reading Graphic and Electronic Sources

Getting Started with . . .

Reading Graphic and Electronic Sources

This student is using a variety of sources to write a paper. In the sources he uses, he will no doubt encounter a variety of graphics, including maps, tables, charts, and photographs. The student is using both print and electronic sources; specialized skills are required for reading each. This chapter focuses on reading graphics effectively as well as on reading electronic sources, such as Web sites.

Students sometimes complain that reading graphics (tables, charts, diagrams, and photographs) is time-consuming. Others complain about assignments that require Internet research. These students do not realize that graphic aids are designed to make the chapter itself easier to read and that they summarize and condense information and actually save you time. In addition, Web sites and other electronic sources provide access to current, up-to-date information.

Try reading the following paragraph *without* looking at the diagram shown in Figure 10-1.

Skeletal muscle fibers, like most living cells, are soft and surprisingly fragile. Yet skeletal muscles can exert tremendous power—how so? The reason they are not ripped apart as they exert force is that thousands of their fibers are bundled together by connective tissue, which provides strength and support to the muscle as a whole. Each muscle fiber is enclosed in a delicate connective tissue called an **endomysium**. Several sheathed muscle fibers are then wrapped by a coarser fibrous membrane called a **perimysium** to form a bundle of fibers called a **fascicle**. Many fascicles are bound together by an even tougher "overcoat" of connective tissue called an **epimysium**, which covers the entire muscle. The epimysia blend into strong cordlike **tendons**, or sheetlike **aponeuroses**, which attach muscles indirectly to bones, cartilages, or connective tissue coverings of each other.

—Marieb, *Essential of Human Anatomy & Physiology*, pp. 162, 164.

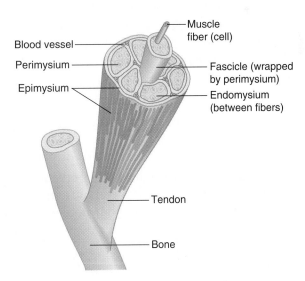

Figure 10-1   Diagram of connective tissue wrappings of skeletal muscles

—Marieb, *Essentials of Human Anatomy & Physiology*, p. 164.

Did you find the paragraph difficult and confusing? Now study Figure 10-1 and then reread the paragraph.

Now the paragraph is easier to understand. You can see that graphics are a valuable aid, not a hindrance. This chapter will describe the various types of graphics commonly included in college textbooks. You will learn how to approach and interpret each kind. You will also learn about various types of electronic learning aids.

A GENERAL APPROACH TO GRAPHICS

Graphics include tables, charts, graphs, diagrams, photographs, and maps. Here is a general step-by-step approach to reading graphics. As you read, apply each step to the graph shown in Figure 10-2 (Step 7 does not apply to this example).

1. **Read the title or caption.** The title will identify the subject and may suggest the relationship being described.

2. **Discover how the graphic is organized.** Read the column headings or labels on the horizontal and vertical axes.

3. **Identify the variables.** Decide what comparisons are being made or what relationship is being described.

4. **Analyze the purpose.** Based on what you have seen, predict what the graphic is intended to show. Is its purpose to show change over time, describe a process, compare costs, or present statistics?

5. **Determine scale, values, or units of measurement.** The scale is the ratio that a graphic has to the thing it represents. For example, a map may be scaled so that one inch on the map represents one mile.

6. **Study the data to identify trends or patterns.** Note changes, unusual statistics, or unexplained variations.

7. **Read the graphic along with corresponding text.** Refer to the paragraphs that discuss the graphic. These paragraphs may explain certain features of the graphic and identify trends or patterns.

8. **Make a brief summary note.** In the margin, jot a brief note summarizing the trend or pattern the graphic emphasizes. Writing will crystallize the idea in your mind, and your note will be useful for reviewing.

In Figure 10-2 the title indicates the purpose of the graph: to report high school students' use of alcohol. The vertical axis lists percentage points in ten-point intervals. The horizontal axis lists three categories of alcohol use:

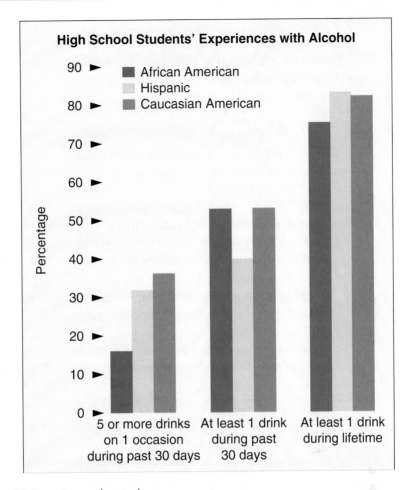

Figure 10-2   A sample graph

—Fabes and Martin, *Exploring Child Development,* p. 454.

five or more drinks on one occasion, at least one drink in the past 30 days, and at least one drink in a lifetime. The graph compares African American, Hispanic, and Caucasian American alcohol use. On the horizontal axis, the graph arranges the categories of alcohol use from greatest use to least use. In two categories fewer African American and Hispanic high school students use alcohol than do Caucasian Americans. The graph also reveals that a fairly high number of all students have tried alcohol at least once. A summary note might read "most adolescents have had some experience with alcohol, and about one-third have engaged in heavy consumption in the last month."

TYPES OF GRAPHICS

This section will describe six types of graphics: tables, graphs, charts, diagrams, maps, and photographs.

Tables

A table is an organized arrangement of facts, usually numbers or statistics. A table condenses large amounts of data to allow you to read and interpret it easily. Use the steps listed below as well as those listed on p. 344 to read the table in Figure 10-3.

1. **Determine how the information is divided and arranged.** The table in Figure 10-3 is divided into three columns: date, estimated world population, and time required for population to double.

2. **Make comparisons and look for trends.** Do this by surveying rows and columns, noting how each compares with the others. Look for similarities, differences, or sudden or unexpected variations. Underline or highlight unusual or outstanding figures. For Figure 10-3, note that from 1650 on, dramatically less time has been required for each doubling of the world population—from 200 years in 1650 to only 40 years in 1990.

3. **Draw conclusions.** Decide what the numbers mean and what they suggest about the subject. This table appeared in a section of a biology textbook dealing with the growth of human population. You can conclude that since

Doubling Times of the Human Population*

Date Double	Estimated World Population	Time Required for Population to
8000 B.C.	5 million	1,500 years
A.D. 1650	500 million	200 years
A.D. 1850	1,000 million (1 billion)	80 years
A.D. 1930	2,000 million (2 billion)	45 years
A.D. 1990	5,300 million (5.3 billion)	40 years
A.D. 2010	8,000 million (8 billion)	?

Figure 10-3   A sample table

—Wallace, *Biology,* p. 774

the world population will have doubled in less than 40 more years, in 40 years we also will need to double our material goods just to maintain present living standards.

4. **Look for clues in corresponding text.** The textbook paragraph that corresponds to the table in Figure 10-3 is reprinted below.

> Some countries have a much firmer grip on their population problems than others, as evidenced by their doubling times (see table). To go from five million people on earth (the present number in only three of New York City's five boroughs) in 8000 B.C. to 500 million in A.D. 1650 took six or seven doublings over a period of 9,000 to 10,000 years. During that time, the human population doubled on an average of about every 1,500 years. A glance at the table will show that, all other things being equal, in only about 40 years, we will need two cars, two schools, two roads, two wells, two houses, and two cities throughout the world for every one that presently exists. And that will only maintain our status quo as far as material goods are concerned.

Notice the author explains and interprets the data presented in the table. He provides real-life examples (two cars, two schools, two wells) of what doubling the population means. Also, at the end of the paragraph, he interprets the data, questioning whether there are enough natural resources to support continued population growth.

EXERCISE 10-1

Directions: The table in Figure 10-4 (p. 348) lists the fitness potential for many popular sports. Study the table and answer the questions that follow.

1. How is the table arranged?

_____

_____

_____

2. Which sport is rated highest for cardiorespiratory endurance?

_____

3. Which sport uses the least number of calories per hour?

_____

4. Which sport is rated highest for flexibility?

_____

Fitness Potential for Popular Sports

Sport	Cardiorespiratory Endurance	Muscular Strength and Endurance		Flexibility	Caloric Range	
		Upper Body	Lower Body		Calories per Minute	Calories per Hour
Back packing[a]	2–3	2	3	2	5–10	300–600
Badminton	2–3	2	2	2	5–10	300–600
Baseball/Softball	1–2	2	2	2	4–7.5	240–450
Basketball	3	2	3	2	10–12.5	600–750
Bowling	1	2	1	1	2.5–4	150–240
Canoeing	2–3	3	1	1	4–10	240–600
Football (touch)	1–2	2	2	2	5–10	300–600
Golf	1	2	3	2	4–5	240–300
Handball	3	3	3	2	10–12.5	600–750
Karate	2	3	3	4	7.5–10	450–600
Racquetball	4	3	3	2	7.5–12.5	450–750
Scuba diving	1	2	2	2	5–7.5	300–450
Skating (ice)	4	1	2–3	2	5–10	300–600
Skating (roller)	2–3	1	2–3	2	5–10	300–600
Skiing (alpine)	2	3	3	3	6–10	360–600
Skiing (nordic)	4–5	3	4	3	7.5–15	450–900
Soccer	3–4	2	3–4	3	7.5–15	450–900
Surfing[b]	2	3	3	3	5–12.5	300–750
Tennis	2–3	2–3	3	2	5–10	300–600
Volleyball	2–3	2	2–3	2	5–10	300–600
Waterskiing	1	3	3	2	5–7.5	300–450

[a]Benefits depend on walking terrain and weight of pack.
[b]Paddling the board out beyond the breaking waves can be demanding.
1 = poor, 2 = fair, 3 = good, 4 = excellent.

Figure 10-4   A table for use in Exercise 10-1

—Getchell, *The Fitness Book*, p. 63.

Graphs

There are four types of graphs: bar, multiple bar, stacked bar, and linear. Each plots a set of points on a set of axes.

Bar Graphs   A bar graph is often used to make comparisons between quantities or amounts, and is particularly useful in showing changes that occur with passing time. Bar graphs usually are constructed to emphasize differences. The graph shown in Figure 10-5 compares the efficiency of producing five common types of animal products. You can readily see that beef, which requires 16 pounds of feed to produce 1 pound of meat, is by far the least efficient.

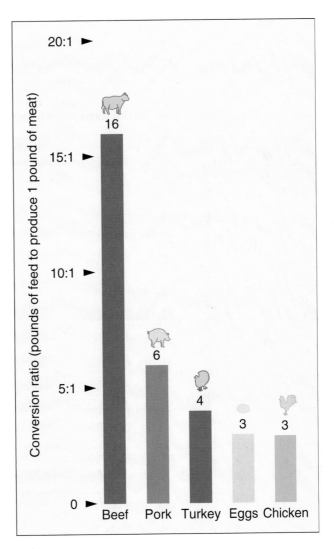

A Comparison of Five Animal Products

Figure 10-5   A sample bar graph

—Lappé, *Diet for a Small Planet*, p. 172.

Multiple Bar Graphs   A multiple bar graph makes at least two or three comparisons simultaneously. As you read them, be sure to identify exactly what comparisons are being made. Figure 10-6 compares percentages of mortgages denied to whites, Latinos, and African Americans according to the percentage of the median income.

Stacked Bar Graphs   A stacked bar graph is an arrangement of data in which bars are placed one on top of another rather than side by side. This variation is often used to emphasize whole/part relationships. Stacked bar

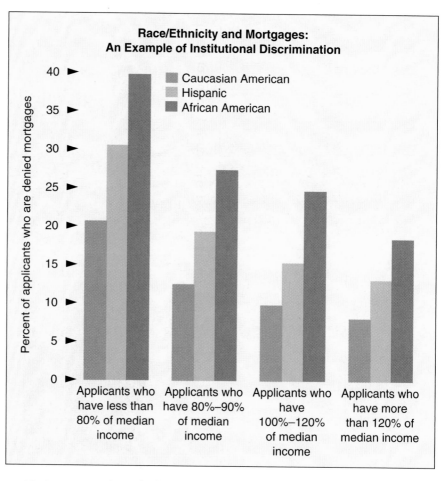

Figure 10-6   A sample multiple bar graph

—Henslin, *Social Problems*, p. 259.

graphs show the relationship of a part to an entire group or class. The graph in Figure 10-7 shows day care arrangements by three ethnic groups: Caucasian American, African American, and Hispanic. Stacked bar graphs also allow numerous comparisons. The graph in Figure 10-7 compares five different day care arrangements for the three ethnic groups: parent, relative, nanny, family child care, and center-based care.

Linear Graphs A linear, or line, graph plots and connects points along a vertical and a horizontal axis. A linear graph allows more data points than a

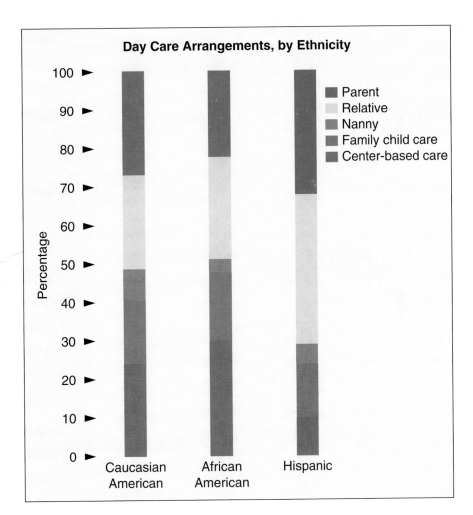

Figure 10-7   A sample stacked bar graph

—Fabes and Martin, *Exploring Child Development*, p. 196.

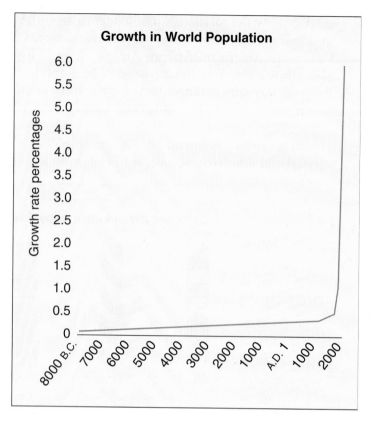

Figure 10-8   A sample linear graph

—Thompson and Hickey, *Society in Focus,* p. 485.

bar graph. Consequently, it is used to present more detailed and/or larger quantities of information. A linear graph may compare two variables; if so, then it consists of a single line. More often, however, linear graphs are used to compare relationships among several sets of variables, and multiple lines are included. The graph shown in Figure 10-8 compares world population in billions of people every thousand years.

    Linear graphs are usually used to display continuous data—data connected in time or events occurring in sequence. The data in Figure 10-8 are continuous, as they move from 8000 B.C. to A.D. 2000.

EXERCISE 10-2 | **Directions:** Study the graphs shown in Figures 10-9 through 10-11 (p. 354), and answer the corresponding questions.

Figure 10-9   Marriage and Increasing Life Expectancies

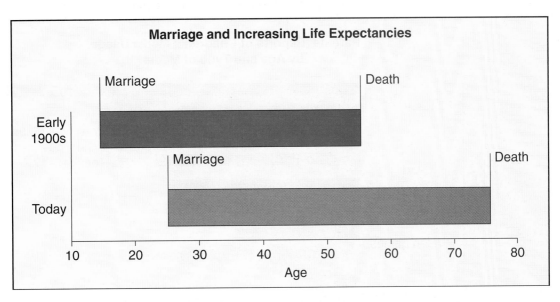

—Byer and Shainberg, *Living Well,* Fig. 65.

1. What is the purpose of the graph?

   _____

   _____

2. About how many years earlier did couples marry in the early 1900s than they do today?

   _____

   _____

3. Approximately how long were couples in the early 1900s married before they died? What about couples of today?

   _____

   _____

4. About how much longer do married couples of today live compared to couples of the early 1900s?

   _____

   _____

Figure 10-10   **Parent's Report of Children's Media Usage**

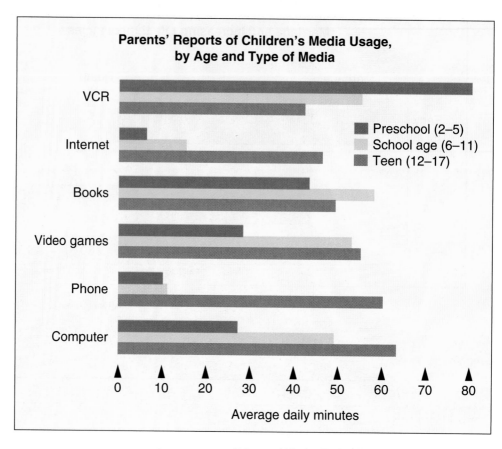

—Fabes and Martin, *Exploring Child Development,* p. 281.

1. What comparisons does this graph allow you to make?

   _____

2. How is this graph organized?

   _____

   _____

3. What patterns are evident?

   _____

   _____

   _____

   _____

Figure 10-11   Rate of Technological Change

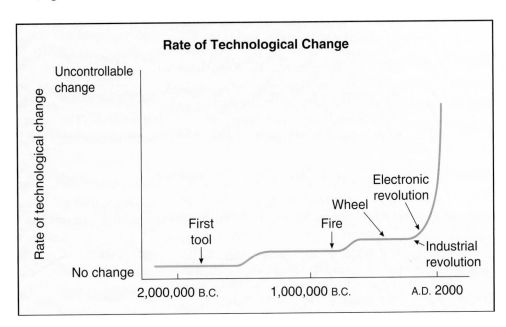

—Dunham and Pierce, *Management,* p. 721.

1. Describe the purpose of the graph.

   _____

   _____

2. What trend is evident?

   _____

   _____

3. Think of some examples of technological changes that have occurred over the past 50 years that may account for the dramatic upswing near the year 2000.

   _____

   _____

Charts

Three types of charts are commonly used in college textbooks: pie charts, organizational charts, and flowcharts.

Pie Charts   Pie charts, sometimes called circle graphs, are used to show whole/part relationships or to depict how given parts of a unit have been divided or classified. They enable the reader to compare the parts to each other as well as to compare each part to the whole. The chart in Figure 10-12 shows the U.S. population divided by race and ethnic group for 2000, 2025, and 2050.

Organizational Charts   An organizational chart divides an organization, such as a corporation, a hospital, or a university, into its administrative parts, staff positions, or lines of authority. Figure 10-13 shows the organization of the American political party. It reveals that party members belong to precinct and ward organizations. From these organizations, county committees are formed. County committee members are represented on state committees, and state delegates are chosen for national positions.

Flowcharts   A flowchart is a specialized type of chart that shows how a process or procedure works. Lines or arrows are used to indicate the direction (route or routes) through the procedure. Various shapes (boxes, circles, rectangles) enclose what is done at each stage or step. You could

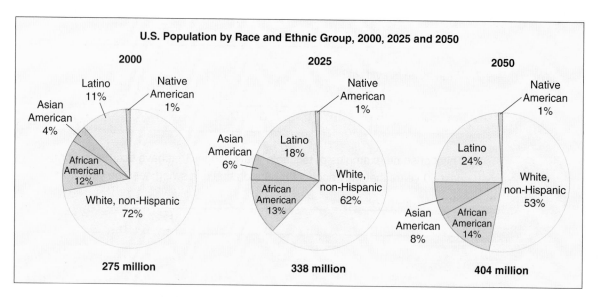

Figure 10-12   Sample pie charts

—Henslin, *Social Problems,* p. 454.

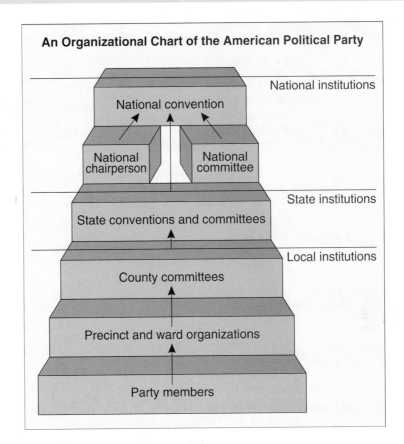

Figure 10-13   A sample organizational chart

—Lineberry and Edwards III, *Government in America,* p. 253.

draw, for example, a flowchart to describe how to apply for and obtain a student loan or how to locate a malfunction in your car's electrical system. Refer to the flowchart shown in Figure 10-14 (p. 358), taken from a business management textbook. It describes the steps in the decision-making process.

To read flowcharts effectively, use the following suggestions:

1. **Decide what process the flowchart shows.**
2. **Next, follow the chart, using the arrows and reading each step.** Start at the top or far left of the chart.
3. **When you have finished, summarize the process in your own words.** Try to draw the chart from memory without referring to the text. Compare your drawing with the chart and note discrepancies.

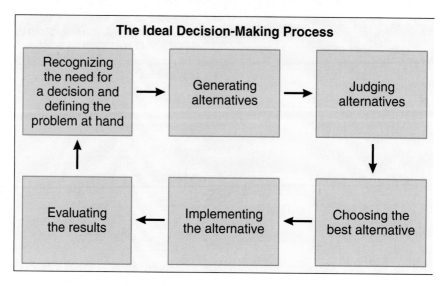

Figure 10-14   A sample flowchart

—Fleet, *Contemporary Management*, p. 187.

Now study the flowchart shown in Figure 10-14, and try to express each step in your own words. You might have said something like: (1) know what has to be decided, (2) think of all possibilities, (3) weigh each possibility, (4) select one, (5) try it out, and (6) decide if it worked.

EXERCISE 10-3 **Directions:** Study the charts shown in Figures 10-15 through 10-17 and answer the corresponding questions.

Figure 10-15   What Are the Living Arrangements of U.S. Children?

1. What is the purpose of these charts?

_____

_____

2. What living arrangement changes least from group to group?

_____

_____

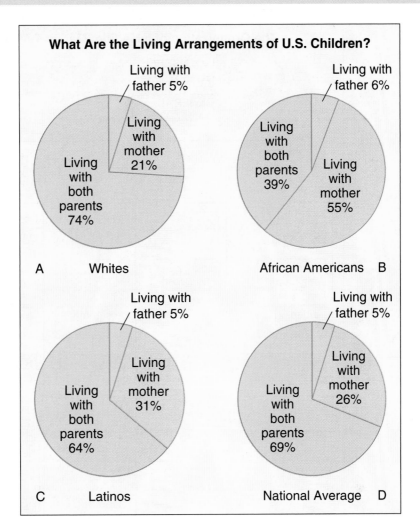

What Are the Living Arrangements of U.S. Children?

A — Whites

Living with father 5%
Living with mother 21%
Living with both parents 74%

B — African Americans

Living with father 6%
Living with mother 55%
Living with both parents 39%

C — Latinos

Living with father 5%
Living with mother 31%
Living with both parents 64%

D — National Average

Living with father 5%
Living with mother 26%
Living with both parents 69%

Figure 10-15

—Henslin, *Social Problems,* p. 368.

3. What other patterns are evident?

_____

_____

_____

_____

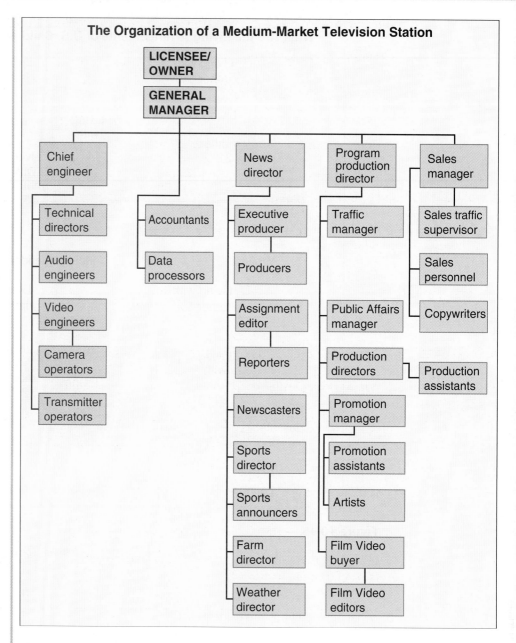

Figure 10-16

—Merrill et al., *Modern Mass Media*, p. 207.

Figure 10-16   The Organization of a Medium Market Television Station

1. What is the purpose of the chart?

_____

_____

2. To which person or office would the artists report directly?

_____

_____

3. Who is in charge of the department in which sports announcers and newscasters work?

_____

_____

Figure 10-17 (p. 362)   The Component of the Criminal Justice System

1. What is the purpose of the chart?

_____

_____

2. Summarize its organization.

_____

_____

3. After a person's "Initial Appearance," what happens next if the charges against him are not dropped or dismissed?

_____

_____

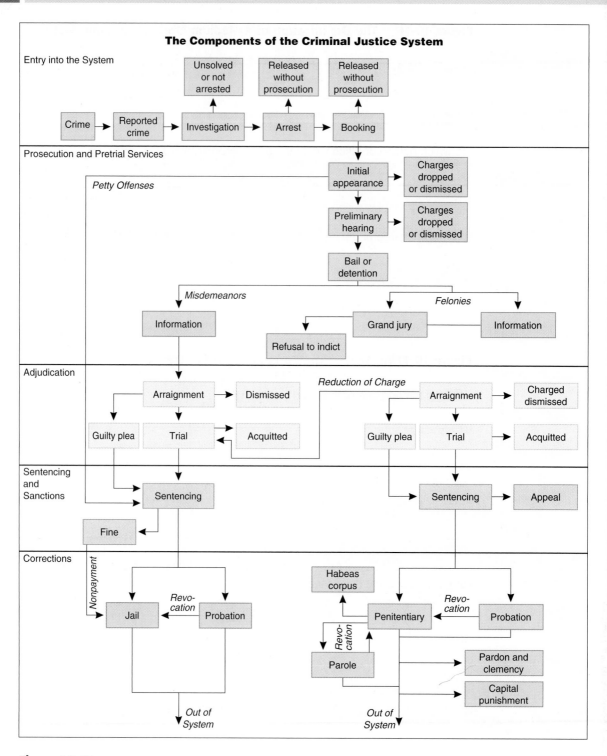

The Components of the Criminal Justice System

Entry into the System

Crime → Reported crime → Investigation → Arrest → Booking

Investigation → Unsolved or not arrested

Arrest → Released without prosecution

Booking → Released without prosecution

Prosecution and Pretrial Services

Initial appearance → Charges dropped or dismissed

Preliminary hearing → Charges dropped or dismissed

Bail or detention

Petty Offenses

Misdemeanors → Information

Felonies → Grand jury → Information

Grand jury → Refusal to indict

Adjudication

Arraignment → Dismissed

Reduction of Charge

Arraignment → Charged dismissed

Guilty plea   Trial → Acquitted

Guilty plea   Trial → Acquitted

Sentencing and Sanctions

Sentencing

Sentencing → Appeal

Fine

Corrections

Nonpayment

Jail ← Revocation ← Probation

Habeas corpus

Penitentiary ← Revocation ← Probation

Revocation

Parole

Pardon and clemency

Capital punishment

Out of System

Out of System

Figure 10-17

—Thompson and Hickey, *Society in Focus*, p. 179.

Diagrams

Diagrams often are included in technical and scientific as well as many other college texts to explain processes. Diagrams are intended to help you visualize relationships between parts and understand sequences. They may also be used to illustrate ideas or concepts. Figure 10-18, taken from a biology textbook, shows the structure of a nail. It accompanies the following text:

> A **nail** is a scalelike modification of the epidermis that corresponds to the hoof or claw of other animals. Each nail has a *free edge*, a *body*, (visible attached portion), and a *root* (embedded in the skin). The borders of the nail are overlapped by skin folds, called *nail folds*. The thick proximal nail is commonly called the *cuticle* [Figure 10-18]. The stratus basale of the epidermis extends beneath the nail as the *nail bed*. Its thickened proximal area, called the *nail matrix*, is responsible for nail growth. The region over the thickened nail matrix that appears as a white crescent is called the *lunula*.
>
> —Marieb, *Essentials of Human Anatomy & Physiology*, p. 106.

Reading diagrams differs from reading other types of graphics in that diagrams often correspond to fairly large segments of text, requiring you to switch back and forth frequently between the text and the diagram to determine which part of the process each paragraph refers to.

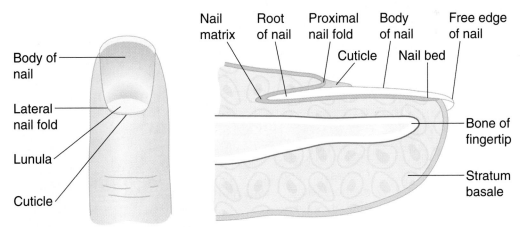

Structure of a nail. Surface view (left) and longitudinal section of the distal part of a finger (right), showing nail parts and the nail matrix that forms the nail.

Figure 10-18   A sample diagram

—Marieb, *Essentials of Human Anatomy & Physiology*, p. 106.

Because diagrams of processes and their corresponding text are often difficult, complicated, or highly technical, plan on reading these sections more than once. Read first to grasp the overall process. In subsequent readings, focus on the details of the process, examining each step and understanding its progression.

One of the best ways to study a diagram is to redraw it in as much detail as possible without referring to the original. Or, test your understanding and recall of the process outlined in a diagram by explaining it, step by step in writing, using your own words.

EXERCISE 10-4

Directions: Study the diagram and accompanying text shown in Figure 10-19 and answer the following questions.

In this personal computer system, the input device is a keyboard or a mouse. The input device feeds data to the central processing unit, which is inside the computer housing, the vertical box to the left of the screen. The output devices in this example are the screen, the printer, and the speakers. The secondary storage devices are hard drive, a 3 1/2-inch disk drive, and a CD-ROM drive, all within the computer housing. This popular configuration, with the housing standing on end, is called a minitower.

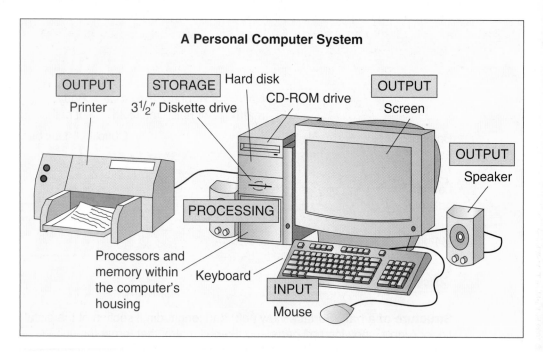

A Personal Computer System

Figure 10-19

—Capron, *Computers*, p. 19.

1. What is the purpose of the diagram?

_____

_____

2. Which parts of personal computers are considered input devices?

_____

_____

3. What type of devices are printers, screens, and speakers?

_____

_____

4. Where is data from input devices sent next?

_____

_____

Maps

Maps describe relationships and provide information about location and direction. They are commonly found in geography and history texts, and also appear in ecology, biology, and anthropology texts. While most of us think of maps as describing distances and locations, maps also are used to describe the placement of geographical and ecological features such as areas of pollution, areas of population concentration, or political data (voting districts).

When reading maps, use the following steps:

1. **Read the caption.** This identifies the subject of the map.
2. **Use the legend or key to identify the symbols or codes used.**
3. **Note distance scales.**
4. **Study the map, looking for trends or key points.** Often the text that accompanies the map states the key points the map illustrates.
5. **Try to visualize, or create a mental picture of, the map.**
6. **As a learning and study aid, write, in your own words, a statement of what the map shows.**

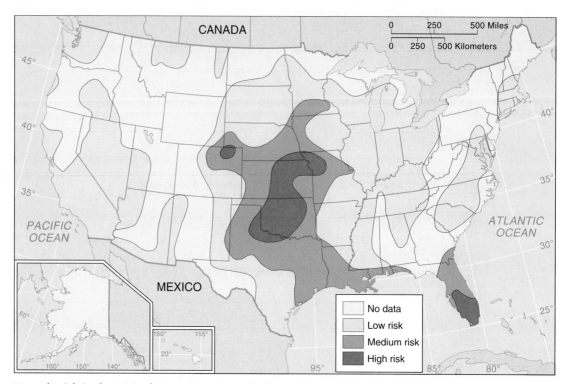

Tornado risk in the United States is greatest in the southern plains, the Southeast (especially central Florida), and the Midwest. (Alaska and Hawaii not to scale.)

Figure 10-20   A sample map

The map in Figure 10-20 shows the degree of risk for tornadoes in the United States.

Photographs

Although sometimes considered an art form instead of a graphic, photographs are used in place of words. Their purpose is similar to other graphics—to replace verbal descriptions in presenting information. Photographs also are used to spark interest, and, often, to draw out an emotional response or feeling. Use these suggestions when studying a photograph:

1. **Read the caption.** It often provides a clue to the photographer's intended meaning.
2. **Ask: What is my first overall impression?** What details did I notice first? These questions will lead you to discover the purpose of the photograph.

Directions: Study the photograph in Figure 10-21, and answer these questions.

1. Describe what is happening in the picture.

   _____

   _____

2. Describe the feeling of each person.

   _____

   _____

3. What does this picture reveal about the relationship between these two people?

   _____

   _____

Figure 10-21

USING ELECTRONIC STUDY AIDS

College instructors are increasingly using a variety of instructional media to supplement their textbook and lecture material. A CD-ROM may be included with the textbook when you purchase it, or it may be available in your college's academic computer labs. (Not all textbooks have CD-ROM accompaniments.) Your textbook may have its own Web site, as this book does. Or, an online tutorial or software program may be available. These sources contain a wealth of information, activities, and learning resources. They may contain a review of key topics, a "click here" function for more information on terms and concepts, demonstrations and experiments, and review quizzes, for example. Many of the activities are interactive—you get involved with the material by responding, rather than just reading it.

Here are a few guidelines for using electronic materials along with textbooks:

1. **Use them with, but *not in place of*, your text.** CD-ROMs and online resources are supplements. Although they are fun to use, you must still read your textbook.

2. **Use the electronic aids for review and practice.** After you have read the text, use them to help you learn the material. Use the quiz or self-test modules when studying for an exam. Keep a record of your progress. Many programs will do this for you and allow you to print a progress report. This record will enable you to see your strengths and weaknesses, plan further study, and review troublesome topics.

3. **If there is a notepad (a place where you can write your own notes), use it.** You will learn more efficiently if you express what you have learned in your own words.

4. **Consolidate your learning.** When you finish a module or program segment, stop and reflect on what you have learned. If you worked on an algebra module about the multiplication of polynomials, then stop and recall the techniques you have learned. Write notes or summarize the process in a separate section of your course notebook reserved for this purpose.

READING AND EVALUATING INTERNET SOURCES

The Internet is a worldwide network of computers through which you can access a wide variety of information and services. Through the Internet, you can access the World Wide Web (a network of networks), a service that connects this vast array of resources. Many instructors use the Internet and have begun requiring their students to do so. It is important to develop effective ways of reading and evaluating the wide range of Internet sources available to you.

Developing New Ways of Thinking and Reading

The first step to reading electronic text easily and effectively is to understand how it is different from print text. A print source is linear—it goes in a straight line from idea to idea. Electronic sources, however, tend to be multidirectional. Using links, you can follow numerous paths. (See Figure 10-22.) Therefore, reading electronic sources demands a different type of thinking than reading print sources.

Using electronic text also requires new reading strategies. Use the following suggestions to change and adapt how you read.

1. **Focus on your purpose.** Focus clearly on your purpose for visiting the site. What information do you need? Because you must create your own path through the site, fix in your mind what you are looking for. If you do not, you may wander aimlessly, waste valuable time, or even become lost, following numerous links that lead you farther and farther away from the site at which you began.

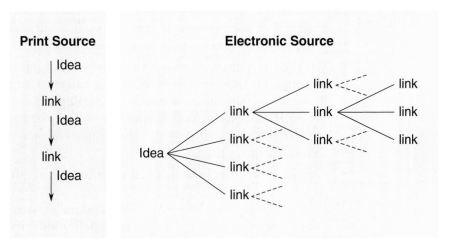

Figure 10-22   The differences between print and electronic sources

2. **Get used to the site's design and layout.** Each Web site has unique features and arranges information differently. Use the following suggestions to help you get used to a site's design and layout.

   • **When you reach a new site, spend a few minutes getting used to it and discovering how it is organized.** Scroll through it quickly to determine how it is organized and what information is available. Ask yourself the following questions:

     • What information is available?

     • How is it arranged on the screen?

     • Can I search the site using a search option or box?

     • Is there a site map?

   • Especially on large and complex sites, you will have a number of different choices for locating the information you need.

   • **Expect the first screen to grab your attention and make a main point.** Web site authors know that many people who read a Web page do not scroll down to see the next page. Therefore, they try to make their first page interesting and memorable.

   • **Consider both the focus of and limitations of your learning style.** Are you a spatial learner? If so, you may have a tendency to focus too heavily on the graphic elements of the screen. If, on the other hand, you tend to focus on words, you may ignore important visual elements or signals. If you focus *only* on the words and ignore color and graphics on a particular screen, you probably will miss information or may not move through the site in the most efficient way.

3. **Pay attention to how information is organized.** Because you can navigate through a Web site in many different ways, it is important to have the right expectations and to make several decisions before you begin.

   • **Use the site map, if provided, to discover what information is available and how it is organized.** A sample site map for the Consumer Reports Web site, http://www.ConsumerReports.org, is shown in Figure 10-23. Notice that the links are categorized according to the types of information (ratings, subscription information, products, etc.) a consumer may need.

   • **Consider the order in which you want to take in information.** Choose an order in which to explore links; avoid randomly clicking on link buttons. Doing so is somewhat like randomly choosing pages to read out of a reference book. Do you need definitions first? Do you want historical background first? Your decision will be partly influenced by your learning style.

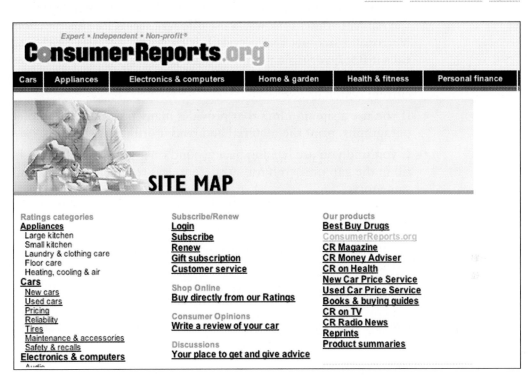

Figure 10-23   The site map of the Consumer Reports Web site (http://www.consumerreports.org)

- **Expect shorter, less detailed sentences and paragraphs.** Much online communication tends to be briefer and more concise than in traditional sources. As a result, you may have to mentally fill in transitions and make inferences about the relationships among ideas. For example, you may have to infer similarities and differences or recognize cause-and-effect connections on your own.

4. **Use links to find the information you need.** Links are unique to electronic text. The suggestions below will help you use links to find the information you need.

- **Plan on exploring links to find complete and detailed information.** Both remote links (those that take you to another site) and related links (within a site) are intended to provide more detailed information on topics introduced on the home page.

- **As you follow links, be sure to bookmark your original site and other useful sites you come across so you can find them again.** Bookmarking is a feature on your Internet browser that allows you to record Web site addresses and access them later by simply clicking on the site name. Different browsers use different terms for this function. Microsoft's Internet Explorer calls it *Favorites*. Mozilla's Firefox calls it *Bookmarks*. In addition, these browsers also have *History* and *Back* functions that allow a user to retrace the steps of a current search.

- **If you use a site or a link that provides many pages of continuous paragraphs, print the material and read it offline.**
- If you find you are lacking background on a topic, use links to help fill in the gap or search for a different, less technical Web site on the same topic.

EXERCISE 10-6   **Directions:** Visit one of the following Web sites. Locate the information needed and take brief notes to record what you find.

URL	Information to Locate
1. **http://www.consumer.gov**	List three tips for buying a used car.

_____

_____

_____

| 2. **http://www.bls.gov.oco** | What is the job outlook for Graphic Designers? |

_____

| 3. **http://thomas.loc.gov/home/ lawsmade.toc.html** | Why are lights and ringing bells used in parts of the Capitol Building and U.S. House and Senate Office Buildings? |

_____

_____

_____

Types of Web Sites

There are thousands of Web sites, and they vary widely in purpose. Table 10-1 summarizes five primary types of Web sites.

TABLE 10-1   Types of Web Sites

Type	Purpose	Description	URL Suffix
Informational	To present facts, information, and research data	May contain reports, statistical data, results of research studies, and reference materials	.edu or .gov
News	To provide current information on local, national, and international news	Often supplements print newspapers, periodicals, and television news programs	.com
Advocacy	To promote a particular cause or point of view	May be concerned with a controversial issue; often sponsored by nonprofit groups	.org
Personal	To provide information about an individual and his or her interests and accomplishments	May list publications or include the individual's résumé	URL will vary. May contain .com or .org or may contain a tilde (~)
Commercial	To promote goods or services	May provide news and information related to a company's products	.com

Evaluating Web Sites

Once you have become familiar with the organization of a Web site and determined its purpose, you should evaluate it. To do this, consider its content, accuracy, and timeliness.

Evaluating the Content of a Web Site   When evaluating the content of a Web site, evaluate its appropriateness, its source, its level of technical detail, its presentation, its completeness, and its links.

Evaluate the Appropriateness.   To be worthwhile, a Web site should contain the information you need. It should answer one or more of your search questions. If the site only touches upon answers to your questions but does not address them in detail, check the links on the site to see if they will lead you to more detailed information. If they do not, search for a more useful site.

Evaluate the Source.   Another important step in evaluating a Web site is to determine its source. Ask yourself, "Who is the sponsor?" and "Why was this site put up on the Web?" The sponsor of a Web site is the person or organization who paid for it to be created and placed on the Web. The sponsor will often suggest the purpose of a Web site. For example, a Web site sponsored by Nike is designed to promote its products, while a site sponsored by a university library is designed to help students learn to use its resources more effectively.

If you are not sure who sponsors a Web site, check its URL, its copyright, and the links it offers. The ending of the URL often suggests the type of sponsorship. The copyright indicates the owner of the site. Links may also reveal the sponsor. Some links may lead to commercial advertising, while others may lead to sites sponsored by nonprofit groups.

Evaluate the Level of Technical Detail.   A Web site should contain the level of technical detail that is suited to your purpose. Some sites may provide information that is too sketchy for your search purposes; others assume a level of background knowledge or technical sophistication that you lack. For example, if you are writing a short, introductory-level paper on threats to the survival of marine animals, the Web site of the Scripps Institution of Oceanography (http://www.sio.ucsd.edu) may be too technical and contain more information than you need. Unless you have some previous knowledge in that field, you may want to search for a different Web site.

Evaluate the Presentation.   Information on a Web site should be presented clearly and should be well written. If you find a site that is not clear and well written, you should be suspicious of it. If the author did not take time to present ideas clearly and correctly, he or she may not have taken time to collect accurate information, either.

Evaluate the Completeness.   Determine whether the site provides complete information on its topic. Does it address all aspects of the topic that you feel it should? For example, if a Web site on Important Twentieth-Century American Poets does not mention Robert Frost, then the site is incomplete. If you discover that a site is incomplete, search for sites that provide a more thorough treatment of the topic.

Evaluate the Links.   Many reputable sites supply links to other related sites. Make sure that the links work and are current. Also check to see if the sites to which you were sent are reliable sources of information. If the links do not work or the sources appear unreliable, you should question the reliability of the site itself. Also determine whether the links provided are comprehensive or only present a representative sample. Either is acceptable, but the site should make clear the nature of the links it is providing.

EXERCISE 10-7 **Directions:** Evaluate the content of two of the following sites. Explain why you would either trust or distrust the site for reliable content.

1. **http://www.geocities.com/RainForest/6243/index.html**

   _____

   _____

   _____

2. **http://www1.umn.edu/ohr/careerdev/resources/resume**

   _____

   _____

   _____

3. **http://www.hoosierherbalremedy.com**

   _____

   _____

Evaluating the Accuracy of a Web Site   When using information on a Web site for an academic paper, it is important to be sure that you have found accurate information. One way to determine the accuracy of a Web site is to compare it with print sources (periodicals and books) on the same topic. If you find a wide discrepancy between the Web site and the printed sources, do not trust the Web site. Another way to determine accuracy of the information on a site is to compare it with other Web sites that address the same topic. If discrepancies exist, further research is needed to determine which site is more accurate.

The site itself will also provide clues about the accuracy of its information. Ask yourself the following questions:

1. **Are the author's name and credentials provided?** A well-known writer with established credentials is likely to author only reliable, accurate information. If no author is given, you should question whether the information is accurate.

2. **Is contact information for the author included on the site?** Often, a site provides an e-mail address where the author may be contacted.

3. **Is the information complete, or in summary form?** If it is a summary, use the site to find the original source. Original information has less chance of containing errors and is usually preferred in academic papers.

4. **If opinions are offered, are they clearly presented as opinions?** Authors who disguise their opinions as facts are not trustworthy.

5. **Does the site provide a list of works cited?** As with any form of research, sources used to put information up on a Web site must be documented. If sources are not credited, you should question the accuracy of the Web site.

It may be helpful to determine if the information is available in print form. If it is, try to obtain the print version. Errors may occur when the article or essay is put up on the Web. Web sites move, change, and delete information, so it may be difficult for a reader of an academic paper to locate the Web site that you used in writing it. Also, page numbers are easier to cite in print sources than in electronic ones.

EXERCISE 10-8   **Directions:** Evaluate the accuracy of two of the following Web sites.

1. **http://gunscholar.com**

   _____

   _____

   _____

2. **http://www.aps.edu/aps/petroglyph/fifth/Yessak/Bones/Social_Studies.html**

   _____

   _____

   _____

3. **http://www.theonion.com/content/news/thousands_lose_jobs_as_michigan**

   _____

   _____

   _____

Evaluating the Timeliness of a Web Site   Although the Web is well-known for providing up-to-the-minute information, not all Web sites are current. Evaluate the timeliness by checking:

- the date on which the Web site was posted (put on the Web).
- the date when the document you are using was added.

- the date when the site was last revised.
- the date when the links were last checked.

This information is usually provided at the end of the site's home page or at the end of the document you are using.

EXERCISE 10-9 **Directions:** Evaluate the timeliness of two of the following Web sites, using the directions given for each site.

1. **http://www.state.gov/r/pa/ei/bgn**
   Choose a geographic region, such as Africa, and evaluate whether information is up-to-date.

   _____

   _____

   _____

2. **http://www.netcat.org/trojan.html**
   Evaluate whether this paper as a whole and the references within it are timely.

   _____

   _____

   _____

3. **http://www.mountainbikepa.com/trails/trails.asp**
   Click on a county to find out about its bike trails. Evaluate the timeliness of the information and discuss why current information on this topic is crucial.

   _____

   _____

   _____

SELF-TEST SUMMARY

How do you read a graphic?	To read a graphic, follow these eight steps: 1. Read the title. 2. Discover how the graphic is organized. 3. Identify variables. 4. Analyze its purpose. 5. Determine the scale of measurement. 6. Identify trends and patterns. 7. Read corresponding text. 8. Write a summary note.
How many types of graphics are there, what are they, and how are they used?	There are six major types of graphics: 1. **Tables** are used to arrange and organize facts. 2. **Graphs**—including bar, multiple bar, stacked bar, and linear graphs—are used to make comparisons between or among sets of information. 3. **Charts**—including pie charts, organizational charts, and flowcharts, present visual displays of information. 4. **Diagrams** demonstrate physical relationships between parts and display sequences. 5. **Maps** describe information about location and direction. 6. **Photographs** are used to spark interest or to draw out an emotional response.
What types of electronic learning aids accompany textbooks?	CD-ROMs and online Web sites often accompany textbooks.
How is reading electronic text different from reading print text?	Electronic text is multidirectional, while print text follows a single direction.
List five different types of Web sites.	The five types are informational, news, advocacy, personal, and commercial.
What factors should you consider when evaluating a Web site?	The factors are content, accuracy, and timeliness.

Getting More Practice with . . .
Reading Graphic and Electronic Sources

WORKING TOGETHER

Directions: Bring a copy of your local newspaper or of *USA Today* to class. After your instructor forms groups, each group should select and tear out four or five graphics. For each graphic, the group should identify the type of graphic, analyze its purpose, and identify the trend or pattern it reveals. Groups should then discuss what other types of graphics could be used to accomplish the author's purpose. Each group should submit one graphic to the instructor along with a brief summary of the members' analysis.

GOING ONLINE

Internet Activities

1. Charts and Graphs

   http://mcckc.edu/longview/ctac/GRAPHS.HTM

   The Critical Thinking Across the Curriculum Project from Longview Community College invites you to analyze the way statistical information is represented visually. Look through some newspapers and magazines with a friend to locate charts and graphs. Analyze their reliability based on the information presented in this site. What is your perception of the media's use of statistics?

2. Web Site Evaluation Worksheet

   http://appserv.pace.edu/execute/page.cfm?doc_id=20964

   Print out this worksheet from Pace University Library, and use it to evaluate a Web site that you use regularly. Notice that at the bottom of the site there are links to specialized criteria for specific types of Web pages. You might want to incorporate some of these into the worksheet you printed out.

Companion Website

For additional readings, exercises, and Internet activities, visit this book's Companion Website at:

http://www.ablongman.com/mcwhorter

If you need a user name and password, please see your instructor.

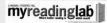

My Reading Lab

For more practice with reading graphics, visit MyReadingLab, click on the Reading Skills tab, and then click on Graphics and Visuals—Wall Street, NY.

http://www.ablongman.com/myreadinglab

Name _____

Section _____ Date _____

Number right _____ × 10 points = Score _____

Directions: Use the graphic below from a sociology text to answer the following questions.

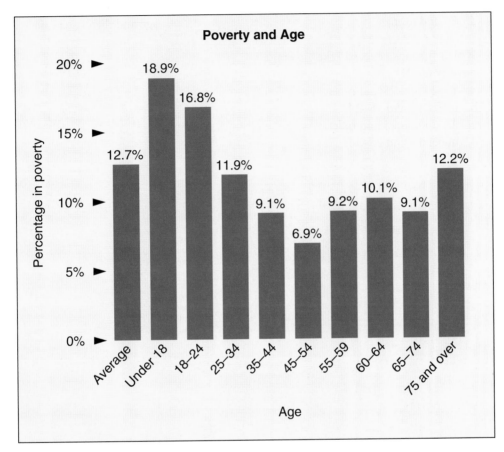

Poverty and Age

Percentage in poverty

- 20% ► 18.9%
- 16.8%
- 15% ► 12.7%
- 11.9%
- 10% ► 9.1%
- 6.9%
- 9.2%
- 10.1%
- 9.1%
- 12.2%
- 5% ►
- 0% ►

Average · Under 18 · 18–24 · 25–34 · 35–44 · 45–54 · 55–59 · 60–64 · 65–74 · 75 and over

Age

— Henslin, *Sociology,* p. 402.

_____ 1. This type of graph is known as
   a. an organizational chart.
   b. a pie chart.
   c. a bar graph.
   d. a flowchart.

_____ 2. The purpose of this graph is to
   a. compare the percentage of various age groups in poverty.
   b. show the increase in poverty in the United States.
   c. compare the income levels of various groups.
   d. predict that poverty will be a continuing problem in the twenty-first century.

381

_____ 3. According to the graph, the group with the largest percentage living in poverty is
   a. under 18.
   b. 18–24.
   c. 55–59.
   d. 75 and over.

_____ 4. Which groups exceed the average poverty level?
   a. 18–24 and 75 and older.
   b. under 18 and 18–24.
   c. 25–34 and 75 and older.
   d. under 18 and 25–34.

_____ 5. Which trend is generally true?
   a. Levels of poverty fall throughout life.
   b. Levels of poverty remain unchanged.
   c. Poverty levels are unpredictable.
   d. Poverty levels decrease until middle age and then rise again.

Name _____

Section _____ Date _____

Number right _____ × 10 points = Score _____

Directions: Use the text and graph below to answer the questions that follow.

TABLE A   Commitment in Cohabitation: Does It Make a Difference?

Level of Commitment	Percent of Couples	Split Up	Still Together	After 5 to 7 Years Of Those Still Together	
				Married	Cohabiting
Substitute for Marriage	10%	35%	65%	25%	40%
Step toward Marriage	46%	31%	69%	52%	17%
Trial Marriage	15%	51%	49%	28%	21%
Coresidential Dating	29%	46%	54%	33%	21%

Source: Bianchi and Casper 2000.

—Henslin, *Sociology,* p. 480.

From the outside, all cohabitation may look the same. And certainly cohabitation has common features, especially that of an unmarried man and woman living together in a sexual relationship. But sociologists have found essential differences in what cohabitation means for the couples. Table A shows the four types of cohabitation sociologists have identified. For about 10 percent of couples, cohabitation is a substitute for marriage. These couples consider themselves married, but for some reason don't want a marriage certificate. Some object to marriage on philosophical grounds ("What difference does a piece of paper make?"); others do not yet have a legal divorce from a spouse. In the most common type of cohabitation, however—involving almost half of cohabiters—the couples view cohabitation as one of a series of steps on the path to marriage. For them, cohabitation is more than "going steady," but less than engagement. Another 15 percent of couples are simply "giving it a try." They want to see what marriage to one another might be like. For the least committed, about 29 percent, cohabitation is a form of dating. It provides a more dependable source of sex and some emotional support.

_____ 1. The purpose of the table is to compare
   a. marital success of those who cohabitate (live together) with those who marry.
   b. levels of commitment of couples who cohabitate with the status of the relationship after 5 to 7 years.
   c. couples who cohabitate and couples who end up getting a divorce.
   d. characteristics of couples who split up with those of couples that stay together.

_____ 2. According to the table, the level of commitment that is most common is
   a. substitute for marriage.
   b. trial marriage.
   c. step toward marriage.
   d. coresidential dating.

_____ 3. Most couples who cohabitate regard cohabitation as
   a. simpler than marriage.
   b. a convenient way to share expenses.
   c. emotionally draining.
   d. connected to marriage.

_____ 4. Couples in the coresidential dating category regard cohabitation as source of
   a. sex and emotional support.
   b. a means of going steady.
   c. a way to give marriage a try without the legal issues.
   d. a step toward marriage.

_____ 5. Of the following facts, the only one that appears _both_ in the text and in the graphic is
   a. sixty-five percent of couples who regard cohabitation as a substitute for marriage are still together five years later.
   b. of trial marriages, only 28 percent of the couples actually marry after five years.
   c. fifteen percent of couples who cohabitate are doing so to give marriage a try.
   d. coresidential dating results in the second largest number of split-ups.

Name _____

Section _____ Date _____

Number right _____ × 10 points = Score _____

Directions: Study the graph below from a sociology text and answer the questions that follow.

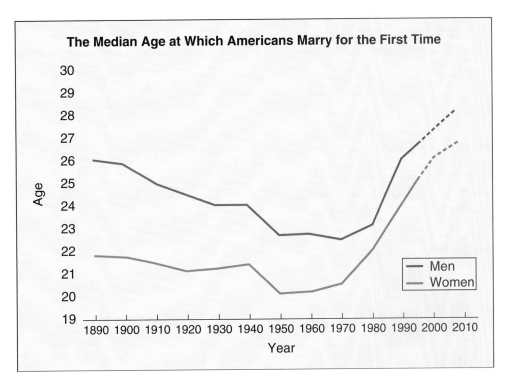

The Median Age at Which Americans Marry for the First Time

—Henslin, *Sociology,* p. 489.

_____ 1. What is the purpose of the graph?
   a. to compare the ages at which men and women marry from 1890 to 2010
   b. to show that the age at which Americans marry is decreasing
   c. to show that men and women marry at similar ages
   d. to compare how men and women have changed from 1890 to 2010

_____ 2. In which of the following years was there the largest difference in ages between men and women?
   a. 1910
   b. 1930
   c. 1970
   d. 1990

3. Which of the following statements describes the trend shown between 1890 and 1990?
   a. Women married at an older age than men.
   b. Men married at an older age than women.
   c. Men married older women.
   d. Women married younger men.

4. Which marriage trend does the graph show?
   a. The age gap between men and women has been gradually narrowing.
   b. Women's average age has been steadily decreasing throughout history.
   c. Men's average age has shown little change.
   d. Women's average age has shown a steady decline.

Directions: Study the pie chart below, and answer the questions that follow.

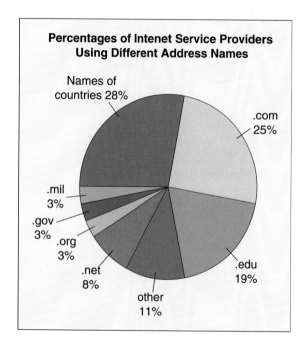

Percentages of Intenet Service Providers Using Different Address Names

Names of countries 28%
.com 25%
.mil 3%
.gov 3%
.org 3%
.net 8%
other 11%
.edu 19%

5. Which of the following address names is used by the second largest percentage of Internet service providers?
   a. .edu
   b. other
   c. .com
   d. names of countries

6. Which of the following address names contain the same percentages of Internet service providers?
   a. .mil and .net
   b. .edu and .com
   c. .gov and .org
   d. .com and names of countries

7. What percentage of Internet service providers use the name of a country in their addresses?
   a. 25 percent
   b. 8 percent
   c. 10 percent
   d. 28 percent

Directions: Study the following chart and answer the questions that follow.

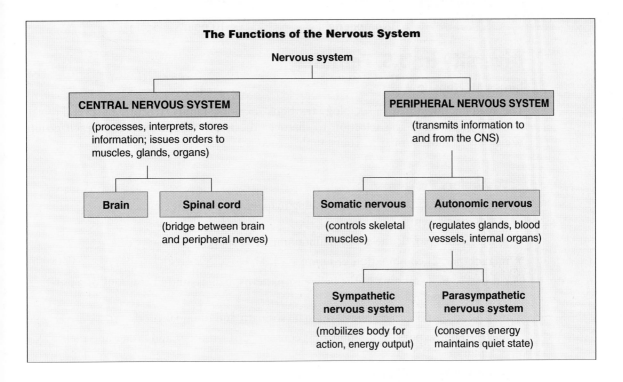

The Functions of the Nervous System

Nervous system

CENTRAL NERVOUS SYSTEM
(processes, interprets, stores information; issues orders to muscles, glands, organs)

PERIPHERAL NERVOUS SYSTEM
(transmits information to and from the CNS)

Brain

Spinal cord
(bridge between brain and peripheral nerves)

Somatic nervous
(controls skeletal muscles)

Autonomic nervous
(regulates glands, blood vessels, internal organs)

Sympathetic nervous system
(mobilizes body for action, energy output)

Parasympathetic nervous system
(conserves energy maintains quiet state)

_____ 8. The brain is part of the
   a. spinal cord.
   b. autonomic nervous system.
   c. peripheral nervous system.
   d. central nervous system.

_____ 9. Which of the following nervous systems controls muscles?
   a. somatic nervous system
   b. autonomic nervous system
   c. brain
   d. central nervous system

_____ 10. Which of the following nervous systems has the greatest number of divisions?
   a. autonomic
   b. spinal cord
   c. peripheral
   d. sympathetic

Name _____

Section _____ Date _____

Number right* _____ × 10 points = Score _____

Diversity in U.S. Families

James M. Henslin

This reading, taken from a sociology textbook, explores family structure of several racial-ethnic groups. Read the selection to discover the family characteristics of each group. Which one is most similar to your family structure?

> ### Vocabulary Preview
>
> **diversity** (par. 1) the condition of being made up of different characteristics, qualities, or elements
>
> **preservation** (par. 2) the act of maintaining or keeping
>
> **merger** (par. 2) combination or union
>
> **cultural** (par. 4) relating to the behavior patterns, beliefs, and institutions of a particular population
>
> **machismo** (par. 7) an emphasis on male strength and dominance
>
> **nuclear family** (par. 10) a family unit consisting of a mother and father and their children
>
> **permissive** (par. 10) tolerant or lenient
>
> **assimilate** (par. 11) to become part of

1   It is important to note that there is no such thing as *the* American family. Rather, family life varies widely throughout the United States. The significance of social class, noted earlier, will continue to be evident as we examine diversity in U.S. families.

African American Families

2   Note that the heading reads African American *families*, not *the* African American family. There is no such thing as *the* African American family any more than there is *the* white family or *the* Latino family. The primary distinction is not between African Americans and other groups, but between social classes. Because African Americans who are members of the upper class follow the class interests—preservation of privilege and family fortune—they are especially concerned about the family background of those whom their children marry (Gatewood 1990). To them, marriage is viewed as a merger of family lines. Children of this class marry later than children of other classes.

---

*To calculate the number right, use items 1–10 under "Mastery Test Skills Check."

3   Middle-class African American families focus on achievement and respectability. Both husband and wife are likely to work outside the home. A central concern is that their children go to college, get good jobs, and marry well—that is, marry people like themselves, respectable and hardworking, who want to get ahead in school and pursue a successful career.

This African American family is observing Kwanzaa, a relatively new festival, that celebrates African heritage.

4   African American families in poverty face all the problems that cluster around poverty (Wilson 1987, 1996; Anderson 2001). Because the men are likely to have few skills and to be unemployed, it is difficult for them to fulfill the cultural roles of husband and father. Consequently, these families are likely to be headed by a woman and to have a high rate of births to single women. Divorce and desertion are also more common than among other classes. Sharing scarce resources and "stretching kinship" are primary survival mechanisms. That is, people who have helped out in hard times are considered brothers, sisters, or cousins to whom one owes obligations as though they were blood relatives (Stack 1974). Sociologists use the term *fictive kin* to refer to this stretching of kinship.

5   From Figure A, you can see that, compared with other groups, African American families are the least likely to be headed by married couples and the most likely to be headed by women. Because of a *marriage squeeze*—an imbalance in the sex ratio, in this instance fewer unmarried men per 1,000 unmarried women—African American women are more likely than other racial-ethnic groups to marry men who are less educated than themselves (South 1991).

Latino Families

6   As Figure A (p. 390) shows, the proportion of Latino families headed by married couples and women falls in between that of whites and that of African Americans. The effects of social class on families, which I just sketched, also apply to Latinos. In addition, families differ by country of origin. Families from Cuba, for example, are more likely to be headed by a married couple than are families from Puerto Rico (*Statistical Abstract* 2000: Table 45).

7   What really distinguishes Latino families, however, is culture—especially the Spanish language, the Roman Catholic religion, and a strong family orientation coupled with a disapproval of divorce. Although there is some debate among the experts, another characteristic seems to be **machismo**—an emphasis on male strength and dominance. In Chicano families (those originating from Mexico), the husband-father plays a stronger role than in either white

Although there is no such thing as *the* Latino family, in general, Latinos place high emphasis on extended family relationships.

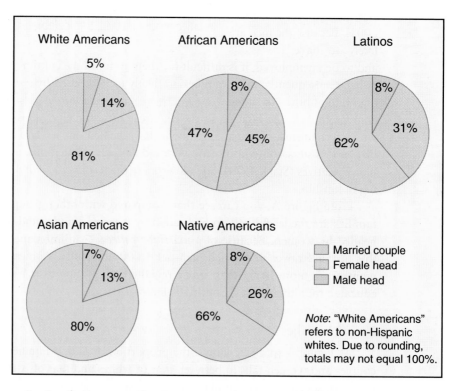

Figure A   Family Structure: The Percentage of U.S. Households Headed by Men, Women, and Married Couples

Source: Statistical Abstract 2000: Tables 41, 32, 44, 45.

or African American families (Vega 1990). Machismo apparently decreases with each generation in the United States (Hurtado et al. 1992; Wood 2001). The wife-mother, however, generally makes most of the day-to-day decisions for the family and does the routine disciplining of the children. She is usually more family centered than her husband, displaying more warmth and affection for her children.

8   Generalizations have limits, of course, and as with other ethnic groups, individual Latino families vary considerably from one to another (Baca Zinn 1994; Carrasquillo 1994).

Asian American Families

9   As you can see from Figure A, the structure of Asian American families is almost identical to that of white families. Apart from this broad characteristic, because Asian Americans come from twenty countries, their family life varies considerably, reflecting their many cultures. In addition, as with Latino families, the more recent their immigration, the more closely their family life reflects the family life of their country of origin (Kibria 1993; Glenn 1994).

10   Despite such differences, sociologist Bob Suzuki (1985), who studied Chinese American and Japanese American families, identified several distinctive characteristics. Although Asian Americans have adopted the nuclear family, they have retained Confucian values that provide a distinct framework for family life: humanism, collectivity, self-discipline, hierarchy, respect for the elderly, moderation, and obligation. Obligation means that each individual owes respect to other family members and is responsible for never bringing shame on the family. Asian Americans tend to be more permissive than Anglos in child rearing and more likely to use shame and guilt rather than physical punishment to control their children's behavior.

Native American Families

11   Perhaps the single most significant issue that Native American families face is whether to follow traditional values or to assimilate into the dominant culture (Yellowbird and Snipp 1994; Garrett 1999). This primary distinction creates vast differences among families. The traditionals speak native languages and emphasize distinctive Native American values and beliefs. Those that have assimilated into the broader culture do not.

12   Figure A depicts the structure of Native American families. You can see how close it is to that of Latinos. In general, Native American parents are permissive with their children and avoid physical punishment. Elders play a much more active role in their children's families than they do in most U.S. families: They not only provide child care, but also they teach and discipline children. Like others, Native American families differ by social class.

In Sum . . .

13   From this brief review, you can see that race-ethnicity signifies little for understanding family life. Rather, social class and culture hold the keys. The more resources a family has, the more it assumes the characteristics of a middle-class nuclear family. Compared with the poor, middle-class families have fewer children and fewer unmarried mothers, and place greater emphasis on educational achievement and deferred gratification.

To search for the Native American family would be fruitless. There are rural, urban, single parent, extended, nuclear, rich, poor, traditional, and assimilated Native American families, to name just a few. Shown here is an Apache family in Whiteriver, Arizona.

MASTERY TEST SKILLS CHECK

Directions: Choose the best answer for each of the following questions.

Checking Your Comprehension

_____ 1. The purpose of this selection is to
   a. describe the typical American family.
   b. summarize the achievements of successful families in America.
   c. describe the characteristics of families in various racial-ethnic groups in America.
   d. list statistics about marriage and divorce among racial-ethnic groups in America.

_____ 2. According to the selection, the primary interest of the upper class is
   a. preservation of privilege and family fortune.
   b. acquisition of real estate and material possessions.
   c. strengthening of extended family relationships.
   d. assimilation into the dominant culture.

_____ 3. According to the reading, a "marriage squeeze" refers to
   a. an overemphasis on marriage.
   b. an imbalance in the ratio of women to men.
   c. a disapproval of divorce.
   d. a decline in the number of married couples.

_____ 4. According to the selection, the primary distinction among families in the U.S. is determined by
a. race.
b. ethnicity.
c. social class.
d. geographic location.

_____ 5. In Asian American families, the term "obligation" specifically means that
a. Asian Americans must marry other Asian Americans only.
b. Asian American children are responsible for taking care of their elderly parents.
c. each family is obliged to maintain the traditions of its country of origin.
d. each individual owes respect to other family members and must never bring shame on the family.

_____ 6. Native American families and Asian American families are similar in that both
a. are permissive with their children and avoid physical punishment.
b. downplay the role of elders in the family.
c. emphasize male strength and dominance.
d. focus on achievement and respectability.

Applying Your Skills

_____ 7. The structure of white (non-Hispanic) American families is most similar to that of
a. Asian American families.
b. African American families.
c. Native American families.
d. Latino families.

_____ 8. Among which group are female headed families most common?
a. African Americans
b. Asian Americans
c. Native Americans
d. White Americans

_____ 9. Which family structure varies least from racial/ethnic group to racial/ethnic group?
a. married couples
b. male headed families
c. female headed families

_____ 10. Which family structure varies most from racial/ethnic group to racial/ethnic group?
a. married couples
b. female headed families
c. male headed families

Studying Words

_____ 11. The word "privilege" (paragraph 2) originated from which of the following languages?
a. Greek
b. German
c. Middle English
d. Spanish

_____ 12. What is the best definition of the word "poverty" as it is used in paragraph 4?
a. unproductiveness
b. infertility
c. state of being poor
d. renunciation of the right to own property

_____ 13. The prefix of the word "imbalance" (paragraph 5) means
   a. against.
   b. toward.
   c. within.
   d. not.

_____ 14. What is the correct pronunciation of the word "machismo" (paragraph 7)?
   a. match IZ moe
   b. maw CHEEZ moe
   c. MACK iz moe
   d. MATCH iz moe

_____ 15. What is the best definition of the word "assumes" as it is used in paragraph 13?
   a. pretends
   b. seizes
   c. takes for granted
   d. takes on

> For more practice, ask your instructor for an opportunity to work on the mastery tests that appear in the Test Bank.

Chapter 11

Organizing and Remembering Information

THIS CHAPTER WILL SHOW YOU HOW TO

1 Highlight and mark important information in textbook chapters

2 Outline information to show its organization

3 Draw maps to organize information

4 Summarize ideas for review purposes

5 Review for maximum retention

Getting Started with . . .
Organizing and Remembering Information

This stack of textbooks demonstrate the heavy reading load expected of many college students. How can you ever remember everything in all of these books? This chapter offers suggestions for organizing and remembering textbook content.

Copyright © 2009 by Kathleen T. McWhorter

395

Suppose you are planning a cross-country trip next summer. To get ready you begin to collect all kinds of information: maps, newspaper articles on various cities, places to visit, names of friends' friends, and so forth. After a while, you find that you have a great deal of information and that it is difficult to locate any one item. You begin to realize that the information you have collected will be of little or no use unless you organize it in some way. You decide to buy large envelopes and put different kinds of information into separate envelopes, such as information on individual states.

In this case, you found a practical, commonsensical solution to a problem. The rule or principle that you applied was this: When something gets confusing, organize it.

This rule also works well when applied to college textbooks. Each text contains thousands of pieces of information—facts, names, dates, theories, principles. This information quickly becomes confusing unless it is organized. Once you have organized it, you will be able to find and remember what you need more easily than if your text were still an unsorted heap of facts.

Organizing information requires sifting, sorting, and in some cases rearranging important facts and ideas. There are five common methods of organizing textbook materials:

- Highlighting
- Marking
- Outlining
- Mapping
- Summarizing

In this chapter you will learn techniques for doing each. You will also see how to study and review more effectively.

HIGHLIGHTING AND MARKING

Highlighting and marking important facts and ideas as you read are effective methods of identifying and organizing information. They are also the biggest time-savers known to college students. Suppose it took you four hours to read an assigned chapter in sociology. One month later you need to review that chapter to prepare for an exam. If you did not highlight or mark as you read the first time, then, in order to review the chapter once, you would have to spend another four hours rereading it. However, if you had highlighted and marked as you read, you could review the chapter in an hour or less—a savings of 300 percent. This means you can save many hours each semester. More important, the less time you spend identifying what to learn, the more thoroughly you can learn the necessary information. This strategy can help improve your grades.

Highlighting Effectively

Here are a few basic suggestions for highlighting effectively:

1. **Read a paragraph or section first.** Then go back and highlight what is important.
2. **Highlight important portions of the topic sentence.** Also highlight any supporting details you want to remember (see Chapters 6 and 7).
3. **Be accurate.** Make sure your highlighting reflects the content of the passage. Incomplete or hasty highlighting can mislead you as you review the passage and may cause you to miss the main point.
4. **Use a system for highlighting.** There are several from which to choose: for instance, using two or more different colors of highlighters to distinguish between main ideas and details, or placing a bracket around the main idea and using highlighter to mark important details. No one system is more effective than another. Try to develop a system that works well for you.
5. **Highlight as few words as possible in a sentence.** Seldom should you highlight an entire sentence. Usually highlighting the key idea along with an additional phrase or two is sufficient. Read the following paragraph. Notice that you can understand its meaning from the highlighted parts alone.

> Obviously, everybody spends part of his or her life as a single person. Traditionally, it was common that as adolescents entered adulthood, they felt compelled to find both jobs and marriage partners. Today, expectations and goals are changing. As an adolescent moves through high school, and perhaps college, he or she faces a number of decisions regarding the future. Marrying right after school is no longer a top priority for many, and the social stigma against remaining single is rapidly disappearing. In fact, single adults are now one of the fastest-growing factions in the United States; in the past two decades, the number of singles has more than doubled, and now represents more than one-fourth of all households.

6. **Use headings to guide your highlighting** (see Chapter 9). Use the headings to form questions that you expect to be answered in the section (see Chapter 5). Then highlight the answer to each question.

Highlighting the Right Amount

If you highlight either too much or too little, you defeat the purpose. By highlighting too little, you miss valuable information, and your review and study of the material will be incomplete. On the other hand, if you highlight too much, you are not identifying the most important ideas and eliminating less important facts. The more you highlight, the more you will have to reread when studying and the less of a time-saver the procedure will prove to be. As a general rule of thumb, highlight no more than 20 to 30 percent of the material.

Here is a paragraph highlighted in three different ways. First read the paragraph that has not been highlighted; then look at each highlighted version. Try to decide which version would be most useful if you were rereading it for study purposes.

Money (or actually the lack of it) is a major source of stress for many people. In a sense, this is one of the most "valid" stressors because so many of our basic survival needs require money. Anyone struggling to survive on a small income is likely to feel plenty of stress. But money has significance beyond its obvious value as a medium of exchange. Even some of the wealthiest people become stressed over money-related issues. To some people, wealth is a measurement of human value and their self-esteem is based on their material assets. Stress management for such people requires taking an objective look at the role money plays for them

— Byer and Shainberg, *Living Well*, pp. 78–79.

Example 1:

Money (or actually the lack of it) is a major source of stress for many people. In a sense, this is one of the most "valid" stressors because so many of our basic survival needs require money. Anyone struggling to survive on a small income is likely to feel plenty of stress. But money has significance beyond its obvious value as a medium of exchange. Even some of the wealthiest people become stressed over money-related issues. To some people, wealth is a measurement of human value and their self-esteem is based on their material assets. Stress management for such people requires taking an objective look at the role money plays for them.

Example 2:

Money (or actually the lack of it) is a major source of stress for many people. In a sense, this is one of the most "valid" stressors because so many of our basic survival needs require money. Anyone struggling to survive on a small income is likely to feel plenty of stress. But money has significance beyond its obvious value as a medium of exchange. Even some of the wealthiest people become stressed over money-related issues. To some people, wealth is a measurement of human value and their self-esteem is based on their material assets. Stress management for such people requires taking an objective look at the role money plays for them.

Example 3:

Money (or actually the lack of it) is a major source of stress for many people. In a sense, this is one of the most "valid" stressors because so many of our basic survival needs require money. Anyone struggling to survive on a small income is likely to feel plenty of stress. But money has significance beyond its obvious value as a medium of exchange. Even some of the wealthiest people become stressed over money-related issues. To some people, wealth is a measurement of human value and their self-esteem is based on their material assets. Stress management for such people requires taking an objective look at the role money plays for them.

The last example is the best example of effective highlighting. Only the most important information has been highlighted. In the first example, too little of the important information has been highlighted, while what *has* been highlighted is either unnecessary or incomplete. The second example, on the other hand, has too much highlighting to be useful for review.

EXERCISE 11-1

Directions: Read and highlight the following passage using the guidelines presented in this section.

Tailoring the Marketing Mix for Global Markets

Marketers have several options as to the products they present in the global arena. They can sell the same product abroad that they sell at home, they can modify the product for foreign markets, or they can develop an entirely new product for foreign markets.

The simplest strategy is product extension, which involves offering the same product in all markets, domestic and foreign. This approach has worked successfully for companies including Pepsico, Coca-Cola, Kentucky Fried Chicken, and Levis. Pepsi and Coke are currently battling for market share in both Russia and Vietnam, countries with small but growing soft-drink markets. Both firms are producing and selling the same cola to the Russian and Vietnamese markets that they sell to other markets around the world. Not all companies that have attempted it, however, have found success with product extension. When Duncan Hines introduced its rich, moist American cakes to England, the British found them too messy to hold while sipping tea. Japanese consumers disliked the coleslaw produced by Kentucky Fried Chicken; it was too sweet for their tastes. KFC responded by cutting the sugar in half.

The strategy of modifying a product to meet local preferences or conditions is product adaptation. Cosmetics companies produce different colors to meet the differing preferences of European consumers. French women like bold reds while British and German women prefer pearly pink shades of lipstick and nail color. Nestle's sells varieties of coffee to suit local tastes worldwide. Unilever produces frozen versions of local delicacies such as Bami Goreng and Madras Curry for markets in Indonesia and India.

Product invention consists of developing a new product to meet a market's needs and preferences. The opportunities that exist with this strategy are great since many unmet needs exist worldwide, particularly in developing and less-developed economies. Marketers have not been quick, however, to attempt product invention. For example, despite the fact that an estimated 600 million people worldwide still scrub clothes by hand, it was the early 1980s before a company (Colgate-Palmolive) developed an inexpensive, all plastic, manual washing machine with the tumbling action of an automatic washer for use in homes without electricity.

—Kinnear et al., *Principles of Marketing*, p. 132.

EXERCISE 11-2   **Directions:** Read or reread and highlight Chapter 5 in this book. Follow the guidelines suggested in this chapter.

Testing Your Highlighting

As you highlight, check to be certain your highlighting is effective and will be helpful for review purposes. To test the effectiveness of your highlighting, take any passage and reread only the highlighted portions. Then ask yourself the following questions:

- Does the highlighting tell what the passage is about?
- Does it make sense?
- Does it indicate the most important idea in the passage?

EXERCISE 11-3   **Directions:** Test the effectiveness of your highlighting for the material you highlighted in Exercises 11-1 and 11-2. Make changes, if necessary.

Marking

Highlighting alone will not clearly identify and organize information in many types of textbooks. Also, highlighting does not allow you to react to or sort ideas. Try making notes in the margin in addition to highlighting. Notice how the marginal notes in the following passage organize the information in a way that highlighting cannot.

The Source of Energy

Within the biosphere itself several forms of energy are produced: hydraulic energy, created by water in motion (a river pouring over a dam, storm waves striking a shoreline); electrical energy (lightning); and geothermal energy (underground water converted to steam by hot rock formations). Powerful as these sources of energy can be, they are insignificant compared with the huge flow of energy that comes to earth from the sun.

The sun's energy begins with reactions like that of a hydrogen bomb. Nuclear fusion deep in the sun's core creates radiation, which makes its way to the sun's surface and is then radiated away—most of it as visible light, some as ultraviolet light and infrared light and X rays. This sunlight is the dominant form of energy in our world, one that primitive peoples recognized eons ago as the giver of life. All the energy humans produce in a single year from our many energy sources— coal, oil, hydraulic power, nuclear power—amounts, according to our present estimates, to only two ten-thousandths of the total energy coming to us each day from the sun.

—Laetsch, *Plants*, p. 8.

Margin notes:

4 forms of energy
1. hydraulic
2. electrical
3. geothermal
4. sun

Radiation
↓
light
↓
energy

Here are a few examples of useful types of marking:

1. **Circle words you do not know.**

   Sulfur is a yellow, solid substance that has several (allotropic) forms.

2. **Mark definitions with an asterisk.**

   * *Chemical reactivity* is the tendency of an element to participate in chemical reactions.

3. **Write summary words or phrases in the margin.**

   reaction w/air

   Some elements, such as aluminum (Al) or Copper (Cu), tarnish just from sitting around in the air. They react with oxygen (O_2) in the air.

4. **Number lists of ideas, causes, and reasons.**

   ① ② ③

   Metallic properties include conductivity, luster, and ductility.

5. **Place brackets around important passages.**

   In Group IVA, carbon (C) is a nonmetal, silicon (Si) and germanium (Ge) are metaloids, and tin (Sn) and lead (Pb) are metals.

6. **Draw arrows or diagrams to show relationships or to clarify information.**

graphite

Graphite is made up of a lot of carbon layers stacked on top of one another, like sheets of paper. The layers slide over one another, which makes it a good lubricant.

7. **Make notes to yourself, such as "good test question," "reread," or "ask instructor."**

Test!

Carbon is most important to us because it is a basic element in all plant and animal structures.

8. **Put question marks next to confusing passages or when you want more information.**

why?

Sometimes an element reacts so violently with air, water, or other substances that an explosion occurs.

Try to develop your own code or set of abbreviations. Here are a few examples:

Types of Marking	Examples
ex	example
T	good test question
sum	good summary
def	important definition
RR	reread later

EXERCISE 11-4   **Directions:** Read each of the following passages and then highlight and mark each. Try various ways of highlighting and marking.

Passage A:

Dieting

1   Millions of people in the United States want to lose weight without sacrificing* their favorite foods, without pain, and without great effort. If only we could be thin and firm by waving a magic wand!

2   It's very popular to resort to well-publicized weight-loss programs that involve special food requirements such as high-fat, high-protein, low-carbohydrate, or liquid protein. There are hundreds of such programs that continue to come and go; many

*Boxed words appear in the Mastering Vocabulary exercise on p. 416.

of them are reported as "breakthroughs," but if this were the case, even newer breakthroughs would not be needed. The problem is that most diet plans focus on short-term (and often futile) weight loss, which results in weight cycling, or "yo-yo" dieting, and psychological problems that result from repeated failures to keep weight off. Only 5 percent of people who try are able to maintain their weight losses. Much better is a program of lifetime weight management, which involves learning new eating and exercise habits.

3   Unwilling or unable to lose weight through diet and exercise, many people in the United States pour over $5 billion each year into diet pills, water pills, diet drugs, hormones, health spas, surgery, and fad diets. Many of these products and procedures, if they work at all, may commit a person to a cycle of quick weight loss, rebound weight gain when normal eating is resumed, and then greater difficulty with weight loss in the next diet attempt. Weight loss has become a fertile field for quick-fix methods, gimmicks, and quackery. We will discuss fad diets, chemical strategies, and surgical procedures in the following sections.

Fad Diets

4   There is usually at least one fad diet book on the best-seller list in any given week. Some fad diets are simple variations of a basic 1000–1100-calorie balanced diet. Others may be dangerous because they emphasize one food or food group and the elimination of others, and advise people to follow diets low in energy and nutrients. Some fad diets are more hazardous to a person's health than the obesity they propose to cure, creating adverse reactions ranging from headaches to death. Of 29,000 claims, treatments, and therapies for losing weight, fewer than 6 percent are effective, and 13 percent are downright dangerous.

Diet Books

5   Fad diet books are long on advertising and packaging and short on unique approaches. Many of them are products of advertising specialists, not of scientists who are experts in dietetics. Although they list "degrees" after their names, the writers/practitioners sometimes have no training in nutrition or food science, or have credentials from unaccredited schools. "Doctor" Robert Hass, author of *Eat to Win,* was awarded a Ph.D. by Columbia Pacific University, in San Rafael, California, from which students could earn degrees in one year or less. "Doctor" Harry Diamond, author of *Fit for Life,* was a graduate of the former American College of Health Science in Austin, Texas, which stopped awarding degrees after the State of Texas said it was not qualified to operate as a college. Even a legitimate degree may not prevent a person from authoring scientifically inaccurate advice. Such was the case with Robert Atkins, a medical doctor, who authored *Diet Revolution,* which advised meals rich in animal fats and cholesterol and almost devoid of carbohydrates. Fad diets may be neither dangerous nor beneficial to a person's health, although this is not always the case.

—Byer and Shainberg, *Living Well*, p. 311.

Passage B:

Melting Point

1   The particles (atoms or molecules) of a solid are held together by attractive forces. . . . Heating up a solid, such as a piece of ice, gives its molecules more energy and makes them move. Pretty soon they are moving fast enough to overcome the attractive forces that were holding them rigidly together in the solid. The temperature at which this happens is the *melting point* of the solid. When a liquid, such as water, is cooled, the reverse process happens. We take energy away from the molecules, and pretty soon the molecules are moving slowly enough for their attractive forces to hold them rigidly together again and form a solid. The temperature at which this happens is the *freezing point* of the liquid. Melting point and freezing point are really the same thing, approached from opposite directions. To melt a substance, we supply heat; to freeze it, we remove heat.

2   While a solid is melting, its temperature stays constant at its melting point. Even though we keep heating a solid as it melts, we won't increase its temperature until all of the solid has changed to liquid. When a solid starts to melt, all of the heat that is put into it from then on goes into breaking up the attractive forces that hold the atoms or molecules together in the solid. When the solid is all melted, then the heat that is put in can once more go into increasing the temperature of the substance. The amount of heat that it takes to melt one gram of any substance at its melting point is called the *heat of fusion.* If we let the substance freeze, then it will give off heat in the amount of the heat of fusion. Freezing is a process that releases energy.

3   Every substance has a melting (or freezing) point except diamond, which no one has been able to melt yet. The stronger the attractive forces that hold atoms or molecules together in the solid, the higher its melting (or freezing) point will be. The forces holding a diamond together in the solid state are so strong that they can't be overcome by heating. Most elements are solids at "room temperature," a vague term meaning a range of about 20°C to 30°C. A substance that's a solid at room temperature has a melting point higher than room temperature. Some substances are borderline, and they can be either liquids or solids depending on the weather: we've all seen tar melt on a hot day. Olive oil will solidify (freeze) on a cold day. . . .

—Newell, *Chemistry,* pp. 47–48.

OUTLINING

Outlining is a good way to create a visual picture of what you have read. In making an outline, you record the writer's organization and show the relative importance of and connection between ideas.

Outlining has a number of advantages:

- It gives an overview of the topic and enables you to see how various subtopics relate to one another.
- Recording the information in your own words tests your understanding of what you read.
- It is an effective way to record needed information from reference books you do not own.

How to Outline

Generally, an outline follows a format like the one below.

```
I. First major idea
    A. First supporting detail
        1. Detail
        2. Detail
    B. Second supporting detail
        1. Detail
            a. Minor detail or example
            b. Minor detail or example
II. Second major idea
    A. First supporting idea
```

Notice that the most important ideas are closer to the left margin. Less important ideas are indented toward the middle of the page. A quick glance at an outline shows what is most important, what is less important, and how ideas support or explain one another.

Here are a few suggestions for using the outline format:

1. **Do not be overly concerned with following the outline format exactly.** As long as your outline shows an organization of ideas, it will work for you.
2. **Write words and phrases rather than complete sentences.**
3. **Use your own words.** Do not lift words from the text.
4. **Do not write too much.** If you need to record numerous facts and details, underlining rather than outlining might be more effective.
5. **Pay attention to headings.** Be sure that all the information you place underneath a heading explains or supports that heading. Every heading indented the same amount on the page should be of equal importance.

Now read the following passage on franchising and then study its outline.

Franchising

Franchising is an arrangement whereby a supplier, or franchiser, grants a dealer, or franchisee, the right to sell products in exchange for some type of consideration. For example, the franchiser may receive some percentage of total sales in exchange for furnishing equipment, buildings, management know-how, and marketing assistance to the franchisee. The franchisee supplies labor and capital, operates the franchised business, and agrees to abide by the provisions of the franchise agreement. In the next section we look at the major types of retail franchises, the advantages and disadvantages of franchising, and trends in retailing.

I. Franchising
- A. Arrangement betw. franchiser (supplier) and franchisee (dealer)
  1. Right to sell products exchanged for type of consideration
  2. Franchiser may receive percentage of sales for supplying equip., building, or services
  3. Franchisee supplies labor and capital, and operates business
- B. Types
  1. Manufacturer authorizes stores to sell brand-name items
     a. Ex: cars, shoes, gasoline
  2. Producer licenses distributors to sell product to retailers
     a. Ex: soft-drink industry
  3. Franchiser supplies brand-names or services but not complete product
     a. Primary role is marketing
     b. Ex: Hertz, McDonald's
     c. Most commonly used type of franchise

Major Types of Retail Franchises

Retail franchise arrangements can generally be classified as one of three general types. In the first arrangement, a manufacturer authorizes a number of retail stores to sell a certain brand-name item. This franchise arrangement, one of the oldest, is common in the sales of passenger cars and trucks, farm equipment, shoes, paint, earth-moving equipment, and petroleum. About 90 percent of all gasoline is sold through franchised independent retail service stations, and franchised dealers handle virtually all sales of new cars and trucks. The second type of retail franchise occurs when a producer licenses distributors to sell a given product to retailers. This franchising arrangement is common in the soft-drink industry. Most national manufacturers of soft-drink syrups—Coca-Cola, Dr Pepper, Pepsi-Cola—franchise independent bottlers, which then serve retailers. In the third type of retail franchise, a franchiser supplies brand names, techniques, or other services, instead of a complete product. The franchiser may provide certain production and distribution services, but its primary role in the arrangement is the careful development and control of marketing strategies. This approach to franchising, which is the most typical today, is used by many organizations, including Holiday Inn, AAMCO, McDonald's, Dairy Queen, Avis, Hertz, Kentucky Fried Chicken, and H&R Block.

—Pride and Ferrell, *Marketing*, p. 380.

EXERCISE 11-5

Directions: Read the following passage and the incomplete outline that follows. Fill in the missing information in the outline.

Changing Makeup of Families and Households

The traditional definition of a typical U.S. household was one that contained a husband, a nonworking wife, and two or more children. That type of household accounts for only about nine percent of households today. In its place we see many single-parent households, households without children, households of one person, and other nontraditional households. A number of trends have combined to create these changes in families and households. Americans are staying single longer— more than one-half of the women and three-quarters of the men between 20 and 24 years old in the United States are still single. Divorce rates are at an all-time high. It is predicted that almost two-thirds of first marriages may end up in divorce. There is a widening gap between the life expectancy of males and females. Currently average life expectancy in the United States is 74 years for men and 78 years for women. Widows now make up more than one-third of one-person households in the United States. These trends have produced a declining average size of household.

The impact of all these changes is significant for marketers. Nontraditional households have different needs for goods and services than do traditional households. Smaller households often have more income per person than larger households, and require smaller houses, smaller cars, and smaller package sizes for food products. Households without children often spend more on personal entertainment and respond more to fads than do traditional households. More money may be spent on travel as well.

—Kinnear et al., *Principles of Marketing*, pp. 39–40.

I. Typical U.S. household has changed

   A. Used to consist of

      1. husband

      2. nonworking wife

      3. two or more children

    B. _____

       1. _____

       2. _____

       3. _____

II. Trends that created this change

    A. _____

       1. _____

       2. _____

    B. Divorce rates higher

       1. maybe two-thirds of marriages

    C. _____

       1. _____

       2. _____

III. Impact of changes for marketers

    A. Different goods and services needed

    B. _____

    C. _____

    D. _____

    E. _____

MAPPING

Mapping is a visual method of organizing information. It involves drawing diagrams to show how ideas in an article or chapter are related. Some students prefer mapping to outlining because they feel it is freer and less tightly structured.

Maps can take numerous forms. You can draw them in any way that shows the relationships of ideas. Figure 11-1 shows two sample maps. Each was drawn to show the overall organization of Chapter 6 in this book. First refer back to Chapter 6 and then study each map.

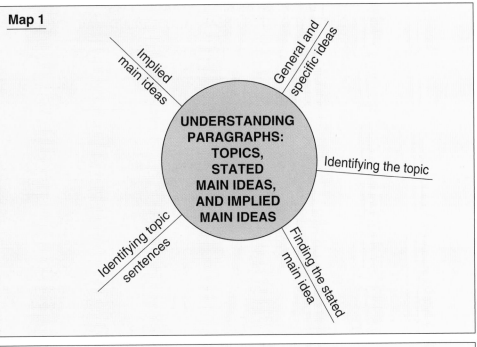

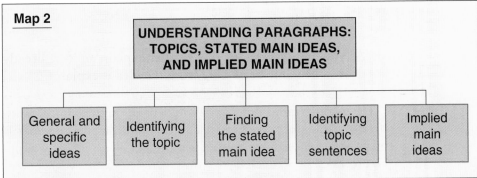

Figure 11-1   Sample maps

How to Draw Maps

Think of a map as a picture or diagram that shows how ideas are connected. Use the following steps in drawing a map.

1. **Identify the overall topic or subject.** Write it in the center or at the top of the page.
2. **Identify major supporting information that relates to the topic.** Draw each piece of information on a line connected to the central topic.

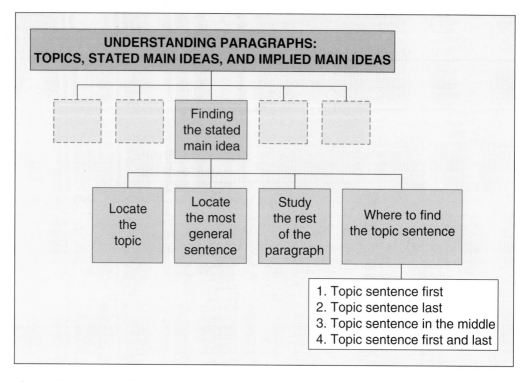

Figure 11-2   Map with greater detail

3. **As you discover details that further explain an idea already mapped, draw a new line branching from the idea it explains.**

How you arrange your map will depend on the subject matter and how it is organized. Like an outline, it can be quite detailed or very brief, depending on your purpose. A portion of a more detailed map of Chapter 6 is shown in Figure 11-2.

Once you are skilled at drawing maps, you can become more creative, drawing different types of maps to fit what you are reading. For example, you can draw a time line (see Figure 11-3) that shows historical events, or a process diagram to show processes and procedures (see Figure 11-4).

EXERCISE 11-6   **Directions:** Draw a map of the excerpt "Tailoring the Marketing Mix for Global Markets" on p. 399.

EXERCISE 11-7   **Directions:** Draw a map of Chapter 7 of this book.

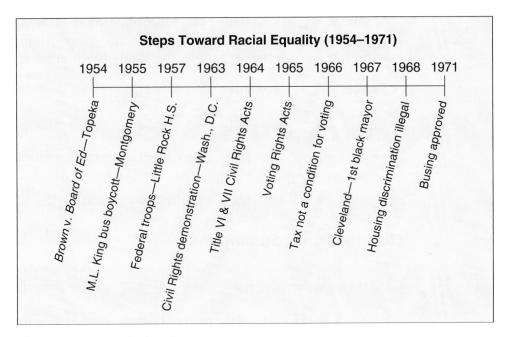

Figure 11-3   Sample time line

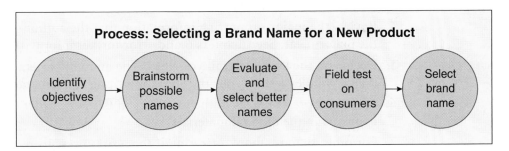

Figure 11-4   Sample process map

SUMMARIZING

A summary is a brief statement that reviews the major idea of something you have read. Its purpose is to make a record of the most important ideas in condensed form. A summary is much shorter than an outline and contains less detailed information.

A summary goes one step beyond recording what the writer says. It pulls together the writer's ideas by condensing and grouping them. Numerous situations in college courses require the ability to summarize, such as:

- Answering an essay question
- Reviewing a film or videotape
- Writing a term paper
- Recording results of a laboratory experiment or demonstration
- Summarizing the plot (main events) of a short story before analyzing it
- Quickly reviewing large amounts of information

How to Write a Summary

Before writing a summary, be sure you understand the material and have identified the writer's major points.

1. **Write a brief outline of the material or underline each major idea.**
2. **Write one sentence that states the writer's overall concern or most important idea.** To do this, ask yourself what one topic the material is about. Then ask what point the writer is trying to make about that topic. This sentence will be the topic sentence of your summary.
3. **Be sure to use your own words rather than those of the author.**
4. **Review the major supporting information that the author gives to explain the major ideas.** See Chapters 6 and 7 for further information.
5. **Decide on the level of detail you need.** The amount of detail you include, if any, will depend on your purpose for writing the summary.
6. **Normally, present ideas in the summary in the same order in which they appeared in the original materials.**
7. **For other than textbook material, if the writer presents a clear opinion or expresses an attitude toward the subject matter, include it in your summary.**
8. **Do not concentrate on correctness when writing summaries for your own use.** Some students prefer to write summaries using words and phrases rather than complete sentences.

Read the following summary of "Changing Makeup of Families and Households," which appeared on p. 407.

Notice that this summary contains only the broadest, most important ideas. Details are not included. The first sentence shows how the typical household has changed, the second sentence lists the three trends that are causing this change, and the last sentence details the implications for marketers.

> The typical U.S. household has changed from a husband, nonworking wife, and two or more children to a smaller-sized unit that might contain a single parent, no children, or even only one person. Three trends that have caused this change are: people are staying single longer, divorce rates are higher, and women are outliving men by more. Because of these changes, marketers have found that the current, smaller household needs different goods and services, has more income per person, tends to purchase smaller items, and spends more on entertainment, fads, and travel than the typical household of the past.

EXERCISE 11-8

Directions: On a separate sheet of paper, write a summary of a television show you recently viewed.

EXERCISE 11-9

Directions: On a separate sheet of paper, write a summary of one of the reading selections in Part Five of this text.

EXERCISE 11-10

Directions: Write a summary of the article "Franchising" on p. 406. When you have finished, compare it with the sample summary shown in Figure 11-5 on p. 414. Then answer the following questions.

1. How does your summary differ from the sample?

2. Did your summary begin with a topic sentence? How does it compare with the one in the sample?

3. Did your summary include ideas in the order they were given in the article?

> franching is an arrangement between a supplier (franchiser) and
> a dealer (franchisee). the franchiser supplies products or services
> and receives a percentage of the profits. the franchisee supplies
> labor and capital, and operates the business. there are three
> types of franchises: 1) authorized stores sell brand-name products,
> 2) distributors are licensed by producer to sell product to retailers,
> and 3) franchiser supplies brand name and/or services but does not
> supply the product.

Figure 11-5   Sample summary: "Franchising"

IMMEDIATE AND PERIODIC REVIEW

Once you have read and organized information, the last step is to learn it. Fortunately, this is not a difficult task if you have organized the information effectively. In fact, through underlining, outlining, and/or summarizing, you have already learned a large portion of the material. Review, then, is a way to fix, or store, information in your memory for later recall. There are two types of review, immediate and periodic.

How Immediate Review Works

Immediate review is done right after you have finished reading an assignment or writing an outline or summary. When you finish any of these, you may feel like breathing a sigh of relief and taking a break. However, it is worth the time and effort to spend another five minutes reviewing what you just read and refreshing your memory. The best way to do this is to go back through the chapter and reread the headings, graphic material, introduction, summary, and any underlining or marginal notes.

Immediate review works because it consolidates, or draws together, the material just read. It also gives a final, lasting impression of the content. Considerable research has been done on the effectiveness of immediate review. Results indicate that review done immediately rather than delayed until a later time makes a large difference in the amount remembered.

How Periodic Review Works

Although immediate review will increase your recall of information, it will not help you retain information for long periods of time. To remember information over time, periodically refresh your memory. This is known as **periodic review.** Go back over the material on a regular basis. Do this by looking again at those sections that carry the basic meaning and reviewing your underlining, outlining, and/or summaries. Here is an example of a schedule one student set up to periodically review assigned chapters in a psychology textbook. You can see that this student reviewed each chapter the week after reading it and again two weeks later. This schedule is only an example. You will need to make a schedule for each course that fits the course requirements. For math and science courses, for example, you may need to include a review of previous homework assignments and laboratory work. In other courses, less or more frequent review of previous material may be needed.

```
Week 1  Read ch. 1
Week 2  Review ch. 1
        Read ch. 2
Week 3  Review ch. 2
        Read ch. 3
Week 4  Review ch. 3
        Review ch. 1
        Read ch. 4
Week 5  Review ch. 4
        Review ch. 2
        Read ch. 5
```

EXERCISE 11-11

Directions: Choose one of your courses that involves regular textbook reading assignments. Plan a reading and periodic review schedule for the next three weeks. Assume that new chapters will be assigned as frequently as in previous weeks and that you want to review whatever has been covered over the past three weeks.

LEARNING STYLE TIPS

If you tend to be a . . .	Strengthen your review strategies by . . .
Creative learner	Brainstorming before and after each assignment to discover new ways to tie the material together
Pragmatic learner	Creating, writing, and answering review questions; preparing and taking self-tests

MASTERING VOCABULARY

Directions: Select the choice that best provides the meaning of each word as it was used in this chapter. Use context clues, word parts, and a dictionary, if necessary.

_____ 1. sacrificing (p. 402)
   a. buying
   b. eating
   c. giving up
   d. saving

_____ 2. futile (p. 403)
   a. routine
   b. ineffective
   c. extreme
   d. careful

_____ 3. maintain (p. 403)
   a. keep
   b. change
   c. show off
   d. slow down

_____ 4. fertile (p. 403)
   a. academic
   b. challenging
   c. new
   d. productive

_____ 5. variations (p. 403)
   a. alternatives
   b. changes
   c. diets
   d. charts

_____ 6. adverse (p. 403)
   a. changing
   b. uplifting
   c. bad
   d. helpful

_____ 7. unique (p. 403)
   a. technical
   b. nutritional
   c. difficult
   d. new

_____ 8. unaccredited (p. 403)
   a. not appreciated
   b. not approved
   c. unstructured
   d. nonexistent

_____ 9. legitimate (p. 403)
   a. genuine
   b. medical
   c. college
   d. useful

_____ 10. devoid (p. 403)
   a. built on
   b. afraid
   c. lacking
   d. full

SELF-TEST SUMMARY

There is so much information in textbooks. How can you organize it all?

Five methods for organizing textbook information are:

1. **Highlighting**—a way of sorting important information from less important information. It eliminates the need to reread entire textbook chapters in order to review their major content. It also has the advantage of helping you stay active and involved with what you are reading.

2. **Marking**—a system that involves using signs, symbols, and marginal notes to react to, summarize, or comment on the material.

3. **Outlining**—a method of recording the most important information and showing the organization and relative importance of ideas. It is particularly useful when you need to see how ideas relate to one another or when you want to get an overview of the subject.

4. **Mapping**—a visual method of organizing information. It involves drawing diagrams to show how ideas in an article or chapter are related.

5. **Summarizing**—a way to pull together the most important ideas in condensed form. It provides a quick review of the material and forces you to explain the writer's ideas in your own words.

Getting More Practice with . . .
Organizing and Remembering Information

WORKING TOGETHER

Directions: Your instructor will choose a reading from Part Five and will then divide the class into three groups. Members of one group should outline the material, another group should draw maps, and the third should write summaries. When the groups have completed their tasks, the class members should review each other's work. Several students can read their summaries, draw maps, and write outlines on the chalkboard. Discuss which of the three methods seemed most effective for the material and how well prepared each group feels for (a) an essay exam, (b) a multiple-choice exam, and (c) a class discussion.

GOING ONLINE

Internet Activities

1. Kinds of Concept Maps

   http://www.classes.aces.uiuc.edu/ACES100/Mind/c-m2.html

   View these examples of the different types of concept maps. Using ideas, relationships, situations, and experiences from your own life, create a simple concept map of each type.

2. Textbook Marking

   http://ccc.byu.edu/learning/txt-mkg.php

   Learn some strategies and actual markings from this Brigham Young University site. Use them during your next textbook reading assignment.
   Write a paragraph about the advantages of highlighting and marking. Imagine you are trying to sway someone who thinks it is wrong to write in books.

Companion Website

For additional readings, exercises, and Internet activities, visit this book's Companion Website at:

http://www.ablongman.com/mcwhorter

If you need a user name and password, please see your instructor.

myreadinglab | **My Reading Lab**

For more practice with organizing and remembering information, visit MyReadingLab, click on the Reading Skills tab, and then click on:

1. Outlining and Summarizing—Spring Break in Florida
2. Memorization and Concentration—Mount Rushmore, South Dakota
3. Notetaking and Highlighting—Seattle, Washington

http://www.ablongman.com/myreadinglab

TEST-TAKING TIPS

Using Highlighting and Summarizing

Highlighting and summarizing can be helpful in certain test-taking situations. Use the following suggestions:

- As you read a lengthy passage on a test, it may be helpful to quickly mark important ideas. For example, if a passage states that there are four key factors that contribute to building a successful Web site, as you find each of the factors, quickly mark or circle them. Then, as you answer detail questions, you can move back quickly to the appropriate section of the passage. (Be sure that you are allowed to write in your test booklet.)

- If a question asks you to choose a statement that best summarizes the paragraph or passage, choose the statement that is the best restatement of the paragraph or passage's main idea.

- If you are having trouble finding the main idea of a paragraph or passage, look away from it and try to summarize it in one sentence in your own words. Your summary statement will be the main idea. Try to find a choice that comes closest to your summary.

Name _____

Section _____ Date _____

Number right _____ x 20 points = Score _____

Directions: Read each of the following sentences; then choose the answer that indicates the most important words to highlight in each sentence.

_____ 1. Unlike group therapies, which are usually supervised by a licensed therapist, self-help groups are not regulated by law or by professional standards, and they vary widely in their philosophies and methods.

—Wade and Tavris, *Invitation to Psychology*, p. 392.

    a. Unlike / therapies / usually / supervised regulated / vary widely

    b. self-help groups / not regulated by law or / professional standards / vary / in / philosophies and methods

    c. unlike group therapies / usually supervised / licensed therapist self-help groups / not regulated / law / professional standards / vary / in philosophies and methods

    d. self-help groups / not / law / standards / philosophies / methods

_____ 2. In 1629 a number of English Puritans formed the Massachusetts Bay Company and settled near Boston, where their charter gave them the rights to virtual self-government.

—Brummett et al., *Civilization*, p. 446.

    a. In 1629 / number of English Puritans formed / Massachusetts Bay Company / settled / Boston where / charter gave / rights to / self-government

    b. 1629 / Puritans / Massachusetts Bay Company / Boston / charter / self-government

    c. In 1629 / English Puritans formed Massachusetts Bay Company / near Boston / charter gave / rights to / self-government

    d. In 1629 a number / formed Massachusetts Bay Company / settled near Boston / gave them / self-government

_____ 3. Since that landmark opening of the first true theme park (Disneyland) in 1955, the operations of amusement parks have become more sophisticated, with technology playing a far more important role.

—Cook et al., *Tourism*, p. 156.

    a. landmark opening of / true theme park Disneyland / operations of amusement parks have become more sophisticated with technology playing / role

    b. Since / opening / Disneyland in 1955 / operations of amusement parks / more sophisticated / technology / more important

    c. landmark opening / first / Disneyland in 1955 / amusement parks / become more sophisticated / with technology / more important role

    d. theme park / Disneyland in 1955 / amusement parks / sophisticated / technology / role

_____ 4. The primary reason that it is important to understand the underlying
source of stress and to come to grips
with it is that there is a well-established scientific connection between
too much stress and the incidence of
disease.

—Pruitt and Stein, *Health Styles*, p. 81.

a. primary reason / it is important /
understand / underlying source of
stress and / come to grips with it is /
well-established scientific connection between / much stress and /
incidence of disease
b. reason / important / source of
stress/ scientific connection / stress /
incidence of disease
c. important to understand / stress /
come to grips / there is / well-
established scientific connection /
stress and / incidence of disease
d. important to understand / underlying source of stress and to come to
grips with it / scientific connection
between / stress and / disease

_____ 5. The best ways to avoid inconsiderate
behavior are to try to see the other
person's point of view; listen actively;
avoid interrupting the other person;
and avoid making any gestures, such
as head shaking or finger pointing,
that indicate disagreement or that are
threatening in nature.

—Donatelle and Davis,
Access to Health, p. 120.

a. avoid inconsiderate behavior / try
to see the other person's point of
view / listen actively / avoid interrupting / avoid / gestures / that
indicate disagreement or / are
threatening
b. best ways to avoid inconsiderate
behavior / to try to see the other
person's point of view / listen
actively / avoid interrupting / other
person / avoid making any gestures /
head shaking / finger pointing / indicate disagreement / threatening in
nature
c. avoid inconsiderate behavior /
point of view / listen / avoid
interrupting / avoid gestures
d. best ways / inconsiderate behavior /
other / point of view / listen / interrupting / making any gestures /
head shaking / finger pointing / indicate disagreement / threatening in
nature

Chapter 11
Mastery Test 2
Mapping and
Summarizing Skills

Name _____

Section _____ Date _____

Number right _____ x 20 points = Score _____

Directions: Read the passage below and then complete the map and the summary by answering the questions that follow each of them.

The first thing good listeners must do is figure out why they're listening. Researchers have identified five kinds of listening that reflect purposes you may have when communicating with others: appreciative, discriminative, empathic, comprehension, and critical.

Appreciative listening focuses on something other than the primary message. Some listeners enjoy seeing a famous speaker. Others relish a good speech, a classic movie, or a brilliant performance. On these occasions, you listen primarily to entertain yourself.

Discriminative listening requires listeners to draw conclusions from the way a message is presented rather than from what is said. In discriminative listening, people seek to understand the meaning behind the message. You're interested in what the speaker really thinks, believes, or feels. You're engaging in discriminative listening when you draw conclusions about how angry your parents are with you, based not on what they say but on how they say it. You draw inferences from the presentation of the message rather than from the message itself.

Empathic or therapeutic listening is intended to provide emotional support for the speaker. Although it is more typical of interpersonal than public communication, empathic listening does occur in public speaking situations, for example, when you hear an athlete apologize for unprofessional behavior or a classmate reveal a personal problem to illustrate a speech. In each case, your role is supportive.

Listening for comprehension occurs when you want to gain additional information or insights from the speaker. You are probably most familiar with this form of listening because you've relied heavily on it for your education. When you listen to a radio newscast, to a classroom lecture on marketing strategies, or to an elections official explaining new registration procedures, you're listening to understand—to comprehend information, ideas, and processes.

Critical listening is the most difficult kind of listening because it requires you to both interpret and evaluate the message. It demands that you go beyond understanding the message to interpreting it and evaluating its strengths and weaknesses. You'll practice this sort of listening in class. A careful consumer also uses critical listening to evaluate television commercials, political campaign speeches, or arguments offered by salespeople. When you are listening critically, you decide whether to accept or reject ideas and whether to act on the message.

—German and Gronbeck,
Principles of Public Speaking, pp. 38–39.

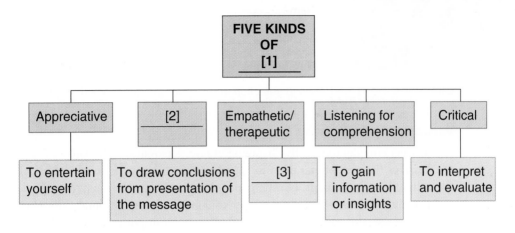

Refer to the map to answer questions 1–3.

_____ 1. The word that correctly fills in blank
[1] is
a. purposes.
b. listening.
c. communicating.
d. responding.

_____ 2. The word that correctly fills in blank
[2] is
a. conclusive.
b. emotional.
c. comprehensive.
d. discriminative.

_____ 3. The phrase that correctly fills in blank
[3] is
a. to apologize for behavior.
b. to reveal a personal problem.
c. to illustrate a speech.
d. to provide emotional support.

Refer to the following summary of the passage to
answer questions 4 and 5.

Summary: In communication, there are
five types of listening. Appreciative listening

is mainly for your own entertainment. Discriminative listening is when you have to figure out what the speaker means by _____[4]_____. Empathic or therapeutic listening requires you to give emotional support to the speaker; it happens more in interpersonal communication than in public speaking situations. Listening for comprehension is when you are trying to learn information or gain understanding. Critical listening is the most difficult because you have to interpret and then _____[5]_____ the message.

_____ 4. The phrase that correctly fills in blank
[4] is
a. how the message is presented.
b. what the speaker says.
c. how you feel about the speaker.
d. what you want to hear.

_____ 5. The phrase that correctly fills in blank
[5] is
a. understand.
b. repeat.
c. evaluate.
d. respond to.

Name _____

Section _____ Date _____

Number right _____ x 20 points = Score _____

Directions: Read the following selection and answer the questions that follow.

Participatory and Passive Listening

The general key to effective listening in interpersonal situations is active participation. Perhaps the best preparation for participatory listening is to act (physically and mentally) like a participant. For many people, this may be the most abused rule of effective listening. Recall, for example, how your body almost automatically reacts to important news: Almost immediately, you assume an upright posture, cock your head to the speaker, and remain relatively still and quiet. You do this almost reflexively because this is the way you listen most effectively. Even more important than this physical alertness is mental alertness. As a listener, participate in the communication interaction as an equal partner with the speaker, as one who is emotionally and intellectually ready to engage in the sharing of meaning.

Effective participatory listening is expressive. Let the listener know that you are participating in the communication interaction. Nonverbally, maintain eye contact, focus your concentration on the speaker rather than on others present, and express your feelings facially. Verbally, ask appropriate questions, signal understanding with "I see" or "yes," and express agreement or disagreement as appropriate.

Passive listening is, however, not without merit and some recognition of its value is warranted. Passive listening—listening without talking or directing the speaker in any obvious way—is a powerful means of communicating acceptance. This is the kind of listening that people ask for when they say, "Just listen to me." They are essentially asking you to suspend your judgment and "just listen." Passive listening allows the speaker to develop his or her thoughts and ideas in the presence of another person who accepts but does not evaluate, who supports but does not intrude. By listening passively, you provide a supportive and receptive environment. Once that has been established, you may wish to participate in a more active way, verbally and nonverbally.

—DeVito, *The Interpersonal Communication Book*, p. 141.

_____ 1. Which of the following is the best outline for paragraph 1?

a. A. Actions of a participant
   1. physical
   2. interaction

b. A. Actions of a participant
   1. sit straight
   2. be quiet
   3. head cocked
   4. be alert

c. A. Physical actions
   1. sit straight
   2. be quiet
   a. B. mental actions

d. A. Active participation in listening
   1. physical alertness
      a. sit straight
      b. quiet
      c. head cocked
   2. mental alertness

_____ 2. Which of the following is the best outline for paragraph 2?

a. B. Listening is expressive
   1. eye contact—maintain
   2. facial expressions verbally
   3. ask questions

b. B. Communication interaction
   1. nonverbal
      a. agree / disagree
      b. signal understanding
   2. verbal
      a. eye contact
      b. facial expression
      c. ask questions

c. B. Expressive participation
   1. nonverbal
      a. eye contact
      b. focus on speaker
      c. facial expressions
   2. verbal
      a. ask questions
      b. signal understanding
      c. agree / disagree

d. B. Expressions of a participant
   C. Nonverbal expressions
   D. Verbal expressions

_____ 3. Which of the following is the best outline for paragraph 3?

a. C. Active listening
   1. definition
   2. reasons

b. C. Reasons for passive listening
   D. Definition of passive listening

c. C. Meaning of passive listening
   1. no talking or directing of speaker
   2. communicates acceptance
   3. suspend judgment and "just listen"
   D. Results of passive listening
   1. speaker can develop thoughts and ideas
   2. you provide supportive, receptive environment

d. C. Passive listening
   1. judgmental
   2. supportive
   3. definition

_____ 4. Which group of words is best to highlight in the first sentence of the selection?

a. key / effective listening / active participation

b. general / interpersonal / participation

c. general / key / situations / active

d. key / interpersonal situations / is

_____ 5. Which of the following phrases from the first paragraph would be most important to highlight?

a. cock your head

b. for many people

c. Recall, for example

d. active participation

_____ 6. Which group of words is best to highlight in the last sentence of paragraph 2?
   a. ask / questions / disagreement / as / appropriate
   b. verbally / questions / signal / understanding / express / agreement / disagreement
   c. ask / questions / signal / agreement / appropriate
   d. verbally / I see / yes

_____ 7. Which of the following sentences from the last paragraph defines passive listening?
   a. first
   b. second
   c. third
   d. last

_____ 8. Which of the following marginal notations would be most useful for paragraph 1?
   a. alert vs. engaged
   b. still and quiet
   c. physical actions / mental actions
   d. physically alert

_____ 9. Which of the following marginal notations would be the best for paragraph 3?
   a. passive listening = nonjudgmental & supportive
   b. just listen = nonverbal
   c. passive vs. active listening
   d. listening vs. hearing

_____ 10. Which of the following maps best presents the ideas in the selection?

   a.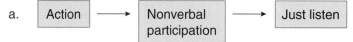

   b.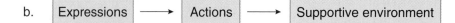

   c.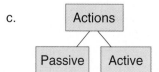

   d.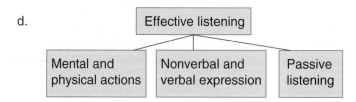

Name _____

Section _____ Date _____

Number right* _____ x 20 points = Score _____

Planning a Fitness Program

Rebecca J. Donatelle

This article discusses the benefits of exercise and the importance of creating a fitness program that suits your needs. The article was taken from a health textbook titled *Access to Health*.

Vocabulary Preview

sedentary (par. 1) characterized by sitting; not physically active

sporadically (par. 1) occurring now and then; infrequently

prudent (par. 2) sensible

debilitating (par. 2) causing disability

monotonous (par. 6) boringly repetitive

rigorously (par. 1 in box) characterized by difficulty or strictness

reneging (par. 6 in box) going back on a commitment

chronicle (par. 8 in box) keep a record

1   Regular physical activity and exercise can help you avoid preventable diseases and add to both the quality and length of your life. If you are currently active, you are aware of the benefits of regular physical activity and should be motivated to continue your efforts. If you are sedentary or sporadically active, you realize that you should not delay one day longer in making the behavior changes necessary to improve your fitness. You should also be aware of the importance of creating a program you love and motivating yourself through positive self-talk. (See the Skills for Behavior Change box.)

Following a fitness plan

*To calculate the number right, use items 1–10 under "Mastery Test Skills Check."

Identifying Fitness Goals

2 Before you initiate a fitness program, analyze your personal needs, limitations, physical activity likes and dislikes, and daily schedule. Your primary reason for exercising may be to lower your risks for health problems. This goal is prudent, particularly for those who have a family history of cardiovascular diseases (heart attack, stroke, high blood pressure), diabetes, obesity, and/or substance abuse. If you have inherited no major risks for fatal or debilitating diseases, then your primary reason for exercising may be to improve the quality of your life. Your specific goal may be to achieve (or maintain) healthy levels of body fat, cardiovascular fitness, muscular strength and endurance, or flexibility and mobility.

3 Once you become committed to regular physical activity and exercise, you will observe gradual changes in your functional abilities and note progress toward your goals. Unfortunately, all the benefits gained through regular physical activity will be lost if you stop exercising. You can't get fit for a couple of years while you're young and expect the positive changes to last the rest of your life. Perhaps your most vital goal will be to become committed to fitness for the long haul—to establish a realistic schedule of diverse exercise activities that you can maintain and enjoy throughout your life.

Designing the Program

4 Once you commit yourself to becoming physically active, you must decide what type of fitness program is best suited to your needs. The amounts and types of exercises required to yield beneficial results vary with the age and physical condition of the exerciser. Men over age 40 and women over age 50 should consult their physicians before beginning a fitness program.

5 Good fitness programs are designed to improve or maintain cardiorespiratory fitness, flexibility, muscular strength and endurance, and body composition. A comprehensive program could include a warm-up period of easy walking followed by stretching activities to improve flexibility, then selected strength development exercises, followed by performance of an aerobic activity for 20 minutes or more, and concluding with a cool-down period of gentle flexibility exercises.

6 The greatest proportion of exercise time should be spent developing cardiovascular fitness, but you should not exclude the other components. Choose an aerobic activity you think you will like. Many people find cross training—alternate-day participation in two or more aerobic activities (i.e., jogging and swimming)—less monotonous and more enjoyable than long-term participation in only one aerobic activity. Cross training is also beneficial because it strengthens a variety of muscles, thus helping you avoid overuse injuries to muscles and joints.

7 Jogging, walking, cycling, rowing, step aerobics, and cross-country skiing are all excellent activities for developing cardiovascular fitness. Responding to the exercise boom, fitness equipment manufacturers have made it easy for you to participate in these activities. Most colleges and universities now have recreation centers where students can use stair-climbing machines, stationary bicycles, treadmills, rowing machines, and ski-simulators.

What Do You Think?

8   You now have the ability to design your own fitness program. Which two activities would you select for a cross-training program? Do the activities you selected exercise different major muscle groups? What may happen to you if they don't?

Skills for Behavior Change

Starting an Exercise Routine

1   Beginners often start their exercise programs too rigorously. The most successful exercise program is one that is realistic and appropriate for your skill level and needs. Be realistic about the amount of time you will need to get into good physical condition. Perhaps the most significant factor early on in an exercise program is personal comfort. You'll need to experiment to find an activity that you truly enjoy. Be open to exploring new activities and new exercise equipment.

2   • *Start slow as a beginning exerciser.* For the sedentary, first-time exerciser, any type and amount of physical activity will be a step in the right direction. If you are extremely overweight or out of condition, you might be able to walk for only five minutes at a time. Don't be discouraged; you're on your way!

3   • *Make only one life change at a time.* Success at one major behavioral change will encourage you to make other positive changes.

4   • *Have reasonable expectations for yourself and your fitness program.* Many people become exercise dropouts because their expectations were too high to begin with. Allow sufficient time to reach your fitness goals.

5   • *Choose a specific time to exercise and stick with it.* Learning to establish priorities and keeping to a schedule are vital steps toward improved fitness. Experiment by exercising at different times of the day to learn what schedule works best for you.

6   • *Exercise with a friend.* Reneging on an exercise commitment is much more difficult if you exercise with someone else. Partners can motivate and encourage each other, provided they remember that the rate of progress will not be the same for them both.

7   • *Make exercise a positive habit.* Usually, if you are able to practice a desired activity for three weeks, you will be able to incorporate it into your lifestyle.

8   • *Keep a record of your progress.* Include various facts about your physical activities (duration, intensity) and chronicle your emotions and personal achievements as you progress.

9   • *Take lapses in stride.* Physical deconditioning—a decline in fitness level—occurs at about the same rate as physical conditioning. First, renew your commitment to fitness, and then restart your exercise program.

MASTERY TEST SKILLS CHECK

Directions: Choose the best answer for each of the following questions.

Checking Your Comprehension

_____ 1. The main point of the selection is that people
   a. do not exercise enough.
   b. have unrealistic fitness goals.
   c. are unaware of the benefits of exercise.
   d. should have a regular exercise program.

_____ 2. The main idea of paragraph 2 is that
   a. people should identify their exercise goals before beginning a fitness program.
   b. the most important goal of exercise should be to increase endurance.
   c. people who have inherited health risks should see a doctor before beginning a fitness program.
   d. the most common fitness goal is to achieve healthy levels of body fat.

_____ 3. According to the article, the greatest proportion of exercise time should be spent
   a. strengthening muscles.
   b. improving flexibility.
   c. developing cardiovascular fitness.
   d. maintaining body composition.

_____ 4. Cross training is defined in the article as
   a. a warm-up period followed by aerobic activity.
   b. aerobic activity followed by a cool-down period.
   c. participation in two or more aerobic activities on alternate days.
   d. participation in one aerobic activity in the morning and a different one in the evening.

_____ 5. According to the information in the Behavior Change box, beginning exercisers should do all of the following *except*
   a. start slowly.
   b. always exercise alone.
   c. keep a record of their progress.
   d. establish an exercise schedule.

_____ 6. The author recommends all of the following activities for cardiovascular fitness except
   a. rowing
   b. tennis
   c. walking
   d. cycling

Applying Your Skills

_____ 7. The most useful summary marginal notation for paragraph 2 would be
   a. analyze lifestyle and set goals.
   b. identify family patterns of illness.
   c. cardiovascular diseases, diabetes, obesity, substance abuse.
   d. body fat, cardiovascular fitness, muscle strength & endurance, flexibility & mobility

_____ 8. The following is an outline of the section titled "Identifying Fitness Goals" (paragraphs 2 and 3). The phrase that belongs in the blank line is

> I. Identifying fitness goals
>   A. Before you begin
>   1. Analyze your needs, preferences, limitations, and schedule
>   2. Primary reason may be to lower health risks
>   3. If no family history of illness goal may be to improve quality of life
>   B. Once you are committed
>   1. Observe gradual changes and note progress
>   2. _____
>   3. Build a fitness program that will last a lifetime

a. All benefits are lost if you stop.
b. Try to get fit for at least a couple of years.
c. Expect positive changes.
d. Positive changes are easy to achieve.

_____ 9. The best paraphrase of paragraph 4 is
a. Men over age 40 and women over age 50 should consult their doctors before beginning an exercise program.
b. When you have decided to begin an exercise program, you need to figure out what type would suit you best. Your age and physical condition affect the type and amount of exercise you need in order to get good results. Before starting an exercise program, women older than 50 and men older than 40 should consult their doctors.
c. Once you commit yourself to physical activity, you have to decide what type of fitness program is best for you. Men and women over age 40 should talk to their physicians before beginning a fitness program.
d. After you have decided to become physically active, you must decide which fitness program you will be able to stick with. The age and physical condition of the exerciser are not as important as the type of exercise chosen.

_____ 10. The phrase that belongs in place of [A] in the following map of paragraph 5 is
a. Improve cardiorespiratory fitness.
b. Cross training.
c. Twenty minutes of aerobic activity.
d. Avoid overuse injuries.

Comprehensive Fitness Program

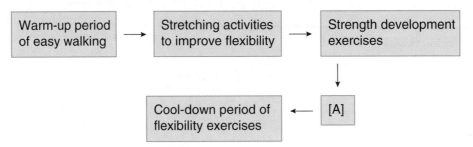

Studying Words

_____ 11. What is the correct pronunciation of the word "sedentary" (paragraph 1)?
a. sed EN tare ee
b. SED en tare ee
c. see DEN tare ee
d. SEE den tare ee

_____ 12. What is the best definition of the word "initiate" as it is used in paragraph 2?
a. begin
b. achieve
c. admit
d. instruct

_____ 13. The word "prudent" (paragraph 2) originated from which of the following languages?
a. Middle English
b. Greek
c. German
d. Spanish

_____ 14. The root of the word "beneficial" (paragraph 4) means
a. body.
b. time.
c. good or well.
d. stretch or strain.

_____ 15. The best definition of the word "boom" in paragraph 7 is
a. a loud noise.
b. a rapid increase in activity or popularity.
c. to grow in value.
d. to make a deep, hollow sound.

For more practice, ask your instructor for an opportunity to work on the mastery tests that appear in the Test Bank.

Chapter 12
Interpreting the Writer's Message and Purpose

THIS CHAPTER WILL SHOW YOU HOW TO

1 Recognize words that suggest positive or negative attitudes

2 Make inferences about what you read

3 Understand figurative language

4 Discover the author's purpose

5 Recognize tone

Getting Started with . . .
Interpreting the Writer's Message and Purpose

GREGORY

"Is this a bad time to talk about global warming?"

What point or message does this cartoon convey? While the point is clear, it is not directly stated. You had to use the information in the cartoon to reason out its point. This chapter concentrates on the reasoning processes readers must use to figure out ideas that are not directly stated.

Up to this point, we have been primarily concerned with building vocabulary, understanding a writer's basic organizational patterns, acquiring factual information, and organizing that information for learning and recall. So far, each chapter has been concerned with understanding what the author *says,* with factual content. Now our focus must change. To read well, you must go beyond what the author says and also consider what he or she *means.*

Many writers directly state some ideas but only hint at others. It is left to the reader to pick up the clues or suggestions and use logic and reasoning skills to figure out the writer's unstated message as you did in the cartoon on p. 433. This chapter will explain several features of writing that suggest meanings. Once you are familiar with these, you will better understand the writer's unstated message. This chapter will also discuss how to discover the author's purpose, recognize tone, and understand context.

CONNOTATIVE MEANINGS

Which of the following would you like to be a part of: a crowd, mob, gang, audience, congregation, or class? Each of these words has the same basic meaning: "an assembled group of people." But each has a different *shade* of meaning. *Crowd* suggests a large, disorganized group. *Audience,* on the other hand, suggests a quiet, controlled group. Try to decide what meaning each of the other words in the list suggests.

This example shows that words have two levels of meaning—a literal meaning and an additional shade of meaning. These two levels of meaning are called denotative and connotative. A word's **denotative meaning** is the meaning stated in the dictionary—its literal meaning. A word's **connotative meaning** is the additional implied meanings, or nuances, that a word may take on. Often the connotative meaning carries either a positive or negative, favorable or unfavorable impression. The words *mob* and *gang* have a negative connotation because they imply a disorderly, disorganized group. *Congregation, audience,* and *class* have a positive connotation because they suggest an orderly, organized group.

Here are a few more examples. Would you prefer to be described as "slim" or "skinny"? As "intelligent" or "brainy"? As "heavy" or "fat"? As "particular" or "picky"? Notice that each pair of words has a similar literal meaning, but that each word within the pair has a different connotation.

Depending on the words they choose, writers can suggest favorable or unfavorable impressions of the person, object, or event they are describing. For example, through the writer's choice of words, the two sentences below create two entirely different impressions. As you read them, underline words that have a positive or negative connotation.

The unruly crowd forced its way through the restraint barriers and ruthlessly attacked the rock star.

The enthusiastic group of fans burst through the fence and rushed toward the rock star.

When reading any type of informative or persuasive material, pay attention to the writer's choice of words. Often a writer may communicate subtle or hidden messages, or he or she may encourage the reader to feel positive or negative toward the subject.

Read the following paragraph on violence in sports and, as you read, underline words that have a strong positive or negative connotation.

So it goes. Knifings, shootings, beatings, muggings, paralysis, and death become part of our play. Women baseball fans are warned to walk with friends and avoid taking their handbags to games because of strong-arm robberies and purse snatchings at San Francisco's Candlestick Park. A professional football coach, under oath in a slander case, describes some of his own players as part of a "criminal element" in his sport. The commissioner of football proclaims* that playing field outlaws and bullies will be punished, but to anybody with normal eyesight and a working television set the action looks rougher than ever. In Europe and South America—and, chillingly, for the first time in the United States—authorities turn to snarling attack dogs to control unruly mobs at athletic events.

—Yeager, *Seasons of Shame,* p. 6.

EXERCISE 12-1

Directions: For each of the following pairs of words, underline the word with the more positive connotation.

1. request   demand

2. overlook   neglect

3. ridicule   tease

4. glance   stare

5. display   expose

6. garment   gown

---

*Boxed words appear in the Mastering Vocabulary exercise on pp. 462–463.

7. gaudy   showy

8. clumsy   awkward

9. artificial   fake

10. token   keepsake

Directions: For each word listed below, write a word that has a similar denotative meaning but a negative connotation. Then write a word that has a positive connotation. Use your dictionary or thesaurus, if necessary.

	Negative	**Positive**
Example: eat	gobble	dine
1. take		
2. ask		
3. look at		
4. walk		
5. dress		
6. music		
7. car		
8. laugh		
9. large		
10. woman		

IMPLIED MEANINGS

An **inference** is an educated guess or prediction about something unknown based on available facts and information. It is the logical connection that you draw between what you observe or know and what you do not know.

Suppose that you arrive ten minutes late for your sociology class. All the students have papers in front of them, and everyone is busily writing. Some students have worried or concerned looks on their faces. The instructor is seated and is reading a book. What is happening? From the known information you can make an inference about what you do not know. Did you figure out that the instructor had given the class a surprise quiz? If so, then you made a logical inference.

While the inference you made is probably correct, you cannot be sure until you speak with the instructor. Occasionally a logical inference can be wrong. Although it is unlikely, perhaps the instructor has laryngitis and has written notes on the board for the students to copy. Some students may look worried because they do not understand what the notes mean.

Here are a few more everyday situations. Make an inference for each.

> You are driving on an expressway and you notice a police car with flashing red lights behind you. You check your speedometer and notice that you are going ten miles an hour over the speed limit.

> A woman seated alone in a bar nervously glances at everyone who enters. Every few minutes she checks her watch.

In the first situation, a good inference might be that you are going to be stopped for speeding. However, it is possible that the officer only wants to pass you to get to an accident ahead or to stop someone driving faster than you. In the second situation, one inference is that the woman is waiting to meet someone who is late.

The following paragraphs are taken from a book by Bill Cosby titled *Time Flies*. First, read them for factual content.

> When I was twenty-five, I saw a movie called *The Loneliness of the Long Distance Runner,* in which a young man running for a reform school was far ahead in a cross-country race and then suddenly stopped as an act of rebellion. That young runner had been struck by the feeling that he had to go his own way and not the way demanded by society.
>
> That young runner was me.
>
> I hadn't been doing time, of course, just *marking* time at Temple, where my mind was not on books but bookings; and so, I had dropped out to go into show business,

a career move as sound as seeking my future as a designer of dirigibles. Although my mother and father kept telling me that I should finish college before I flopped in show business, I felt that only I, with the full wisdom of a north Philadelphia jock, knew what was best for me. I empathized with the hero of *The Loneliness of the Long Distance Runner*, who had said about his race, "You have to run, run, run without knowing *why*."

Cosby, *Time Files*, pp. 169–170.

These paragraphs are primarily factual—they tell who did what, when, and where. However, some ideas are not directly stated and must be inferred from the information given. Here are a few examples. Some are fairly obvious inferences; others are less obvious.

1. The runner did not finish the race.
2. The runner could have won the race.
3. Cosby was *not* the young runner from reform school.
4. Cosby thought he was like the runner.
5. Temple is a university or college.
6. Cosby did not do well academically at Temple.
7. A career in show business is impractical.
8. Cosby's parents thought he would fail in show business.
9. Cosby felt it was acceptable to act without having specific reasons.
10. Cosby now realizes that he was not as wise as he thought he was at the time.

Although none of the above ideas is directly stated, they can be inferred from clues provided in the passage. Some of the statements could be inferred from actions, others by adding facts together, and still others by the writer's choice of words.

Now read the following passage to find out why Cindy Kane is standing on the corner of Sheridan and Sunnyside.

An oily midnight mist had settled on the city streets . . . asphalt mirrors from a ten-o'-clock rain now past . . . a sleazy street-corner reflection of smog-smudged neon . . . the corner of Sheridan and, incongruously, Sunnyside . . . Chicago.

A lone lady lingers at the curb . . . but no bus will come.

She is Cindy Kane, twenty-eight. Twenty-eight hard years old. Her iridescent dress clings to her slender body. Her face is buried under a technicolor avalanche of makeup.

She is Cindy Kane.

And she has a date.

With someone she has never met . . . and may never meet again.

Minutes have turned to timelessness . . . and a green Chevy four-door pulls slowly around the corner.

The driver's window rolls down. A voice comes from the shadow . . .

"Are you working?"

Cindy nods . . . regards him with vacant eyes.

He beckons.

She approaches the passenger side. Gets in. And the whole forlorn, unromantic ritual begins all over again. With another stranger.

—Aurandt, *Paul Harvey's The Rest of the Story,* p. 116.

If you made the right inferences, you realized that Cindy Kane is a prostitute and that she is standing on the corner waiting for a customer. Let us look at the kinds of clues the writer gave that led to this inference.

1. **Description.** By the way the writer describes Cindy Kane, you begin to suspect that she is a prostitute. She is described as "hard." She is wearing an iridescent, clinging dress and "a technicolor avalanche of makeup." These descriptive details convey an image of a gaudy, unconventional appearance.

2. **Action.** The actions, although few, also provide clues about what is happening. The woman is lingering on the corner. When the car approaches, she gets in.

3. **Conversation.** The only piece of conversation, the question, "Are you working?" is one of the strongest clues the writer provides.

4. **Writer's commentary/details.** As the writer describes the situation, he slips in numerous clues. He establishes the time as around midnight ("An oily midnight mist"). His reference to a "reflection of smog-smudged neon" suggests an area of bars or nightclubs. The woman's face is "buried under . . . makeup." Covering or hiding one's face is usually associated with shame or embarrassment. In the last paragraph, the reference to a "forlorn, unromantic ritual" provides a final clue.

How to Make Inferences

Making an inference is a thinking process. As you read, you are following the author's thoughts. You are also alert for ideas that are suggested but not directly stated. Because inference is a logical thought process, there is no simple, step-by-step procedure to follow. Each inference depends entirely on the situation, the facts provided, and the reader's knowledge and experience.

However, here are a few guidelines to keep in mind as you read. These will help you get in the habit of looking beyond the factual level to the inferential.

1. **Be sure you understand the literal meaning.** You should have a clear grasp of the key idea and supporting details of each paragraph.

2. **Notice details.** Often a detail provides a clue that will help you make an inference. When you spot a striking or unusual detail, ask yourself: Why did the writer include this piece of information?

3. **Add up the facts.** Consider all the facts taken together. Ask yourself: What is the writer trying to suggest from this set of facts? What do all these facts and ideas point toward?

4. **Watch for clues.** The writer's choice of words and detail often suggest his or her attitude toward the subject. Notice, in particular, descriptive words, emotionally charged words, and words with strong positive or negative connotations.

5. **Be sure your inference is supportable.** An inference must be based on fact. Make sure there is sufficient evidence to justify any inference you make.

EXERCISE 12-3   **Directions:** Read each of the following passages. Then answer the questions that follow. You will need to reason out, or infer, the answers.

Passage A:

Eye-to-eye contact and response are important in real-life relationships. The nature of a person's eye contact patterns, whether he or she looks another squarely in the eye or looks to the side or shifts his gaze from side to side, tells a lot about the person. These patterns also play a significant role in success or failure in human relationships. Despite its importance, eye contact is not involved in television watching. Yet children spend several hours a day in front of the television set. Certain children's programs pretend to speak directly to each individual child. (Mr. Rogers is an example, telling the child "I like you, you're special," etc.) However, this is still one-way communication and no response is required of the child. How might such a distortion of real-life relationships affect a child's development of trust, or openness, or an ability to relate well to other people?

Weaver, *Understanding Interpersonal Communication*, p. 291.

1. How would the author answer the question asked in the last sentence of the paragraph?

_____

2. What is the author's attitude toward television?

_____

3. To develop a strong relationship with someone, should you look directly at him or her or shift your gaze?

_____

4. What activities, other than television, do you think this author would recommend for children?

_____

Passage B:

There is little the police or other governmental agencies can't find out about you these days.

For starters, the police can hire an airplane and fly over your backyard filming you sunbathing and whatever else is visible from above. A mail cover allows the post office, at the request of another government or police agency, to keep track of people sending you mail and organizations sending you literature through the mail. A pen register at the phone company may be installed at police request to collect the numbers dialed to and from your home telephone. Police or other governmental agencies may have access to your canceled checks and deposit records to find out who is writing checks to you and to whom you are writing checks. Library and film rental records disclose what you are reading and what you are watching. Even the trash you discard may be examined to see what you are throwing away.

No doubt by now you've realized that the accumulation of this information provides a fairly complete and accurate picture about a person, including her health, friends, lovers, political and religious activities, and even beliefs. Figure that, if the Gillette razor company knows when it's your eighteenth birthday to send you a sample razor, your government, with its super, interconnecting computers, knows much more about you.

—Katz, _Know Your Rights,_ p. 54.

1. What is the author's attitude toward government agencies?

_____

2. For what reason might a police agency request a pen register?

_____

3. Where do you think the author stands on the issue of right to privacy? (What rights to privacy do we or should we have?)

_____

Passage C:

George Washington is remembered not for what he was but for what he should have been. It doesn't do any good to point out that he was an "inveterate land-grabber," and that as a young man he illegally had a surveyor stake out some prize territory west of the Alleghenies in an area decreed off limits to settlers. Washington is considered a saint, and nothing one says is likely to make him seem anything less. Though he was a wily businessman and accumulated a fortune speculating in frontier lands, he will always be remembered as a farmer—and a "simple farmer" at that.

Even his personal life is misremembered. While Washington admitted despising his mother and in her dying years saw her infrequently, others remembered his mother fondly and considered him a devoted son. While his own records show he was something of a dandy and paid close attention to the latest clothing designs, ordering "fashionable" hose, the "neatest shoes," and coats with "silver trimmings," practically no one thinks he was vain. Though he loved to drink and dance and encouraged others to join him, the first President is believed to have been something of a prude.

—Shenkman, *Legends, Lies,and Cherished Myths of American History,* pp. 37–38.

1. Describe how Washington is usually remembered.

   _____

   _____

2. Describe the author's attitude toward Washington.

   _____

   _____

3. Does the author think attitudes toward Washington are likely to change?

   _____

4. Explain the term "inveterate landgrabber."

   _____

   _____

5. Why do you think there is such a discrepancy between what Washington did and how he is remembered?

   _____

   _____

Passage D:

I am a peace-loving woman. But several events in the past 10 years have convinced me I'm safer when I carry a pistol. This was a personal decision, but because handgun possession is a controversial subject, perhaps my reasoning will interest others.

I live in western South Dakota on a ranch 25 miles from the nearest large town; for several years I spent winters alone here. As a freelance writer, I travel alone a lot—more than 100,000 miles by car in the last four years. With women freer than ever before to travel alone, the odds of our encountering trouble seem to have risen. And help, in the West, can be hours away. Distances are great, roads are deserted, and the terrain is often too exposed to offer hiding places.

A woman who travels alone is advised, usually by men, to protect herself by avoiding bars and other "dangerous situations," by approaching her car like an Indian scout, by locking doors and windows. But these precautions aren't always enough. I spent years following them and still found myself in dangerous situations. I began to resent the idea that just because I am female, I have to be extra careful. . . .

When I got my pistol, I told my husband, revising the old Colt slogan, "God made men *and women,* but Sam Colt made them equal." Recently I have seen a gunmaker's ad with a similar sentiment. Perhaps this is an idea whose time has come, though the pacifist inside me will be saddened if the only way women can achieve equality is by carrying weapons.

We must treat a firearm's power with caution. "Power tends to corrupt, and absolute power corrupts absolutely," as a man (Lord Acton) once said. A pistol is not the only way to avoid being raped or murdered in today's world, but, intelligently wielded, it can shift the balance of power and provide a measure of safety.

—Hasselstrom, *Land Circle.*

1. Predict the author's position on the issue of gun control.

   _____

   _____

2. What does the author think of the advice that women should avoid dangerous situations?

   _____

   _____

   _____

3. The author lives on a ranch in South Dakota and describes the particular problems she faces there. What problems might a resident of a large city describe to justify carrying a gun?

_____

_____

4. What was the original Colt slogan?

_____

_____

EXERCISE 12-4 **Directions:** Read each of the following passages and answer the questions that follow.

Passage A:

"Oprah Winfrey—A Woman for All Seasons"

Oprah Winfrey—actress, talk-show host, and businesswoman—epitomizes the opportunities for America's women entrepreneurs. From welfare child to multimillionaire, Ms. Winfrey—resourceful, assertive, always self-assured, and yet unpretentious—has climbed the socioeconomic ladder by turning apparent failure into opportunities and then capitalizing on them.

With no playmates, Oprah entertained herself by "playacting" with objects such as corncob dolls, chickens, and cows. Her grandmother, a harsh disciplinarian, taught Oprah to read by age 2 ½, and as a result of speaking at a rural church, her oratory talents began to emerge.

At age 6, Winfrey was sent to live with her mother and two half-brothers in a Milwaukee ghetto. While in Milwaukee, Winfrey, known as "the Little Speaker," was often invited to recite poetry at social gatherings, and her speaking skills continued to develop. At age 12, during a visit to her father in Nashville, she was paid $500 for a speech she gave to a church. It was then that she prophetically announced what she wanted to do for a living: "get paid to talk."

Her mother, working as a maid and drawing available welfare to make ends meet, left Oprah with little or no parental supervision and eventually sent her to live with her father in Nashville. There Oprah found the stability and discipline she so desperately needed. "My father saved my life," Winfrey reminisces. Her father—like her grandmother—a strict disciplinarian, obsessed with properly educating his daughter, forced her to memorize 20 new vocabulary words a week and turn in a weekly book report. His guidance and her hard work soon paid off, as she began to excel in school and other areas.

—Mosley et al., *Management,* p. 555.

1. What is the author's attitude toward Winfrey?

   _____

   _____

2. What is the author's attitude toward strict discipline for children?

   _____

   _____

3. Is the author optimistic about business opportunities for women? How do you know?

   _____

   _____

4. What factors contributed to Winfrey's success?

   _____

   _____

Passage B:

Private Pains

The damnedest thing happened while I was driving down Pioneer Avenue last week. I was passing an intersection and noticed a middle-aged lady stopped in her car waiting to enter the road. There was nothing remarkable about the car, but I happened to look at just the right time and saw she was crying.

Her cheeks were wet and her mouth was sort of twisted in that sorrowful half-smile people sometimes get when they cry. She didn't seem to be in any kind of predicament, and I'd never seen her before, so I did what we usually do when we see people crying; I looked away and drove on.

I kept thinking about it as I drove down the road. What could have driven this woman to tears in the middle of the day while waiting at a stop sign? Maybe she'd just gotten some terrible news about something. Maybe a parent had died or her husband left her. Perhaps a child was hurt at school and she was panicked and on her way there at that very moment. It could have been her birthday or anniversary, and her family had gone off to work and school without saying anything about it. Who could tell?

It might even have been something rather silly. She may have been coming from her hairdresser, who'd done an absolutely horrible job on her, and she didn't know how she'd face people. Or found that she'd inadvertently *not* been invited to her club luncheon that day. Maybe she was just having one of those days we all have from time to time, and trying to make a left turn onto Pioneer Avenue in lunch-hour traffic was the last straw this poor woman could bear.

I wanted to turn around and go ask her what was wrong, but I knew she'd be gone by then. Even if she wasn't, I didn't think she'd talk to a stranger about it. I had a brief vision of opening her car door and holding her, telling her it would be all right. But I knew I would never do that, and would probably get arrested if I did.

It bugged the heck outa me. [I kept] Wondering what kind of tragedy this woman was carrying with her and enduring by herself. I thought about the sadness we all carry with us every day, and take to bed with us at night. The small pains and disappointments that keep us off our mark a little. They make us snap at store clerks without meaning to, or beep our horns at a slowpoke even when we're in no particular hurry. The sadness that sits like a chip on our shoulders, daring anyone to touch it. It makes our mouths taut and our eyes steely. We move stiffly, looking at our feet when we walk, lost in our own little worlds.

This woman, all alone in her car and for no apparent reason, had let her taut mouth fold and her steely eyes fill with tears. The tears came easier with every car that rolled by and left her there, myself included.

Possibly she was the store clerk someone had snapped at, or the slowpoke that got honked at. I don't know, I'm just guessing. It seems we spend so much time torturing each other to get to the head of the line or maneuver into that last parking space. Maybe we should forget about all that stuff every once in a while and just keep our eyes peeled for the tears of a stranger.

—Bodett, *As Far as You Can Go Without a Passport,* pp. 79–81.

1. What inferences did the author make about the woman who was crying?

_____

_____

2. Which inferences seem least plausible?

_____

_____

3. Does the author regret not stopping to comfort the woman? Justify your answer.

_____

_____

_____

4. Explain the meaning of the last line of the selection.

_____

_____

FIGURATIVE LANGUAGE

Read each of the following statements:

The cake tasted like a moist sponge.

The wilted plants begged for water.

Jean wore her heart on her sleeve.

You know that a cake cannot really have the same taste as a sponge, that plants do not actually request water, and that a person's heart cannot really be attached to her sleeve. However, you know what message the writer is communicating in each sentence. The cake was soggy and tasteless, the plants were extremely dry, and Jean revealed her feelings to everyone around her.

Each of these sentences is an example of figurative language. **Figurative language** is a way of describing something that makes sense on an imaginative level but not on a factual or literal level. Notice that while none of the above expressions is literally true, each is meaningful. In many figurative expressions, one thing is compared with another for some quality they have in common. Take, for example, the familiar expression in the following sentence:

Sam eats like a horse.

The diagram below shows the comparison being made in this figurative expression:

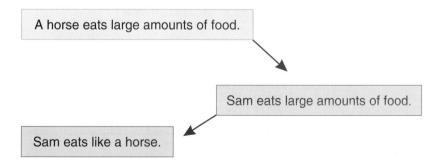

You can see that two unlike things—Sam and a horse—are compared because they are alike in one particular way—the amount they eat.

The purpose of figurative language is to paint a word picture—to help you visualize how something looks, feels, or smells. Figurative language is a device writers use to express an idea or feeling and, at the same time, allow the reader the freedom of imagination. Since it is not factual, figurative language allows the writer to express attitudes and opinions without directly stating them. Depending on the figurative expression chosen, a writer can create a variety of impressions.

When reading an article that contains figurative language, be sure to pay close attention to the images and feelings created. Be sure you recognize that the writer is shaping your response to the topic or subject.

Figurative language is used in many types of articles and essays. It is also used in everyday speech and in slang expressions. Various types of literature, especially poetry, also use figurative language. Notice its use in the following excerpt from a play by William Shakespeare.

> All the world's a stage,
> And all the men and women merely players;
> They have their exits and entrances;
> And one man in his time plays many parts.
>
> (Shakespeare, *As You Like It*, II, vii,139)

Here are a few more examples from other sources. Notice how each creates a visual image of the person, object, or quality being described.

> The red sun was pasted in the sky like a wafer.
>
> (Stephen Crane, *The Red Badge of Courage*)

> In plucking the fruit of memory,
> one runs the risk of spoiling its bloom.
>
> (Joseph Conrad)

> "I will speak daggers to her, but use none."
>
> (Shakespeare, *Hamlet*)

> Life, like a dome of many-colored glass,
> Stains the white radiance of Eternity.
>
> (Shelley, "Adonais")

> Float like a butterfly, sting like a bee.
>
> (Muhammad Ali)

EXERCISE 12-5 **Directions:** Each of the following sentences includes a figurative expression. Read each sentence and explain in your own words what the expression means.

1. My psychology quiz was a piece of cake.

   _____

2. My life is a junkyard of broken dreams.

   _____

3. "Life is as tedious as a twice-told tale." (Shakespeare, *King John III*)

   _____

4. "A sleeping child gives me the impression of a traveler in a very far country." (Ralph Waldo Emerson)

   _____

5. "I refuse to accept the notion that nation after nation must spiral down a militaristic stairway into the hell of nuclear war." (Martin Luther King, Jr.)

   _____

EXERCISE 12-6 **Directions:** Read each of the following passages and answer the questions that follow.

Passage A:

Love in the Afternoon—In a Crowded Prison Hall

1   Each time I visit my man in prison, I relive the joy of reunion—and the anguish of separation.

2   We meet at the big glass door at the entrance to the small visitors' hall at Lompoc Federal Correctional Institution. We look at each other silently, then turn and walk into a room jammed with hundreds of molded fiberglass chairs lined up side by side. Finding a place in the crowded hall, we sit down, appalled that we're actually in a prison. Even now, after four months of such clocked, supervised, regulated visits, we still can't get used to the frustrations.

3   Yet, as John presses me gently to his heart, I feel warm and tender, and tears well up inside me, as they do each weekend. I have seven hours to spend with the

man I love—all too brief a time for sharing a lifetime of emotion: love and longing, sympathy and tenderness, resentment and anger.

4   The guard's voice jars us: "Please keep the chairs in order!"

5   We can't keep from laughing, for we're struck by the absurdity of the scene: 60 couples, some with families, packed in a single room—each trying, somehow, to create an atmosphere of intimacy. And what's demanded by the single guard who's assigned to oversee us? *Chairs in a straight line.*

6   Nevertheless, John and I abide by the rules, holding each other as close as we can—without moving our chairs—and the loneliness of the past week gradually subsides.

7   We break our silent communion with small talk much like the kind we shared at home for the past three years. Like: *Should we have the van repaired, or sell it?*

8   Then we speak of our separate needs and fears. He feels defeated—by confinement, by prison life, by the 20 months left to serve on a two-year sentence for a drug-related charge that we think should never have come to trial. He feels deeply insecure, too, doubting my fidelity and hating himself for doubting me. He wants support and reassurance.

9   But what about me? *Doesn't he understand that this has been an ordeal for me, too?* My whole life fell apart when he went to prison. Our wedding plans were canceled; I had to quit school, sell everything, find a job, and move in with relatives.

10   Prison has become my second full-time occupation. Each weekend I spend 10 hours traveling. Always I must save money—money for my motel room in Lompoc, money for his collect phone calls to supplement the letters we write, money for his supplies at the prison commissary.

11   Worst of all, there's the almost unbearable burden of conducting my home life alone. At least in prison he has no decisions to make, no meals to worry about, no rent. So I, too, need reassurance and emotional support.

—King, *Los Angles Times.*

1. Answer each of the following questions by making an inference.

   a. Who is visiting the man in prison?

   _____

   b. Why is she there?

   _____

   c. Does she go there often? How do you know?

   _____

   d. Why do they break the silence with small talk?

   _____

e. Why does the guard insist that the chairs be kept in a straight line?

_____

f. Why did the woman have to quit school?

_____

g. Does the writer feel sorry for herself? How do you know?

_____

2. List several words with negative connotations that suggest how the writer feels about the prison.

_____

3. List several words with positive connotations that suggest how the woman feels about the man she is visiting.

_____

4. What main point do you think the writer is trying to make?

_____

_____

Passage B:

Stop Junk Mail Forever

Every American, on average, receives 677 sales pitches in his or her mailbox every year—thanks to low-cost, third-class postal rates. While the direct mailers who produce and distribute those 40 million tons of sales pitches take in over $200 billion annually, taxpayers bear the burden of some $320 million to cart their unsolicited promos, pleas, and promises to and from incinerators, garbage dumps (on land and sea), and recycling centers. Sixty-eight million trees and 28 billion gallons of water (and the animals who lived there) are used to produce each year's crop of catalogs and come-ons. Nearly half get trashed unopened.

Many of the environmental organizations that you'd expect to speak up for the trees, rivers, and wildlife are silent about junk mail. Why? Because they support themselves just like the other mailbox fishermen do . . . by casting an extremely wide net to catch a couple of fish. A "response rate" of 1% or 2%—that's 1 or 2 of every 100 pieces mailed—is considered typical, no matter if the mailer is a worthy charity . . . or the distributor of yet one more vegetable slicer.

There's another issue of great concern to us: Privacy. We think Americans should have the right to choose how personal information about them is marketed, if at all.

What follows are some clear instructions on how to keep your name, business, address, and other personal information private—off of those thousands upon thousands of mailing lists that are regularly bought and sold, without our approval, for pennies a name.

Eisenson, *Mother Earth News,* p. 18.

1. Underline three words in the passage that carry positive or negative connotative meanings.

   _____

2. What is the author's attitude toward environmental organizations?

   _____

3. What is the author's attitude toward vegetable slicers? Why does he or she use them as an example?

   _____

   _____

4. Explain why the phrase "mailbox fishermen" is an example of figurative language.

   _____

   _____

UNDERSTANDING THE AUTHOR'S PURPOSE

Writers have many different reasons or purposes for writing. Read the statements below and try to decide why each was written:

1. About 14,000 ocean-going ships pass through the Panama Canal each year. This averages about three ships per day.
2. *New Unsalted Dry Roasted Almonds.* Finally, a snack with a natural flavor and without salt. We simply shell the nuts and dry-roast them until they're crispy and crunchy. Try a jar this week.
3. Man is the only animal that blushes or has a need to.
4. If a choking person has fallen down, first turn him or her face up. Then knit together the fingers of both your hands and apply pressure with the heel of your bottom hand to the victim's abdomen.
5. If your boat capsizes, it is usually safer to cling to the boat than to try to swim ashore.

Statement 1 was written to give information, 2 to persuade you to buy almonds, 3 to amuse you and make a comment on human behavior, 4 to explain, and 5 to give advice.

In each of the examples, the writer's purpose was fairly clear, as it will be in most textbooks (to present information), newspaper articles (to communicate daily events), and reference books (to compile facts). However, in many other types of writing, authors have varied, sometimes less obvious, purposes. In these cases, an author's purpose must be inferred.

Often a writer's purpose is to express an opinion indirectly. Or the writer may want to encourage the reader to think about a particular issue or problem. Writers achieve their purposes by manipulating and controlling what they say and how they say it. This section will focus on techniques writers use and features of language that writers control to achieve the results they want.

Style and Intended Audience

Are you able to recognize a friend just by his or her voice? Can you identify family members by their footsteps? You are able to do so because each person's voice and footsteps are unique. Have you noticed that writers have unique characteristics as well? One author may use many examples; another may use few. One author may use relatively short sentences, another may use long, complicated ones. The characteristics that make a writer unique are known as **style**. By changing style, writers can create different effects.

Writers may vary their styles to suit their intended audiences. A writer may write for a general-interest audience (anyone who is interested in the subject but is not considered an expert). Most newspapers and periodicals, such as *Time* and *Newsweek*, appeal to a general-interest audience. On the other hand, a writer may have a particular interest group in mind. A writer may write for medical doctors in the *Journal of American Medicine*, for skiing enthusiasts in *Skiing Today*, or for antique collectors in *The World of Antiques*. A writer may also target his or her writing for an audience with particular political, moral, or religious attitudes. Articles in the *New Republic* often appeal to a particular political viewpoint, whereas the *Catholic Digest* appeals to a specific religious group.

Depending on the group of people for whom the author is writing, he or she will change the level of language, choice of words, and method of presentation. One step toward identifying an author's purpose, then, is to ask yourself the question: Who is the intended audience? Your response will be your first clue to determining why the author wrote the article.

EXERCISE 12-7

Directions: Read each of the following statements and decide for whom each was written. Write a sentence that describes the intended audience.

1. Chances are you're going to be putting money away over the next five years or so. You are hoping for the right things in life. Right now, a smart place to put your money is in mutual funds or bonds.

   _____

   _____

2. Think about all the places your drinking water has been before you drink another drop. Most likely it has been chemically treated to remove bacteria and chemical pollutants. Soon you may begin to feel the side effects of these treatments. Consider switching to filtered, distilled water today.

   _____

   _____

3. Introducing the new, high-powered Supertuner III, a stereo system guaranteed to keep your mother out of your car.

   _____

   _____

4. Bright and White laundry detergent removes dirt and stains faster than any other brand.

   _____

   _____

5. As a driver, you're ahead if you can learn to spot car trouble before it's too late. If you can learn the difference between drips and squeaks that occur under normal conditions and those that mean big trouble is just down the road, then you'll be ahead of expensive repair bills and won't find yourself stranded on a lonely road.

   _____

   _____

Tone

The tone of a speaker's voice helps you interpret what he or she is saying. If the following sentence were read aloud, the speaker's voice would tell you how to interpret it: "Would you mind closing the door?" In print you cannot tell whether the speaker is polite, insistent, or angry. In speech you could tell by whether the speaker emphasized the word *would, door,* or *mind.*

Just as a speaker's tone of voice tells how the speaker feels, so does a writer convey a tone, or feeling, through his or her writing. Tone refers to the attitude or feeling a writer expresses about his or her subject. A writer may adopt a sentimental tone, an angry tone, a humorous tone, a sympathetic tone, an instructive tone, a persuasive tone, and so forth. Here are a few examples of different tones. How does each make you feel?

- Instructive

  When purchasing a piece of clothing, one must be concerned with quality as well as with price. Be certain to check for the following: double-stitched seams, matched patterns, and ample linings.

- Sympathetic

  The forlorn, frightened-looking child wandered through the streets alone, searching for someone who would show an interest in helping her find her parents.

- Persuasive

  Child abuse is a tragic occurrence in our society. Strong legislation is needed to control the abuse of innocent victims and to punish those who are insensitive to the rights and feelings of others.

- Humorous

  "Those people who study animal behavior professionally must dread those times when their cover is blown at a dinner party. The unfortunate souls are sure to be seated next to someone with animal stories. The conversation will invariably be about some pet that did this or that, and nonsense is the polite word for it. The worst stories are about cats. The proud owners like to talk about their ingenuity, what they are thinking, and how they 'miss' them while they're at the party. Those cats would rub the leg of a burglar if he rattled the Friskies box."

  —Wallace, *Biology*, p. 659.

- Nostalgic

  "Things change, times change, but when school starts, my little granddaughter will run up the same wooden stairs that creaked for all of the previous generations and I will still hate it when the summer ends."

  —Hastreiter, "Not Every Mother is Glad Kids Are
  Back in School," *Buffalo Evening News.*

In the first example, the writer offers advice in a straightforward, informative style. In the second, the writer wants you to feel sorry for the child. This is done through description. In the third example, the writer tries to convince the reader that action must be taken to prevent child abuse. The use of such words as *tragic, innocent,* and *insensitive* establish this tone.

The tone of an article directly affects how the reader interprets and responds to it. If, as in the fourth example, the writer's tone is humorous and you do not recognize this, you will miss the point of the entire selection. If the writer's tone is sympathetic, it is important to know that an appeal to your feelings is being made. You can begin to suspect, then, that you may not receive an objective, unbiased treatment of the subject.

The author's tone is intended to rub off on you, so to speak. If a writer's tone is humorous, the writer hopes you will be amused. If a writer's tone is persuasive, the writer hopes you will accept his or her viewpoint. You can see how tone can be important in determining an author's purpose. Therefore, a second question to ask when trying to determine an author's purpose is: What tone does the writer use? Or: How is the writer trying to make me feel about the subject?

EXERCISE 12-8   **Directions:** Read each of the following statements, paying particular attention to the tone. Then write a sentence that describes the tone. Prove your point by listing some of the words that reveal the author's feelings.

1. No one says that nuclear power is risk-free. There are risks involved in all methods of producing energy. However, the scientific evidence is clear and obvious. Nuclear power is at least as safe as any other means used to generate electricity.

   _____

   _____

2. The condition of our city streets is outrageous. The sidewalks are littered with paper and other garbage—you could trip while walking to the store. The streets themselves are in even worse condition. Deep potholes and crumbling curbs make it unsafe to drive. Where are our city tax dollars going if not to correct these problems?

   _____

   _____

3. I am a tired American. I am tired of watching criminals walk free while they wait for their day in court. I'm tired of hearing about victims getting as much as or more hassle than criminals. I'm tired of reading about courts of law that even accept a lawsuit in which a criminal sues his or her intended victim.

_____

_____

4. Cross-country skis have heel plates of different shapes and materials. They may be made of metal, plastic, or rubber. Be sure that they are tacked on the ski right where the heel of your boot will fall. They will keep snow from collecting under your foot and offer some stability.

_____

_____

5. We in the United States have made great progress in lowering our birth rates. But now, because we have been responsible, it seems to some that we have a great surplus. There is, indeed, waste that should be eliminated, but there is not as much fat in our system as most people think. Yet we are being asked to share our resources with the hungry peoples of the world. But why should we share? The nations having the greatest needs are those that have been the least responsible in cutting down on births. Famine is one of nature's ways of telling profligate peoples that they have been irresponsible in their breeding habits.

—Montgomery, *The Norton Sampler*, p. 310.

_____

_____

6. In July of 1986 my daughter, Lucy, was born with an underdeveloped brain. She was a beautiful little girl—at least to me and my husband—but her disabilities were severe. By the time she was two weeks old we knew that she would never walk, talk, feed herself, or even understand the concept of mother and father. It's impossible to describe the effect that her five-and-a-half-month life had on us; suffice it to say that she was the purest experience of love and pain that we will ever have, that she changed us forever, and that we will never cease to mourn her death, even though we know that for her it was a triumphant passing.

—Armstrong, *The Choices We Made*, p. 165.

_____

_____

Language

One important feature that writers adjust to suit their purpose is the kind of language they use. There are two basic types of language: objective and subjective.

Objective and Subjective Language **Objective language** is factual, whereas **subjective language** expresses attitudes and feelings.

Read each of the following descriptions of the death penalty. As you read, decide how they differ.

> The death penalty is one of the most ancient of all types of formal punishment for crime. In early criminal codes, death was the penalty for a wide range of offenses, such as kidnapping, certain types of theft, and witchcraft. Today, in the United States, the death penalty is reserved for only the most serious of crimes—murder, kidnapping, and treason.

> The death penalty is a prime example of man's inhumanity to man. The death penalty violates the Eighth Amendment to the Constitution, which prohibits cruel and unusual punishment.

You probably noticed that the first paragraph gave facts about the death penalty and that the second paragraph seemed to state a case against it. These two paragraphs are examples of two different types of writing.

The first paragraph is an example of objective language. The writer reported information without showing feelings. You cannot tell whether the writer favors or is opposed to the death penalty.

The second paragraph is an example of subjective language. Here, the writer expresses freely his or her own attitudes and feelings. You know exactly how the author feels about the death penalty. Through choice of words and selection of facts, a tone of moral disapproval is evident. Such words as *inhumanity, violates,* and *cruel* have negative connotations.

EXERCISE 12-9   **Directions:** Choose a topic that interests you, or use one of the topics listed below. On a separate sheet of paper, write two brief paragraphs. In the first, use only objective, factual information. In the second, try to show your feelings about the topic by using subjective language.

1. One of your college instructors

2. Managing your time

3. Current fashion fads

Descriptive Language Descriptive language is a particular type of subjective language. It is the use of words that appeal to one or more of the reader's senses. Descriptive words help the reader create an imaginary picture of the object, person, or event being described. Here is a paragraph that contains numerous descriptive words and phrases. As you read, underline words and phrases that help you to imagine what the Oregon desert is like.

> You can camp in the Oregon desert for a week and see no one at all, no more than the glow of headlights hovering over a dirt road miles distant, disappearing soundlessly over the curve of the Earth. You can see, as you wander over those dry flats, that man has been there, that vast stretches of sagebrush have replaced the bunchgrass grazed off by his cattle and sheep. Against a hill you can find the dry-rotting foundation of a scuttled homestead. But the desert is not scarred by man's presence. It is still possible to be alone out there, to stare at your hands for an hour and have no one ask why. It is possible to feel the cracks in the earth, to sense the enormity of space, to roll, between the tips of your fingers, the dust of boulders gone to pieces.
>
> —Lopez, "Weekend," *Audubon.*

Through descriptive language, a writer often makes you feel a certain way about the topic. In the preceding paragraph, the writer is trying to suggest that the desert is lonely, peaceful, and a good place to think or relax. Did you notice such words and phrases as *soundlessly, enormity of space, distant, wander, vast stretches?*

EXERCISE 12-10 **Directions:** Read each of the following articles and answer the questions that follow.

Article 1:

Americans and the Land

I have often wondered at the savagery and thoughtlessness with which our early settlers approached this rich continent. They came at it as though it were an enemy, which of course it was. They burned the forests and changed the rainfall; they swept the buffalo from the plains, blasted the streams, set fire to the grass, and ran a reckless scythe through the virgin and noble timber. Perhaps they felt that it was limitless and could never be exhausted and that a man could move on to new wonders endlessly. Certainly there are many examples to the contrary, but to a large extent the early people pillaged the country as though they hated it, as though they held it temporarily and might be driven off at any time.

—Steinbeck, *America and Indians,* pp. 127–128.

1. Is this selection an objective or subjective account of the early settlement of America? Give examples to support your choice.

_____

_____

_____

2. Describe the writer's tone. How does it make you feel?

_____

_____

_____

3. Why do you think the author wrote this selection?

_____

_____

_____

Article 2:

Eat It Raw

Raw food is not just for hippies anymore. It is being embraced by hip-hop stars and New York restaurateurs.

The raw-food diet, once the exclusive domain of '70s food faddists, is making a comeback for the same reasons it flourished 30 years ago: health and politics. Many find it helpful in relieving a variety of maladies—including allergies, fibromyalgia, obesity, gum disease, and mood swings—while others see raw food as a way to resist the unhealthy products of an industrialized food system. No matter how you slice it, excitement about a diet of uncooked food is running high.

"Anecdotally, there's been a definite rise in interest in raw-foods diets," says nutritionist Suzanne Havala Hobbs, adjunct assistant professor at the University of North Carolina–Chapel Hill's School of Public Health. "There's been a lot of information out about celebrities that are eating raw foods, and naturally many younger people are interested in trying it out. There's also been a wave of raw-foods cookbooks and restaurants." Hobbs, who also serves as nutrition advisor to the Baltimore-based Vegetarian Resource Group, is currently conducting a research survey on the topic, called the Raw Foods Project.

A raw-food diet consists of foods that have not been processed or heated above 118 degrees Fahrenheit. These might include fresh fruits, vegetables, cold-pressed oils, sprouted grains, nuts, seeds, and even organic wine—but not meat or fish. According to June Butlin in *Positive Health* (Aug. 2001), a proper raw-food diet provides high levels of natural, essential nutrients such as fiber, essential oils, antimicrobials, plant hormones, bioflavonoids, vitamins, minerals, chlorophyll, digestive enzymes, and antioxidants. . . .

New York's raw foodists even have their own restaurant, Quintessence, a Manhattan bistro whose proprietors, Tolentin Chan and her husband, Dan Hoyt, understand the political and the personal power of the raw-food diet. "Major corporations are poisoning people with overprocessed, denatured food," says Hoyt. As for Chan, she suffered frequent colds and asthma attacks before trying a raw-food "cleanse" the way most raw foodists get started to see if she could get some relief. "My health improved tremendously," she says. "Now I'm 100 percent raw and my asthma is completely gone. I never get sick, and my energy is really high." Hoyt followed her lead and found relief from hay fever and food allergies. But both of them know how unappetizing raw food can seem at first.

"People think eating raw is gonna be like chewing on weeds," Hoyt says. But in the right hands, he says, it can be a refreshing culinary experience. "Raw food is very vibrant. We use lots of spices and sauces. The flavors are very strong and clean." Somebody out there must agree: Raw foods restaurants have sprung up across the United States, from Berkeley, Las Vegas, and Chicago to Minneapolis, Philadelphia, and Washington, D.C. It appears more are in the works.

—Olson, *Utne Reader,* pp. 20–22.

1. What is the author's purpose?

   _____

2. For whom is this article written?

   _____

3. Explain the figurative expression "People think eating raw is gonna be like chewing on weeds."

   _____

4. Describe the tone of the article.

   _____

5. List several words or phrases that have a somewhat negative connotation. List several words or phrases with positive connotations.

   _____

   _____

6. This reading is an excerpt from a larger article. What do you expect the rest of the article to contain?

_____

_____

If you tend to be a(n) . . .	Then build your interpretive reading skills by . . .
Applied learner	Asking the questions, How can I use this information? Of what value is this information?
Conceptual learner	Studying to see how the ideas fit together, looking for connections and relationships, as well as inconsistencies

MASTERING VOCABULARY

Directions: Determine the meaning of each of the following words used in this chapter. Then insert each one in the sentence in which it makes the most sense.

proclaims (p. 435)

unruly (p. 435)

empathized (p. 438)

distortion (p. 440)

accumulation (p. 441)

inveterate (p. 442)

precautions (p. 443)

abide (p. 450)

vast (p. 459)

enormity (p. 459)

1. There was a great _____ of trash in the vacant lot.

2. The tourists were surprised by the _____ areas of uninhabited land.

3. They were surprised at the _____ of the Grand Canyon.

4. The store clerk _____ with the crying, lost child.

5. The boy was an _____ liar, spinning tales and unbeliev-
able stories with every opportunity.

6. The child's _____ behavior made it impossible for her
parents to take her to restaurants.

7. You should take a number of _____ before lighting a
barbecue grill.

8. After the election board _____ a winner, there will be a
press conference.

9. Both teams must _____ by the referee's decision.

10. The defendant's story was filled with _____.

SELF-TEST SUMMARY

How do authors suggest their ideas without directly stating them?	Authors use three features to state their ideas indirectly. These three features are: 1. **Connotative meaning**—the shades of meaning a word may have in addition to its literal meaning 2. **Implied meaning**—ideas suggested based on facts and information given by the author 3. **Figurative language**—a way of describing things that make sense on an imaginative level, but not on a factual level
How can you identify the author's purpose?	There are four ways to identify the author's purpose. These are: 1. **Style**—A writer will change his or her style (level of language, choice of words, and method of presentation) to suit the intended audience. 2. **Audience**—Analyzing the style and identifying the intended audience are the first steps toward identifying an author's purpose. 3. **Tone**—A writer's tone (serious, humorous, angry, sympathetic) is a clue to how the writer wants you to feel about the topic. 4. **Language**—A writer's language may be objective or subjective, depending on whether the writer is simply presenting facts or expressing an opinion or feelings. This language presents one or more clues to the writer's purpose.

Getting More Practice with . . .
Interpreting the Writer's Message and Purpose

WORKING TOGETHER

Directions: Bring a magazine ad to class. Working in groups of three or four students, make as many inferences as possible about each ad. For example, answer questions such as "What is happening?" "How does each person feel?" and "How will this ad sell the product?" Group members who differ in their opinions should present evidence to support their own inferences. Each group should then state to the class, as specifically as possible, the purpose of each ad. Be specific; try to say more than "To sell the product."

GOING ONLINE

Internet Activities

1. Writing as a Social Act

   http://writing.colostate.edu/guides/processes/writingsituations/graphic.cfm

   Explore this site about the ways in which authors and readers create and react to the written word. Then make your own graphic representation of the material using a concept map or other type of diagram.

2. Selling Yourself

   One of the most important arguments you will have to make is in your cover letter for job applications. Read over this information about selling yourself:

   http://owl.english.purdue.edu/handouts/pw/p_applettr.html

   Print out the sample cover letter and analyze it according to the site's tips.

Companion Website

For additional readings, exercises, and Internet activities, visit this book's Companion Website at:

http://www.ablongman.com/mcwhorter

If you need a user name and password, please see your instructor.

myreadinglab

My Reading Lab

For more practice with critical reading skills, visit MyReadingLab, click on the Reading Skills tab, and then click on:

1. Purpose and Tone—The Getty Museum, California
2. Inference—Great Lakes Region

http://www.ablongman.com/myreadinglab

TEST-TAKING TIPS

Answering Inference Questions

Reading comprehension tests usually ask questions that require you to make inferences. Answers to these questions, unlike questions about details, are not directly stated in the passage. Instead, you have to reason out the answers. Use the following suggestions to answer inferential questions correctly.

- Remember, all questions are answerable if you use the information contained in the passage.

- To answer an inferential question, you need to add up the facts and ideas contained in the passage and come to your own conclusion. Unless you can point to some evidence in the passage to support a particular answer, do not choose it.

- To answer a question about the author's purpose, ask yourself the following question: What does the writer intend to accomplish by writing this? Then match your answer to the available choices.

- You may also be asked questions about tone. To find the tone of a passage, ask yourself the following question: How does the author feel toward his or her subject? Also pay particular attention to connotative language. Words with emotional meanings often reveal tone.

- Questions about intended audience are often worded as follows: "This passage is written for. . . ." or "This passage is intended to appeal to . . ." To answer this type of question, consider each choice and look for evidence in the passage that supports one of the choices.

Name _____

Section _____ Date _____

Number right _____ x 20 points = Score _____

Directions: Read each statement and answer the questions that follow.

_____ 1. "Before the meeting began, several staff members stood in a corner of the room and **chatted** about the new organizational chart." Replace the boldfaced word in this sentence with one of the words below that has a *negative* connotative meaning.
   a. conversed
   b. wondered
   c. gossiped
   d. talked

_____ 2. "Gordon is so **cheap** that he always uses coupons at the grocery store and dines out only once a year." Replace the boldfaced word in this sentence with one of the words below that has a *positive* connotative meaning.
   a. stingy
   b. miserly
   c. tightfisted
   d. thrifty

_____ 3. Of the following sentences, the only one that does *not* contain figurative language is
   a. I worked my fingers to the bone on this project.
   b. I stayed up past midnight in order to finish the project on time.
   c. The project took on a life of its own.
   d. My professor said the project looked like a million bucks.

_____ 4. "When you are hitting a baseball, it's important to see the ball as soon as it leaves the pitcher's hand." The tone in this sentence can best be described as
   a. sympathetic.
   b. sentimental.
   c. instructive.
   d. persuasive.

_____ 5. "Even though I grew up in the Midwest, to me Christmas will always mean bright sunshine, warm breezes, and the thrill of splashing in the ocean near my grandparents' house in San Diego." The tone in this sentence can best be described as
   a. sympathetic.
   b. humorous.
   c. persuasive
   d. nostalgic.

Name _____

Section _____ Date _____

Number right _____ x 20 points = Score _____

Directions: Read each of the following paragraphs and answer the questions that follow.

Paragraph 1:

Over the past 20 years, psychologists have made a science of the joys and devastations of couples' relationships. They've come to understand, at least in part, why some relationships happily endure and what contributes to the hellhole interactions that claim over half of all first marriages, usually within the first seven years. Although these same psychologists note that most marriages start with great optimism and true love, they get into trouble for a very humbling reason: we just don't know how to handle the negative feelings that are a result of the differences between two people, the very differences that formed the basis for attraction in the first place.

—Donatelle and Davis,
Access to Health, p. 146.

_____ 1. One inference that can be made from this paragraph is that
   a. the author disapproves of divorce.
   b. more than half of all first marriages end in divorce.
   c. the author is a marriage counselor.
   d. all divorces occur within the first seven years of marriage.

Paragraph 2:

Alas, all is not perfect in the virtual world. E-commerce does have its limitations. Security is one important concern. We hear horror stories of consumers whose credit cards and other identity information have been stolen. While an individual's financial liability in most theft cases is limited to $50, the damage to one's credit rating can last for years. Some shady companies are making money by prying and then selling personal information to others. Pretty scary. Almost daily we hear of hackers getting into a business or even a government Web site and causing havoc. Businesses risk the loss of trade secrets and other proprietary information. Many must spend significant amounts to maintain security and conduct regular audits to ensure the integrity of their sites.

—Soloman and Stuart, *The Brave New World of E-Commerce*, p. 17.

_____ 2. In this paragraph, an example of *objective* language is
   a. "horror stories."
   b. "individual liability."
   c. "shady companies."
   d. "Pretty scary."

Paragraph 3:

If we want to create safe classrooms in which teachers and students have the right to question existing knowledge and produce new knowledge, we must prepare you, who are planning to teach, for the problems you will face. One of your most frustrating problems will revolve around your discovery that power can shape and even dominate your life and your school. Power is a basic reality of human existence, present in all human relationships, including those of lovers, business partners, basketball teams, teachers and students, college faculties, courts, government bodies and so on.

—Kincheloe, *Contextualizing Teaching*, pp. 90–91.

_____ 3. For this paragraph, the authors' intended audience is
    a. parents of school-age children.
    b. people who work in positions of power.
    c. college professors.
    d. people who are planning to become teachers.

Paragraph 4:

Computer games are big business, but many of the best-sellers are filled with gore and violence that are not the best things for children to see. Is there an alternative? A company formed by five young people in Sweden thinks so, and they're succeeding by offering product alternatives that prove you don't need to be bloody to be the best. The company, called Daydream Software, got its start when one of the programmers gave a computer to his little sister for Christmas. He had a hard time finding appropriate games she could play, however. This frustrating discovery led to discussions with friends about finding methods to push players' thrill buttons other than endless blood and splatter. All of Daydream's founders have children, and they design games they would want their own kids to play. They want the player to come away with more than just the echo of machine guns and a sore trigger finger.

—Soloman and Stuart, _Marketing_, p. 59.

_____ 4. One inference that can be made from this paragraph is that
    a. Daydream's computer games are nonviolent.
    b. Daydream's computer games are more expensive than other computer games.
    c. the people who produce violent computer games do not have children.
    d. violent computer games are always more exciting than nonviolent games.

Paragraph 5:

Another shameful abandonment of human rights affected Native Americans. Between 1700 and 1763, thousands of white settlers poured into Indian lands west of the mountains. The result was bloody warfare, marked by barbarous atrocities on both sides. Looking to the British for protection, most of the tribes fought against Americans during the Revolution, only to have their territories put under control of their enemies in the peace of 1783. Protracted negotiations with the American government led to more surrenders and numerous treaties, all of which were broken as the flood of white land speculators and settlers moved westward. In desperation, the Indians attempted unification and a hopeless resistance. By 1800 enforced living on land set aside for Indians was already promoting the disintegration of Native American cultures.

—Brummett et al., _Civilization_, pp. 578–579.

_____ 5. The authors' purpose in this paragraph is to
    a. explain the role of Native Americans in the settling of the west.
    b. describe the effect of westward expansion on Native Americans.
    c. criticize Native Americans for their treatment of whites in the 18th century.
    d. defend the actions of whites against Native Americans in the 18th century.

Name _____

Section _____ Date _____

Number right _____ × 10 points = Score _____

Directions: After reading the selection, choose the best answer for each of the questions that follow.

Scar

The mark on my face made me who I am

1   Growing up, I had a scar on my face—a perfect arrow in the center of my cheek, pointing at my left eye. I got it when I was 3, long before I knew that scars were a bad thing, especially for a girl. I knew only that my scar brought me attention and tenderness and candy.

2   As I got older I began to take pride in my scar, in part to stop bullies from taunting me, but mainly to counter the assumption that I should feel embarrassed. It's true, I was embarrassed the first couple of times someone pointed at my cheek and asked "What's that?" or called me Scarface. But the more I heard how unfortunate my scar was, the more I found myself liking it.

3   When I turned 15, my parents—on the advice of a plastic surgeon—decided it was time to operate on what was now a thick, shiny red scar.

4   "But I don't mind the scar, really," I told my father as he drove me home from the local mall, explaining that I would have the surgery during my summer vacation. "I don't need surgery." It had been years since I'd been teased, and my friends, along with my boyfriend at the time, felt as I did—that my scar was unique and almost pretty in its own way. After so many years, it was part of me.

5   "You do need surgery," my father said, his eyes on the road, his lips tight.

6   "But I like it," I told him. "I don't want to get rid of it."

7   "You need surgery," he said again, and he lowered his voice. "It's a deformity."

8   I don't know what hurt more that day: hearing my father call my scar a deformity or realizing that it didn't matter to him how I felt about it.

9   I did have plastic surgery that summer. They cut out the left side of the arrow, leaving a thinner, zigzag scar that blended into the lines of my face when I smiled. The following summer they did the same to the right side of the arrow. Finally, when I was 18, the surgeon sanded my cheek smooth.

10   In my late 20s, I took a long look at my scar, something I hadn't done in years. It was still visible in the right light, but no one asked me about it anymore. I examined the small steplike pattern and the way it made my cheek dimple when I smiled. As I leaned in awkwardly toward the mirror, I felt a sudden sadness.

11   There was something powerful about my scar and the defiant, proud person I became because of it. I have never been quite so strong since they cut it out.

—Audet, "Scar," *The Sun*, Issue 325, p. 96.

_____ 1. The central thought of the reading is that
    a. the author's scar contributed to her self-identity and gave her power.
    b. parents should not make decisions for their children.
    c. people really do not notice deformities.
    d. beauty is in the eye of the beholder.

_____ 2. The writer's primary purpose is to
    a. provide autobiographical information.
    b. explain how she feels about her scar.
    c. give a general overview of plastic surgery.
    d. criticize her father.

_____ 3. What does the author mean when she says "scars were a bad thing, especially for a girl"?
    a. Faces reveal the inner person.
    b. Girls poke fun at other girls.
    c. Beauty is important for girls, and a scar is thought to detract.
    d. Boys do not care about how they look.

_____ 4. The connotation of the word "deformity" (paragraph 7) is
    a. strong and forceful act.
    b. frequently recurring problem.
    c. unsightly, unpleasant disability.
    d. unfortunate accident.

_____ 5. This article seems written primarily for which of the following audiences?
    a. plastic surgery patients
    b. audiences interested in personal stories
    c. children with serious physical disabilities
    d. parents who make decisions for their children

_____ 6. The meaning of the word "taunting" in paragraph 2 is
    a. complimenting.
    b. arguing with.
    c. teasing.
    d. accompanying.

_____ 7. Which word best describes the author's attitude toward her scar?
    a. positive
    b. negative
    c. uncertain
    d. hateful

_____ 8. Based on the reading, the author is likely to agree that
    a. plastic surgeons should be more sensitive to their patients' needs.
    b. parents seldom have their children's best interests in mind.
    c. disabled people should be pitied.
    d. disabilities can be a source of strength.

_____ 9. The father probably wanted his daughter to have surgery because he
    a. thought she would look better without the scar.
    b. thought the scar disturbed her.
    c. blamed himself that she had a scar.
    d. knew she would be happier in the long run.

_____ 10. The author helps readers make inferences about the father's attitude toward the scar by providing
    a. examples.
    b. opinions of others.
    c. dialogue.
    d. comparisons.

Name _____

Section _____ Date _____

Number right* _____ x 20 points = Score _____

Chapter 12
Mastery Test 4
Reading Selection

His Name Is Michael

Donna M. Marriott

This reading from *Education Week* magazine describes how a teacher learned an important lesson from a child who did not assert his identity in her classroom. The author is an early-literacy program manager in the San Diego, California, city schools.

Vocabulary Review

full-inclusion (par. 2) the practice of including children with disabilities in a regular classroom full-time

curriculum (par. 2) a set of courses

la maestra (par. 10) in Spanish, "the teacher"

complicity (par. 11) involvement as an accomplice in a questionable act

1   This is a true story—one that both haunts and inspires me. I wish I could say that the names have been changed to protect the innocent. The names were changed, but, sadly, no one was protected.

2   I was teaching that year in a full-inclusion, multi-age class. My teaching partner and I had 43 children ranging in age from 5 to 9, ranging in ability from average to labeled, ranging in experience from indulged to adequate. I boasted about being a progressive teacher—a teacher bent on changing the system. As I looked around my classroom, I could see evidence of all the latest and greatest in education: child-directed learning, meaning-driven curriculum, responsive teaching, authentic assessment. It took a little boy to show me what I couldn't see: Beneath this veneer of "best practice," there was a layer of fundamental ignorance.

3   He appeared at my classroom door in the middle of a busy morning gripping the hand of a harried school secretary. He was a tiny child with carefully combed hair, wearing a crisply pressed shirt, tightly clutching his lunch money. The secretary handed this child to me and rattled off the institutional essentials: "His name is Michael. He is a bus rider. He doesn't speak English." Not much of an introduction, but that's how it happens in schools. New students appear in the office at times that make sense in their lives—not in our lives. These children are unceremoniously placed in whatever classroom has an extra chair. It's not very welcoming—but that's the drill. We did all the usual new-kid things that day. We played the name game. The kid of the day gave him the grand tour of our room. He got to sit on the couch even though

*To calculate the number right, use items 1–10 under "Mastery Test Skills Check."

471

it wasn't really his turn. The children insisted that Michael have a buddy for absolutely everything—learning buddy, recess buddy, bathroom buddy, lunch buddy, cubby buddy, line buddy, water buddy, rug buddy, bus buddy. They thought it would be great if he had a sleepover buddy, too, but I was able to convince them otherwise. We were genuinely glad to have this youngster in our learning family. But Michael didn't become part of our family.

4   Michael existed marginally on the outside of the group. Sometimes he was on the outside looking in; sometimes he was on the outside looking out. I often saw him with his eyes closed—looking somewhere hidden. He was well-mannered, punctual, respectful, cute-as-a-button—but completely detached from me, from the children, and from the learning.

5   I met with the bilingual resource teacher to chat about concerns and possibilities. She told me she could come do an informal observation "a week from tomorrow." It was a long wait, but that's how it is in schools. She came. She watched. She listened. On her way out she said, "You might have better results, dear, if you call him Miguel."

6   I could not have been more embarrassed or confused. How could I have been calling this child the wrong name? I was a progressive teacher: How could I have made such a mistake? How could the school secretary have made such a mistake? Why hadn't the parents corrected her? Why hadn't the child corrected me?

7   Miguel didn't stay with us for long. His family moved on to follow their own calendar of opportunities. We didn't get to say goodbye, but that's how it happens in schools.

8   Miguel's paperwork arrived about three weeks after he had moved away. I was going through the folder, updating it for his next teacher, when I noticed something that made me catch my breath. His name wasn't Michael. It wasn't Miguel. His name was David.

9   I wondered how it was that this child could have been part of my classroom for more than a month, and in that entire time he never had enough personal power to tell me that his name was David. What was it about me, about the other children, about the school that made David feel he had to give up his name? No child should have to forfeit his identity to walk through our classroom doors. No child. Ever. It is much too high a price to pay.

10   I have to do a bit of guessing about what was going on in David's head. I am guessing that he was told to respect la maestra—to "be good" in school. I am guessing that he thought if the teacher decided to change his name, well then . . . that was that. I am guessing that he didn't connect school to any known reality. He could be David at home, but at school he was expected to become someone else.

11   I don't have to do much guessing at my own complicity. It never occurred to me that his name would be anything other than Michael. In the entire breadth of my experience, people had called me by my given name. In those few instances when someone mispronounced my name, I would offer a polite but prompt correction. I was taught to speak up for myself. I was given the power to be me—in my school, in my neighborhood, in my life. I never considered checking in with David

about his name. It was beyond the scope of my experience. It was beyond the lens of my culture.

12   Our power distance was huge. I had all the power. I was white; I was the teacher; I spoke English. David had no power. He was brown; he was a child; he spoke Spanish. Our sense of individualism clashed. I expected him to have a sense of himself—to stand up for himself, to speak up. He denied himself. David expected and accepted that he was "less than" in the culture of school. Our perception of reality was polarized. I trusted in the precision of the system. The name on the registration card just had to be correct. That's how it works in schools. David accepted the imprecision of the system. Having his name changed was just part of the whole befuddling experience.

13   I have learned many difficult lessons in the years since David sat submissively on the edge of my classroom. I have learned lessons about passive racism—the kind that we cannot see in ourselves, don't want to see in ourselves, and vehemently deny. I have learned lessons about implicit power and explicit powerlessness—about those voices we choose to hear and those voices we unknowingly silence. I have learned that being a good teacher is as much about rapport and relationships as it is about progressive curriculum, pedagogy, and assessment.

14   If I could go back to that day when the secretary brought in a little boy with carefully combed hair wearing a crisply pressed shirt, I would shake his hand and say, "Hello. My name is Mrs. Marriott. What's your name?" I believe that if I had simply asked him, he would have told me.

MASTERY TEST SKILLS CHECK

Directions: Select the best answer for each of the following questions.

Checking Your Comprehension

_____ 1. The main point of this selection is that
   a. the procedures for enrolling children in schools should be improved to make new students feel more welcome.
   b. cultural differences and false assumptions can prevent children from having a voice in their own lives.
   c. programs need to teach English as a second language.
   d. overcrowding in classrooms can lead to students getting overlooked by their teachers.

_____ 2. The topic of paragraph 3 is the
   a. classroom.
   b. secretary.
   c. new student, "Michael."
   e. teacher.

_____ 3. The bilingual resource teacher's comment in paragraph 5 indicates that she
   a. understood exactly why the student did not participate in class.
   b. thought the classroom teacher was doing a poor job.
   c. also made an incorrect assumption about the student's name.
   d. did not think the student was having any problems.

_____ 4. The question that the author is trying to answer in paragraph 10 is
  a. Why did David let people call him by the wrong name at school?
  b. Why did David's family remove him from school?
  c. What did David's parents call him at home?
  d. How did the school secretary get the wrong name for David?

_____ 5. The main idea of paragraph 11 is that the teacher
  a. should have known she was calling her student by the wrong name.
  b. made incorrect assumptions about a student based on her own experience.
  c. was taught to speak up for herself in every aspect of her life.
  d. did not even consider asking her student about his name.

Applying Your Skills

_____ 6. The author's primary purpose is to
  a. compare her own experience as a child with that of her students.
  b. criticize parents who move their children during the school year.
  c. describe what she learned from her experience with a particular student.
  d. discuss what it means to be a progressive teacher in an inclusive classroom.

_____ 7. The main audience this article is intended for is
  a. college students.
  b. educators.
  c. bilingual students.
  d. parents who speak English as a second language.

_____ 8. The tone of the selection can best be described as
  a. angry and bitter.
  b. cheerful and optimistic.
  c. honest and sympathetic.
  d. indifferent and resigned.

_____ 9. One inference that can be made from the selection is that the
  a. teacher wishes she had handled her new student differently.
  b. secretary gave the teacher the wrong name on purpose.
  c. students did not like having a new student in their classroom.
  d. student's family left because they did not like how he was treated at school.

_____ 10. The phrase "power distance" in paragraph 12 refers to the
  a. difference between the physical strength of adults compared to children.
  b. distance each student and teacher must travel to come to school.
  c. total amount of power people have when they work together for a common goal.
  d. difference between the amount of power or status that two people possess.

Studying Words

Directions: Use a dictionary to answer the following questions.

_____ 11. A person who is "bilingual" (paragraph 5) is able to speak
  a. one language.
  b. two languages.
  c. three languages.
  d. many languages.

_____ 12. What is the best definition of the word "forfeit" as it is used in paragraph 9?
   a. to give up
   b. to surrender as punishment for a crime
   c. something placed in escrow to be redeemed later
   d. a game in which forfeits are demanded

_____ 13. In the sentence, "I boasted about being a progressive teacher—a teacher bent on changing the system," the word "progressive" has which type of context clue?
   a. definition
   b. synonym
   c. contrast
   d. inference

_____ 14. The word "rapport" (paragraph 13) originated from which of the following languages?
   a. German
   b. Greek
   c. Spanish
   d. French

_____ 15. What is the correct pronunciation of the word "pedagogy" (paragraph 13)?
   a. PED uh gog ee
   b. PED uh go jee
   c. ped uh GOG ee
   d. ped uh GO jee

For more practice, ask
your instructor for an
opportunity to work on the mastery
tests that appear in the Test Bank.

Chapter 13

Evaluating: Asking Critical Questions

Getting Started with . . .
Evaluating

What issue does this photograph address? What position or stance on the issue is presented? What questions should you ask about this issue? This chapter will show you how to read and evaluate persuasive material.

If you were thinking of purchasing a used car from a private owner, you would ask questions before deciding whether to buy it. You would ask about repairs, maintenance, gas mileage, and so forth. When it comes to buying something, most of us have learned the motto "Buyer beware." We have learned to be critical, sometimes suspicious, of a product and its seller. We realize that salespeople will often tell us only what will make us want to buy the item. They will not tell what is wrong with the item or whether it compares unfavorably with a competitor's product.

Although many of us have become wise consumers, few of us have become wise, critical readers. We need to adopt a new motto: Reader beware. You can think of some writers as sellers and their written material as the product to be sold. Just as you would ask questions about a car before buying it, so should you ask questions about what you read before you accept what is said. You should ask questions about who wrote the material and where it came from. You need to decide whether the writer is selling you a one-sided, biased viewpoint. You should evaluate whether the writer provides sufficient support for his or her ideas to allow you to accept them. This chapter will discuss these critical issues and show you how to apply them to articles and essays.

WHAT IS THE SOURCE OF THE MATERIAL?

Just as you might check the brand label on an item of clothing before you buy it, so should you check to see where an article or essay comes from before you read it. You will often be asked to read material that is not in its original form. Many textbooks, such as this one, include excerpts or entire selections borrowed from other authors. Instructors often photocopy articles or essays and distribute them or place them on reserve in the library for students to read.

A first question to ask before you even begin to read is: What is the source; from what book, magazine, or newspaper was this taken? Knowledge of the source will help you judge the accuracy and soundness of what you read. For example, in which of the following sources would you expect to find the most accurate and up-to-date information about computer software?

- An advertisement in *Time*
- An article in *Reader's Digest*
- An article in *Software Review*

The article in *Software Review* would be the best source. This is a magazine devoted to the subject of computers and computer software. *Reader's Digest*, on the other hand, does not specialize in any one topic and often reprints or condenses articles from other sources. *Time*, a weekly newsmagazine, does contain information, but a paid advertisement is likely to provide information on only one line of software.

Knowing the source of an article will give clues to the kind of information the article will contain. For instance, suppose you went to the library to locate information for a research paper on the interpretation of dreams. You found the following sources of information. What do you expect each to contain?

- An encyclopedia entry titled "Dreams"
- An article in *Woman's Day* titled "A Dreamy Way to Predict the Future"
- An article in *Psychological Review* titled "An Examination of Research on Dreams"

You can predict that the encyclopedia entry will be a factual report. It will provide a general overview of the process of dreaming. The *Woman's Day* article will probably focus on the use of dreams to predict future events. You can expect the article to contain little research. Most likely, it will be concerned largely with individual reports of people who accurately dreamt about the future. The article from *Psychological Review*, a journal that reports research in psychology, will present a primarily factual, research-oriented discussion of dreams.

As part of evaluating a source or selecting an appropriate source, be sure to check the date of publication. For many topics, it is essential that you work with current, up-to-date information. For example, suppose you have found an article on the safety of over-the-counter (nonprescription) drugs. If the article was written four or five years ago, it is already outdated. New drugs have been approved and released; new regulations have been put into effect; packaging requirements have changed. The year a book was published can be found on the copyright page. If the book has been reprinted by another publisher or has been reissued in paperback, look to see when it was first published and check the year(s) in the copyright notice.

EXERCISE 13-1

Directions: For each set of sources listed below, choose the one that would be most useful for finding information on the stated topic. Then, in the space provided, give a reason for your choice.

_____ 1. **Topic:** gas mileage of American-made cars

Sources:
a. A newspaper article titled "Gas-Eating American Cars"
b. An encyclopedia article on "Gas Consumption of Automobile Engines"
c. A research report in *Car and Driver* magazine on American car performance

Reason: _____

_____ 2. **Topic:** viruses as a cause of cancer

      Sources:
      a. A textbook titled *Well-Being: An Introduction to Health*
      b. An article in *Scientific American* magazine on controlling viruses
      c. An issue of the *Journal of the American Medical Association* devoted to a review of current research findings on the causes of cancer

      Reason: _____

_____ 3. **Topic:** the effects of aging on learning and memory

      Sources:
      a. An article in *Reader's Digest* titled "Older Means Better"
      b. A psychology textbook titled *A General Introduction to Psychology*
      c. A textbook titled *Adult Development and Aging*

      Reason: _____

IS AN INTERNET SOURCE RELIABLE?

While the Internet contains a great deal of valuable information and resources, it also contains rumor, gossip, hoaxes, and misinformation. In other words, not all Internet sources are trustworthy. You must evaluate a source before accepting it. Unlike print sources, the Internet has no editors or publishers to verify the accuracy of the information presented. As explained in Chapter 10, any individual, company, or organization can put information on a Web site or in a newsgroup posting. Here are some guidelines to follow when evaluating Internet sources.

1. **Check the author.** For Web sites, look for professional credentials or affiliations. If no author is listed, you should be skeptical. For newsgroups or discussion groups, check to see if the author has given his or her name and a signature (a short biographical description included at the end of messages).

2. **Discover the purpose of the posting.** Many Web sites have an agenda such as to sell a product, promote a cause, advocate a position, and so forth. Look for bias in the reporting of information.

3. **Check the date of the posting.** Be sure you are obtaining current information. A Web site usually includes the date on which it was last updated.

4. **Check the sponsoring organization of the site.** If a site is sponsored or provided by a well-known organization, such as a reputable newspaper such as the *New York Times,* the information is apt to be reliable.

5. **Check links (addresses of other sources suggested by the Web site).** If these links are no longer working, the Web site you are visiting may be outdated or not reputable.

6. **Cross-check your information.** Try to find the same information in, ideally, two other sources, especially if the information is vitally important (issues dealing with health, financial discussion, etc.) or if it is at odds with what seems logical or correct.

EXERCISE 13-2 | **Directions:** Visit a Web site and become familiar with its organization and content. Evaluate it using the suggested criteria. Then write a brief paragraph explaining why the Web site is or is not a reliable source.

WHAT IS THE AUTHORITY OF THE AUTHOR?

Another clue to the reliability of the information is the author's qualifications. If the author lacks expertise in or experience with a subject, the material may not be accurate or worthwhile reading.

In textbooks, the author's credentials may appear on the title page or in the preface. In nonfiction books and general market paperbacks, a summary of the author's life and credentials may be included on the book jacket or back cover. In many other cases, however, the author's credentials are not given. You are left to rely on the judgment of the editors or publishers about an author's authority.

If you are familiar with an author's work, then you can anticipate the type of material you will be reading and predict the writer's approach and attitude toward the subject. If, for example, you found an article on world banking written by former President Carter, you could predict it will have a political point of view. If you were about to read an article on John Lennon written by Ringo Starr, one of the other Beatles, you could predict the article might possibly include details of their working relationship from Ringo's point of view.

EXERCISE 13-3 | **Directions:** Read each statement and choose the individual who would seem to be the best authority on the subject.

_____ 1. *General Hospital* is one of the best soap operas on TV.
   a. Rick Levine, a former producer of *General Hospital*
   b. Sally Hastings, a soap-opera fan for two years
   c. Frances Hailey, a TV critic for the *New York Times*

_____ 2. The president's recent news conference was a success.
   a. Peter Jennings, a well-known news commentator
   b. Janet Ferrick, one of the president's advisors
   c. Howard Summers, a professor of economics

_____ 3. Kurt Vonnegut is one of the most important modern American novelists.
   a. James Toth, producer of a TV documentary on Vonnegut's life
   b. John Vilardo, a _Time_ magazine columnist
   c. Cynthia Weinstein, a professor of twentieth-century literature at Georgetown University

DOES THE WRITER MAKE ASSUMPTIONS?

An assumption is an idea, theory, or principle that the writer believes to be true. The writer then develops his or her ideas based on that assumption. Of course, if the assumption is not true or is one you disagree with, then the ideas that depend on that assumption are of questionable value. For instance, an author may believe that the death penalty is immoral and, beginning with that assumption, develop an argument for the best ways to prevent crime. However, if you believe that the death penalty _is_ moral, then from your viewpoint, the writer's argument is invalid.

Read the following paragraph. Identify the assumption the writer makes, and write it in the space provided.

> The evil of athletic violence touches nearly everyone. It tarnishes what may be our only religion. Brutality in games blasphemes* play, perhaps our purest form of free expression. It blurs the clarity of open competition, obscuring our joy in victory as well as our dignity in defeat. It robs us of innocence, surprise, and self-respect. It spoils our fun.
>
> —Yaeger, _Seasons of Shame_, p. 4.

Assumption: _____

Here the assumption is stated in the first sentence—the writer assumes that athletic violence exists. He makes no attempt to prove or explain that sports are violent. He assumes this and goes on to discuss its effects. You may agree or disagree with this assumption.

_____
*Boxed words appear in the Mastering Vocabulary exercise on p. 500.

Directions: For each of the following paragraphs, identify the assumption that is made by the writer and write it in the space provided.

1. Do you have any effective techniques that you use regularly to reduce your level of stress? If not, you may be among the many people who intellectually recognize the dangers of chronic stress—perhaps even have benefited from relaxation exercises—but somehow haven't made stress reduction part of their daily schedule. And you may be especially fascinated by a unique six-second exercise conceived and developed by Charles F. Stroebel, M.D., Ph.D., director of research at The Institute of Living in Hartford, Connecticut, and professor of psychiatry at the University of Connecticut Medical School.

    —Stern, "Calm Down in Six Seconds," *Vogue.*

    Assumption: _____

2. Do boys need to rely on heroes more than girls do as sources of identity while growing up? While no one has gathered statistics, it is true that boys are more often called upon to prove themselves through performance. For example, even today, they're often still judged by how well they can kick and throw a ball. So they may have a greater *dependence* on athletes, if only as models to imitate. The baseball/football trading card ritual is still very common among elementary school–age boys; girls, however, have no equivalent for this practice, nor are they rated for their physical accomplishments the same way. Despite today's increasingly "non-sexist" child rearing, girls are still evaluated more on the basis of how they relate to other people than as solitary, achieving individuals.

    —Fortino, "Why Kids Need Heroes," *Parents Magazine.*

    Assumption: _____

IS THE AUTHOR BIASED?

As you evaluate any piece of writing, always try to decide whether the author is objective or one-sided (biased). Does the author present an objective view of the subject or is a particular viewpoint favored? An objective article presents all sides of an issue, while a biased one presents only one side.

You can decide whether a writer is biased by asking yourself these questions:

1. Is the writer acting as a reporter—presenting facts—or as a salesperson—providing only favorable information?
2. Are there other views toward the subject that the writer does not discuss?

Use these questions to determine whether the author of the following selection is biased:

> Teachers, schools, and parent associations have become increasingly concerned about the effects of television on school performance. Based on their classroom experiences, many teachers have reported mounting incidences of fatigue, tension, and aggressive behavior, as well as lessened spontaneity and imagination.
>
> So what have schools been doing? At Kimberton Farms School in Phoenixville, Pennsylvania, parents and teachers have been following written guidelines for five years which include no television *at all* for children through the first grade. Children in second grade through high school are encouraged to watch no television on school nights and to restrict viewing to a total of three to four hours on weekends. According to Harry Blanchard, head of the faculty, "You can observe the effects with some youngsters almost immediately. . . . Three days after they turn off the set you see a marked improvement in their behavior. They concentrate better, and are more able to follow directions and get along with their neighbors. If they go back to the set you notice it right away."
>
> As Fiske has pointed out, In the final analysis, the success of schools in minimizing the negative effects of television on their (children's) academic progress depends almost entirely on whether the parents share this goal.
>
> —Gander and Gardiner, *Child and Adolescent Development*, p. 384.

The subject of this passage is children's television viewing. The passage expresses concern and gives evidence that television has a negative effect on children. The other side of the issue—the positive effects or benefits—is not mentioned. There is no discussion of such positive effects as the information to be learned from educational television programs or the use of television in increasing a child's awareness of different ideas, people, and places. The author is biased and expresses only a negative attitude toward television.

Occasionally, you may come upon unintentional bias—bias that the writer is not aware of. A writer may not recognize his or her own bias on cultural, religious, or sexual issues.

IS THE WRITING SLANTED?

Slanting refers to the inclusion of details that suit the author's purpose and the omission of those that do not. Suppose you were asked to write a description of a person you know. If you wanted a reader to respond favorably to the person, you might write something like this:

> Alex is tall, muscular, and well-built. He is a friendly person and seldom becomes angry or upset. He enjoys sharing jokes and stories with his friends.

On the other hand, if you wanted to create a less positive image of Alex, you could omit the above information and emphasize these facts instead:

> Alex has a long nose and his teeth are crooked. He talks about himself a lot and doesn't seem to listen to what others are saying. Alex wears rumpled clothes that are too big for him.

While all of these facts about Alex may be true, the writer decides which to include, and which to omit.

Much of what you read is slanted. For instance, advertisers tell only what is good about a product, not what is wrong with it. In the newspaper advice column, Dear Abby gives her opinion on how to solve a reader's problem, but she does not discuss all the possible solutions.

As you read material that is slanted, keep these questions in mind:

1. **What types of facts has the author omitted?**
2. **How would the inclusion of these facts change your reaction or impression?**

EXERCISE 13-5

Directions: Below is a list of different types of writing. For each item, decide whether it has little slant (L), is moderately slanted (M), or is very slanted (V). Write L, M, or V in the space provided.

_____ 1. Help-wanted ads

_____ 2. An encyclopedia entry

_____ 3. A newspaper editorial

_____ 4. A biology textbook

_____ 5. A letter inviting you to apply for a charge account

_____ 6. A college catalog

_____ 7. An autobiography of a famous person

_____ 8. An insurance policy

_____ 9. *Time* magazine

_____ 10. *Catholic Digest* magazine

HOW DOES THE WRITER SUPPORT HIS OR HER IDEAS?

Suppose a friend said he thought you should quit your part-time job immediately. What would you do? Would you automatically accept his advice, or would you ask him why? No doubt you would not blindly accept the advice but would inquire why. Then, having heard his reasons, you would decide whether they made sense.

Similarly, when you read, you should not blindly accept a writer's ideas. Instead, you should ask why by checking to see how the writer supports or explains his or her ideas. Then, once you have examined the supporting information, decide whether you accept the idea.

Evaluating the supporting evidence a writer provides involves using your judgment. The evidence you accept as conclusive may be regarded by someone else as insufficient. The judgment you make depends on your purpose and background knowledge, among other things. In judging the quality of supporting information a writer provides, you should watch for the use of (1) generalizations, (2) personal experience, and (3) statistics as evidence.

Generalizations

What do the following statements have in common?

> Dogs are vicious and nasty.
> College students are more interested in having fun than in learning.
> Parents want their children to grow up to be just like them.

These sentences seem to have little in common. Although the subjects are different, the sentences do have one thing in common: each is a generalization. Each makes a broad statement about a group—dogs, college students, parents. The first statement says that dogs are vicious and nasty. Yet the writer could not be certain that this statement is true unless he or she had seen *every* existing dog. No doubt the writer felt this statement was true based on his or her observation of and experience with dogs.

A generalization is a statement that is made about an entire group or class of individuals or items based on experience with some members of that group. It necessarily involves the writer's judgment.

The question that must be asked about all generalizations is whether they are accurate. How many dogs did the writer observe and how much research did he or she do to justify the generalization? Try to think of exceptions to the generalization, in this instance, a dog that is neither vicious nor nasty.

As you evaluate the supporting evidence a writer uses, be alert for generalizations that are presented as facts. A writer may, on occasion, support a statement by offering unsupported generalizations. When this occurs, treat the writer's ideas with a critical, questioning attitude.

EXERCISE 13-6   **Directions:** Read each of the following statements and decide whether it is a generalization. Place a check mark next to the statements that are generalizations.

_____   1. My sister wants to attend the University of Chicago.

_____   2. Most engaged couples regard their wedding as one of the most important occasions in their lives.

_____   3. Senior citizens are a cynical and self-interested group.

_____   4. People do not use drugs unless they perceive them to be beneficial.

_____   5. Warning signals of a heart attack include pain or pressure in the left side of the chest.

EXERCISE 13-7   **Directions:** Read the following paragraphs and underline each generalization.

1. Teenagers need privacy; it allows them to have a life of their own. By providing privacy, we demonstrate respect. We help them disengage themselves from us and grow up. Some parents pry too much. They read their teenagers' mail and listen in on their telephone calls. Such violations may cause permanent resentment. Teenagers feel cheated and enraged. In their eyes, invasion of privacy is a dishonorable offense. As one girl said: "I am going to sue my mother for malpractice of parenthood. She unlocked my desk and read my diary."

    —Ginott, *Between Parent and Teenager*, pp. 39–41.

2. Farmers are interested in science, in modern methods, and in theory, but they are not easily thrown off balance and they maintain a healthy suspicion of book learning and of the shenanigans of biologists, chemists, geneticists, and other late-rising students of farm practice and management. They are, I think, impressed by education, but they have seen too many examples of the helplessness and the impracticality of educated persons to be either envious or easily budged from their position.

    —White, *One Man's Meat*, pp. 305–306.

3. Although the most commonplace reason women marry young is to "complete" themselves, a good many spirited young women gave another reason: "I did it to get away from my parents." Particularly for girls whose educations and privileges are limited, a jailbreak marriage is the usual thing. What might appear to be an act of rebellion usually turns out to be a transfer of dependence.

—Sheehy, *Passages*, p. 68.

Personal Experience

Writers often support their ideas by describing their own personal experiences. Although a writer's experiences may be interesting and reveal a perspective on an issue, do not accept them as proof. Suppose you are reading an article on drug use and the writer uses his or her personal experience with particular drugs to prove a point. There are several reasons why you should not accept the writer's conclusions about the drugs' effects as fact. First, the effects of a drug may vary from person to person. The drugs' effects on the writer may be unusual. Second, unless the writer kept careful records about times, dosages, surrounding circumstances, and so on, he or she is describing events from memory. Over time, the writer may have forgotten or exaggerated some of the effects. As you read, treat ideas supported only through personal experience as *one person's experience*. Do not make the error of generalizing the experience.

Statistics

People are often impressed by **statistics**—figures, percentages, averages, and so forth. They accept these as absolute proof. Actually, statistics can be misused, misinterpreted, or used selectively to give other than the most objective, accurate picture of a situation.

Here is an example of how statistics can be misused. Suppose you read that magazine *A* increased its readership by 50 percent, while magazine *B* had only a 10 percent increase. From this statistic, some readers might assume that magazine *A* has a wider readership than magazine *B*. The missing but crucial statistic is the total readership of each magazine prior to the increase. If magazine *A* had a readership of 20,000 and this increased by 50 percent, its readership would total 30,000. If magazine *B*'s readership was already 50,000, a 10 percent increase, bringing the new total to 55,000, would still give it the larger readership despite the smaller increase. Even statistics, then, must be read with a critical, questioning mind.

Here is another example:

Americans in the workforce are better off than ever before. The average salary of the American worker is $48,000.

At first the statement may seem convincing. However, a closer look reveals that the statistic given does not really support the statement. The term *average* is the key to how the statistic is misused. An average includes all salaries, both high and low. It is possible that some Americans earn $4,000 while others earn $250,000. Although the average salary may be $48,000, this does not mean that everyone earns $48,000.

EXERCISE 13-8

Directions: Read each of the following statements and decide how the statistic is misused. Write your explanation in the space provided.

1. Classrooms on our campus are not overcrowded. There are ten square feet of floor space for every student, faculty member, and staff member on campus.

   _____

   _____

   _____

2. More than 12,000 people have bought Lincoln Town Cars this year, so it is a popular car.

   _____

   _____

   _____

3. The average water pollution by our local industries is well below the hazardous level established by the Environmental Protection Agency.

   _____

   _____

   _____

IS IT FACT OR OPINION?

Facts are statements that can be verified. They can be proven true or false. **Opinions** are statements that express a writer's feelings, attitudes, or beliefs. They are neither true nor false. Here are a few examples of each:

Facts

1. My car insurance costs $1500.
2. The theory of instinct was formulated by Konrad Lorenz.
3. Greenpeace is an organization dedicated to preserving the sea and its animals.

Opinions

1. My car insurance is too expensive.
2. The slaughter of baby seals for their pelts should be outlawed.
3. Population growth should be regulated through mandatory birth control.

The ability to distinguish between fact and opinion is an essential part of evaluating an author's supporting information. Factual statements from reliable sources can usually be accepted as correct. Opinions, however, must be considered as one person's viewpoint that you are free to accept or reject.

EXERCISE 13-9   **Directions:** Mark each of the following statements as either fact or opinion.

_____ 1. Alligators provide no physical care for their young.

_____ 2. Humans should be concerned about the use of pesticides that kill insects at the bottom of the food chain.

_____ 3. There are 28 more humans living on the earth now than there were ten seconds ago.

_____ 4. We must bear greater responsibility for the environment than our ancestors did.

_____ 5. Nuclear power is the only viable solution to our dwindling natural resources.

_____ 6. Between 1850 and 1900 the death rate in Europe decreased due to industrial growth and advances in medicine.

_____   7. Dogs make the best pets because they can be trained to obey.

_____   8. Solar energy is available wherever sunlight reaches the earth.

_____   9. By the year 2010, many diseases, including cancer, will be preventable.

_____   10. Hormones are produced in one part of the body and carried by the blood to another part of the body where they influence some process or activity.

Judgment Words

When a writer or speaker expresses an opinion he or she often uses words or phrases that can tip you off that a judgment or opinion is being offered. Here are a few examples.

Professor Rodriguez is a *better* teacher than Professor Harrigan.

My sister's behavior at the party was *disgusting*.

Here is a list of words that often suggests that the writer is interpreting, judging or evaluating, or expressing feelings.

bad	good	worthless	amazing	frightening
worse	better	worthwhile	wonderful	
worst	best	disgusting	lovely	

EXERCISE 13-10   **Directions:** For each of the following statements, underline the word or phrase that suggests the statement is an opinion.

1. Purchasing a brand new car is a terrible waste of money.

2. Many wonderful vegetarian cookbooks are available in bookstores.

3. Of all the film versions of Victor Hugo's novel *Les Miserables,* the 1935 version starring Charles Laughton is the best.

4. The introductory biology textbook comes with an amazing CD-ROM.

5. Volunteers for Habitat for Humanity are engaged in a worthwhile activity.

Informed Opinion

The opinion of experts is known as **informed opinion.** For example, the Surgeon General is regarded as an authority on the health of Americans and his or her opinion on this subject is more trustworthy than casual observers or nonprofessionals.

Here are a few examples of expert opinions.

- Diana Baumrind, a psychologist at the University of California at Berkeley: *"Occasional spankings do not damage a child's social or emotional development."*
- Alan Greenspan, former chair of the Federal Reserve Board: *"The period of sub-par economic performance is not yet over."*
- Jane Goodall, primate expert and ethologist: *"Chimps are in massive danger of extinction from dwindling habitats—forests are being cut down at an alarming rate."*

Textbook authors, too, often offer informed opinion. As experts in their fields, they may make observations and offer comments that are not strictly factual. Instead, they are based on years of study and research. Here is an example from an American government textbook:

> The United States is a place where the pursuit of private, particular, and narrow interests is honored. In our culture, following the teachings of Adam Smith, the pursuit of self-interest is not only permitted but actually celebrated as the basis of the good and prosperous society.
>
> —Greenberg and Page, *The Struggle for Democracy*, p. 186.

The author of this statement has reviewed the available evidence and is providing his expert opinion on what the evidence indicates about American political culture. The reader, then, is free to disagree and offer evidence to support an opposing view.

Some authors are careful to signal the reader when they are presenting an opinion. Watch for words and phrases such as:

apparently	this suggests	in my view	one explanation is
presumably	possibly	it is likely that	according to
in my opinion	it is believed	seemingly	

Other authors do just the opposite; they try to make opinions sound like facts.

In the following excerpt from a social problems textbook, notice how the author carefully distinguishes factual statements from opinion by using qualifying words and phrases (underlined here for easy identification).

Economic Change, Ideology, and Private Life

It seems clear that there has been a major change in attitudes and feelings about family relationships since the eighteenth century. It is less clear how and why the change came about. One question debated by researchers is: In what social class did the new family pattern originate—in the aristocracy, as Trumbach (1978) believes, or in the upper gentry, as Stone (1977) argued, or in the working class, as Shorter (1975) contended? Or was the rise of the new domesticity a cultural phenomenon that affected people in all social categories at roughly the same time? Carole Shammas (1980) has found evidence of such a widespread cultural change by looking at the kinds of things people had in their homes at various times in the past, as recorded in probate inventories. She found that in the middle of the eighteenth century all social classes experienced a change in living habits; even working-class households now contained expensive tools of domesticity, such as crockery, teapots, eating utensils, and so on. Thus, according to Shammas, the home was becoming an important center for social interaction, and family meals had come to occupy an important place in people's lives.

—Skolnick, *The Intimate Environment*, p. 96.

EXERCISE 13-11

Directions: Read each of the following statements. In each, underline the word or phrase that suggests that the author is offering an informed opinion.

1. It seems clear that parents who would bring a young child to an R-rated movie are putting their own interests ahead of what's best for the child.

2. Voters rejected the proposed rapid transit system connecting the southern and northern suburbs, possibly because of racial issues.

3. According to the city superintendent of schools, school uniforms lead to improved behavior and fewer disruptions in the classroom.

4. One explanation for low attendance at professional sporting events is the high price of tickets.

5. It is believed that most people practice some form of recycling in their daily lives.

EXERCISE 13-12

Directions: Each of the following paragraphs contains both fact and opinion. Read each paragraph and label each sentence as fact or opinion.

Paragraph 1:

¹Flowering plants that are native to the South include purple coneflower and rose verbena. ²In the view of many longtime gardeners, these two plants are an essential part of the Southern landscape. ³Trees that are native to the South include a variety of oaks, as well as flowering dogwoods and redbuds. ⁴Dogwoods are especially lovely, with their white, pink, or coral blossoms announcing the arrival of spring. ⁵For fall color, the deep red of Virginia willow makes a spectacular show in the native Southern garden.

Sentences:

1. _____

2. _____

3. _____

4. _____

5. _____

Paragraph 2:

¹Today, many companies provide child care assistance, either on- or off-site, for their employees. ²This suggests that employers are becoming aware that their workers' family concerns can affect the company's bottom line. ³The Eli Lilly pharmaceutical company, for example, has built two child-development centers with a total capacity of more than 400 children. ⁴In addition to assistance with daily child care, Bank of America reimburses employees for child-care expenses related to business travel. ⁵It seems clear that other, less progressive employers will have to follow these companies' leads in order to attract and retain the best employees.

Sentences:

1. _____

2. _____

3. _____

4. _____

5. _____

Paragraph 3:

[1]Preparing a will is an important task that millions of people ignore, presumably because they prefer not to think about their own death. [2]However, if you die without a will, the courts will determine how your assets should be distributed, as directed by state law. [3]Even more important than establishing a will, in my opinion, is expressing your willingness to be an organ donor upon your death. [4]Each year, 25,000 new patients are added to the waiting list for organ transplants. [5]The legacy of an organ donor is far more valuable than any material assets put in a will.

Sentences:

1. _____

2. _____

3. _____

4. _____

5. _____

DOES THE WRITER MAKE VALUE JUDGMENTS?

A writer who states that an idea or action is right or wrong, good or bad, desirable or undesirable is making a **value judgment.** That is, the writer is imposing his or her own judgment on the worth of an idea or action. Here are a few examples of value judgments:

Divorces should be restricted to couples who can prove incompatibility.

Abortion is wrong.

Welfare applicants should be forced to apply for any job they are capable of performing.

Premarital sex is acceptable.

You will notice that each statement is controversial. Each involves some type of conflict or idea over which there is disagreement:

1. Restriction versus freedom
2. Right versus wrong
3. Force versus choice
4. Acceptability versus nonacceptability

You may know of some people who would agree and others who might disagree with each statement. A writer who takes a position or side on a conflict is making a value judgment.

As you read, be alert for value judgments. They represent one person's view *only* and there are most likely many other views on the same topic. When you identify a value judgment, try to determine whether the author offers any evidence in support of the position.

EXERCISE 13-13   **Directions:** Read the following passage and answer the questions that follow.

A Welfare Mother

I start my day here at five o'clock. I get up and prepare all the children's clothes. If there's shoes to shine, I do it in the morning. About seven o'clock I bathe the children. I leave the baby with the babysitter and I go to work at the settlement house. I work until twelve o'clock. Sometimes I'll work longer if I have to go to welfare and get a check for somebody. When I get back, I try to make hot food for the kids to eat. In the afternoon it's pretty well on my own. I scrub and clean and cook and do whatever I have to do.

Welfare makes you feel like you're nothing. Like you're laying back and not doing anything and it's falling in your lap. But you must understand, mothers, too, work. My house is clean. I've been scrubbing since this morning. You could check my clothes, all washed and ironed. I'm home and I'm working. I am a working mother.

A job that a woman in a house is doing is a tedious job—especially if you want to do it right. If you do it slipshod, then it's not so bad. I'm pretty much of a perfectionist. I tell my kids, hang a towel. I don't want it thrown away. That is very hard. It's a constant game of picking up this, picking up that. And putting this away, so the house'll be clean.

Some men work eight hours a day. There are mothers that work eleven, twelve hours a day. We get up at night, a baby vomits, you have to be calling the doctor, you have to be changing the baby. When do you get a break, really? You don't. This is an all-around job, day and night. Why do they say it's charity? We're working for our money. I am working for this check. It is not charity. We are giving some kind of home to these children.

I'm so busy all day I don't have time to daydream. I pray a lot. I pray to God to give me strength. If He should take a child away from me, to have the strength to accept it. It's His kid. He just borrowed him to me.

I used to get in and close the door. Now I speak up for my right. I walk with my head up. If I want to wear big earrings, I do. If I'm overweight, that's too bad. I've gotten completely over feeling where I'm little. I'm working now, I'm pulling my weight. I'm gonna get off welfare in time, that's my goal—get off.

It's living off welfare and feeling that you're taking something for nothing the way people have said. You get to think maybe you are. You get to think, Why am I so stupid? Why can't I work? Why do I have to live this way? It's not enough to live on anyway. You feel degraded.

The other day I was at the hospital and I went to pay my bill. This nurse came and gave me the green card. Green card is for welfare. She went right in front of me and gave it to the cashier. She said, "I wish I could stay home and let the money fall in my lap." I felt rotten. I was just burning inside. You hear this all the way around you. The doctor doesn't even look at you. People are ashamed to show that green card. Why can't a woman just get a check in the mail: Here, this check is for you. Forget welfare. You're a mother who works.

This nurse, to her way of thinking, she represents the working people. The ones with the green card, we represent the lazy no-goods. This is what she was saying. They're the good ones and we're the bad guys.

—Terkel, *Working*, pp. 303–304.

1. What do you think is the source of this selection?

_____

_____

_____

2. Do you consider this welfare mother to be an authority? Why or why not?

_____

_____

_____

3. What assumptions does this welfare mother make? Do you agree or disagree? Why?

_____

_____

_____

4. Do you think this view of a welfare mother is biased? Why or why not?

_____

_____

_____

5. Is the writing in this article slanted? If so, give some examples.

_____

_____

_____

6. How does this welfare mother support her ideas?

_____

_____

_____

7. Does this welfare mother make any value judgments? If so, what are they?

_____

_____

_____

8. Does this welfare mother make any generalizations? If so, underline them.

_____

_____

_____

EXERCISE 13-14   **Directions:** Read the passage below and answer the questions that follow.

Consumer Privacy

1   To what extent should a consumer's personal information be available online? This is one of the most controversial ethical questions today. Scott McNealy, CEO of Sun Microsystems, said in 1999: "You already have zero privacy—get over it." Apparently many consumers don't agree: A study of 10,000 Web users found that 84 percent object to reselling of information about their online activity to other companies. One of the highest profile cases is that of DoubleClick Inc., a company that places

"cookies" in your computer to let you receive targeted ads. The trouble began when DoubleClick bought Abacus Direct, a 90-million-name database, and began compiling profiles linking the two sets of data so clients would know who was receiving what kinds of ads.

2   DoubleClick's ability to track what you choose to buy and where you choose to surf is just one isolated example, though. Many companies can trace choices you make online and link them to other information about you. For example, when you register online for a product a Globally Unique Identity (GUID) is linked to your name and e-mail address. That means firms like RealJukebox, with 30 million registered users, can relay information to its parent company RealNetworks about the music each user downloads. Comet Systems, which creates customized cursors for companies featuring characters ranging from Pokemon to Energizer bunnies, reports each time a person visits any of the 60,000 Web sites that support its technology. Still other privacy violations are committed by consumers themselves: A site called disgruntledhousewife.com features a column to which women write to describe in excruciating detail the intimate secrets of former lovers. Be careful how you break off a relationship!

3   How can these thorny ethical issues be solved? One solution is an "infomediary;" an online broker who represents consumers and charges marketers for access to their data. As a Novell executive observed, "Slowly but surely consumers are going to realize that their profile is valuable. For loaning out their identity, they're going to expect something in return." Or, perhaps the solution is to hide your identity: Zero-Knowledge Systems of Montreal sells a software package called Freedom that includes five digital pseudonyms to assign to different identities.

4   All of these precautions may be irrelevant if regulations now being considered are ever implemented. One now being discussed is an "opt in" proposal that would forbid a Web site from collecting or selling personal data unless the user checked a box letting it do so. These efforts are being resisted by the online commerce lobby, which argues these safeguards would drastically reduce ad revenues.

—Solomon, *Consumer Behavior, Having, and Being*, p. 19.

1. What is the main point of the passage?

    _____

    _____

2. What is the author's attitude toward women who use the digruntledhousewife site?

    _____

    _____

3. This passage appeared in a consumer behavior college text. Evaluate it as source for:

   a. a business marketing term paper

   b. computer users who want to learn more about privacy issues on the Internet.

   _____

   _____

4. Is the passage biased? Explain your answer.

   _____

   _____

5. What types of supporting evidence does the author provide? Mark several examples of each type in the passage.

   _____

   _____

6. What assumptions does the author make?

   _____

   _____

7. Describe the tone of the passage.

   _____

   _____

8. Identify the generalization that is contained in paragraph 1. How is it supported?

   _____

   _____

9. Identify a statement of opinion in paragraph 1.

   _____

   _____

10. Identify a value judgment made in the passage.

   _____

   _____

If you tend to be a . . .	Then build your critical reading skills by . . .
Creative learner	Asking "What if . . .?" and "So what?" questions to free new ideas and new ways of looking at the subject
Pragmatic learner	Writing marginal notes, recording your thoughts, reactions, and impressions

MASTERING VOCABULARY

Directions: Match each word in Column A with its meaning in Column B. Determine the meaning from its context in this chapter, its word parts, or use a dictionary, if necessary.

	Column A	Column B
_____	1. blasphemes (p. 481)	a. existing alone
_____	2. chronic (p. 482)	b. disconnect
_____	3. solitary (p. 482)	c. put into effect
_____	4. disengage (p. 486)	d. made to individual specifications
_____	5. shenanigans (p. 486)	e. speaks evil about
_____	6. ethical (p. 497)	f. fictitious names
_____	7. customized (p. 498)	g. concerning right and wrong
_____	8. excruciating (p. 498)	h. continual
_____	9. pseudonyms (p. 498)	i. intensely painful or distressing
_____	10. implemented (p. 498)	j. underhanded acts

SELF-TEST SUMMARY

How can you evaluate what you read?

In order to evaluate what you read, ask yourself nine questions:
1. What is the source of the material?
2. Is an Internet source reliable?
3. What is the authority of the author?
4. Does the author make assumptions?
5. Is the author biased?
6. Is the writing slanted?
7. How does the author support his or her ideas?
8. Is it fact or opinion?
9. Does the author make value judgments?

Getting More Practice with . . .
Evaluating

WORKING TOGETHER

Directions: Bring to class a brief (two- to three-paragraph) newspaper article, editorial, film review, etc. Working in groups of three or four students, each student should read his or her piece aloud. The group can then discuss and evaluate (1) assumptions, (2) bias, (3) slanted writing, (4) methods of support, and (5) value judgments for each article. Each group should choose one representative article and submit its findings to the class or instructor.

GOING ONLINE

Internet Activities

1. Try these online "Fact or Opinion" quizzes:

   http://cuip.uchicago.edu/www4teach/97/jlyman/default/quiz/factopquiz.html

   http://dhp.com/~laflemm/RfT/Tut2.htm

   Pay attention to what you hear during the day and try to keep track of the facts and opinions. When do you hear more of one than the other?

2. Evaluating Sources

   http://library.nyu.edu/research/tutorials/evaluate/printeval.htm

   Read through the information in this tutorial from the New York University Libraries. Print out the page and use it to evaluate a book or article that you are currently reading for school or pleasure.

Companion Website

For additional readings, exercises, and Internet activities, visit this book's Companion Website at:

http://www.ablongman.com/mcwhorter

If you need a user name and password, please see your instructor.

myreadinglab

My Reading Lab

For more practice with critical reading, visit MyReadingLab, click on the Reading Skills tab, and then click on:

1. Critical Thinking—American Southwest
2. Purpose and Tone—The Getty Museum, California

http://www.ablongman.com/myreadinglab

TEST-TAKING TIPS

Answering Questions About Sources

Reading comprehension tests may include questions that ask you to identify the most likely source from which the selection was taken.

Example: This passage most likely originally appeared in a(n)

a. popular press magazine.

b. textbook.

c. newspaper editorial.

d. biography.

To answer questions like the sample above, consider the following:

• Writing style. How is the material written? Where does it sound like it might have come from? Textbooks are written in a straightforward, somewhat formal style while articles in popular press magazines may be more casual.

• Bias and opinion. Is the material factual, or does it express bias and opinions? While a newspaper editorial may express opinion, usually textbooks do not.

• Tone. Consider the attitude the writer takes toward the subject. Textbooks are helpful and instructive, while a popular news magazine may be more light and entertaining, for example.

Name _____

Section _____ Date _____

Number right _____ x 10 points = Score _____

Directions: Read each sentence and decide whether it can best be described as a fact, an opinion, an informed opinion, or a generalization.

_____ 1. Although the president nominates individuals to fill positions on the Supreme Court, the nomination must be confirmed by a majority vote in the Senate.
   a. fact
   b. opinion
   c. informed opinion
   d. generalization

_____ 2. A five-ounce cup of regular brewed coffee contains almost twice as much caffeine as a six-ounce cup of hot steeped tea.
   a. fact
   b. opinion
   c. informed opinion
   d. generalization

_____ 3. There should be a law against using a cell phone while driving.
   a. fact
   b. opinion
   c. informed opinion
   d. generalization

_____ 4. Australians are friendly and gregarious people.
   a. fact
   b. opinion
   c. informed opinion
   d. generalization

_____ 5. According to child psychologist Lawrence Kohlberg, the moral development of children takes place in three stages: preconventional morality, conventional morality, and postconventional (or principled) morality.
   a. fact
   b. opinion
   c. informed opinion
   d. generalization

503

Name _____

Section _____ Date _____

Number right _____ x 20 points = Score _____

Directions: Read each of the passages below and answer the questions that follow.

Passage 1:

Tuition vouchers have been proposed as a way to improve the quality of public schools. Under a tuition voucher program, the government gives parents of school-age children a set amount of money to pay for school tuition. Parents can use the money at either a public or private school. In order to attract students, public schools will have to improve their meager offerings dramatically; competition from more adaptive private schools will force public schools to wake up and pay better attention to the needs of students.

—Edwards III et al., *Government in America*, p. 685.

_____ 1. The author's bias is revealed in the
   a. first sentence.
   b. second sentence.
   c. third sentence.
   d. last sentence.

Passage 2:

Although the president's wife does not have an official government position, each First Lady of the past forty years has become known for her attention to a particular issue. For example, Lady Bird Johnson supported highway beautification, Rosalyn Carter was a mental health advocate, Barbara Bush promoted literacy, and Hillary Rodham Clinton was involved in health care reform during her husband's first term. During her husband's second term, however, Ms. Clinton took advantage of her position to launch her own political career as a U.S. senator. In doing so, Ms. Clinton became the first First Lady to run for political office.

_____ 2. The only sentence in this paragraph that contains an opinion is the
   a. first sentence.
   b. second sentence.
   c. third sentence.
   d. last sentence.

Passage 3:

Traveling through Europe presents countless opportunities to meet people from other countries. Unfortunately, many of them don't speak English. Of course, that's part of the fun, as I discovered when I went to Europe as a senior in high school. My efforts to communicate with a Greek sailor, an Italian bus driver, and an Austrian bank teller at various times during that trip convinced me that with persistence, and a sense of humor, you can usually make yourself understood. It's not so important to be able to say the words correctly or to say them with the right accent, and it truly does not help to say the same words slowly and loudly. What works best, both abroad *and* at home, is to say them with a smile.

_____ 3. The author supports the ideas in this paragraph primarily with
   a. statistics.
   b. personal experience.
   c. generalizations
   d. facts.

Passage 4:

Welfare and related programs are expensive. Our country has amassed a large public debt, partially due to past spending on social services. Each year, welfare spending continues to increase. Despite the costs of welfare, it is unfair to blame welfare recipients for the past debt problems welfare programs created.

_____ 4. The statement in this paragraph that is a value judgment is the
   a. first sentence.
   b. second sentence.
   c. third sentence.
   d. last sentence.

Passage 5:

Most of us believe that racism is a bad thing. However, when we are at a party or in another social setting where someone tells a racist joke, we often find it difficult to voice our objections. Why is that? Are we against racism only when it is convenient or easy? Our dilemma is that we see ourselves two ways: as polite people who would never purposely embarrass a friend or even an acquaintance, and as socially aware individuals who know racist comments are wrong. This moral inconsistency is even more troubling when we become parents and must serve as role models for our children. How do we explain the difference between "right" and "polite"—or is there really a difference?

_____ 5. The assumption that the author makes in this paragraph is that most people
   a. would rather not embarrass another person.
   b. believe children know right from wrong.
   c. want their children to behave properly at parties.
   d. enjoy racist jokes.

Name _____

Section _____ Date _____

Number right _____ x 10 points = Score _____

Directions: Read each of the passages below and choose the best answer for each of the questions that follow.

Passage 1

Having built four new elementary schools in the last five years, members of the Palmville School Board were convinced they had solved the problem with overcrowding that had plagued the public schools ever since the mid-1980s. As a result, they were disappointed when School Superintendent Marisa LaRoux made her mid-July Projected Enrollment Report. She pointed out that the town's population has expanded by several hundred more families than were projected because the good weather this year spurred home building and the low mortgage rates encouraged buyers. In addition, more families are deciding to have two or more children, bringing the average number of children per family to 1.9, much higher than the figure of 1.65 used in the past to calculate demands for school services. The superintendent also admitted that the decades-old policy of calculating a family of two as a family without children has proven to be a serious mistake because it ignored the many children growing up in single-parent families. Based on this information, the superintendent concluded that the overcrowding problem would continue this year and probably for many years in the future. Chairperson Clifton Washington summed up the school board's response this way: "The schools are overcrowded now and if more students are going to be coming to us asking for instruction, then we'd better get back into the school-building business."

1. Which of the following types of evidence does the school superintendent use in her report?
   a. opinions
   b. personal experiences
   c. facts and statistics
   d. generalizations

2. Which of the following is a value judgment that the school board seems to have made?
   a. Public school boards should not study projected enrollments.
   b. Previous enrollment studies were always wrong.
   c. Overcrowding in schools helps education.
   d. Education and schools are important.

3. Which of the following sentences is *not* an assumption used by the school board when they studied school enrollment in the past?
   a. A household of two people does not have any children.
   b. The average number of children per family was 1.9.
   c. Low mortgage rates encourage home buying.
   d. Good weather increased new home building.

_____ 4. Which of the following, if added to the evidence, would *not* support the author's ideas?

     a. Reducing overcrowding is a good idea because students usually learn better in less crowded classrooms.

     b. The recent plant closing in the area has forced many people to move away from Palmville.

     c. All the teachers support building new schools over expanding the school year.

     d. If we build new schools, the best teachers will apply for the new jobs.

_____ 5. Which of the following is a conclusion reached by the school board?

     a. They need to build more schools.

     b. Schools will always be overcrowded.

     c. Four new elementary schools would solve overcrowding.

     d. Most families in the area have more than two children.

Passage 2

The latest state proposal to divert more water from agricultural to residential uses might be expected to gain support from rapidly urbanizing Palmville. Speaking through their Town Meeting, however, the citizens of the town argue that the state should not meddle with arrangements that have contributed so much to the economic and social health of the region. The report of the Town Meeting contained these arguments: (1) Farming in the Palmville area constitutes an important element in the state's food supply, which would be expensive to replace. (2) Farms and support industries provide a large proportion of the jobs of Palmville residents. (3) The farms are an important part of the social fabric of the town and the region, providing, among other things, healthful summer employment for many of the town's youth. (4) Diverting water from the farms would cause many to be sold to real estate developers, thus increasing the population *and* the demand for water. (5) The town's zoning plan will limit growth over the next decade and should slow the increasing demand for water. Whether state officials will be persuaded by these arguments remains to be seen, but Palmville residents hope to prevent changes that might threaten the community they have built so carefully.

_____ 6. Which of the following types of evidence do the town citizens rely on in their arguments?

     a. statistics

     b. personal experiences

     c. facts

     d. generalizations

_____ 7. Which of the following value judgments seems to be the reason behind the arguments by the Palmville citizens?

     a. Residential areas are more important than farm areas.

     b. Proposals by the state should be supported.

     c. Changes will destroy the community.

     d. Water is not important to Palmville.

_____ 8. Which of the following sentences is an assumption (rather than an argument) made by the citizens?
   a. Farms are important to the town.
   b. The town's zoning plan will limit growth over the next decade.
   c. Farms and support industries provide jobs for Palmville residents.
   d. Farms provide summer employment for youths from Palmville.

_____ 9. Which of the following sentences would *not* provide evidence for the Palmville citizens' ideas?
   a. The state proposals should not be supported because this is a local issue.
   b. Fewer farms will probably increase unemployment in the area.
   c. Because farms are beautiful, they are productive.
   d. Diverting the water will cause taxes to rise.

_____ 10. Which of the following is supported by the evidence presented by the citizens of Palmville?
   a. State officials will be persuaded by the citizens' arguments.
   b. Change will occur even if Palmville residents fight it.
   c. Farming around Palmville is an important part of the economy of the region.
   d. The town's zoning plan is worse than the state's latest proposal.

Name _____

Section _____ Date _____

Number right* _____ x 10 points = Score _____

Arming Myself with a Gun Is Not the Answer

Bronwyn Jones

After a terrifying experience with a stalker, the author discusses why she chooses not to protect herself with a gun. This article first appeared in *Newsweek* magazine in 2000.

Vocabulary Preview

harried (par. 1) stressful, busy, rushed

idyllic (par. 1) simple and peaceful

incoherently (par. 3) not expressed clearly or logically

paranoia (par. 8) feelings of persecution or extreme distrust of others

corrupt (par. 8) to ruin or spoil the integrity of something

deterrent (par. 9) something that prevents or discourages an action

incarcerated (par. 11) jailed or imprisoned

1   When my father died 15 years ago, my brother and I inherited the old Midwestern farmhouse our grandparents had purchased in the 1930s. I was the one who decided to give up my harried existence as a teacher in New York City and make a life in this idyllic village, population 350, in northern Michigan.

2   A full-time job in the English department of a nearby college quickly followed. I settled into small-town life, charmed by a community where your neighbors are also your friends and no one worries about locking a door. Eventually I forgot about the big-city stress of crowds, noise and crime.

3   I felt safe enough to keep my phone number listed so colleagues and students could reach me after hours. I was totally unprepared when I returned home one evening to an answering machine filled with incoherently and horribly threatening messages. I could identify the voice—it belonged to a former student of mine. Shocked and frightened I called 911, and an officer arrived in time to pick up the phone and hear the man threaten to rape and kill me. The cop recognized the caller as the stalker in a similar incident that had been reported a few years before, and immediately rushed me out of the house. I soon learned that my would-be assailant had been arrested, according to police, drunk, armed with a 19-inch double-edged knife and just minutes from my door.

_____

*To calculate the number right, use items 1–10 under "Mastery Test Skills Check."

4   It was revealed in court testimony that my stalker was a schizophrenic who had fallen through the cracks of the mental-health system. In spite of my 10-year personal-protection order, I live with the fear that he will return unsupervised to my community. Time and again, colleagues and friends have urged me to get a gun to protect myself.

5   And why shouldn't I? This part of rural Michigan is hometown to an avid gun culture. Nov. 15, the opening day of deer-hunting season, is all but an official holiday. It is not uncommon to see the bumper sticker CHARLTON HESTON IS MY PRESIDENT displayed, along with a gun rack on the back of local pickup trucks.

6   A good friend recommended several different handguns. The assistant prosecutor on the case told me I'd have no problem getting a concealed-weapon permit. A female deputy offered to teach me how to shoot.

7   But I haven't gotten a gun, and I'm not going to. When I questioned them, my friends and colleagues had to admit that they've used guns only for recreational purposes, never for self-defense. The assistant prosecutor said that he would never carry a concealed weapon himself. And an ex-cop told me that no matter how much you train, the greatest danger is of hurting yourself.

8   The truth is when you keep a gun for self-protection, you live with constant paranoia. For me, owning a gun and practicing at a target range would be allowing my sense of victimization to corrupt my deepest values.

9   Contrary to all the pro-gun arguments, I don't believe guns are innocent objects. If they were, "gunnies" wouldn't display them as badges of security and freedom. When someone waves a gun around, he or she is advertising the power to snuff out life. But guns are no deterrent. Like nuclear weapons, they only ensure greater devastation when conflict breaks out or the inevitable human error occurs.

10   I never needed a weapon in the years prior to my terrifying experience. And while I learned not to flinch at the sight of men and women in fluorescent orange carrying rifles into the woods at the start of deer season, owning a gun for play or protection didn't occur to me. But I've learned firsthand that even small, close-knit communities are subject to the kind of social problems—like disintegrating families and substance abuse—that can propel a troubled person toward violence. So I now carry pepper spray and my cell phone at all times.

11   In Michigan—and elsewhere—as federal funding for state mental-health care continues to shrink and state psychiatric hospitals are forced to close, the numbers of untreated, incarcerated and homeless mentally ill are rising. People with serious mental illness and violent tendencies need 24-hour care. It costs less to house them in group homes with trained counselors than it does to keep them in prisons or hospitals. But until states fund more of this kind of care, people like my stalker will continue to return unsupervised to our communities.

12   And people like me will be forced to consider getting guns to protect ourselves. I am lucky. I survived, though not unchanged. I know my fear cannot be managed with a gun. The only reasonable response is to do what I can to help fix the mental-health system. Awareness, education and proper funding will save more lives and relieve more fears than all the guns we can buy.

MASTERY TEST SKILLS CHECK

Directions: Choose the best answer for each of the following questions.

Checking Your Comprehension

_____ 1. The main point of this selection is that
   a. small towns are just as dangerous as big cities.
   b. mentally ill people belong in 24-hour care facilities.
   c. today's culture promotes gun ownership.
   d. keeping a gun for self-protection was not a solution for the author.

_____ 2. The main idea of paragraph 2 is that the author
   a. missed living in New York City.
   b. worked in the English department.
   c. felt safe living in the small town.
   d. made many new friends in the small town.

_____ 3. The person who threatened the author was
   a. a complete stranger.
   b. an ex-boyfriend from New York City.
   c. a former student.
   d. an escaped convict.

_____ 4. As a result of being threatened, the author decided to
   a. carry a gun for protection.
   b. move back to New York City.
   c. carry pepper spray and a cell phone at all times.
   d. take shooting lessons from a female deputy.

_____ 5. The main idea of paragraph 11 is that
   a. group homes, not prisons, are the proper place for mentally ill people.
   b. communities are endangered by the lack of funding for mental-health care.
   c. states should enact stricter laws against stalking.
   d. even small towns are subject to violence.

_____ 6. The term "gunnies" in paragraph 9 refers to
   a. hunters.
   b. criminals.
   c. police officers.
   d. gun owners.

Applying Your Skills

_____ 7. The author's bias is revealed in the statement
   a. "A good friend recommended several different handguns."
   b. "This part of Michigan is home to an avid gun culture."
   c. "Time and again, colleagues and friends have urged me to get a gun to protect myself."
   d. "Contrary to all the pro-gun arguments, I don't believe guns are innocent objects."

_____ 8. The author supports her ideas primarily through
   a. facts
   b. personal experience.
   c. statistics.
   d. generalizations.

_____ 9. Of the following sentences from the selection, the only one that is a *fact* is
   a. "When my father died 15 years ago, my brother and I inherited the old Midwestern farmhouse our grandparents had purchased in the 1930s."
   b. "And why should I?"
   c. "I know my fear cannot be managed with a gun."
   d. "The truth is when you keep a gun for self-protection, you live with constant paranoia."

_____ 10. Of the following sentences from the selection, the only one that is an *opinion* is
   a. "But guns are no deterrent."
   b. "The cop recognized the caller as the stalker in a similar incident that had been reported a few years before."
   c. "It was revealed in court testimony that my stalker was a schizophrenic."
   d. "November 15 [is] the opening day of deer-hunting season."

Studying Words

_____ 11. The word "idyllic" (paragraph 1) originated from which of the following languages?
   a. French
   b. Latin
   c. Spanish
   d. German

_____ 12. What part of speech is the word "assailant" (paragraph 3)?
   a. verb
   b. adverb
   c. noun
   d. adjective

_____ 13. The best synonym for the word "avid" as it is used in paragraph 5 is
   a. enthusiastic.
   b. afraid.
   c. official.
   d. uncommon.

_____ 14. The prefix of the word "disintegrating" (paragraph 10) means
   a. extra.
   b. former.
   c. wrongly.
   d. not.

_____ 15. What is the correct pronunciation of the word "incarcerated" (paragraph 11)?
   a. in CAR kur ate ed
   b. in CAR suh rate ed
   c. in car sur ATE ed
   d. in SAR kur ate ed

> For more practice, ask your instructor for an opportunity to work on the mastery tests that appear in the Test Bank.

PART **FIVE** **A Fiction Minireader**

Reading and Interpreting Short Stories

READING AND INTERPRETING SHORT STORIES

A short story is a creative or imaginative work describing a series of events for the purpose of entertainment and/or communicating a serious message. It has six basic elements. The next section describes each. But first, read the following short story, "The Story of an Hour," and then refer back to it as you read about each of the six elements.

The Story of an Hour

Kate Chopin

1   Knowing that Mrs. Mallard was afflicted with heart trouble, great care was taken to break to her as gently as possible the news of her husband's death.

2   It was her sister Josephine who told her, in broken sentences; veiled hints that revealed in half concealing. Her husband's friend Richards was there, too, near her. It was he who had been in the newspaper office when intelligence of the railroad disaster was received, with Brently Mallard's name leading the list of "killed." He had only taken the time to assure himself of its truth by a second telegram, and had hastened to forestall any less careful, less tender friend in bearing the sad message.

3   She did not hear the story as many women have heard the same, with a paralyzed inability to accept its significance. She wept at once, with sudden, wild abandonment, in her sister's arms. When the storm of grief had spent itself she went away to her room alone. She would have no one follow her.

4   There stood, facing the open window, a comfortable, roomy armchair. Into this she sank, pressed down by a physical exhaustion that haunted her body and seemed to reach into her soul.

5   She could see in the open square before her house the tops of trees that were all aquiver with the new spring life. The delicious breath of rain was in the air. In the street below a peddler was crying his wares. The notes of a distant song which someone was singing reached her faintly, and countless sparrows were twittering in the eaves.

6   There were patches of blue sky showing here and there through the clouds that had met and piled one above the other in the west facing her window.

7   She sat with her head thrown back upon the cushion of the chair, quite motionless, except when a sob came up into her throat and shook her, as a child who has cried itself to sleep continues to sob in its dreams.

8   She was young, with a fair, calm face, whose lines bespoke repression and even a certain strength. But now there was a dull stare in her eyes, whose gaze was fixed away off yonder on one of those patches of blue sky. It was not a glance of reflection, but rather indicated a suspension of intelligent thought.

9   There was something coming to her and she was waiting for it, fearfully. What was it? She did not know; it was too subtle and elusive to name. But she felt it, creeping out of the sky, reaching toward her through the sounds, the scents, the color that filled the air.

10   Now her bosom rose and fell tumultuously. She was beginning to recognize this thing that was approaching to possess her, and she was striving to beat it back with her will—as powerless as her two white slender hands would have been.

11   When she abandoned herself a little whispered word escaped her slightly parted lips. She said it over and over under her breath: "free, free, free!" The vacant stare and the look of terror that had followed it went from her eyes. They stayed keen and bright. Her pulses beat fast, and the coursing blood warmed and relaxed every inch of her body.

12   She did not stop to ask if it were or were not a monstrous joy that held her. A clear and exalted perception enabled her to dismiss the suggestion as trivial.

13   She knew that she would weep again when she saw the kind, tender hands folded in death; the face that had never looked save with love upon her, fixed and gray and dead. But she saw beyond that bitter moment a long procession of years to come that would belong to her absolutely. And she opened and spread her arms out to them in welcome.

14   There would be no one to live for her during those coming years; she would live for herself. There would be no powerful will bending hers in that blind persistence with which men and women believe they have a right to impose a private will upon a fellow-creature. A kind intention or a cruel intention made the act seem no less a crime as she looked upon it in that brief moment of illumination.

15   And yet she had loved him—sometimes. Often she had not. What did it matter! What could love, the unresolved mystery, count for in face of this possession of self-assertion which she suddenly recognized as the strongest impulse of her being!

16   "Free! Body and soul free!" she kept whispering.

17   Josephine was kneeling before the closed door with her lips to the keyhole, imploring for admission. "Louise, open the door! I beg; open the door—you will make yourself ill. What are you doing, Louise? For heaven's sake open the door."

18   "Go away. I am not making myself ill." No; she was drinking in a very elixir of life through that open window.

19   Her fancy was running riot along those days ahead of her. Spring days, and summer days, and all sorts of days that would be her own. She breathed a quick prayer that life might be long. It was only yesterday she had thought with a shudder that life might be long.

20   She arose at length and opened the door to her sister's importunities. There was a feverish triumph in her eyes, and she carried herself unwittingly like a goddess of Victory. She clasped her sister's waist, and together they descended the stairs. Richards stood waiting for them at the bottom.

21   Someone was opening the front door with a latchkey. It was Brently Mallard who entered, a little travel-stained, composedly carrying his grip-sack and umbrella. He had been far from the scene of the accident, and did not even know there had been one. He stood amazed at Josephine's piercing cry; at Richards' quick motion to screen him from the view of his wife.

22   But Richards was too late.

23   When the doctors came they said she had died of heart disease—of joy that kills.

Plot

The plot is the basic story line—the sequence of events as they occur in the work. The plot focuses on conflict and often follows a predictable structure. The plot frequently begins by setting the scene, introducing the main characters, and providing the background information needed to follow the story. Next, there is often a complication or problem that arises. Suspense builds as the problem or conflict unfolds. Near the end of the story, events reach a climax—the point at which the outcome (resolution) of the conflict will be decided. A conclusion quickly follows as the story ends.

The plot of "The Story of an Hour" involves a surprise ending: Mrs. Mallard learns that her husband has been killed in an railroad disaster. She ponders his death and relishes the freedom it will bring. At the end of the story, when Mrs. Mallard discovers that her husband is not dead after all, she suffers a heart attack and dies.

Setting

The setting is the time, place, and circumstances under which the action occurs. The setting provides the mood or atmosphere in which the characters interact. The setting of "The Story of an Hour" is one hour in the Mallards' home.

Characterization

Characters are the actors in a narrative story. The characters reveal themselves by what they say—the dialogue—and by their actions, appearance, thoughts, and feelings. The narrator, or person who tells the story, may also comment on or reveal information about the characters. As you read, analyze the characters' traits and motives. Also analyze their personalities and watch for character changes. Study how the characters relate to one another.

In "The Story of an Hour" the main character is Mrs. Mallard; her thoughts and actions after learning of her husband's supposed death are the crux of the story.

Point of View

The point of view refers to the way the story is presented or the person from whose perspective the story is told. Often the story is not told from the narrator's perspective. The story may be told from the perspective of one of the characters, or that of an unknown narrator. In analyzing point of view, determine the role and function of the narrator. Is the narrator reliable and knowledgeable? Sometimes the narrator is able to enter the minds of some or all of the characters, knowing their thoughts and understanding their actions and motivations. In other stories, the narrator may not understand the actions or implications of the events in the story.

"The Story of an Hour" is told by a narrator not involved in the story. The story is told by a third-person narrator who is knowledgeable and understands the characters' actions and motives. In the story's last line, the narrator tells us that doctors assumed Mrs. Mallard died of "the joy that kills."

Tone

The tone or mood of a story reflects the author's attitude. Like a person's tone of voice, tone suggests feelings. Many ingredients contribute to tone, including the author's choice of detail (characters, setting, etc.) and the language that is used. The tone of a story may be, for example, humorous, ironic, or tragic. The author's feelings are not necessarily those of the characters or the narrator. Instead, it is through the narrator's description of the characters and their actions that we infer tone. In "The Story of an Hour," the tone might be described as serious. Serious events occur that dramatically affect Mrs. Mallard's life. The story also has an element of surprise and irony. We are surprised to learn that Mr. Mallard is not dead after all, and it is ironic, or the opposite of what we expect, to learn that Mrs. Mallard dies "of the joy that kills."

Theme

The theme of the story is its meaning or message. The theme of a work may also be considered its main idea or main point. Themes are often large, universal ideas dealing with life and death, human values, or existence. To establish the theme, ask yourself, "What is the author trying to say about life by telling the story?" Try to explain it in a single sentence. One theme of "The Story of an Hour" is freedom. Mrs. Mallard experiences a sense of freedom upon learning of her husband's supposed death. She sees "a long procession of years to come that would belong to her absolutely." There is also a theme of rebirth, suggested by references to springtime; her life without her husband was just beginning. The author also may be commenting on the restrictive or repressive nature of marriage during the time the story was written. After Mr. Mallard's death, "There will be no powerful will bending hers. . . ." Mrs. Mallard, after all, dies not from losing her husband but from the thought of losing her newly found freedom.

If you are having difficulty stating the theme, try the following suggestions:

1. **Study the title.** Now that you have read the story, does it take on any new meanings?
2. **Analyze the main characters.** Do they change? If so, how and in reaction to what?
3. **Look for broad general statements.** What do the characters or the narrator say about life or the problems they face?
4. **Look for symbols, figurative expressions, meaningful names (example: Mrs. Goodheart), or objects that hint at larger ideas.**

Thank You, M'am

Langston Hughes

This short story was written by a well-known African American poet and writer of fiction, nonfiction, biography, humor, and drama. Before his death in 1967, Hughes had published 39 volumes of literature. This story, written in 1958, explores a common conflict that crosses all racial boundaries.

1   She was a large woman with a large purse that had everything in it but a hammer and nails. It had a long strap, and she carried it slung across her shoulder. It was about eleven o'clock at night, dark, and she was walking alone, when a boy ran up behind her and tried to snatch her purse. The strap broke with a sudden single tug the boy gave it from behind. But the boy's weight and the weight of the purse combined caused him to lose his balance. Instead of taking off full blast as he had hoped, the boy fell on his back on the sidewalk and his legs flew up. The large woman simply turned around and kicked him right square in his blue-jeaned sitter. Then she reached down, picked the boy up by his shirt front, and shook him until his teeth rattled.

2   After that the woman said, "Pick up my pocketbook, boy, and give it here."

3   She still held him tightly. But she bent down enough to permit him to stoop and pick up her purse. Then she said, "Now ain't you ashamed of yourself?"

4   Firmly gripped by his shirt front, the boy said, "Yes'm."

5   The woman said, "What did you want to do it for?"

6   The boy said, "I didn't aim to."

7   She said, "You a lie!"

8   By that time two or three people passed, stopped, turned to look, and some stood watching.

9   "If I turn you loose, will you run?" asked the woman.

10   "Yes'm," said the boy.

11   "Then I won't turn you loose," said the woman. She did not release him.

12   "Lady, I'm sorry," whispered the boy.

13   "Um-hum! And your face is dirty. I got a great mind to wash your face for you. Ain't you got nobody home to tell you to wash your face?"

14   "No'm," said the boy.

15   "Then it will get washed this evening," said the large woman, starting up the street, dragging the frightened boy behind her.

16   He looked as if he were fourteen or fifteen, frail and willow-wild, in tennis shoes and blue jeans.

17   The woman said, "You ought to be my son. I would teach you right from wrong. Least I can do right now is to wash your face. Are you hungry?"

18   "No'm," said the being-dragged boy. "I just want you to turn me loose."

19   "Was I bothering *you* when I turned that corner?" asked the woman.

20   "No'm."

21   "But you put yourself in contact with *me*," said the woman. "If you think that that contact is not going to last awhile, you got another thought coming. When I get through with you, sir, you are going to remember Mrs. Luella Bates Washington Jones."

22   Sweat popped out on the boy's face and he began to struggle. Mrs. Jones stopped, jerked him around in front of her, put a half nelson about his neck, and continued to drag him up the street. When she got to her door, she dragged the boy inside, down a hall, and into a large kitchenette-furnished room at the rear of the house. She switched on the light and left the door open. The boy could hear other roomers laughing and talking in the large house. Some of their doors were open, too, so he knew he and the woman were not alone. The woman still had him by the neck in the middle of her room.

23   She said, "What is your name?"

24   "Roger," answered the boy.

25   "Then, Roger, you go to that sink and wash your face," said the woman, whereupon she turned him loose—at last. Roger looked at the door—looked at the woman—looked at the door—*and went to the sink.*

26   "Let the water run till it gets warm," she said. "Here's a clean towel."

27   "You gonna take me to jail?" asked the boy, bending over the sink.

28   "Not with that face, I would not take you anywhere," said the woman. "Here I am trying to get home to cook me a bite to eat, and you snatch my pocketbook! Maybe you ain't been to your supper either, late as it be. Have you?"

29   "There's nobody home at my house," said the boy.

30   "Then we'll eat," said the woman. "I believe you're hungry—or been hungry—to try to snatch my pocketbook!"

31   "I want a pair of blue suede shoes," said the boy.

32   "Well, you didn't have to snatch *my* pocketbook to get some suede shoes," said Mr. Luella Bates Washington Jones. "You could of asked me."

33   "Ma'am?"

34   The water dripping from his face, the boy looked at her. There was a long pause. A very long pause. After he had dried his face, and not knowing what else to do, dried it again, the boy turned around, wondering what next. The door was open. He could make a dash for it down the hall. He could run, run, run, *run*!

35   The woman was sitting on the daybed. After a while she said, "I were young once and I wanted things I could not get."

36   There was another long pause. The boy's mouth opened. Then he frowned, not knowing he frowned.

37   The woman said, "Um-humm! You thought I was going to say *but*, didn't you? You thought I was going to say, *but I didn't snatch people's pocketbooks.* Well, I wasn't going to say that." Pause. Silence. "I have done things, too, which I would not tell you, son—neither tell God, if He didn't already know. Everybody's got something in common. So you set down while I fix us something to eat. You might run that comb through your hair so you will look presentable."

38   In another corner of the room behind a screen was a gas plate and an icebox. Mrs. Jones got up and went behind the screen. The woman did not watch the boy to see if he was going to run now, nor did she watch her purse, which she left behind her on the daybed. But the boy took care to sit on the far side of the room, away from the purse, where he thought she could easily see him out of the corner of her eye if she wanted to. He did not trust the woman *not* to trust him. And he did not want to be mistrusted now.

39   "Do you need somebody to go to the store," asked the boy, "maybe to get some milk or something?"

40   "Don't believe I do," said the woman, "unless you just want sweet milk yourself. I was going to make cocoa out of this canned milk I got here."

41   "That will be fine," said the boy.

42   She heated some lima beans and ham she had in the icebox, made the cocoa, and set the table. The woman did not ask the boy anything about where he lived, or his folks, or anything else that would embarrass him. Instead, as they ate, she told him about her job in a hotel beauty shop that stayed open late, what the work was like, and how all kinds of women came in and out, blondes, redheads, and Spanish. Then she cut him a half of her ten-cent cake.

43   "Eat some more, son," she said.

44   When they were finished eating, she got up and said, "Now here, take this ten dollars and buy yourself some blue suede shoes. And next time, do not make the mistake of latching onto *my* pocketbook *nor nobody else's*—because shoes got by

devilish ways will burn your feet. I got to get my rest now. But from here on in, son, I hope you will behave yourself."

45   She led him down the hall to the front door and opened it. "Good night! Behave yourself, boy!" she said, looking out into the street as he went down the steps.

46   The boy wanted to say something other than, "Thank you, m'am," to Mrs. Luella Bates Washington Jones, but although his lips moved, he couldn't even say that as he turned at the foot of the barren stoop and looked up at the large woman in the door. Then she shut the door.

Directions: Choose the best answer for each of the following questions.

Checking Your Comprehension

_____   1. Roger says he steals because he wants blue suede shoes. The blue suede shoes may represent
   a. a gang symbol.
   b. a reference to a song.
   c. a fashion trend.
   d. things well-off people have that Roger wants.

_____   2. When Mrs. Washington takes Roger to her home, the first thing she does is to
   a. direct him to wash his face.
   b. threaten to call the police.
   c. comb his hair.
   d. prepare food.

_____   3. Mrs. Washington reveals that
   a. she knew Roger's family but would not tell them about the incident.
   b. she has a son the age of Roger.
   c. she has made mistakes in her life.
   d. she regretted that she did not have a son.

_____   4. The expression "Shoes got by devilish ways will burn your feet" means
   a. people should select shoes carefully.
   b. wrongful deeds are often discovered by those you hurt.
   c. if you do devilish things, they will eventually harm you.
   d. if you steal, you will hurt others.

_____ 5. At the end of the story, we find out that Roger
    a. finally escapes.
    b. is lost for words to express his appreciation.
    c. admits that he is a criminal.
    d. repents and vows to avoid criminal activities.

The Elements of a Short Story

_____ 6. The story is told from the perspective of
    a. Mrs. Washington.
    b. Roger.
    c. a passerby.
    d. an observer not involved in the story.

_____ 7. One possible theme of the story is
    a. Crime does not pay.
    b. Treat others as you have been treated.
    c. Try to help those who have done something wrong.
    d. If you get caught telling a lie, it is best to admit it.

_____ 8. The climax of the story occurs when
    a. Roger attempts to steal Mrs. Washington's purse.
    b. Mrs. Washington takes Roger home with her.
    c. Mrs. Washington gives Roger ten dollars and a piece of advice.
    d. Mrs. Washington grabs Roger.

_____ 9. The story takes place primarily
    a. in Mrs. Washington's house.
    b. in Mrs. Washington's furnished room.
    c. on the street.
    d. in Roger's parents' home.

_____ 10. The tone of this story can best be described as
    a. distant and impersonal.
    b. angry and distraught.
    c. cynical and critical.
    d. positive and uplifting.

Discussion Questions

1. Why is Mrs. Washington a survivor rather than a victim? What qualities or characteristics make her so?

2. Have you ever been the victim of a crime? Describe how you reacted and whether your behavior helped or hurt your situation.

3. How would the story be different if told from another perspective, say, from Roger's point of view?

4. Create a modern day version of this story. You may change the ending if you wish.

5. Roger says he is sorry. Discuss whether he means it, or comes to mean it. Give evidence from the story to support your viewpoint.

Route 23: 10th and Bigler to Bethlehem Pike

Becky Birtha

Becky Birtha was named after her great grandmother, a slave. Birtha is a current and popular writer, poet, and children's book author. This short story appeared in a collection of fiction titled *Lovers' Choice*.

1 Ain't no reason for you to be gaping at me. I pay my taxes, just like everybody else. And it just don't make no sense. The mayor and all them city council men sitting up in all them little offices over in City Hall, ain't never been cold in they life. And me and my little ones freezing to death up on Thirteenth Street.

2 Last time I was down to City Hall to try and talk to one of them men, heat just pouring out the radiator in that office. I had to yell at Kamitra and Junie not to touch it, scared they was gonna burn theyself. Man I'm talking to done took off his jacket and drape it over the back of his chair. Wiping his forehead off with his hanky, talking bout, "No, Miz Moses, we can't do nothing for you. Not a thing. Not as long as you living in a privately-own residence and you not in the public housing. . . ."

3 I'm thinking how they only use them offices in the day time. Ain't nobody in em at night. And my babies is sleeping in the kitchen, even since the oil run out two weeks ago and they ain't deliver no more. Landlord claim he outta town.

4 Hasan, my baby here, he don't hardly even know what warm is. He so little he can't remeber last summer. All the others done had colds all winter. Noses ain't stopped running since last October. And Kleenex just one more thing I can't afford to buy em. Scuse me a minute.

5 —I know, Junie. I see it. Yeah, I see the swings. Can't get off and play today. Too cold out there. Maybe so, honey. Maybe tomorrow, if the sun come out. Lamont, let your sister have a turn to sit by the window now.—

6 Don't you be thinking I'm homeless, cause I ain't. You ever see a bag lady with all these kids? These here shopping bags is just a temporary measure. Like I said, I live up on Thirteenth Street. Seventeen hundred block. North. Top floor.

You don't believe me you go look. My name on the mailbox: Leona Mae Moses. And all the rest of the stuff belong to us is right where we left it. The kids is got other clothes, and we got beds and dishes and all the same stuff you got in your house. We ain't planning to make this no permanent way of life. Just till this cold spell break.

7   —Cherise, honey, would you get the baby bottle out that bag you got up there? Right next to that box of Pampers. And you and Lamont gonna have to get off and get some more milk. Next time we come up to the A & P. Junie, get your hands away from that buzzer. We ain't there yet. We got to go all the way up to Chestnut Hill, and then turn around and come back down. Anyway, it's Kamitra turn to ring the bell this time.—

8   Ain't nobody got no call to stare at me like I'm some kinda freak. My kids got the same rights as other people kids. They got a right to spend the night some-place warm and dry. Got a right to get some sleep at night. Last night, along about eleven o'clock, when the man on the radio say the temperature gone down to fifteen below, he didn't have to tell me nothing. The pipes is froze, and the wind lifting the curtains right up at the windows in my kitchen. And my little girl crying, "Mama, I'm cold." Air so icy I can see a little cloud come out her mouth, every time she cry.

9   —Kamitra, sugar, don't sing so loud. Mama trying to talk. Anyway, other people on here besides us. They don't want to be bother listen to all that racket.—

10   You got kids? Well, think a minute what you would do if you was in my place. Last night I'm trying so hard to think what to do, feel like my head gonna split wide open. Nobody in my building ain't got no more heat than we do. I don't know no neighbors got space enough for all of us. They be sleep anyway. All my people still down south.

11   Kamitra crying done waked up the others, too. Then all of em crying they cold. I ain't crazy yet, but I like to went crazy last night trying to think what I'm gonna do. I just thinking theys got to be some place in this great big city that I can carry these children to, where it's warm, where it stay warm, even in the middle of the night. And then it come to me.

12   "Mama, where we going?" the kids is all asking. I just tell em to hush and go get they blankets and towels and sweaters and stuff. Comb everybody hair and dress em real warm. Start packing up some food to last us for a couple days. "Mama, what we gonna do? Where we taking all this stuff?" And Junie, he tickle me. Say, "Mama, we can't go no place. It's dark outside."

13   I just hush em all up and hustle em down to the corner. Little ones start crying again, cause even with all them layers on, they ain't warm enough for no fifteen below. Lamont done lost his gloves last week, and Cherise just got one a my scarf wrap around her head, cause it ain't enough hats to go round. Ain't one of em got boots. Cherise still asking me where we going, while we standing at the corner, waiting. I tell em, "Mama got a surprise for you all. We taking a trip. We going on a nice, long ride."

14   —Get outta that bag, Kamitra. You can't have no more crackers. Mama gonna fix you some tuna fish for supper, pretty soon. What's the matter Junie? You gotta pee? You sure? Well then, sit still. Lamont, next time we come up to our corner, I want you to take him in to the bathroom, anyway. It don't hurt to try.—

15   I guess that explain how come we here. We intend to stay here, too, right where we at, up till the weather break. Or the oil come. Whatever happen first. It ain't no laws against it. I pay my taxes to keep these things running, just like everybody else. And I done paid our fare. The ones under six rides for free, just like the sign say. I got enough quarters here to last us a long time.

16   My kids is clean—all got washed up at the library just this morning. And look how nice and well-behave they is. I ain't got nothing to be ashamed of.

17   I hope your curiosity satisfied, cause I really ain't got no more to say. This car big enough for all of us. You better find something else to gawk at. Better look on out the window, make sure you ain't miss your stop.

18   —Cherise, sugar, we at the end of the line again. Go up there and put these quarters in the man box. No, Junie. This trolley gonna keep running all night long. Time just come for the man to turn the thing around. We ain't getting off. This trip ain't over yet.

Directions: Choose the best answer for each of the following questions.

Checking Your Comprehension

_____   1. Why are the mother and her children riding the trolley?
    a. They are on their way to the airport to go on vacation.
    b. The children are going to stay with family in another part of town.
    c. They are moving from their apartment to public housing.
    d. The mother is trying to help her children stay warm.

_____   2. The mother is telling her story to
    a. her friend.
    b. her landlord.
    c. a city councilman.
    d. a stranger on the trolley.

_____   3. The heat is not working at the family's apartment because the
    a. mother did not pay her bills.
    b. landlord apparently did not have oil delivered.
    c. whole city is having a power outage.
    d. furnace overheated and stopped working.

_____   4. How many children are mentioned in the story?
    a. five
    b. four
    c. three
    d. two

_____   5. The mother intends for her family to ride the trolley until
    a. they get to their destination.
    b. the police make them get off the trolley.
    c. they run out of quarters.
    d. either the weather breaks or the heat starts working at her apartment.

The Elements of a Short Story

_____   6. The story is told from the perspective of
    a. the children.
    b. the mother.
    c. the trolley driver.
    d. an unknown passenger on the trolley.

_____   7. Which statement best expresses the theme of the story?
    a. People should mind their own business.
    b. Desperate times call for creative solutions.
    c. Don't judge a book by its cover.
    d. Never underestimate the power of prayer.

_____   8. The story takes place primarily
    a. at City Hall.
    b. at the park.
    c. on the trolley.
    d. in the family's apartment.

_____   9. The tone of this story can best be described as
    a. pleasant and optimistic.
    b. lighthearted and humorous.
    c. hopeless and sad.
    d. defiant and determined.

_____   10. The title is a reference to the
    a. family's home address.
    b. address of City Hall.
    c. trolley route.
    d. children's school bus route.

Discussion Questions

1. How do you know what kind of mother the narrator is? Describe her attitude and how she has chosen to cope with her circumstances.

2. Discuss how Birtha inspires readers to feel sympathy and respect for the narrator.

3. Why is it important to the narrator that she not be mistaken for a homeless person? Discuss what this reveals about her character.

4. Evaluate the effectiveness of the story's title. Can you think of other titles that would work for this story?

5. Discuss what you think will happen to this family.

6. How would this story be different if it were told from the perspective of one of the children?

The Tell-Tale Heart

Edgar Allan Poe

Edgar Allan Poe was born in Boston in 1809 and was orphaned at the age of two. He was raised by wealthy foster parents who provided him with a privileged upbringing, including education and travel. He embarked upon a successful literary career as both editor and contributor to several major journals. However, after his wife died in 1847, Poe's personal problems and heavy drinking became worse. This led to unemployment, poverty, and eventually to his death in Baltimore at the age of 40. Poe is most famous for his macabre poems and short stories, and he is considered by many to be the inventor of the modern detective story.

Vocabulary Preview

hearken (par. 1) listen or pay attention

dissimulation (par. 3) disguising one's true intentions

profound (par. 3) insightful

sagacity (par. 4) wisdom

suppositions (par. 7) assumptions or beliefs

crevice (par. 8) a narrow opening or crack

scantlings (par. 13) small pieces of lumber

suavity (par. 14) pleasantness; showing politeness and charm

deputed (par. 14) assigned or delegated

audacity (par. 15) boldness

gesticulations (par. 17) gestures or movements

derision (par. 17) ridicule or contempt

1   True!—nervous—very, very dreadfully nervous I had been and am; but why *will* you say that I am mad? The disease had sharpened my senses—not destroyed—not dulled them. Above all was the sense of hearing acute. I heard all things in the heaven and in the earth. I heard many things in hell. How, then, am I mad? Hearken! and observe how healthily—how calmly I can tell you the whole story.

2   It is impossible to say how first the idea entered my brain; but once conceived, it haunted me day and night. Object there was none. Passion there was none. I loved the old man. He had never wronged me. He had never given me insult. For his gold I had no desire. I think it was his eye! Yes, it was this! One of his eyes resembled that of a vulture—a pale blue eye, with a film over it. Whenever it fell upon me, my blood ran cold; and so by degrees—very gradually—I made up my mind to take the life of the old man, and thus rid myself of the eye for ever.

3   Now this is the point. You fancy me mad. Madmen know nothing. But you should have seen *me*. You should have seen how wisely I proceeded—with what caution—with what foresight—with what dissimulation I went to work! I was never kinder to the old man than during the whole week before I killed him. And every night, about midnight, I turned the latch of his door and opened it—oh, so gently! And then, when I had made an opening sufficient for my head, I put in a dark lantern, all closed, closed, so that no light shone out, and then I thrust in my head. Oh, you would have laughed to see how cunningly I thrust it in! I moved it slowly—very, very slowly, so that I might not disturb the old man's sleep. It took me an hour to place my whole head within the opening so far that I could see him as he lay upon his bed. Ha!—would a madman have been so wise as this? And then, when my head was well in the room, I undid the lantern cautiously—oh, so cautiously—cautiously (for the hinges creaked)—I undid it just so much that a single thin ray fell upon the vulture eye. And this I did for seven long nights—every night just at midnight—but I found the eye always closed; and so it was impossible to do the work; for it was not the old man who vexed me, but his Evil Eye. And every morning, when the day broke, I went boldly into the chamber, and spoke courageously to him, calling him by name in a hearty tone, and inquiring how he had passed the night. So you see he would have been a very profound old man, indeed, to suspect that every night, just at twelve, I looked in upon him while he slept.

4   Upon the eighth night I was more than usually cautious in opening the door. A watch's minute hand moves more quickly than did mine. Never before that night had I *felt* the extent of my own powers—of my sagacity. I could scarcely contain my feelings of triumph. To think that there I was, opening the door, little by little, and he not even to dream of my secret deeds or thoughts. I fairly chuckled at the idea; and perhaps he heard me; for he moved on the bed suddenly, as if startled. Now you may think that I drew back—but no. His room was as black as pitch with the thick darkness, (for the shutters were close fastened, through fear of robbers), and so I knew that he could not see the opening of the door, and I kept pushing it on steadily, steadily.

5   I had my head in, and was about to open the lantern, when my thumb slipped upon the tin fastening, and the old man sprang up in bed, crying out—"Who's there?"

6   I kept quite still and said nothing. For a whole hour I did not move a muscle, and in the meantime I did not hear him lie down. He was still sitting up in the bed, listening;—just as I have done, night after night, hearkening to the death watches* in the wall.

7   Presently I heard a slight groan, and I knew it was the groan of mortal terror. It was not a groan of pain or of grief—oh, no!—it was the low stifled sound that arises from the bottom of the soul when overcharged with awe. I knew the sound very well. Many a night, just at midnight, when all the world slept, it has welled up from my own bosom, deepening, with its dreadful echo, the terrors that distracted me. I say I knew it well. I knew what the old man felt, and pitied him, although I chuckled at heart. I knew that he had been lying awake ever since the first slight noise, when he had turned in the bed. His fears had been ever since growing upon him. He had been trying to fancy them causeless, but could not. He had been saying to himself—"It is nothing but the wind in the chimney—it is only a mouse crossing the floor," or "It is merely a cricket which has made a single chirp." Yes, he had been trying to comfort himself with these suppositions; but he had found all in vain. *All in vain;* because Death, in approaching him, had stalked with his black shadow before him, and enveloped the victim. And it was the mournful influence of the unperceived shadow that caused him to feel—although he neither saw nor heard—to *feel* the presence of my head within the room.

8   When I had waited a long time, very patiently, without hearing him lie down, I resolved to open a little—a very, very little crevice in the lantern. So I opened it— you cannot imagine how stealthily, stealthily—until, at length, a single dim ray, like the thread of the spider, shot from out the crevice and fell upon the vulture eye.

9   It was open—wide, wide open—and I grew furious as I gazed upon it. I saw it with perfect distinctness—all a dull blue, with a hideous veil over it that chilled the very marrow in my bones; but I could see nothing else of the old man's face or person: for I had directed the ray as if by instinct, precisely upon the damned spot.

10   And now have I not told you that what you mistake for madness is but over-acuteness of the senses?—now, I say, there came to my ears a low, dull, quick sound, such as a watch makes when enveloped in cotton. I knew *that* sound well, too. It was the beating of the old man's heart. It increased my fury, as the beating of a drum stimulates the soldier into courage.

11   But even yet I refrained and kept still. I scarcely breathed. I held the lantern motionless. I tried how steadily I could maintain the ray upon the eye. Meantime the hellish tattoo of the heart increased. It grew quicker and quicker, and louder and louder every instant. The old man's terror *must* have been extreme! It grew louder, I say, louder every moment!—do you mark me well? I have told you that

---

death watches: beetles that infest timbers. Their clicking sound was thought to be an omen of death.

I am nervous: so I am. And now at the dead hour of the night, amid the dreadful silence of that old house, so strange a noise as this excited me to uncontrollable terror. Yet, for some minutes longer I refrained and stood still. But the beating grew louder, louder! I thought the heart must burst. And now a new anxiety seized me—the sound would be heard by a neighbor! The old man's hour had come! With a loud yell, I threw open the lantern and leaped into the room. He shrieked once—once only. In an instant I dragged him to the floor, and pulled the heavy bed over him. I then smiled gaily, to find the deed so far done. But, for many minutes, the heart beat on with a muffled sound. This, however, did not vex me; it would not be heard through the wall. At length it ceased. The old man was dead. I removed the bed and examined the corpse. Yes, he was stone, stone dead. I placed my hand upon the heart and held it there many minutes. There was no pulsation. He was stone dead. His eye would trouble me no more.

12   If still you think me mad, you will think so no longer when I describe the wise precautions I took for the concealment of the body. The night waned, and I worked hastily, but in silence. First of all I dismembered the corpse. I cut off the head and the arms and the legs.

13   I then took up three planks from the flooring of the chamber, and deposited all between the scantlings. I then replaced the boards so cleverly, so cunningly, that no human eye—not even *his*—could have detected anything wrong. There was nothing to wash out—no stain of any kind—no bloodspot whatever. I had been too wary for that. A tub had caught all—ha! ha!

14   When I had made an end of these labors, it was four o'clock—still dark as midnight. As the bell sounded the hour, there came a knocking at the street door. I went down to open it with a light heart,—for what had I *now* to fear? There entered three men, who introduced themselves, with perfect suavity, as officers of the police. A shriek had been heard by a neighbor during the night; suspicion of foul play had been aroused; information had been lodged at the police office, and they (the officers) had been deputed to search the premises.

15   I smiled,—for *what* had I to fear? I bade the gentlemen welcome. The shriek, I said, was my own in a dream. The old man, I mentioned, was absent in the country. I took my visitors all over the house. I bade them search—search *well*. I led them, at length, to *his* chamber. I showed them his treasures, secure, undisturbed. In the enthusiasm of my confidence, I brought chairs into the room, and desired them *here* to rest from their fatigues, while I myself, in the wild audacity of my perfect triumph, placed my own seat upon the very spot beneath which reposed the corpse of the victim.

16   The officers were satisfied. My *manner* had convinced them. I was singularly at ease. They sat, and while I answered cheerily, they chatted of familiar things, But, ere long, I felt myself getting pale and wished them gone. My head ached, and I fancied a ringing in my ears: but still they sat and still chatted. The ringing became more distinct:—it continued and became more distinct: I talked more freely to get rid of the feeling: but it continued and gained definitiveness—until, at length, I found that the noise was *not* within my ears.

17   No doubt I now grew *very* pale—but I talked more fluently, and with a heightened voice. Yet the sound increased—and what could I do? It was *a low, dull, quick sound—much such a sound as a watch makes when enveloped in cotton.* I gasped for breath—and yet the officers heard it not. I talked more quickly—more vehemently; but the noise steadily increased. I arose and argued about trifles, in a high key and with violent gesticulations; but the noise steadily increased. Why *would* they not be gone? I paced the floor to and fro with heavy strides, as if excited to fury by the observations of the men—but the noise steadily increased. Oh God! what *could* I do? I foamed—I raved—I swore! I swung the chair upon which I had been sitting, and grated it upon the boards, but the noise arose over all and continually increased. It grew louder—louder—*louder!* And still the men chatted pleasantly and smiled. Was it possible they heard not? Almighty God!—no, no! They heard!—they suspected!—they *knew!*—they were making a mockery of my horror!—this I thought and this I think. But anything was better than this agony! Anything was more tolerable than this derision! I could bear those hypocritical smiles no longer! I felt that I must scream or die!—and now—again!—hark! louder! louder! louder! *louder!*—

18   "Villains!" I shrieked, "dissemble no more! I admit the deed!—tear up the planks!—here, here!—it is the beating of his hideous heart!"

Directions: Choose the best answer for each of the following questions.

Checking Your Comprehension

_____   1. In this story, the main character describes how
   a. an old man tried to murder him.
   b. he prevented an old man's murder.
   c. he caught and arrested a murderer.
   d. he murdered an old man.

_____   2. The character was inspired to kill the old man because
   a. he wanted the old man's gold.
   b. the old man had wronged him.
   c. the old man had insulted him.
   d. he was disturbed by one of the old man's eyes.

_____   3. Once the character decided to kill the old man, he
   a. killed him later that day.
   b. waited until the next day to kill him.
   c. waited a whole week before killing him.
   d. waited almost a year and then changed his mind.

_____   4. The reason the killer waited was that he
   a. wanted to find someone to help him kill the old man.
   b. could not kill the old man unless the old man's eye was open.
   c. needed to find a weapon.
   d. was afraid of being caught.

_____   5. When the police came to the house, they
   a. immediately found the old man's body and arrested the killer.
   b. searched for clues but left without making an arrest.
   c. were suspicious of the man's story and took him in for questioning.
   d. were satisfied with the man's story.

The Elements of a Short Story

_____   6. The tone of the story can best be described as
   a. suspenseful.
   b. humorous.
   c. ironic.
   d. sad.

_____   7. The setting of the story is
   a. the old man's house.
   b. the police station.
   c. prison.
   d. an insane asylum.

_____   8. This story is told from the perspective of
   a. the old man.
   b. the police.
   c. the killer.
   d. a neighbor.

_____   9. The title is a reference to how the
   a. killer imagined the old man's heart beating so loudly that it gave him away.
   b. old man knew that he was going to be murdered.
   c. police officers found the old man's heart and knew he had been murdered.
   d. killer gave himself away by the loud beating of his own heart.

_____ 10. Which statement best expresses the theme of the story?
   a. Murder is immoral.
   b. Madness is a social disease.
   c. Law enforcement personnel deserve respect.
   d. Guilt is powerful and self-destructive.

Discussion Questions

1. How does Poe create feelings of suspense in this story?

2. How does Poe convince us that the narrator is mad?

3. What do you think is the relationship between the old man and his killer?

4. Why do you think Poe chose to tell this story from the killer's point of view?

PART SIX A Contemporary Issues Minireader

READING ABOUT CONTROVERSIAL ISSUES

A controversial issue is one about which people disagree and hold different opinions. This section offers suggestions for how to read articles about controversial issues. But first, read "The High Cost of Having Fun," below, and then refer back to it as you read the guidelines that follow it.

The High Cost of Having Fun

A majority of Americans follow at least one professional sport. Unfortunately, rising costs are making it impossible for the average fan to watch his or her favorite athlete or team in person. According to *Team Marketing Report,* the average ticket price in the NFL is $58.95, and in the NBA it's $45.28. For professional baseball, the average ticket price is $22.21, while in hockey, it's $43.13. Some argue that the high prices are justified. After all, they say, in order to please fans, teams must win more games than they lose. The best way to win is to have the top players, but teams must spend large amounts of money to get these players. These costs are passed on to the fans through ticket prices and merchandising. However, instead of raising ticket prices, team owners should raise the fees paid by corporations who sponsor stadiums and put their logo on the TV next to the score or advertise in the arena, making use of the real money in the hands of big business. The love of sports cuts across socioeconomic lines; the ability to enjoy a game in person should too.

Guidelines for Reading About Controversial Issues

Use the following suggestions when reading about controversial issues:

1. **Plan on reading the article several times.** Read the article once to get a first impression. Read it another time to closely follow the author's line of reasoning. Read it again to analyze and evaluate it.

2. **Identify the issue.** The issue is the problem or controversy that the article discusses. In "The High Cost of Having Fun," the issue is the high cost of tickets to sporting events.

3. **Identify the author's position on the issue.** In many articles, the author takes one side of the issue. In the paragraph above, the author's position is that the ticket cost is too high. A different author could take the opposite view—the tickets are reasonably priced for the level of entertainment provided. Or another article could examine and discuss both sides of the issue, explaining why some people feel the cost is too high and why others think it is reasonable.

4. **Examine the reasons and evidence.** As you read, look closely at the reasons and types of evidence the author provides in support of the position or positions presented in the article. In "The High Cost of Having Fun," the author presents statistics about the cost of tickets and recognizes that running a professional sports team is expensive. The

author argues that the costs are being unfairly passed on to the fans and suggests an alternate means of financing the teams—passing the costs on to sponsors. The author also argues that sports should not be only for wealthy people who can afford high ticket prices.

5. **Evaluate the evidence.** Once you have examined the evidence offered, decide whether it is of good quality and whether there is enough evidence to be convincing. In "The High Cost of Having Fun," the statistics about the cost of tickets is useful. However, the author does not present any information about how much cost sponsors already assume and how much additional costs they would need to assume in order to maintain or lower ticket prices.

6. **Opposing viewpoints.** If the writer presents only one viewpoint on the issue, be sure to consider the opposing viewpoints. Sometimes the author will recognize opposing viewpoints, and sometimes even refute (present arguments against) them. In "The High Cost of Having Fun," the writer does recognize that some feel the high ticket prices are justified in order to get and keep top players.

Issue 1: Smokers' Rights
Should People Be Allowed to Smoke at Home?
Daniel B. Wood

Originally published in the *Christian Science Monitor* in February 2007, this article examines one aspect of smokers' rights—the right to smoke in one's own home. As you read, identify the writer's position on the issue and evaluate the evidence offered in support of this position.

Vocabulary Preview

scenarios (par. 2) possible situations

mandate (par. 2) to require or order

communal (par. 3) shared; used by all members of a group

susceptible (par. 3) easily influenced or affected

intrusion (par. 4) an unwelcome presence or disturbance

precedent (par. 4) an action or decision that can later be used as an example to justify a similar action/decision

statistics (par. 9) a collection of numerical data

ire (par. 9) anger

proliferate (par. 9) to increase greatly in number

intervening (par. 10) taking action in order to change or prevent something

Prereading

1. Do you think the article will be based primarily on research or personal experience?

_____

2. Do you know anyone who is bothered by secondhand smoke? Why do you think secondhand smoke bothers some people more than others?

_____

1   After retiree Judy Wilson moved from Georgia back to her hometown of Sault Ste. Marie, Mich., in 1997, life was sweet: fresh air, beautiful scenery, quiet neighbors. A year later, a heavy smoker moved in across the hall at Ms. Wilson's second-floor apartment in Arlington Town Apartments. Wilson says her life changed. "I started having all kinds of breathing problems and eye irritations," says Wilson, a retired assembly-line worker. After maintenance personnel tried and failed to stop the smoke in several ways, including ventilation changes, air filters, and intake fans, she was moved to an apartment down the hall. Everything was fine—until more smokers moved in across the hall. "My doctor told me . . . that I'd better move away from it or else," says Wilson.

2   As similar scenarios play out in apartment and condominium complexes across the country, they are resulting in a new frontier in antismoking policies: private dwellings. Not only are some condos and apartment houses banning smoking inside private units, but there is talk in Belmont, Calif., of a city law next month that would mandate that all complexes keep a portion of their units smoke-free. The war against smoking first ramped up in the 1980s when some of America's public buildings became smoke-free. Then, in the 1990s, a slew of restaurants and bars in U.S. cities banned smoking.

3   Now, seniors are leading the way in the new battle in part because many live in communal environments and they feel they are susceptible to the health and safety hazards of smoking. "The primary drive for smoke-free housing in America is coming from the elderly," says Jim Bergman, director of the Smoke-Free Environments Law Project in Ann Arbor, Mich.

4   Smoke-free policies in private dwellings are also taking hold because state and federal laws do not protect smokers in the same way that they protect people from discrimination based on race, ethnicity, and national origin, say experts. But banning a legal behavior in someone's own home is an intrusion of privacy that could set a dangerous precedent that, taken to extremes, could allow government to regulate too much in private life, opponents say.

5   Smoking can also be safety issue, particularly in close quarters, some say. "There is a great deal of growing interest in the senior housing community about senior smokers because seniors become forgetful and careless about smoking,"

says Serena Chen, policy director for the American Lung Association of California. Although cigarettes cause 10 percent of apartment fires, 40 percent of apartment fire deaths are attributed to smoking. Such fires cause death because they occur while more people are asleep.

6   Giving more teeth to the push is a finding in the U.S. Surgeon General report last June that there are no safe levels of secondhand smoke. Last year, the California Air Resources Board declared secondhand smoke to be a toxic air contaminant on par with other industrial pollutants.

7   For their part, condo and apartment owners are beginning to realize the additional costs of getting units ready for new tenants after smokers have lived there. Across the state of Michigan, 12 of 132 housing commissions have banned smoking in multiunit apartments and condos in the past two years, Mr. Bergman says. Two-and-a-half years ago, no one could find a smoke-free apartment listing anywhere in the state; now there are more than 5,000, he says. About two or three public housing commissions in Michigan are adopting smoke-free policies each month; elsewhere in the U.S., Bergman says, perhaps another one commission per month is doing the same. So far, that means that the public buildings owned and run by such commissions—such as Arlington Courts in Sault Ste. Marie—are taking such actions voluntarily.

8   But that could change next month in California. In Belmont, the city attorney and city council are expected to break new ground by passing a law that affects all public and private apartment and condominium owners in the city, requiring them to adopt smoke-free policies for a certain percentage of their units. "Belmont will be watched nationally to see how far it goes in requiring apartment owners to have smoke-free policies," says Bergman. "Since no other city has passed a law requiring private apartment owners or condo associations to have a percentage of their units be smoke-free, this will be unique in the nation and other cities will seriously consider taking the step as well."

9   If Belmont's and Michigan's measures are being fueled in part by statistics showing that 80 percent of Americans don't smoke, they are also drawing ire from many among the 20 percent who do. Smokers wonder where they'll be allowed to smoke if new laws proliferate. Even top proponents of smoke-free policies question whether scientific evidence overstates the dangers of being exposed to secondhand smoke, and chases smokers into an ever-shrinking portion of the great outdoors.

10   "There really is no evidence that even a fleeting whiff of cigarette smoke will give you lung cancer, but that's how proponents of these policies seem to be advancing their cause," says Jacob Sullum, senior editor at *Reason Magazine*, who authored a book about the antismoking movement. If smokers are banned from apartments and condos, parks, and other public spaces, the only space left for them to smoke will be single-family homes, a place where children reside. "The next angle we are going to see on this is how to protect children from respiratory problems in the home, and that is not the kind of place where I think the government ought to be intervening," says Mr. Sullum.

Checking Your Comprehension

1. According to Judy Wilson, why did she start experiencing health problems?

   _____

2. When did the trend toward smoke-free public buildings begin
   in the United States?

   _____

3. What law is being considered in Belmont, California?

   _____

   _____

4. Give two reasons that seniors are leading the movement for smoke-free housing.

   _____

   _____

   _____

5. Why do opponents of antismoking laws for private dwellings think that such
   laws are a bad idea?

   _____

   _____

6. According to the article, smokers are responsible for what percentage
   of apartment fire deaths?

   _____

7. What is the U.S. Surgeon General's position on the safety of secondhand smoke ?

   _____

8. What is one reason that apartment and condominium owners might support
   antismoking policies in their complexes?

   _____

   _____

Critical Reading and Thinking

1. What is the author's main purpose in writing this article?

   _____

   _____

2. What types of information are used to support the main points of the article?

_____

3. How do the first two paragraphs relate to the rest of the article?

_____

_____

4. What is the tone of the reading?

_____

Words in Context

Directions: Locate each word in the paragraph indicated and reread that paragraph. Then, based on the way the word is used, write a synonym or brief definition. You may use a dictionary, if necessary.

1. slew (par. 2)

_____

2. drive (par. 3)

_____

3. regulate (par. 4)

_____

4. advancing (par. 10)

_____

5. angle (par. 10)

_____

Vocabulary Review

Directions: Match each word in Column A with its correct meaning in Column B.

Column A	Column B
_____ 1. scenarios	a. anger
_____ 2. mandate	b. an unwelcome presence or disturbance
_____ 3. susceptible	c. shared; used by all members of a group
_____ 4. communal	d. to require or order
_____ 5. intrusion	e. a collection of numerical data

_____   6. precedent   f. easily influenced or affected

_____   7. statistics   g. taking action in order to change or prevent
                                    something

_____   8. ire   h. an action or decision that can later be used as an
                                    example to justify a similar action/decision

_____   9. proliferate   i. to increase greatly in number

_____ 10. intervening   j. possible situations

Summarizing the Reading Selection

Directions: Read the following incomplete summary. Then, using information in
the article, fill in the blanks.

In the war against smoking, _____ are leading a movement to ban
smoking in apartment and condominium complexes. Supporters of the movement cite
the health risks of breathing secondhand smoke and the hazard of
_____ caused by careless smokers. In recent years, a growing number
of apartment and condominium complexes have voluntarily _____
smoking in private units. One city is considering _____ that would
require all apartment and condominium complexes to designate a portion of the units as
_____ dwellings. _____ of the movement maintain that
people should be allowed to smoke in their own homes. From this perspective, a legal
ban on smoking in private dwellings would violate _____ and discrimi-
nate against the _____ percent of U.S. citizens who smoke. Some
observers even question the validity of scientific research on secondhand smoke, maintaining that the dangers have been _____.

Writing Exercises

1. Many seniors are concerned about secondhand smoke in communal environments such as apartment and condominium complexes. Do you think that the
seniors' concerns are justified? Write a paragraph explaining your point of view.

2. Do you think that U.S. citizens who smoke are victims of discrimination? Write
a paragraph explaining why or why not.

3. Would you support a law requiring all apartment and condominium complexes
in your community to make some of their units smoke-free? Write an essay
explaining your position on this issue.

4. Do you think that the government has a responsibility to protect children from secondhand smoke in single-family homes? Write an essay explaining your point of view.

Issue 2: Cell Phones and Driving Safety
Driving While on Cell Phone Worse Than Driving While Drunk
Forbes.com

Published by Forbes.com, this article examines the use of cell phones while driving. As you read, identify the writer's position on the issue and evaluate the evidence offered in support of this position.

> **Vocabulary Preview**
>
> **tolerating** (par. 2) putting up with
>
> **simulator** (par. 3) a device used for testing or training that models actual operational conditions
>
> **impairments** (par. 3) weakened physical functions
>
> **inebriated** (par. 4) intoxicated; drunk
>
> **rear-ending** (par. 4) crashing into another vehicle from behind
>
> **aggressive** (par. 5) energetic and assertive
>
> **compensating** (par. 8) making up for
>
> **multi-task** (par. 10) to perform two or more activities at the same time

Prereading

1. Do you expect this article to be based primarily on fact or opinion?

_____

2. Have you ever used a cell phone while driving or observed another driver using a cell phone? Do you feel that use of the phone was distracting or potentially unsafe?

_____

1   Thursday, June 29 (HealthDay News)—Maneuvering through traffic while talking on the phone increases the likelihood of an accident fivefold and is actually more dangerous than driving drunk, U.S. researchers report. That finding held true whether the driver was holding a cell phone or using a hands-free device, the researchers noted.

2   "As a society, we have agreed on not tolerating the risk associated with drunk driving," said researcher Frank Drews, an assistant professor of psychology at the University of Utah. "This study shows us that somebody who is conversing on a cell phone is exposing him or herself and others to a similar risk—cell phones actually are a higher risk," he said. His team's report appears in the summer issue of the journal *Human Factors*.

3   In the study, 40 people followed a pace car along a prescribed course, using a driving simulator. Some people drove while talking on a cell phone, others navigated while drunk (meaning their blood-alcohol limit matched the legal limit of 0.08 percent), and others drove with no such distractions or impairments. "We found an increased accident rate when people were conversing on the cell phone," Drews said. Drivers on cell phones were 5.36 times more likely to get in an accident than non-distracted drivers, the researchers found.

4   The phone users fared even worse than the inebriated, the Utah team found. There were three accidents among those talking on cell phones—all of them involving a rear-ending of the pace car. In contrast, there were no accidents recorded among participants who were drunk, or the sober, cell-phone-free group. The bottom line: Cell-phone use was linked to "a significant increase in the accident rate," Drews said.

5   He said there was a difference between the behaviors of drunk drivers and those who were talking on the phone. Drunk drivers tended to be aggressive, while those talking on the phone were more sluggish, Drews said. In addition, the researchers found talking on the cell phone reduced reaction time by 9 percent in terms of braking and 19 percent in terms of picking up speed after braking. "This is significant, because it has an impact on traffic as a system," Drews said. "If we have drivers who are taking a lot of time in accelerating once having slowed down, the overall flow of traffic is dramatically reduced," he said.

6   In response to safety concerns, some states have outlawed the use of hand-held cell phones while driving. But that type of legislation may not be effective, because the Utah researchers found no difference in driver performance whether the driver was holding the phone or talking on a hands-free model. "We have seen again and again that there is no difference between hands-free and hand-held devices," Drews said. "The problem is the conversation," he added.

7   According to Drews, drivers talking on the phone are paying attention to the conversation—not their driving. "Drivers are not perceiving the driving environment," he said. "We found 50 percent of the visual information wasn't processed at all—this could be a red light. This increases the risk of getting into an accident dramatically," he said.

8   The reason that there aren't more accidents linked to cell phone use is probably due to the reactions of other—more alert—drivers, Drews said, "Currently, our system seems to be able to handle 8 percent of cell-phone drivers, because other drivers *are* paying attention," he said. "They are compensating for the errors these drivers are causing," he speculated.

9   This is a growing public health problem, Drews said. As more people are talking and driving, the accident rate will go up, he said. One expert agreed that driving and cell phone use can be a deadly mix. "We don't believe talking on a cell phone while driving is safe," said Rae Tyson, a spokesman for the U.S. National Highway Traffic Safety Administration (NHTSA). "It is a level of distraction that can affect your driving performance," he said. NHTSA has just completed a study that showed that 75 percent of all traffic accidents were preceded by some type of driver distraction, Tyson said. Tyson pointed out that talking on the phone is very different than talking to the person in the passenger seat. "If you are engaged in a conversation with a passenger, the passenger has some situational awareness, whereas a person on the phone has no idea what you are dealing with on the road," he said.

10   "Our recommendation is that you should not talk on the phone while driving, whether it's a hand-held or hand-free device," Tyson said. "We realize that a lot of people believe that they can multi-task, and in a lot of situations they probably can, but it's that moment when you need your full attention, and it's not there because you are busy talking, that you increase the likelihood that you are going to be involved in a crash," he said.

11   Tyson also sees this as a growing public health issue. "Every time we do a survey, there are more people using cell phones while driving," he said. "And the popularity of hand-held devices like Palm Pilots or Blackberries, and people using them in the car, is another problem," he added.

12   An industry spokesman said cell phones don't cause accidents, people do. "If cell phones were truly the culprit some studies make them out to be, it's only logical that we'd see a huge spike in the number of accidents [since their introduction]," said John Walls, a vice president at the industry group, the Cellular Telecommunications & Internet Association-The Wireless Association. "To the contrary, we've experienced a decline in accidents, and an even more impressive decline in the accident rate per million miles driven," he said. "We believe educating drivers on how to best handle all of the possible distractions when you're behind the wheel is the most effective means to make better drivers, and that legislation focusing on a specific behavior falls short of that well-intended goal and creates a false sense of security," Walls said.

Checking Your Comprehension

1. What is the main point of this article?

_____

_____

2. In the Utah study led by Frank Drews, how much did use of a cell phone while driving increase the risk of an accident?

_____

_____

3. In the Utah study, what kinds of accidents did drivers using cell phones experience?

_____

4. According to the Utah study, how were the reactions of drunk drivers different from the reactions of drivers using cell phones?

_____

_____

5. According to Frank Drews, why is the use of a hands-free cell phone while driving just as dangerous as the use of a handheld cell phone?

_____

_____

_____

6. How does Frank Drews explain the fact that the number of traffic accidents has not increased since people began using cell phones while driving?

_____

_____

7. According to the NHTSA study, what proportion of all traffic accidents were preceded by some type of driver distraction?

_____

8. According to Rae Tyson, why are driver conversations with passengers less distracting than cell phone conversations?

_____

_____

Critical Reading and Thinking

1. What kind of evidence does the author present?

_____

2. How does the author organize the article?

_____

_____

3. Does the author recognize or refute opposing viewpoints?

_____

4. What kind of information is not included in this selection that might help readers evaluate the issue?

_____

_____

5. What is the tone of the reading?

_____

Words in Context

Directions: Locate each word or phrase in the paragraph indicated and reread that paragraph. Then, based on the way the word is used, write a synonym or brief definition. You may use a dictionary, if necessary.

1. prescribed (par. 3)

_____

2. situational awareness (par. 9)

_____

3. culprit (par. 12)

_____

4. spike (par. 12)

_____

Vocabulary Review

Directions: Match each word in Column A with its correct meaning in Column B.

Column A	Column B
_____ 1. tolerating	a. crashing into another vehicle from behind
_____ 2. simulator	b. intoxicated; drunk
_____ 3. impairments	c. energetic and assertive
_____ 4. inebriated	d. to perform two or more actions at the same time
_____ 5. rear-ending	e. a device used for testing or training that models actual operational conditions
_____ 6. aggressive	f. making up for
_____ 7. compensating	g. weakened physical functions
_____ 8. multitask	h. putting up with

Summarizing the Reading Selection

Directions: Read the following incomplete summary. Then, using information in the article, fill in the blanks.

A recent research study in Utah used _____ to compare the driving

performance of three groups of drivers: drivers talking on handheld or hands-free cell

phones, intoxicated drivers without cell phones, and _____.

The drivers using cell phones were five times more likely to have an accident than the

_____ drivers without cell phones. The study concluded that using any type

of cell phone while driving is even more dangerous than driving drunk. The U.S. National

Highway Traffic Safety Administration (NHTSA) _____ the findings of the

Utah researchers. A _____ showed that 75 percent of traffic accidents

were caused by _____ drivers, and the NHTSA recommends that all

drivers refrain from using cell phones while driving.

   A spokesman for the _____ disagrees, pointing out that the

number of accidents has _____ since cell phones were introduced. The

industry recommends educating drivers on ways to manage _____

rather than _____ cell phone use for drivers, which could give drivers

a _____.

Writing Exercises

1. After reading this article, what advice would you give someone who routinely talks on a cell phone while driving? Write your advice in paragraph form.

2. Do you think there should be a law against using cell phones while driving? Write an essay explaining your answer.

Issue 3: Campus Violence
Preventing Violence on Campuses
Ron Scherer and Amanda Paulson

Originally published by the *Christian Science Monitor* in April 2007, this article examines ways to prevent violence on campuses. As you read, identify the writer's position on the issue and evaluate the evidence offered in support of this position.

Vocabulary Preview

daunting (par. 1) discouraging; intimidating

bucolic (par. 1) rural

aftermath (par. 2) the time following a terrible event

feasible (par. 6) possible; reasonable

intercede (par. 8) take action to alter a situation

protocol (par. 10) a set of rules

negotiate (par. 10) discuss in an effort to reach agreement

hyper-vigilant (par. 11) very cautious and alert to danger

Prereading

1. What security measures have you noticed on your campus? Do you think these measures are sufficient? Why or why not?

    _____

2. Do you think most colleges are doing enough to prevent and respond to violent crime on campus? Why or why not?

    _____

1   University officials are starting to ask tough questions about what they can learn from the worst shooting in United States history [the shootings at Virginia Tech on April 16, 2007]. Many colleges adopted new security plans and procedures in the wake of the 1999 Columbine high school and other mass shootings. But preventing—and reacting to—such attacks poses a daunting challenge to campuses that treasure open environments and often bucolic settings that encompass hundreds of buildings. "The world has changed and we now have to think about balancing the open campus with the secure campus," says Dennis Black, a vice president at the University at Buffalo, noting that this is a wake-up call. "It's Charles Whitman [who killed 16 at the University of Texas in 1966] and Columbine rolled into one."

2   Already, Virginia Tech, where 32 people were killed by a student who then killed himself, is under attack for not locking down campus after the first of two shootings. But experts note that tighter security in the aftermath of violence isn't always effective. Instead, some argue, universities must focus more on preventive measures like outreach and helping students identify early signs of trouble.

3   "For a period of time, colleges and universities will take the law-and-order approach, and it will make students and professors and administrators feel safer. They won't be safer, but they'll feel safer, and that isn't a small thing," says Jack Levin, director of the Brudnick Center on Violence and Conflict at Northeastern

University. Determined shooters will always find a way to get to people, he says, noting that in at least one past case, shooters pulled a fire alarm and waited until students filed out before opening fire. "You can't make college buildings into safe havens," he adds. While most people who exhibit warning signs will never pick up a gun, trying to reach them early on to make them feel less isolated can only help, he says. "If we wait until they want to kill a lot of people, it's too late."

4   Random mass shootings have generally been rare at colleges. Before the Virginia Tech massacre, the worst campus shooting took place in 1966 at the University of Texas at Austin, when Charles Whitman killed 16 people from the observation deck of a clock tower before he was gunned down. Instead, colleges have tended to focus on assaults, rapes, and other violent crimes. Since the "Clery Act" was enacted in 1990—named for Jeanne Clery, raped and murdered in her Lehigh University dorm room—colleges have been required to report violent crimes on campus and notify students when it takes place. Such crimes have tended to mirror national statistics, dropping sharply between 1994 and 2002 and edging up since then, says Lori Sudderth, director of Quinnipiac University's criminal justice program.

5   "We are in a better situation than we were 10 to 20 years ago," Professor Sudderth says. "Victims of violence have more ways to report it than before." In 2005, FBI statistics show that Virginia Tech, with a student body of 27,619, had only four reported violent crimes—fairly typical for a large university. However, Sudderth says, the reported numbers usually underestimate the problem, with crimes like sexual assaults often vastly underreported.

6   Like Levin, Sudderth hopes the Virginia Tech incident makes universities look more closely at security and ways to treat students with mental-health problems. "I would hope we at least ask, 'What do you look for in a violent offender? How do you intervene earlier?'" While locking down an entire campus or putting metal detectors in every building may not be feasible, there are some physical security measures universities can do. Many have already locked dormitories, for instance.

7   Installing monitored TV systems could also help, says Paul Viollis, CEO of Risk Control Strategies. That could have helped police at Virginia Tech target the shooter after the first incident was called in, he says, since stopping and frisking thousands of students isn't feasible. "The security architecture of college campuses needs to be improved," Mr. Viollis says. "But for the most part, that will assist in reacting. . . . The preventative part is really the key. . . . When you put a Band-Aid on the outside, the cause is still there."

8   Faculty and students, he says, could be educated on what signs to look for—someone who's socially isolated, has low self-worth, doesn't take criticism well, and may have put out early signals about his intentions in the hope of getting someone to intercede. In the case of Virginia Tech, the shooter, a senior from South Korea, may have posted worrisome comments in his online profile. The Associated Press reported that his creative writing in class was so disturbing that he was referred for counseling. That's the sort of thing that should be report[ed] to authorities, says Beverly Glenn, director of George Washington University's Hamilton Fish Institute

on School and Community Violence. Her organization has trained resident assistants in dorms in understanding warning signs—something she'd like to see more of. She'd also like to see universities create rules outlawing possession of weapons. That issue arose at the University of Utah last year, when a law was passed allowing students 21 or older to bring firearms to campus if they have a permit.

9   "We have a lot of boys and young men who don't know how to deal with their feelings of rage or depression or being broken-hearted or any of the other kinds of normal emotions," Dr. Glenn notes. "You have to try to teach people that guns are not a way to resolve things." Some campuses have already taken significant steps to boost security, and many more say they'll revisit their plans now.

10   Mr. Black says that before Columbine, protocol was to wait out the shooter and try to negotiate. "Now, we've discovered every second could be a death, so training has changed—we need to get in quickly, effectively, and safely. We need to take risks to save lives." Now, he expects campuses to install more cameras and practice their "active shooter response." "We will begin to close buildings that don't need to be open to the public," he says. "The library, concert halls will be open, but our laboratories and our classroom buildings may need swipe cards for access, just like residence halls."

11   At Arizona State University in Tempe, officials expect to review what happened at Virginia Tech, and possibly adjust their current crisis plans. The university sends out flyers and updates its website when there are situations, such as armed robberies. "We also have general safety briefings for students and residence assistants," says Police Commander Jim Hardina. "People tend not to take security seriously until [an incident like Virginia Tech] happens, and then we find they are hyper-vigilant. But, after a few days or months, they go back to their everyday ways."

Checking Your Comprehension

1. What is the main point of this article?

   _____

   _____

2. According to the article, what is one important factor that limits the ability of college officials to increase security on campus?

   _____

   _____

3. What mistake do some people think Virginia Tech officials made?

   _____

   _____

4. What does the Clery Act require?

_____

_____

5. List three characteristics that can be early warning signs of a student's potential to become violent.

_____

_____

6. What is the University of Utah's policy about possession of weapons on campus?

_____

7. According to Dennis Black, how did guidelines for responding to shooting incidents change after the tragedy at Columbine High School?

_____

_____

8. List two security measures implemented by Arizona State University at Tempe.

_____

_____

_____

Critical Reading and Thinking

1. What is the author's purpose for writing this article?

_____

_____

2. Does the author take a position on the issue of campus violence?

_____

_____

3. What kinds of information are used to support the main points of the article?

_____

4. How does the first paragraph relate to the rest of the article?

_____

_____

_____

5. Is the author biased or objective?

_____

Words in Context

Directions: Locate each word in the paragraph indicated and reread that paragraph. Then, based on the way the word is used, write a synonym or brief definition. You may use a dictionary, if necessary.

1. secure (par. 1)

_____

2. outreach (par. 2)

_____

3. intervene (par. 6)

_____

4. frisking (par. 7)

_____

5. revisit (par. 9)

_____

Vocabulary Review

Directions: Match each word in Column A with its correct meaning in Column B.

	Column A	Column B
_____	1. daunting	a. the period following a terrible event
_____	2. bucolic	b. take action to alter a situation
_____	3. aftermath	c. very cautious and alert to danger
_____	4. feasible	d. discuss in an effort to reach agreement
_____	5. intercede	e. a set of rules
_____	6. protocol	f. rural
_____	7. negotiate	g. possible; reasonable
_____	8. hypervigilant	h. discouraging; intimidating

Summarizing the Reading Selection

Directions: Read the following incomplete summary. Then, using information in the article, fill in the blanks.

In the aftermath of the tragic shootings at _____, many college officials are reevaluating _____ plans and procedures and considering ways to maintain a safe yet _____ campus. Guidelines for responding to violent incidents are changing, shifting from an emphasis on patient _____ to a recognition that quick action may save _____. Use of _____ _____ and monitored _____ systems also could curtail violence by enabling officials to locate suspects after an incident has occurred. An effective crisis plan should include methods for keeping the campus community _____ about violent incidents.

Some experts recommend that college officials focus primarily on _____, rather than just reacting to, violence on campus. Prevention strategies include physical safety measures, such as _____ classroom buildings and _____, and rules prohibiting possession of _____ on campus. In addition, colleges and universities should provide members of the campus community with information to help them recognize _____ signs that a student could become violent.

Writing Exercises

1. Write a paragraph describing one security measure that you think colleges and universities should use, and explain why this measure would be effective in helping prevent violence on campus.

2. Do you think colleges and universities should create rules outlawing possession of weapons on campus? Write a paragraph explaining your answer.

3. Do you agree with Jack Levin's conclusion that "You can't make college buildings into safe havens"? Write an essay explaining your answer.

4. Do you agree with Beverly Glenn's recommendation that students whose creative writing is "disturbing" should be "reported to authorities"? Write an essay explaining your answer.

Issue 4: Employee Rights and Surveillance
Wal-Mart and Target Spy on Their Employees
Barbara Ehrenreich

Published by AlterNet on April 6, 2007, this article examines the alleged mistreatment of employees by corporate giants Wal-Mart and Target. As you read, identify the writer's position on the issue and evaluate the evidence offered in support of this position.

Vocabulary Preview

surveillance (par. 1) prolonged observation of a suspect

fraternization (par. 2) participation in inappropriate socializing

allegedly (par. 2) supposedly

ferret out (par. 3) to discover something hidden

interrogation (par. 4) aggressive questioning

unavailing (par. 7) useless; unsuccessful

detention (par. 7) confinement

browbeating (par. 8) bullying

sweatshop (par. 9) a small factory that mistreats employees

Prereading

1. Do you expect this article to examine one or both sides of the issue of employee rights?

_____

2. Do your expect this article to be primarily fact or opinion?

_____

1   It reads like a cold war thriller: The spy follows the suspects through several countries, ending up in Guatemala City, where he takes a room across the hall from his quarry. Finally, after four days of surveillance, including some patient ear-to-the-keyhole work, he is able to report back to headquarters that he has the goods on them. They're guilty!

2   But this isn't a John Le Carré novel, and the powerful institution pulling the strings wasn't the USSR or the CIA. It was Wal-Mart, and the two suspects weren't carrying plans for a shoulder-launched H-bomb. Their crime was "fraternization." One of them, James W. Lynn, a Wal-Mart factory inspection manager, was traveling with a female subordinate, with whom he allegedly enjoyed some

intimate moments behind closed doors. At least the company spy reported hearing "moans and sighs" within the woman's room.

3   Now you may wonder why a company so famously cheap that it requires its same-sex teams to share hotel rooms while on the road would invest in international espionage to ferret out mixed-sex fraternizers. Unless, as Lynn argues, they were really after him for what is a far worse crime in Wal-Mart's books: Openly criticizing the conditions he found in Central American factories supplying Wal-Mart stores. In fact, the cold war thriller analogy is not entirely fanciful. *New York Times* reporter Michael Barbaro, who related the story of Wal-Mart's stalking of Lynn and his colleague, also reports that the company's security department is staffed by former top officials of the CIA and the FBI. Along the same lines, Jeffrey Goldberg provides a chilling account of his visit to Wal-Mart's Bentonville "war room" in the April 2nd *New Yorker*. Although instructed not to write down anything he saw, he found a "dark, threadbare room . . . its walls painted battleship gray," where only two out of five of the occupants will even meet his eyes. In general, he found the Bentonville fortress "not unlike the headquarters of the National Security Agency."

4   We've always known that Wal-Mart is as big, in financial terms, as many sizable nations. It may even have begun to believe that [it] is one, complete with its own laws, security agency, and espionage system. But the illusion of state power is not confined to Wal-Mart. Justin Kenward, who worked at a Target store in Chino CA for three years, wrote to tell me about his six hour interrogation, in 2003, by the store's "Asset Protection" agents, who accused him of wrongly giving a fellow employee a discount on a video game a year earlier:

5   After about an hour of trying to tell them that I don't remember anything about that day let alone that transaction, I had to use the restroom. I asked if I could and was denied. This goes on for about another hour when I say "Look I have to pee, bad, can I go to the restroom?" Once more I was told no. So I stand up and start walking out the door, and was stopped. At this point I thought to myself "They're looking to fire me!" So I start to think of ways that transaction might have came to be. I say something like "I would never give a discount unless an L.O.D. (Leader On Duty, aka: a manager) or a Team Lead (aka: supervisor) told me to. . . ." I was interrupted and told that it sounds like I was trying to place my mistake on other people. Three hours into this and still needing to pee I was told that I need to write an apologetic letter to the company with the details, every detail, that we just went over and then I could use the rest room. . . .

6   Kenward not only lost his job, but faced charges of theft.

7   My efforts to get a comment from Target were unavailing, but I did manage to track down a person who worked in security for the Chino store at the time of Kenward's detention. Because she still depends on Target for her health

insurance, she asked not to be named, but she writes that Kenward's experience was not unusual:

8   What I know for a fact is that they took each of the twelve youngsters [Target employees] to their office separately. They locked them in an office without a telephone, would not let them phone their parents or anyone, and kept them there browbeating them for six to ten hours. They never told them they were being arrested . . . only that Target was disappointed in them and if they would write a letter of apology that they'd dictate they could go and all would be forgotten. None of these children knew their rights . . . all of them ended up writing the stupid letter. Of course this too was a lie . . . as soon as they had the letter in hand the police were called and that person was hauled off in handcuffs and arrested.

9   This is the workplace dictatorship at its brass-knuckled best. When companies start imagining that they are nation-states, entitled to spy on, stalk, and imprison their own employees, then we are well down the road to an actual, full-scale dictatorship. As for those "moans and sighs" that issued from the hotel room in Guatemala City: Maybe Lynn and his companion were reflecting on the sweatshop conditions they encountered in a Wal-Mart subcontractor's factory. Or maybe they were aware of the man spying on them, and were mourning the decline of democracy.

Checking Your Comprehension

1. What is the main point of the article?

_____

_____

_____

2. According to James Lynn, what is the real reason that Wal-Mart was spying on him?

_____

_____

_____

3. According to reporter Michael Barbaro, what are the professional backgrounds of some staff members in Wal-Mart's security department?

_____

_____

4. Justin Kenward claims that Target wrongly accused him of what offense?

_____

5. What happened after Justin Kenward's interrogation by Target's Asset Protection agents?

_____

6. What position at Target did the author's unnamed source hold?

_____

_____

7. According to the unnamed source, what happened after the 12 young Target employees wrote letters of apology?

_____

Critical Reading and Thinking

1. What is the author's main purpose in writing this article?

_____

_____

2. What kinds of evidence does the author present?

_____

3. How does the author construct her argument?

_____

_____

_____

4. Why does the author suggest that the Wal-Mart employees were "mourning the decline of democracy"?

_____

_____

5. Does the article present an objective or biased view of the issue of employee surveillance?

_____

Words in Context

Directions: Locate each word or phrase in the paragraph indicated and reread that paragraph. Then, based on the way the word or phrase is used, write a synonym or brief definition. You may use a dictionary, if necessary.

1. the goods (par. 1)

   _____

2. pulling the strings (par. 2)

   _____

3. fanciful (par. 3)

   _____

4. chilling (par. 3)

   _____

5. threadbare (par. 3)

   _____

Vocabulary Review

Directions: Match each word or phrase in Column A with its correct meaning in Column B.

	Column A	Column B
_____	1. surveillance	a. to discover something hidden
_____	2. fraternization	b. useless; unsuccessful
_____	3. allegedly	c. bullying
_____	4. ferret out	d. participation in inappropriate socializing
_____	5. interrogation	e. a small factory that mistreats employees
_____	6. unavailing	f. prolonged observation of a suspect
_____	7. detention	g. aggressive questioning
_____	8. browbeating	h. supposedly
_____	9. sweatshop	i. confinement

Summarizing the Reading Selection

Directions: Read the following incomplete summary. Then, using information in the article, fill in the blanks.

Two giant corporations, _____ and _____, have

been accused of mistreating and spying on their own employees. James Lynn, a

Wal-Mart _____, and a female colleague traveled to

_____ for the company. When they shared a hotel room, Wal-Mart's

corporate spies charged the two employees with "_____." Lynn claims

that the company was attempting to discredit him because he criticized conditions at

Central American _____ supplying Wal-Mart stores.

Former Target _____ also have complained about corporate

harassment. _____ alleges that he was wrongly charged with granting

an unauthorized _____ for a fellow employee. According to Kenward,

he was detained and _____ by company agents for six hours; after

submitting a forced _____, he was fired and charged with

_____. Kenward's account was supported by a former Target

_____ official, who describes similar treatment of

_____, who also were wrongfully detained,

harassed, and arrested. Such cases cause some observers to wonder whether large

companies such as Wal-Mart and Target are headed toward "workplace

_____."

Writing Exercises

1. Have you experienced or observed surveillance, unfair treatment, or invasion of privacy in the workplace? Describe the situation and your response to it.

2. Do you agree with the author's conclusion that Wal-Mart and Target are guilty of "workplace dictatorship"? Write a paragraph explaining your point of view.

3. Do you think large American companies are justified in conducting surveillance of their employees? Write an essay explaining your answer.

Issue 5: Media Image of Women
Beauty and Body Image in the Media
Media Awareness Network

Published by Media Awareness Network, this article examines the portrayal of women in the media. As you read, identify the writer's position on the issue and evaluate the evidence offered in support of this position.

Vocabulary Preview

criterion (par. 2) a standard used in making judgments

anorexia nervosa (par. 4) an eating disorder marked by an abnormal fear of gaining weight and an unwillingness to eat

activist (par. 5) a person who vigorously supports or opposes a cause

chronic (par. 6) recurring often or lasting a long time

malnutrition (par. 6) a condition of being poorly nourished due to a lack of healthy foods

devastating (par. 7) severely destructive

buck the trend (par. 10) to resist a general tendency or current fashion

barrage (par. 12) an attack or outpouring

internalize (par. 13) to absorb beliefs or attitudes and make them one's own

---

Prereading

1. What position do you expect this article to take on the portrayal of women in the media?

   _____

   _____

2. What magazine do you read most often? How do you feel about the way women are portrayed in this magazine?

   _____

1   Images of female bodies are everywhere. Women—and their body parts—sell everything from food to cars. Popular film and television actresses are becoming younger, taller and thinner. Some have even been known to faint on the set from lack of food. Women's magazines are full of articles urging that if they can just lose those last twenty pounds, they'll have it all—the perfect marriage, loving children, great sex, and a rewarding career.

2   Why are standards of beauty being imposed on women, the majority of whom are naturally larger and more mature than any of the models? The roots, some

analysts say, are economic. By presenting an ideal difficult to achieve and maintain, the cosmetic and diet product industries are assured of growth and profits. And it's no accident that youth is increasingly promoted, along with thinness, as an essential criterion of beauty. If not all women need to lose weight, for sure they're all aging, says the Quebec Action Network for Women's Health in its 2001 report *Changements sociaux en faveur de la diversité des images corporelles*. And, according to the industry, age is a disaster that needs to be dealt with.

> "We don't need Afghan-style burquas to disappear as women. We disappear in reverse—by revamping and revealing our bodies to meet externally imposed visions of female beauty."
>
> *Source:* Robin Gerber, author and motivational speaker.

3   The stakes are huge. On the one hand, women who are insecure about their bodies are more likely to buy beauty products, new clothes, and diet aids. It is estimated that the diet industry alone is worth $100 billion (U.S.) a year. On the other hand, research indicates that exposure to images of thin, young, air-brushed female bodies is linked to depression, loss of self-esteem and the development of unhealthy eating habits in women and girls.

4   The American research group Anorexia Nervosa & Related Eating Disorders, Inc. says that one out of every four college-aged women uses unhealthy methods of weight control—including fasting, skipping meals, excessive exercise, laxative abuse, and self-induced vomiting. And the Canadian Fitness and Lifestyle Research Institute warns that weight control measures are being taken by girls as young as nine. American statistics are similar. In 2003, *Teen* magazine reported that 35 percent of girls 6 to 12 years old have been on at least one diet, and that 50 to 70 percent of normal weight girls believe they are overweight.

5   Media activist Jean Kilbourne concludes that, "Women are sold to the diet industry by the magazines we read and the television programs we watch, almost all of which make us feel anxious about our weight."

Unattainable Beauty

6   Perhaps most disturbing is the fact that media images of female beauty are unattainable for all but a very small number of women. Researchers generating a computer model of a women with Barbie-doll proportions, for example, found that her back would be too weak to support the weight of her upper body, and her body would be too narrow to contain more than half a liver and a few centimeters of bowel. A real woman built that way would suffer from chronic diarrhea and eventually die from malnutrition.

7   Still, the number of real life women and girls who seek a similar underweight body is epidemic, and they can suffer equally devastating health consequences.

The Culture of Thinness

8   Researchers report that women's magazines have ten and one-half times more ads and articles promoting weight loss than men's magazines do, and

over three-quarters of the covers of women's magazines include at least one message about how to change a woman's bodily appearance—by diet, exercise or cosmetic surgery.

9   Television and movies reinforce the importance of a thin body as a measure of a woman's worth. Canadian researcher Gregory Fouts reports that over three-quarters of the female characters in TV situation comedies are underweight, and only one in twenty are above average in size. Heavier actresses tend to receive negative comments from male characters about their bodies ("How about wearing a sack?"), and 80 percent of these negative comments are followed by canned audience laughter.

10   There have been efforts in the magazine industry to buck the trend. For several years the Quebec magazine *Coup de Pouce* has consistently included full-sized women in their fashion pages and *Châtelaine* has pledged not to touch up photos and not to include models less than 25 years of age.

11   However, advertising rules the marketplace and in advertising thin is "in." Twenty years ago, the average model weighed 8 percent less than the average woman—but today's models weigh 23 percent less. Advertisers believe that thin models sell products. When the Australian magazine *New Woman* recently included a picture of a heavy-set model on its cover, it received a truckload of letters from grateful readers praising the move. But its advertisers complained and the magazine returned to featuring bone-thin models. *Advertising Age International* concluded that the incident "made clear the influence wielded by advertisers who remain convinced that only thin models spur the sales of beauty products."

Self-Improvement or Self-Destruction?

12   The barrage of messages about thinness, dieting and beauty tells "ordinary" women that they are always in need of adjustment—and that the female body is an object to be perfected.

13   Jean Kilbourne argues that the overwhelming presence of media images of painfully thin women means that real women's bodies have become invisible in the mass media. The real tragedy, Kilbourne concludes, is that many women internalize these stereotypes, and judge themselves by the beauty industry's standards. Women learn to compare themselves to other women, and to compete with them for male attention. This focus on beauty and desirability "effectively destroys any awareness and action that might help to change that climate."

Checking Your Comprehension

1. What is the main point of this article?

_____

_____

_____

2. What reason is given in the reading to explain the images of female beauty presented in the media?

_____

_____

_____

3. According to the article, what percentage of normal-weight American girls believe they are overweight?

_____

4. Why did researchers generate a computer model of a woman with Barbie-doll proportions?

_____

_____

5. Identify two ways that television and movies imply that a woman's worth depends on her weight.

_____

_____

_____

_____

6. Why did the Australian magazine *New Woman* discontinue its practice of featuring a heavyset model on the cover?

_____

7. According to Jean Kilbourne, what happens when women judge themselves by the beauty industry's standards?

_____

_____

Critical Reading and Thinking

1. What is the author's purpose for writing this article?

_____

_____

2. What do you think Robin Gerber means when she says that women "disappear" (quotation in sidebar, paragraph 1)?

_____

_____

_____

3. What types of information are used to support the main points of the article?

_____

4. Which evidence cited in the article seems most compelling to you? Why?

_____

5. What is the tone of the essay?

_____

6. What generalizations are stated in the article?

_____

_____

Words in Context

Directions: Locate each word in the paragraph indicated and reread that paragraph. Then, based on the way the word is used, write a synonym or brief definition. You may use a dictionary, if necessary.

1. epidemic (par. 7)

_____

2. canned (par. 9)

_____

3. spur (par. 11)

_____

4. climate (par. 13)

_____

Vocabulary Review

Directions: Match each word or phrase in Column A with its correct meaning in Column B.

	Column A	Column B
_____	1. criterion	a. severely destructive
_____	2. anorexia nervosa	b. recurring often or lasting a long time
_____	3. activist	c. a standard used in making judgments
_____	4. chronic	d. to resist a general tendency or current fashion
_____	5. malnutrition	e. a person who vigorously supports or opposes a cause
_____	6. devastating	f. to absorb beliefs or attitudes and make them one's own
_____	7. buck the trend	g. a condition of being poorly nourished due to a lack of healthy foods
_____	8. barrage	h. an eating disorder marked by an abnormal fear of gaining weight and an unwillingness to eat
_____	9. internalize	i. an attack or outpouring

Summarizing the Reading Selection

Directions: Read the following incomplete summary. Then, using the information in the article, fill in the blanks.

The portrayal of women in _____, _____,

_____, and other media reflects _____ standards for

physical beauty. The fashion, cosmetic, and _____ industries actively

promote such standards, depicting the ideal woman as very young and very thin. This

ideal is _____ for most women, who are naturally larger and more

mature than fashion models. Feeling inadequate, many women purchase

_____ and _____ in a quest to conform to the

_____ of female beauty promoted by the _____.

Such images can have _____ effects on women's physical and

_____ health. Many young women use _____ methods of

_____ or develop serious _____. Measuring themselves against media stereotypes of female beauty, some women even question their own worth, experiencing _____ and a loss of self-esteem.

Writing Exercises

1. Write a paragraph describing the way you think women should be portrayed in the media.

2. The article cites examples of magazines that feature women of normal weight rather than models who are excessively thin. Do you think public attitudes about female beauty would change if more magazines followed this practice? Write a paragraph explaining why or why not.

3. One magazine used heavyset models on its cover. Write a description of other ways the public attitude toward female beauty could be changed.

4. Do you agree or disagree with Jean Kilbourne's argument, cited in paragraph 13, that many women internalize media stereotypes of the female body? Write an essay explaining your reasons.

Issue 6: Global Warming
Global Warming
Holli Riebeek

Published by NASA for the "earth observatory" Web site, this article examines global warming. As you read, identify the writer's position on the issue and evaluate the evidence offered in support of this position.

Vocabulary Preview
intergovernmental (par. 1) involving representatives of more than one government

unequivocal (par. 1) certain

greenhouse gases (par. 2) certain gases that trap solar radiation and warm the earth's atmosphere

virtually (par. 3) almost

infectious (par. 4) contagious

infestation (par. 8) invasion by insects

malaria (par. 9) a disease spread by infected mosquitoes

ozone (par. 9) a form of oxygen that pollutes the earth's lower atmosphere

emissions (par. 10) substances that are released into the air

Prereading

1. Does this article appear to be primarily fact or opinion?

_____

2. Why is global warming important?

_____

1 Over the last five years, 600 scientists from the Intergovernmental Panel on Climate Change [IPCC] sifted through thousands of studies about global warming published in forums ranging from scientific journals to industry publications and distilled the world accumulated knowledge into this conclusion: "Warming of the climate system is unequivocal."

2 Far from being some future fear, global warming is happening now, and scientists have evidence that humans are to blame. For decades, cars and factories have spewed billions of tons of greenhouse gases into the atmosphere, and these gases caused temperatures to rise between 0.6°C and 0.9°C (1.08°F to 1.62°F) over the past century. The rate of warming in the last 50 years was double the rate observed over the last 100 years. Temperatures are certain to go up further.

3 But why should we worry about a seemingly small increase in temperature? . . . Even the temperature change of a degree or two that has occurred over the last century is capable of producing significant changes in our environment and way of life. In the future, it is very likely that rising temperatures will lead to more frequent heat waves, and virtually certain that the seas will rise, which could leave low-lying nations awash in seawater. Warmer temperatures will alter weather patterns, making it likely that there will be more

Cars, factories, and power plants pump billions of tons of carbon dioxide into the atmosphere every year. . . .

intense droughts and more intense rain events. Moreover, global warming will last thousands of years. To gain an understanding of how global warming might impact humanity, it is necessary to understand what global warming is, how scientists measure it, and how forecasts for the future are made.

Potential Effects of Global Warming

4 The most obvious impact of global warming will be changes in both average and extreme temperature and precipitation, but warming will also enhance

coastal erosion, lengthen the growing season, melt ice caps and glaciers, and alter the range of some infectious diseases, among other things.

Climate Changes

5   For most places, global warming will result in more hot days and fewer cool days, with the greatest warming happening over land. Longer, more intense heat waves will become more frequent. High latitudes and generally wet places will tend to receive more rainfall, while tropical regions and generally dry places will probably receive less rain. Increases in rainfall will come in the form of bigger, wetter storms, rather than in the form of more rainy days. In between those larger storms will be longer periods of light or no rain, so the frequency of drought will increase. Hurricanes will likely increase in intensity due to warmer ocean surface temperatures.

6   It is impossible to pin any one unusual weather event on global warming, but evidence is emerging that suggests that global warming is already influencing the weather. The IPCC reports that both heat waves and intense rain events have increased in frequency during the last 50 years, and human-induced global warming more likely than not contributed to the trend. Satellite-based rainfall measurements show tropical areas got more rain in the form of large storms or light rainfall instead of moderate storms between 1979 and 2003. Since the 1970s, the area affected by drought and the number of intense tropical cyclones also have increased, trends that IPCC scientists say were more likely than not influenced by human activities, though in the case of cyclones, the record is too sparse to draw any certain conclusions.

Rising Sea Level

7   The weather isn't the only thing global warming will impact: rising sea level will erode coasts and cause more frequent coastal flooding. The problem is serious because as much as 10 percent of the world's population lives in coastal areas less that 10 meters (about 30 feet) above sea level. The IPCC estimates that sea levels will rise between 0.18 and 0.59 meters (0.59 to 1.9 feet) by 2099 because of expanding sea water and melting mountain glaciers. . . .

Ecosystem Effects

8   Global warming is also putting pressure on ecosystems, the plants and animals that co-exist in a particular climate. Warmer temperatures have already shifted the growing season in many parts of the globe. Spring is coming earlier, and that means that migrating animals have to start earlier to follow food sources. And since the growing season is longer, plants need more water to keep growing or they will dry out, increasing the risk of fires. Shorter, milder winters fail to kill insects, increasing the risk that an infestation will destroy an ecosystem. As the growing season progresses, maximum daily temperatures increase, sometimes beyond the tolerance of the plant or animal. To survive the climbing temperatures, both marine and land-based plants and animals have started to migrate towards the

poles. Those species that cannot migrate or adapt face extinction. The IPCC estimates that 20–30 percent of plant and animal species will be at risk of extinction if temperatures climb more than 1.5° to 2.5°C.

9   The people who will be hardest hit will be residents of poorer countries who do not have the resources to fend off changes in climate. As tropical temperature zones expand, the reach of some infectious diseases like malaria will change. More intense rains and hurricanes, rising sea levels, and fast-melting mountain glaciers will lead to more severe flooding. Hotter summers and more frequent fires will lead to more cases of heat stroke and deaths, and to higher levels of near-surface ozone and smoke, which would cause more 'code red' air quality days. Intense droughts could lead to an increase in malnutrition. On a longer time scale, fresh water will become scarcer during the summer as mountain glaciers disappear, particularly in Asia and parts of North America. On the flip side, warmer winters will lead to fewer cold-related deaths, and the longer growing season could increase food production in some temperate areas.

10   Ultimately, global warming will impact life on Earth in many ways, but the extent of the change is up to us. Scientists have shown that human emissions of greenhouse gases are pushing global temperatures up, and many aspects of climate are responding to the warming in the way that scientists predicted they would. Ecosystems across the globe are already affected and surprising changes have already taken place. Polar ice caps are melting, plants and animals are migrating, tropical rain is shifting, and droughts are becoming more widespread and frequent. Since greenhouse gases are long-lived, the planet will continue to warm and changes will continue to happen, but the degree to which global warming changes life on Earth depends on our decisions.

Checking Your Comprehension

1. What is the main point of this article?

_____

_____

2. According to the article, how large an increase in global temperature is required to produce significant changes in the environment?

_____

3. Why are coastal communities especially at risk as global warming progresses?

_____

_____

4. Why does global warming increase the risk of insect infestation?

_____

5. What changes are some plants and animals making in response to global warming?

_____

6. What are two health problems that global warming will likely cause?

_____

_____

7. According to the article, what are two positive changes that could result from global warming?

_____

_____

8. According to the article, what are two examples of environmental changes that already have occurred as a result of global warming?

_____

_____

Critical Reading and Thinking

1. How does the first paragraph relate to the rest of the selection?

_____

_____

_____

2. What kinds of evidence does the author present?

_____

3. How do the photograph and its caption support the author's purpose?

_____

_____

_____

4. What function does the final paragraph serve?

_____

_____

Words in Context

Directions: Locate each word in the paragraph indicated and reread that paragraph. Then, based on the way the word is used, write a synonym or brief definition. You may use a dictionary, if necessary.

1. sifted (par. 1)

_____

2. distilled (par. 1)

_____

3. enhance (par. 4)

_____

4. range (par. 4)

_____

5. ecosystems (par. 8)

_____

5. tolerance (par. 8)

_____

Vocabulary Review

Directions: Match each word or phrase in Column A with its correct meaning in Column B.

Column A	Column B
_____ 1. intergovernmental	a. certain gases that trap solar radiation and warm the earth's atmosphere
_____ 2. unequivocal	b. a disease spread by infected mosquitoes
_____ 3. greenhouse gases	c. contagious
_____ 4. virtually	d. involving representatives of more than one government
_____ 5. infectious	e. substances that are released into the air
_____ 6. infestation	f. certain
_____ 7. malaria	g. a form of oxygen that pollutes the earth's lower atmosphere
_____ 8. ozone	h. an invasion by insects
_____ 9. emissions	i. almost

Summarizing the Reading Selection

Directions: Read the following incomplete summary. Then, using information in the article, fill in the blanks.

Many scientists now agree that the earth has entered a period of _____

_____ that will have dramatic consequences. _____

suggests that global warming is already affecting the environment. In the years ahead,

climate changes are likely to cause more frequent heat waves, _____,

and _____ as well as more intense _____ and

_____. As _____ melt and sea levels rise, densely popu-

lated coastal areas will _____ and flood. _____ and

_____ that have difficulty adapting to climate changes may become

extinct, and infestations of _____ could destroy some

_____. Climate changes also are likely to affect human health, as people

cope with heat-related illnesses, poor air quality, _____ resulting from

drought, and the spread of some _____.

In recent decades, human activities most likely have contributed to global warming,

as factories, _____, and _____ have pumped tons of

_____ into the atmosphere. Now we face the challenge of seeking

productive ways to limit the negative consequences of global warning.

Writing Exercises

1. What evidence about the consequences of global warming did you find most compelling? Write a paragraph explaining your answer.

2. What are some obstacles that individuals and governments face in preparing for possible effects of global warming or in trying to reduce its effects? Write an essay explaining your answer.

3. Write an essay describing actions that you could take to help address problems associated with global warming.

Progress Charts

Directions: As you complete each mastery test, record its chapter number, the date, and your percentage score.

Mastery Test 1

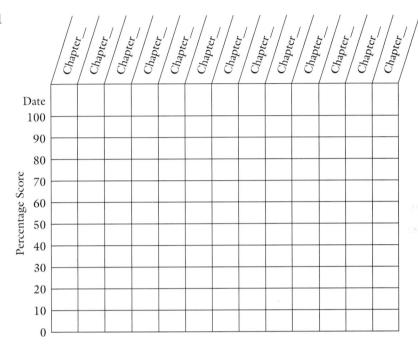

Mastery Test 2

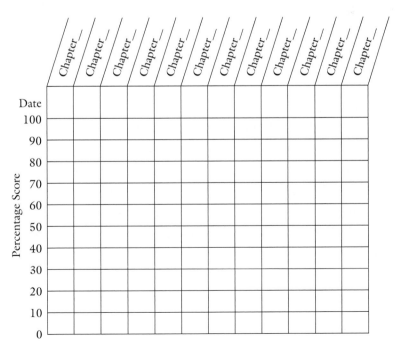

Mastery Test 3

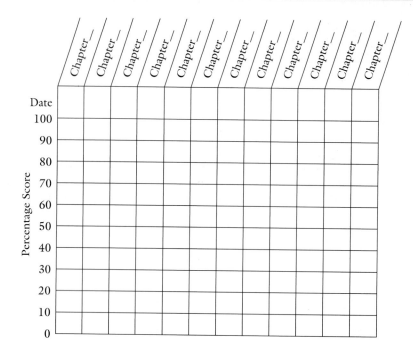

Mastery Test 4

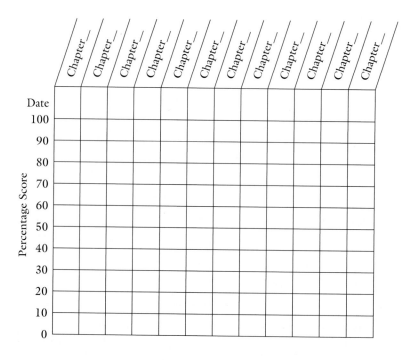

Credits

TEXT CREDITS

Chapter 1

19: Carole Wade and Carol Tavris, *Psychology*, 3/e, p. 82. Copyright © 1993 Prentice-Hall. Reprinted by permission of Pearson Education, Inc., Upper Saddle River, NJ.

19: James Trefil, "Greetings from the Antiworld," *Smithsonian*, June 1998, p. 62. Reprinted by permission.

21: Robert Wallace, *Biology: The World of Life*, 5/e, p. 185. Copyright © 1990 Scott Foresman. Reprinted by permission of Pearson Education, Inc.

23: Kurt Nortstog and Andrew J. Meyerricks, *Biology*, pp. 193. Toronto: Charles E. Merrill, 1985.

23: Ronald White, "Weightlessness and the Human Body," *Scientific American Online*, September 1998, p. 2.

23: Roger Chisholm and Marilu McCarty, *Principles of Economics*, p. 443. Glenview, IL: Scott, Foresman, 1981.

28: Kim McLarin, "Primary Colors" as first appeared in *The New York Times Magazine*, 1998. Reprinted by permission of Inkwell Management.

Chapter 2

44: James Geiwitz, *Psychology: Looking at Ourselves*, 2/e, p. 189. Copyright © 1980. Reprinted by permission of the author.

45: Ross Eshleman, Barbara Cashion, and Laurence Basirico, *Sociology: An Introduction*, 4/e, p. 93. New York: HarperCollins College Publishers, 1993.

46: Eshleman, Cashion, and Basirico, *Sociology: An Introduction*, 4/e, pp. 98–99.

53: H.L. Capron, *Computers: Tools for an Information Age*, 5/e, p. 233. Copyright © 1998. Reprinted by permission of Pearson Education, Inc., Upper Saddle River, NJ.

54: "My Life as an Illegal" by Immigrant X as told to John Spong, *Texas Monthly*, July 2006. Reprinted by permission of Texas Monthly.

Chapter 3

81: Curtis Byer and Louis Shainberg, *Living Well: Health in Your Hands*, 2/e, p. 360. Copyright © 1995 Jones and Bartlett Publishers, Sudbury, MA, www.jbpub.com. Reprinted with permission.

82: Joseph A. DeVito, *Messages: Building Interpersonal Communication Skills*, 3/e, pp. 22–23. New York: HarperCollins College Publishers, 1996.

82: Byer and Shainberg, *Living Well: Health in Your Hands*, 2/e, p. 67.

83: Robert Wallace, *Biology: The World of Life*, 6/e, p. 834. Copyright © 1992 Addison-Wesley Educational Publishers. Reprinted by permission of Pearson Education, Inc.

90: B.E. Pruitt and Jane J. Stein, *HealthStyles: Decisions for Living Well*, 2/e, pp. 127, 131. Copyright © 1999. Reprinted by permission of Pearson Education, Inc.

91: Catharine Skipp and Dan Ephron, "Trouble at Home; The Iraq War Is Taking an Incalculable Toll on Families at Home. How One Military Couple Is Coping with the Strain." From *Newsweek*, October 23, 2006. © 2006 Newsweek, Inc. All rights reserved. Used by

Chapter 4

98: By permission. From *Merriam-Webster Online* © 2007 by Merriam-Webster, Incorporated (www.Merriam-Webster.com)

99: By permission. From *Merriam-Webster Online* © 2007 by Merriam-Webster, Incorporated (www.Merriam-Webster.com)

102: "Curve." Copyright © 2006 by Houghton Mifflin Company. Reproduced by permission from *The American Heritage Dictionary of the English Language, Fourth Edition.*

105: "Pronunciation Key" (abbreviated). Copyright © 1991 by Houghton Mifflin Company. Reproduced by permission from *The American Heritage Dictionary, Second College Edition.*

109: "Green." Copyright © 2006 by Houghton Mifflin Company. Reproduced by permission from *The American Heritage Dictionary of the English Language, Fourth Edition.*

110: "Oblique." Copyright © 2006 by Houghton Mifflin Company. Reproduced by permission from *The American Heritage Dictionary of the English Language, Fourth Edition.*

125: "Articulate." Copyright © 2006 by Houghton Mifflin Company. Reproduced by permission from *The American Heritage Dictionary of the English Language, Fourth Edition.*

126: "Panoply." Copyright © 2006 by Houghton Mifflin Company. Reproduced by permission from *The American Heritage Dictionary of the English Language, Fourth Edition.*

126: "Ventilate." Copyright © 2006 by Houghton Mifflin Company. Reproduced by permission from *The American Heritage Dictionary of the English Language, Fourth Edition.*

127: "Manifest." Copyright © 2006 by Houghton Mifflin Company. Reproduced by permission from *The American Heritage Dictionary of the English Language, Fourth Edition.*

127: "Besiege." Copyright © 2006 by Houghton Mifflin Company. Reproduced by permission from *The American Heritage Dictionary of the English Language, Fourth Edition.*

127: "Facile." Copyright © 2006 by Houghton Mifflin Company. Reproduced by permission from *The American Heritage Dictionary of the English Language, Fourth Edition.*

129: Teresa Audesirk, Gerald Audesirk, and Bruce E. Byers, "Spare Parts for Human Bodies," from *Biology: Life on Earth,* 8/e, pp. 57, 77. Copyright © 2008 by Pearson Education, Inc. Reprinted by permission.

Chapter 5

138: Joseph A. DeVito, *Messages: Building Interpersonal Communication Skills* 4/e, p. 146. Published by Allyn and Bacon, Boston, MA Copyright © 1999 by Pearson Education. Reprinted/adapted by permission of the publisher.

146: Janice Thompson and Melinda Manore, *Nutrition for Life,* pp. 109–111. Copyright © 2007, Pearson Education, Inc., publishing as Benjamin Cummings. Reprinted by permission.

156: Rebecca Donatelle and Lorraine Davis, *Access to Health,* 6/e, pp. 560–561. Copyright © 2000. Reprinted by permission of Pearson Education, Inc.

Chapter 6

171: Curtis Byer and Louis Shainberg, *Living Well: Health in Your Hands,* 2/e, p. 256. Copyright © 1995 Jones and Bartlett Publishers, Sudbury, MA, www.jbpub.com. Reprinted with permission.

171: Tim Curry, Robert Jiobu, and Kent Schwirian, *Sociology for the 21st Century,* 3/e, p. 356. Copyright © 2001. Reprinted by permission of Pearson Education, Inc., Upper Saddle River, NJ.

171: Edward Bergman and William Renwick, *Introduction to Geography,* 2/e, pp. 343–344. Copyright © 2002. Reprinted by permission of Pearson Education, Inc., Upper Saddle River, NJ.

172: Hugh D. Barlow, *Criminal Justice in America,* p. 290. Copyright © 2000. Reprinted by permission of Pearson Education, Inc., Upper Saddle River, NJ.

172: Stephen F. Davis and Joseph J. Palladino, *Psychology*, 3/e, pp. 190. Copyright © 2000. Reprinted by permission of Pearson Education, Inc., Upper Saddle River, NJ.

173: Rebecca Donatelle and Lorraine Davis, *Access to Health*, 6/e, p. 546. Copyright © 2000. Reprinted by permission of Pearson Education, Inc.

173: Richard George, *The New Consumer Survival Kit*, p. 212. Boston: Little, Brown and Company, 1978.

173: John Dorfman et al., *Well Being: An Introduction to Health*, p. 27. Glenview, IL: Scott, Foresman, 1980.

174: K. Warner Schaie and James Geiwitz, *Adult Development and Aging*, pp. 371–372. Boston: Little, Brown and Company, 1982.

174: Dorfman et al., *Well Being: An Introduction to Health*, p. 263.

175: Robert Wallace, *Biology: The World of Life*, 7/e, p. 497. Menlo Park, CA: Benjamin/Cummings, 1997.

176: Richard Campbell, *Media and Culture*, p. 196. New York: St. Martin's Press, 1997.

176: Byer and Shainberg, *Living Well: Health in Your Hands*, 2/e, p. 289.

177: Bob Weinstein, *Jobs for the 21st Century*, p. 118. New York: Macmillan, 1983.

178: Edward Fox and Edward Wheatley, *Modern Marketing*, p. 142. Glenview, IL: Scott, Foresman, 1978.

178: Walter Thompson and Joseph V. Hickey, *Society in Focus*, 4/e, p. 156. Published by Allyn and Bacon, Boston, MA. Copyright © 1994 by Pearson Education. Reprinted by permission of the publisher.

178: Dr. Joyce Brothers, excerpt from column on "What Dirty Words Mean," *Good Housekeeping*, May 1973. Reprinted by permission of the author.

179: Jean Weirch, *Personal Financial Management*, p. 155. Boston: Little, Brown and Company, 1983.

179: Weirch, *Personal Financial Management*, pp. 20–21.

179: William E. Smith and Raymond D. Liedlich, *From Thought to Theme*, 7/e, pp. 281–282. New York: Harcourt Brace Jovanovich, 1983.

180: Donatelle and Davis, *Access to Health*, 6/e, p. 497.

180: Joseph A. DeVito, *The Interpersonal Communication Book*, 9/e, p. 43. Boston: Allyn and Bacon, 2001.

180: Roy Cook, Laura Yale, and Joseph Marqua, *Tourism: The Business of Travel*, p. 151. Copyright © 1999. Reprinted by permission of Pearson Education, Inc., Upper Saddle River, NJ.

180: Barlow, *Criminal Justice in America*, pp. 422–423.

181: Wendy G. Lehnert, *Light on the Internet: Essentials of the Internet and the World Wide Web*, p. 44. Reading, MA: Addison Wesley Longman, Inc., 1999.

189: Bergman and Renwick, *Introduction to Geography*, 2/e, p. 365.

189: Barlow, *Criminal Justice in America*, p. 271.

190: Donatelle and Davis, *Access to Health*, 6/e, pp. 285–286.

191: Kathleen German and Bruce Gronbeck, *Principles of Public Speaking*, 14/e, pp. 190–191. New York: Longman, 2001.

191: Tim Curry, Jiobu, and Schwirian, *Sociology for the 21st Century*, 3/e, p. 138.

192: Michael Solomon and Elnora Stuart, *The Brave New World of E-Commerce* (supplement to *Marketing: Real People, Real Choices*), p. 13. Upper Saddle River, NJ: Prentice-Hall, 2001.

192: German and Gronbeck, *Principles of Public Speaking*, 14/e, p. 70

193: Michael Solomon, *Consumer Behavior*, 4/e, p. 239. Upper Saddle River, NJ: Prentice-Hall, 1999.

193: Donatelle and Davis, *Access to Health*, 6/e, p. 42.

194: Steven A. Beebe and John T. Masterson, *Communicating in Small Groups: Principles & Practice*, 6/e, p. 150. New York: Longman, 2001.

194: Weinstein, *Jobs for the 21st Century*, pp. 110–111.

194: *Science Digest.* Excerpt from "Trees Talk to One Another," *Science Digest*, January 1984, p. 47.

195: John Naisbitt, *Megatrends*, p. 23. New York: Warner Books, 1982.

195: James Geiwitz, *Psychology: Looking at Ourselves*, 2/e, p. 276. Copyright © 1980. Reprinted by permission of the author.

195: Frans Gerritsen, *Theory and Practice of Color*, p. 9. New York: Van Nostrand, 1975.

195: Cook, Yale, and Marqua, *Tourism: The Business of Travel*, pp. 246–247.

196: Donatelle and Davis, *Access to Health*, 6/e, pp. 289–290.

196: Bergman and Renwick, *Introduction to Geography*, 2/e, pp. 384–385.

196: Knut Nortstog and Andrew J. Meyerricks, *Biology*, p. 641. Toronto: Charles E. Merrill, 1985.

197: Joseph A. DeVito, *Messages: Building Interpersonal Communication Skills*, 5/e, pp. 224–225. Boston: Allyn and Bacon, 2002.

203: Michael Solomon and Elnora Stuart, *The Brave New World of E-Commerce* (supplement to *Marketing: Real People, Real Choices*), p. 16. Upper Saddle River, NJ: Prentice-Hall, 2001.

203: Bergman and Renwick, *Introduction to Geography*, 2/e, p. 348.

204: Joseph A. DeVito, *Messages: Building Interpersonal Communication Skills* 4/e, p. 140. Published by Allyn and Bacon, Boston, MA. Copyright © 1999 by Pearson Education. Reprinted/adapted by permission of the publisher.

204: Donatelle and Davis, *Access to Health*, 6/e, p. 78.

204: Cook, Yale, and Marqua, *Tourism: The Business of Travel*, p. 86.

205: Joseph A. DeVito, *The Interpersonal Communication Book*, 8/e, p. 233. New York: Longman, 1998.

207: Deborah Tannen, "Don't Ask" (pp. 61–64) from *You Just Don't Understand* by Deborah Tannen. Copyright © 1990 by Deborah Tannen. Reprinted by permission of HarperCollins Publishers. William Morrow.

Chapter 7

213: Joseph A. DeVito, *Messages: Building Interpersonal Communication Skills* 4/e, p. 150. Published by Allyn and Bacon, Boston, MA. Copyright © 1999 by Pearson Education. Reprinted/adapted by permission of the publisher.

215: DeVito, *Messages: Building Interpersonal Communication Skills* 4/e, p. 159.

216: DeVito, *Messages: Building Interpersonal Communication Skills* 4/e, p. 130.

217: B.E. Pruitt and Jane J. Stein, *HealthStyles: Decisions for Living Well*, 2/e, pp. 108, 110. Copyright © 1999 Allyn & Bacon. Reprinted by permission of Pearson Education, Inc.

218: Hugh D. Barlow, *Criminal Justice in America*, p. 238. Copyright © 2000. Reprinted by permission of Pearson Education, Inc., Upper Saddle River, NJ.

221: James Geiwitz, *Psychology: Looking at Ourselves*, 2/e, p. 512. Copyright © 1980. Reprinted by permission of the author.

222: Geiwitz, *Psychology: Looking at Ourselves*, 2/e, p. 513.

222: Geiwitz, *Psychology: Looking at Ourselves*, 2/e, p. 229.

222: Richard George, *The New Consumer Survival Kit*, p. 114. Boston: Little, Brown and Company, 1978.

223: *U.S. News & World Report.* "ABCs of How a President is Chosen," *U.S. News & World Report*, February 18, 1980.

223: Paul Hewitt, *Conceptual Physics*, 5/e, p. 15. Copyright © 1985 by Paul G. Hewitt. Reprinted by permission of Pearson Education, Inc.

224: James Henslin, *Sociology: A Down-To-Earth Approach*, 6/e, p. 383. Published by Allyn and Bacon, Boston, MA. Copyright © 2003 by Pearson Education. Reprinted by permission of the publisher.

224: Hewitt, *Conceptual Physics*, 5/e, pp. 234–235.

225: Hewitt, *Conceptual Physics*, 5/e, p. 259.

225: Steven E.F. Brown, "Gap Sales Up 13% in February," *San Francisco Business Times*, March 12, 2004.

226: George Edwards III et al., *Government in America*, 9/e, pp. 458–459. New York: Longman, 2000.

226: Stephen F. Davis and Joseph J. Palladino, *Psychology*, 3/e, pp. 563, 564, 566. Copyright © 2000. Reprinted by permission of Pearson Education, Inc., Upper Saddle River, NJ.

226: Rebecca Donatelle and Lorraine Davis, *Access to Health*, 6/e, pp. 358, 371. Copyright © 2000 Allyn and Bacon. Reprinted by permission of Pearson Education, Inc.

227: John A. Garraty and Mark C. Carnes, *The American Nation*, 10/e, p. 706. New York: Longman, 2000.

227: Roy Cook, Laura Yale, and Joseph Marqua, *Tourism: The Business of Travel*, pp. 150, 151. Copyright © 1999. Reprinted by permission of Pearson Education, Inc., Upper Saddle River, NJ.

228: Wendy G. Lehnert, *Light on the Internet: Essentials of the Internet and the World Wide Web*, pp. 112, 131. Reading, MA: Addison Wesley Longman, Inc., 1999.

228: Palmira Brummett et al., *Civilization: Past & Present*, 9/e, p. 348. Copyright © 2000. Reprinted by permission of Pearson Education, Inc.

229: Edward H. Reiley and Carroll L. Shry, *Introductory Horticulture*, p. 114. Albany, NY: Delmar Publishers, 1979.

234: Alex Thio, *Sociology*, p. 374. New York: HarperCollins College Publishers, 1994.

241: Donatelle and Davis, *Access to Health*, 6/e, pp. 446–447.

241: Brummett et al., *Civilization: Past & Present*, 9/e, p. 919.

241: Davis and Palladino, *Psychology*, 3/e, p. 609.

242: Cook, Yale, and Marqua, *Tourism: the Business of Travel*, p. 156.

242: Joseph A. DeVito, *Messages: Building Interpersonal Communication Skills*, 5/e, p. 284. Boston: Allyn and Bacon, 2002.

243: Stephen Kosslyn and Robin Rosenberg, *Psychology: The Brain, The Person, The World*, pp. 180–181. Boston: Allyn and Bacon, 2001.

245: Mary Pipher, "The Beautiful Laughing Sisters—An Arrival Story" from *The Middle of Everywhere*. Copyright © 2002 by Mary Pipher. Reprinted by permission of Harcourt, Inc.

Chapter 8

253: Sydney B. Newell, *Chemistry: An Introduction*, 2/e, pp. 11. Copyright © 1980. Reprinted by permission of the author.

254: Paul Hewitt, *Conceptual Physics*, 5/e, p. 21. Copyright © 1985 by Paul G. Hewitt. Reprinted by permission of Pearson Education, Inc.

254: Richard L. Weaver, *Understanding Interpersonal Communication*, 7/e, p. 24. Published by Allyn and Bacon, Boston, MA. Copyright © 1996 by Pearson Education. Reprinted by permission of the publisher.

255: Hewitt, *Conceptual Physics*, 5/e, p. 56.

255: Hewitt, *Conceptual Physics*, 5/e, p. 224.

257: "Nez Perce." Excerpted from *The World Book Encyclopedia*. Copyright © 2002. By permission of the publisher. www.worldbookonline.com.

258: Hal B. Pickle and Royce L. Abrahamson, *Introduction to Business*, p. 40. Copyright © 1987. Reprinted by permission of Pearson Education, Inc., Upper Saddle River, NJ.

258: Walter Thompson and Joseph V. Hickey, *Society in Focus*, 4/e, p. 70. Published by Allyn and Bacon, Boston, MA. Copyright © 1994 by Pearson Education. Reprinted by permission of the publisher.

259: Pickle and Abrahamson, *Introduction to Business*, p. 119.

261: Hewitt, *Conceptual Physics*, 5/e, pp. 82–84.

262: "New York City." Excerpted from *The World Book Encyclopedia*. Copyright © 2002. By permission of the publisher. www.worldbookonline.com.

263: Robert C. Nickerson, *Fundamentals of Structured COBOL*, p. 2. Copyright © 1984. Reprinted by permission of Little, Brown and Company.

264: Weaver, *Understanding Interpersonal Communication*, 7/e, p. 85

264: Ross Eshleman and Barbara Cashion, *Sociology: An Introduction*, 2/e, pp. 109–111. Copyright © 1985. Reprinted by permission of Allyn and Bacon.

264: Eshleman and Cashion, *Sociology: An Introduction*, 2/e, p. 583.

268: "New York City (Social Problems)." Excerpted from *The World Book Encyclopedia*. Copyright © 2007. By permission of the publisher. www.worldbookonline.com.

269: Pickle and Abrahamson, *Introduction to Business*, p. 123.

269: Bowman O. Davis et al., *Conceptual Human Physiology*, p. 213. Columbus, OH: Charles E. Merrill, 1985.

270: Hewitt, *Conceptual Physics*, 5/e, p. 233.

272: Carole Wade and Carol Tavris, *Psychology*, 3/e, p. 77. Copyright © 1993 Prentice-Hall. Reprinted by permission of Pearson Education, Inc., Upper Saddle River, NJ.

273: Weaver, *Understanding Interpersonal Communication*, 7/e, p. 24.

273: Weaver, *Understanding Interpersonal Communication*, 7/e, p. 291.

274: Hugh D. Barlow, *Criminal Justice in America*, p. 332. Copyright © 2000. Reprinted by permission of Pearson Education, Inc., Upper Saddle River, NJ.

275: Weaver, *Understanding Interpersonal Communication*, 7/e, p. 123.

275: Hewitt, *Conceptual Physics*, 5/e, p. 252.

276: William Kephart and Davor Jedlicka, *The Family, Society, and the Individual*, p. 332. Copyright © 1991. Reprinted by permission of Pearson Education, Inc., Upper Saddle River, NJ.

277: "Marriage." Excerpted from *The World Book Encyclopedia*. Copyright © 2002. By permission of the publisher. www.worldbookonline.com.

277: "Muscle." Excerpted from *The World Book Encyclopedia*. Copyright © 2002. By permission of the publisher. www.worldbookonline.com.

278: Kephart and Jedlicka, *The Family, Society, and the Individual*, pp. 332-333.

278: "Mimosa." Excerpted from *The World Book Encyclopedia*. Copyright © 2002. By permission of the publisher. www.worldbookonline.com.

278: "Morphine." Excerpted from *The World Book Encyclopedia*. Copyright © 2002. By permission of the publisher. www.worldbookonline.com.

279: "Mental Illness." Excerpted from *The World Book Encyclopedia*. Copyright © 2007. By permission of the publisher. www.worldbookonline.com.

279: "Mosquitos." Excerpted from *The World Book Encyclopedia*. Copyright © 2002. By permission of the publisher. www.worldbookonline.com.

280: Wade and Tavris, *Psychology*, 3/e, p. 252.

280: "Magic." Excerpted from *The World Book Encyclopedia*. Copyright © 2002. By permission of the publisher. www.worldbookonline.com.

281: "Mathematics." Excerpted from *The World Book Encyclopedia*. Copyright © 2002. By permission of the publisher. www.worldbookonline.com.

281: Nanda Bandyo-padhyay, *Computing for Non-Specialists*, p. 260. New York: Addison Wesley, 2000.

283: James Henslin, *Sociology: A Down-To-Earth Approach*, 6/e, p. 637. Published by Allyn and Bacon, Boston, MA. Copyright © 2003 by Pearson Education. Reprinted by permission of the publisher.

283: Edward Bergman and William Renwick, *Introduction to Geography*, 2/e, p. 410. Copyright © 2002. Reprinted by permission of Pearson Education, Inc., Upper Saddle River, NJ.

283: William Germann and Cindy Stanfield, *Principles of Human Physiology*, pp. 303–304. San Francisco: Benjamin Cummings, 2002.

292: Michael Solomon and Elnora Stuart, *Marketing: Real People, Real Choices*, 2/e, p. 71. Copyright © 2000. Reprinted by permission of Pearson Education, Inc., Upper Saddle River, NJ.

293: Bruce E. Gronbeck et al., *Principles of Speech Communication*, 13th Brief ed., pp. 32-33. New York: Longman, 1998.

293: Michael C. Mix, Paul Farber, Keith I. King, *Biology: The Network of Life*, p. 262. New York: HarperCollins College Publishers, 1996.

294: Joseph A. DeVito, *The Interpersonal Communication Book*, 9/e, pp. 219–220. Boston: Allyn and Bacon, 2001.

294: John D. Daniels and Lee H. Radebaugh, *International Business: Environments and Operations*, 8/e, p. 679. Reading, MA: Addison-Wesley, 1998.

294: Carole Wade and Carol Tavris, *Psychology*, 5/e, pp. 327–328. New York: Longman, 1998.

295: Thomas Kinnear, Kenneth Bernhardt, and Kathleen Krentler, *Principles of Marketing*, 4/e, pp. 283-284. Copyright © 1995. Reprinted by permission of Pearson Education, Inc., Upper Saddle River, NJ.

295: H.L. Capron, *Computers: Tools for an Information Age*, 5/e, pp. 199. Copyright © 1998. Reprinted by permission of Pearson Education, Inc., Upper Saddle River, NJ.

295: Wade and Tavris, *Psychology*, 5/e p. 494.

295: Wade and Tavris, *Psychology*, 5/e p. 226.

296: James Spradley and David W. McCurdy, *Conformity and Conflict: Readings in Cultural Anthropology*, 9/e, p. 349. New York: Longman, 1997.

297: Alton Fitzgerald White, "Right Place, Wrong Face," originally published as "Ragtime, My Time." Reprinted with permission from the October 11, 1999 issue of *The Nation*. For subscription information, call 1-800-333-8536. Portions of each week's Nation magazine can be accessed at http://www.thenation.com.

Chapter 9

302: Neil A. Campbell et al., page reprint from *Biology: Concepts and Connections*, 5/e, p. 70. Copyright © 2008 Pearson Education, Inc., publishing as Benjamin Cummings. Reprinted by permission.

305: H.L. Capron, *Computers: Tools for an Information Age*, Brief Edition, pp. xxiii, xxiv, xxv. Copyright © 1998. Reprinted by permission of Pearson Education, Inc., Upper Saddle River, NJ.

309: Curtis Byer and Louis Shainberg, *Living Well: Health in Your Hands*, 2/e, p. 311. Copyright © 1995 Jones and Bartlett Publishers, Sudbury, MA, www.jbpub.com. Reprinted with permission.

309: "Control." Copyright © 2006 by Houghton Mifflin Company. Reproduced by permission from *The American Heritage Dictionary of the English Language, Fourth Edition*.

317: Kenneth Budinski, *Engineering Materials: Properties and Selection*, p. 15. Reston, VA: Reston Publishing Co., 1979.

317: Herbert Ellinger, *Auto-Mechanics*, 2/e, p. 183. Englewood Cliffs, NJ: Prentice Hall, 1977.

317: Robert C. Nickerson, *Fundamentals of Structured COBOL*, p. 271. Copyright © 1984. Reprinted by permission of Little, Brown and Company.

321: Nickerson, *Fundamentals of Structured COBOL*, p. 2.

324: Paul Hewitt, *Conceptual Physics*, 5/e, pp. 54-56. Copyright © 1985 by Paul G. Hewitt. Reprinted by permission of Pearson Education, Inc.

332: Rebecca Donatelle and Lorraine Davis, *Access to Health*, 6/e, pp. xix-xxi. Copyright © 2000 Allyn and Bacon. Reprinted by permission of Pearson Education, Inc.

333: Hans Selye, *The Stress of Life*. New York: McGraw-Hill, 1956.

337: DeVito, "Legible Clothing" from *Human Communication: The Basic Course*, 7/e, pp. 139-140. Published by Allyn and bacon, Boston, MA. Copyright © 1997 by Pearson Education. Reprinted by permission of the publisher.

Chapter 10

342: Greenpeace USA web page "Oceans." http://www.greenpeace.org/usa/campaigns/oceans. © Greenpeace. Reprinted by permission of Greenpeace, Inc.

343: Elaine Marieb, *Essentials of Human Anatomy & Physiology*, 7/e, pp. 162, 164. Copyright © 2003 Pearson Education, Inc., publishing as Benjamin Cummings. Reprinted by permission of Pearson Education, Inc.

343: Marieb, *Essentials of Human Anatomy & Physiology*, 7/e, p. 164, Fig 6.1.

345: Richard Fabes and Carol Lynn Martin, *Exploring Child Development*, 2/e., p. 454. Published by Allyn and bacon, Boston, MA. Copyright © 2003 by Pearson Education. Reprinted by permission of the publisher.

346: Robert Wallace, *Biology: The World of Life*, 6/e, p. 774. Copyright © 1992 Addison-Wesley Educational Publishers. Reprinted by permission of Pearson Education, Inc.

347: Wallace, *Biology: The World of Life*, 6/e p. 774.

348: Bud Getchell, *The Fitness Book*. Copyright © 1987. Reprinted by permission of Cooper Publishing Group, PO Box 1129, Traverse City, MI 49685.

349: Frances Moore Lappé, *Diet for a Small Planet*. Copyright © 1971, 1975, 1982, 1991 by Frances Moore Lappé. Used with permission.

350: James Henslin, *Social Problems*, 6/e, p. 259, Fig 8.3. Copyright © 2003. Reprinted by permission of Pearson Education, Inc., Upper Saddle River, NJ.

351: Fabes and Martin, *Exploring Child Development*, 2/e., p. 196.

352: Walter Thompson and Joseph V. Hickey, *Society in Focus*, 4/e, p. 485. Published by Allyn and Bacon, Boston, MA. Copyright © 1994 by Pearson Education. Reprinted by permission of the publisher.

353: Curtis Byer and Louis Shainberg, *Living Well: Health in Your Hands*, 2/e, Fig. G5. Copyright © 1995 Jones and Bartlett Publishers, Sudbury, MA, www.jbpub.com. Reprinted with permission.

354: Fabes and Martin, *Exploring Child Development*, 2/e., p. 281.

355: Randall B. Dunham and Jon L. Pierce, *Management*, p. 721. Copyright © 1989. Reprinted by permission of Pearson Education, Inc., Upper Saddle River, NJ.

356: Henslin, *Social Problems*, 6/e, p. 454, Fig 13.11.

357: Robert L. Lineberry and George Edwards III, *Government in America*, 4/e, p. 253. Copyright © 1989. Reprinted by permission of Scott, Foresman Publishing Company.

358: David Van Fleet, *Contemporary Management*, 2/e, p. 187. Copyright © 1991 by Houghton Mifflin Company. Used with permission.

359: Henslin, *Social Problems*, 6/e, p. 368, Fig 11.5.

360: John C. Merrill et al, *Modern Mass Media*, p. 207. Copyright © 1994 by Addison-Wesley Educational Publishers. Reprinted by permission of Pearson Education, Inc.

362: Thompson and Hickey, *Society in Focus*, 4/e, p. 179.

363: Marieb, *Essentials of Human Anatomy & Physiology*, 7/e, p. 106.

363: Marieb, *Essentials of Human Anatomy & Physiology*, 7/e, p. 106, Fig 4.9.

364: H.L. Capron, *Computers: Tools for an Information Age,* Brief Edition, p. 19. Copyright © 1998. Reprinted by permission of Pearson Education, Inc., Upper Saddle River, NJ.

366: Edward Bergman and William Renwick, *Introduction to Geography: People, Places, and Environment*, 3/e, p. 69. © 2005. Reprinted by permission of Pearson Education, Inc., Upper Saddle River, NJ.

371: Site map. © 2007 by Consumers Union of U.S., Inc. Yonkers, NY 10703-1057, a nonprofit organization. Reprinted with permission from ConsumerReports.org® for educational purposes only. No commercial use or reproduction permitted. www.ConsumerReports.org.

381: James Henslin, *Sociology: A Down-To-Earth Approach*, 6/e, p. 402. Published by Allyn and Bacon, Boston, MA. Copyright © 2003 by Pearson Education. Reprinted by permission of the publisher.

383: Henslin, *Sociology: A Down-To-Earth Approach*, 6/e, p. 480.

385: Henslin, *Sociology: A Down-To-Earth Approach*, 6/e, p. 489.

388: Henslin, *Sociology: A Down-To-Earth Approach*, 6/e, pp. 482–485.

Chapter 11

398: Curtis Byer and Louis Shainberg, *Living Well: Health in Your Hands*, 2/e, Fig. G5. Copyright © 1995 Jones and Bartlett Publishers, Sudbury, MA, www.jbpub.com. Reprinted with permission.

400: Thomas Kinnear, Kenneth Bernhardt, and Kathleen Krentler, *Principles of Marketing*, 4/e, p. 132. Copyright © 1995. Reprinted by permission of Pearson Education, Inc., Upper Saddle River, NJ.

401: Watson M. Laetsch, *Plants: Basic Concepts in Botany*, p. 8. Boston: Little, Brown and Co, 1979.

403: Byer and Shainberg, *Living Well: Health in Your Hands*, 2/e, p. 311.

404: Sydney B. Newell, *Chemistry: An Introduction*, 2/e, pp. 47–48. Copyright © 1980. Reprinted by permission of the author.

407: William M. Pride and O.C. Ferrell, *Marketing: Basic Concepts and Strategies*, p. 380. Boston: Houghton Mifflin, 1991.

407: Kinnear et al., *Principles of Marketing*, 4.e, pp. 39–40.

420: Carole Wade and Carol Tavris, *Invitation to Psychology*, 7/e, p. 392. Upper Saddle River, NJ: Prentice-Hall, 2002.

420: Palmira Brummett et al., *Civilization: Past & Present*, 9/e, p. 446. Copyright © 2000. Reprinted by permission of Pearson Education, Inc.

420: Roy Cook, Laura Yale, and Joseph Marqua, *Tourism: The Business of Travel*, p. 156. Copyright © 1999. Reprinted by permission of Pearson Education, Inc., Upper Saddle River, NJ.

421: B.E. Pruitt and Jane J. Stein, *HealthStyles: Decisions for Living Well*, 2/e, p. 81. Copyright © 1999 Allyn & Bacon. Reprinted by permission of Pearson Education, Inc.

421: Rebecca Donatelle and Lorraine Davis, *Access to Health*, 6/e, p. 120. Copyright © 2000 Allyn and Bacon. Reprinted by permission of Pearson Education, Inc.

422: Kathleen German and Bruce Gronbeck, *Principles of Public Speaking*, 14/e, pp. 38–39. New York: Longman, 2001.

424: Joseph A. DeVito, *The Interpersonal Communication Book*, 8/e, p. 141. New York: Longman, 1998.

427: Rebecca Donatelle, *Access to Health*, 7/e, pp. 305–307. Copyright © 2002 Benjamin/Cummings. Reprinted by permission of Pearson Education, Inc.

Chapter 12

435: Robert C. Yeager, *Seasons of Shame: The New Violence in Sports*, p. 6. New York: McGraw-Hill, 1979.

438: Bill Cosby, *Time Flies*, pp. 169–170. New York: Doubleday, 1987.

439: Paul Aurandt, *Paul Harvey's The Rest of the Story*, edited and compiled by Lynne Harvey, p. 116. New York: Doubleday, 1977.

440: Richard L. Weaver, *Understanding Interpersonal Communication*, 7/e, p. 291. Published by Allyn and Bacon, Boston, MA. Copyright © 1996 by Pearson Education. Reprinted by permission of the publisher.

441: Lewis Katz, *Know Your Rights*, p. 54. Cleveland: Banks Baldwin Law, 1993.

442: Richard Shenkman, *Legends, Lies, and Cherished Myths of American History*, pp. 37–38. New York: William Morrow, 1988.

443: Linda Hasselstrom, "A Peaceful Woman Explains Why She Carries a Gun." Used with permission from *Land Circle: Writings Collected from the Land* by Linda Hasselstrom. Copyright © 1991, Fulcrum Publishing, Inc., Golden, Colorado, USA. All rights reserved.

444: Donald Mosley et al., *Management: Leadership in Action*, 5/e, p. 555. New York: HarperCollins College Publishers, 1996.

446: Tom Bodett, *As Far As You Can Go Without a Passport.* Copyright © 1985 by Tom Bodett. Reprinted by permission of Da Capo Press, a member of Perseus Books Group.

450: Sara King, "Love in the Afternoon-in a Crowded Prison Hall," *Los Angeles Times*, November 5, 1976. Copyright © 1976 Los Angeles Times. Reprinted with permission.

452: Marc Eisenson, excerpt from "Stop Junk Mail Forever" as appeared in *Mother Earth News*, August / September 1994. Copyright © 1994 Mother Earth News. Used with permission.

455: Robert Wallace, *Biology: The World of Life*, 6/e, p. 659. Copyright © 1992 Addison-Wesley Educational Publishers. Reprinted by permission of Pearson Education, Inc.

455: Marge Thielman Hastreiter, "Not Every Mother is Glad Kids Are Back in School," *Buffalo Evening News*, 1991.

457: Johnson C. Montgomery, "The Island of Plenty," *The Norton Sampler: Short Essays for Composition*, Thomas Cooley, ed. p. 310. New York: W.W. Norton, 1985.

457: Bess Armstrong, article from *The Choices We Made*, Angela Bonavoglia, ed. p. 165. New York: Random House, 1991.

459: Barry Lopez, "Weekend," *Audubon*, July 1973.

459: John Steinbeck, *America and Indians*, pp. 127–128. New York: Viking Press, 1966.

461: Karen Olson, from "Eat it Raw," *Utne Reader*, March/April 2002. Reprinted by permission of the author and Utne Reader.

467: Rebecca Donatelle and Lorraine Davis, *Access to Health*, 6/e, p. 146. Copyright © 2000 Allyn and Bacon. Reprinted by permission of Pearson Education, Inc.

467: Michael Solomon and Elnora Stuart, *The Brave New World of E-Commerce* (supplement to *Marketing: Real People, Real Choices*), p. 17. Upper Saddle River, NJ: Prentice-Hall, 2001.

467: Joe L. Kincheloe et al., *Contextualizing Teaching*, pp. 90–91. Boston: Allyn and Bacon, 2000.

468: Michael Solomon and Elnora Stuart, *Marketing: Real People, Real Choices*, 2/e, p. 59. Copyright © 2000. Reprinted by permission of Pearson Education, Inc., Upper Saddle River, NJ.

468: Palmira Brummett et al., *Civilization: Past & Present*, 9/e, pp. 578–579. Copyright © 2000. Reprinted by permission of Pearson Education, Inc.

469: Cynthia Audet, "Scar" from *The Sun*, Issue 325, January 2003. Reprinted by permission of the author.

471: Donna M. Marriott, "His Name is Michael," *Education Week*, October 9, 2002. Reprinted by permission of the author.

Chapter 13

481: Robert C. Yeager, *Seasons of Shame: The New Violence in Sports*, p. 4. New York: McGraw-Hill, 1979.

482: Barbara Stern, "Calm Down in Six Seconds," *Vogue*, October 1981.

482: Denise Fortino, "Why Kids Need Heroes," *Parents*, November 1984.

483: Mary Gander and Harry Gardiner, *Child Adolescent Development*, p. 384. Copyright © 1981 Prentice-Hall. Reprinted by permission of Pearson Education, Inc., Upper Saddle River, NJ.

486: Haim Ginott, *Between Parent and Teenager*, pp. 39–41. New York: Macmillan, 1969.

486: E.B. White, *One Man's Meat*, pp. 305–306. New York: Harper & Row, 1944.

487: Gail Sheehy, *Passages*, p. 68. New York: EP Dutton, 1976.

491: Edward S. Greenberg and Benjamin I. Page, *The Struggle for Democracy*, 2/e, p. 186. New York: HarperCollins College Publishers, 1995.

492: Arlene Skolnick, *The Intimate Environment: Exploring Marriage and the Family*, 6/e, p. 96. New York: HarperCollins College Publishers, 1996.

496: Studs Terkel, from "Jesusita Novarro" in *Working: People Talk About What They Do All Day*. Reprinted by permission of Donadio & Olson, Inc. Copyright 1974 Studs Terkel.

498: Michael Solomon, *Consumer Behavior: Buying, Having, and Being*, 5/e, p. 19. Copyright © 2002. Reprinted by permission of Pearson Education, Inc., Upper Saddle River, NJ.

504: George Edwards III et al., *Government in America*, 9/e, p. 685. New York: Longman, 2000.

506: Edwards III et al., *Government in America*, 9/e, pp. 426–427.

509: Bronwyn Jones, "Arming Myself with a Gun Is Not the Answer." From *Newsweek*, May 22, 2000. © 2000 Newsweek, Inc. All rights reserved. Used by permission and protected by the

Copyright Laws of the United States. The printing, copying, redistribution, or retransmission of the Material without express written permission is prohibited.

Part 5

514: Kate Chopin, "The Story of an Hour," 1894.

518: Langston Hughes, "Thank You Ma'm" from Short Stories by Langston Hughes. Copyright © 1996 by Ramona Bass and Arnold Rampersad. Reprinted by permission of Hill and Wang, a division of Farrar, Straus and Giroux, LLC.

523: Becky Birtha, *Lovers' Choice.* Copyright © 1987 by Becky Birtha. Reprinted by permission of Seal Press, a member of Perseus Books Group.

527: Allen Poe, "The Tell-Tale Heart," 1843.

Part 6

536: Daniel B. Wood, "Should People be Allowed to Smoke at Home?" originally published as "New No-Smoking Frontier: Condos and Apartments" by Daniel B. Wood. Reproduced with permission from the February 7, 2007 issue of *The Christian Science Monitor* (www. csmonitor.com). © 2007 The Christian Science Monitor. All rights reserved.

542: Steven Reinberg, "Driving While on the Cell Phone Worse Than Driving Drunk from *HealthDay*, June 29, 2006. Copyright © 2006. Reprinted by permission of HealthDay.

547: Amanda Paulson and Ron Scherer, "Preventing Violence on Campuses" originally published as "How Safe Are College Campuses?" by Amanda Paulson and Ron Scherer. Reproduced with permission from the April 18, 2007 issue of *The Christian Science Monitor* (www.csmonitor.com). © 2007 The Christian Science Monitor. All rights reserved.

554: Barbara Ehrenreich , "Wal-Mart and Target Spy on Their Employees," posted on *AlterNet*, April 6, 2007. Reprinted by permission of International Creative Management, Inc. Copyright © 2007 by Barbara Ehrenreich.

560: Media Awareness Network, "Beauty and Body Image in the Media."© Media Awareness Network, www.media-awareness.ca. Reproduced with permission.

566: Holli Riebeek, from "Global Warming," NASA's website *Earth Observatory*, May 11, 2007, http://earthobservatory.nasa.gov/Library/GlobalWarming/global_warming_update.html. Original version by John Weier, April 8, 2002.

PHOTO CREDITS

p. 3, top: Les Gibbon/Alamy; **p. 3, bottom:** Pixtal/AGE Fotostock; **p. 29:** David Young Wolf/PhotoEdit; **p. 32:** Elmer Martinez/AFP/Getty Images; **p. 59:** Advertising Archives; **p. 95, left:** Journal Courier/The Image Works; **p. 95, right:** David Young Wolf/PhotoEdit; **p. 131:** BBC Photo Library; **p. 134:** Rocky Widner/Getty Images; **p. 146:** Getty Images; **p. 149:** Quest/Photo Researchers; **p. 161:** Christoph Wilhelm/Taxi/Getty Images; **p. 165:** Ron Koeberer/Getty Images; **p. 182:** ©The New Yorker Collection 1979 Mischa Richter from cartoonbank.com. All Rights Reserved; **p. 205:** Corbis; **p. 207:** Spencer Grant/PhotoEdit; **p. 212:** Mark Avery/AP Photo; **p. 251, top right:** Getty Images; **p 251, top left:** Getty Images; **p. 251, bottom:** Corbis; **p. 298:** Diane Bondareff/AP Photo; **p. 302:** Jeff Mark Cassino/Superstock; **p. 338:** Phil Coale/AP Photo; **p. 342:** Patrick Lynch/Alamy; **p. 367:** Lon C. Diehl/PhotoEdit; **p. 389:** Mark Adams/Getty Images; **p. 390:** Bob Deammrich/The Image Works; **p. 392:** Lawrence Migdale/Getty Images; **p. 395:** © Frank La Bua/Pearson Education/PH College; **p. 427:** David Leahy/Getty Images; **p. 433:** ©The New Yorker Collection 2007 Alex Gregory from cartoonbank.com. All Rights Reserved; **p. 476:** Jeff Greenberg/AGE Fotostock; **p. 513, top:** Getty Images; **p. 513, center:** Library of Congress; **p. 513, bottom:** Tee Corinne; **p. 534:** Getty Images; **p. 567:** Bruce Forster/Getty Images.

Index